GUIDE TO

AMERICAN
ENGLISH

PRENTICE-HALL INTERNATIONAL, INC., LONDON
PRENTICE-HALL OF AUSTRALIA, PTY., LTD., SYDNEY
PRENTICE-HALL OF CANADA, LTD., TORONTO
PRENTICE-HALL OF INDIA (PRIVATE) LTD., NEW DELHI
PRENTICE-HALL OF JAPAN, INC., TOKYO
PRENTICE-HALL DE MEXICO, S.A., MEXICO CITY

GUIDE TO

AMERICAN
ENGLISH

third edition

L. M. MYERS *Professor of
English Arizona State University*

PRENTICE-HALL, INC.,
ENGLEWOOD CLIFFS, N.J.

Third printing. . . . . June, 1964

Library of Congress Catalog Card Number: 63-9823

PRINTED IN THE UNITED STATES OF AMERICA
36920-C

PREFACE

The second edition of this book was a very thorough revision of the first. In this third edition the changes in the text are not nearly so extensive. The chapter on the research paper has, I think, been considerably improved. Otherwise there are only a few minor changes and corrections.

But if the author has done comparatively little for this edition, others have done much. The less expensive format has obvious advantages, especially for a textbook containing so many exercises; and the exercises themselves, by my colleague George Herman, are a very definite improvement. For each chapter there are two kinds: a number, most often twenty-five, of sentences or comparable items to be worked on, and two or three more general questions for class discussion or assigned writing. They are so skillfully devised to help students understand and practice what the text preaches that I am embarrassed when I compare them with my own earlier attempts.

A writer who reissues a book with so little modification of his own is bound to examine very closely his reasons for so doing. Is he moved (or unmoved) by laziness, complacency, or pure ignorance of what has been taking place during the intervening time? I can speak to the first two possibilities quite simply. After a good deal of time spent in contemplating revision I am forced to the conclusion that this book, whatever its quality, is about the best I can do on this subject, and that any considerable reworking would be much more likely to damage it than to improve it. I am supported by the fact that such suggestions for improvement as I have received cancel each other out with almost geometrical regularity.

As for the third point I can only say that recent developments in linguistic theory, fascinating as some of them are, do not seem to me likely to be very helpful to most instructors in teaching most classes. I have commented on some of these developments in more appropriate places. Here I need only say that a trained linguist using this book will no doubt supplement it with material of his own, and that I am not vain enough to think I can create additional linguists by adding a few paragraphs.

L. M. Myers

CONTENTS

GUIDE TO
AMERICAN
ENGLISH

INTRODUCTION:

SEEING THROUGH WORDS

If you can read rapidly and with good understanding, you will probably find it easy to remember a good deal of what you do read. On the other hand, if you find reading a difficult and unpleasant job, even those things that you manage to learn by reading are likely to slip from your memory within a very short time. In other words, the harder and more disagreeable reading is, the less it pays. This does not seem at all fair, but it is generally true.

A very large proportion of freshmen entering college have not learned to read at all well. Some of them realize this and are anxious for help. Others are in about the same position as a man who has needed glasses all his life without knowing it. He is not dissatisfied with his sight, simply because he does not know how much there is to see. You may have heard somebody say that he had never realized that anybody ever saw blades of grass or the leaves of trees until he finally got glasses.

There are many causes of poor reading. Some students require psychological or even medical help. Many others have developed bad mechanical habits from which they can recover with a little training. If your college has a remedial reading clinic you may find it extremely valuable to have yourself tested and to take any training advised, even if it is not required. Few investments of time pay bigger dividends.

But the commonest cause of poor reading is one that you can work on yourself if you make the effort. It is the habit of looking *at* the words on a page without trying to look *through* them. You come across a sentence, for instance, that says:

He had all the tastes and habits of a gentleman.

At first glance this seems perfectly simple. The words are all familiar, and so is their arrangement. If anybody asks you, perhaps in a ten-minute quiz, what kind of tastes and habits he had, you can say that he had those of a gentleman, and probably you will be marked correct. But if somebody asks you to tell him exactly what those tastes and habits were, you may suddenly realize that you don't know whether he liked opera or polo, and whether he drank champagne or tea. As a matter of fact, the sentence means nothing—and I know, because I just wrote it. I didn't have any ideas in mind when I wrote it. I was just playing with echoes.

This may strike you as a low-down trick, and you may very reasonably ask, "How do you expect me to know what a sentence means if the writer himself doesn't know?" The trouble is, people don't ask this question nearly often enough. A good many writers fool themselves that familiar groups of words must mean something, even if they haven't stopped to figure out exactly what. And a good many readers fool themselves in turn.

Let us look at an even simpler sentence:

He is a good man.

Assuming that we know who "he" is, what does the sentence tell us about him? Coach Pasternak might use it to indicate that "he" blocks well, tackles hard, and keeps driving all the time. The Reverend Mr. Gillespie might wish to indicate by the same sentence that "he" is generous, kindly, and sincere, and a faithful member of the church. Or Professor Hubbard might use it to imply that "he" is well grounded in calculus and a quick hand with a slide rule. In fact the sentence might mean so many things that we may suspect it has no meaning of its own.

This may seem like a remarkable idea, since we have been hearing about the meaning of words for years. But the fact is that *words in themselves have no meaning at all*. It takes a mind to mean something. Words are merely the mechanical symbols by which meaning is conveyed from one mind to another. This idea will be discussed more fully in Chapter 12. For the moment you are not asked to accept it as completely true, but merely to see whether it is useful in examining your reading habits.

Many students, if they are asked whether they have understood a paragraph, will say that they do not know what certain words mean. When these words are defined, they relax and ask no further questions. But if the instructor then asks *them* questions, it soon becomes clear that they have little idea of what the writer was saying. The reason is simply that they never expected to get the idea. They think of reading as primarily a matter of recognizing the written symbols. That is, they look at the words and identify them *as words*. If a word is unfamiliar they are puzzled, or perhaps annoyed. If a word is familiar, they feel that they have accomplished something by identifying it, and go on to the next word. But they make little or no effort to look through the word to find the *thing* (or activity or relation) that the writer had in mind when he used the word.

If this sounds like an exaggeration, consider the following evidence. I once gave a freshman class a lecture and exercise on looking through words, and then asked for a short paper discussing the experiment. One of the students began his paper as follows:

This idea of reading and thinking at the same time is new to me. When I read I cannot think. When I try to read and think all at the same time I get confused. This exercise has shown me to read for ideas instead of words. I find that I read faster and remember better.

The man who wrote that was obviously not a genius, but he was by no means a fool, either. Very early in his school life he had been taught "to read" in the simplest mechanical sense. But in twelve years of grade and high school he had never really been taught to read for information, though he was perfectly willing to do it as soon as the possibility was mentioned to him.

The unfortunate thing is that his experience was not unique, or even especially rare. A great many students come to college almost completely unable to learn from a printed page. The reason for this is quite clear, once we stop to think of it.

The first step in reading is to learn what noises certain combinations of letters stand for. This is fairly difficult for a young child, especially in English, with its very irregular spelling. The child is concentrating so hard on discovering what words to pronounce, or at least to think of, when he sees the letters, that he has no energy left over to think of what the words stand for. If a sentence happens to say "The rooster said 'Moo' and laid an egg," he will read it with complete seriousness and rush on to the next one, without stopping to consider the improbabilities involved.

When we get to the point where we recognize words easily, we are supposed to think of what they mean when we see them, and therefore to get some information when we read. But this process is *not* automatic, and many people make very little headway with it. I have had college students tell me with complete seriousness, "I don't see how you expect us to get that just from reading it. You never told us what it meant."

Of course, anybody who has reached college can get some information by reading—if he expects to and is trying to. When even the poorest student reads a comic strip or a personal letter or the report of a football game he expects something he can understand, and he will stretch his mind out to grasp it. But if he is asked to read a chapter on economics or philosophy—anything "deep"—he often goes back to the "rooster said 'Moo'" stage. He will look at the words one after another, and feel mildly virtuous about having done so. He may even memorize some of the statements, because he has learned that he is expected to. But he will not examine them to see what the author had in mind, or to see how they fit in with what he already knows.

A somewhat better student will find out what almost any passage is "about," but will fail rather consistently to notice exactly what it says. Suppose he runs across a sentence like "The economic policy of the administration was characterized by unexampled deficit spending."

Teacher: Do you understand that sentence?
Student: Yes—I guess so.
Teacher: What does it mean?
Student: It's about the policy of the administration.
Teacher: What does it *say* about the policy of the administration?
Student: Well, there was some deficit spending.
Teacher: What is deficit spending?
Student: Why, I guess it's when you spend your deficit.
Teacher: You can't spend a deficit. Maybe you'd better look the word up in your dictionary.
Pause.
Student: Does it mean they spent money they didn't have—that they went into debt?
Teacher: That's right. How much did they go into debt?
Student: I don't know—quite a lot, I guess.
Teacher: Does the sentence say?
Student: It just says "unexampled deficit spending." It doesn't say how much.
Teacher: What does "unexampled" mean?

Student: Quite a lot?
Teacher: No.
Pause.
Student: Does it mean that they went into debt more than any other administration?
Teacher: Yes.
Student: Well why didn't they say so?
Teacher: They did.

Now the sentence was certainly not a very good one; it could have been written more simply and directly. We can hardly blame a poorly trained student for not getting it at the first reading. It isn't the fact that he didn't understand it that bothers us. It's the fact that he "supposed" he did. Any student, no matter how poor his previous training, can learn to find out *whether he understands what the writer means or not.*

One good way to learn to do this is to practice reading with a pencil in hand. If a sentence is clear, put a little check mark at the end of it. If it is not completely clear—so clear that you could say the same thing accurately in your own words and be quite sure what you were saying—put a question mark at the end and examine it again. What you do next depends on how much time you have for the assignment. Obviously, if there are any words you don't know, it might help to look them up. Perhaps even more important, if there are any words that you think you know, but that do not seem to make very good sense in this sentence, look *them* up. They may have additional meanings that you have never suspected. Above all, be sure you see just how the ideas are connected. You wouldn't expect to understand a mathematical equation if you merely looked at the numbers and did not notice whether the signs indicated addition or subtraction, multiplication or division. But a good many people read sentences without paying any attention to the connectives. In fact, in some schools they seem to be taught to do this—to concentrate on the nouns and verbs and skim happily over all those little words that show the exact relations between ideas. This works all right if the author says exactly what you expect him to. But if he says anything new and surprising—in other words, if he gives you any real information—you are likely to miss it.

If you are now a poor reader, you cannot expect to become a good one immediately by any magic formula. But you can begin to make progress almost at once if you learn the one simple fact that intelligent reading is an *active* process. You don't just look at a page like a television screen and passively receive what comes to you. You have to dig away to find out *what the writer had in mind that he tried to express by his sentences.* Sometimes you may find that he had very little. At other times you will find that a passage that seemed dull and unimportant at the first glance is actually very interesting, because the writer has looked at things in a way that had never occurred to you. You are almost certain to find that reading is more fun than it used to be. And, surprising as it may seem, you will probably find that as you read more carefully, you will also read faster. Reading without really trying to understand is such a dull practice that the mind resents it by loafing and wandering. When reading begins to pay off in interest, the mind speeds up.

You may recall that when you were very young you took the air for granted. It seemed to be something that was just there when nothing else was, or a sort of empty place where other things happened. When you first heard that it had weight and a structure of its own, the idea probably seemed absurd. But when you thought about it a little more you could see that only this weight and structure could explain why balloons go up and airplanes fly and cars run on inflated tires, not to mention hundreds of other things. In much the same way, most people ordinarily take our language for granted, as something that has always been there, like the air. They know that we use the language whenever we read, write, listen, or talk, but they seldom think that we could do all these things better if we understood a little about its structure. We have just seen that reading is not the automatic process that some people seem to think it is, and neither are the other uses of language. It will therefore be useful to devote some time to seeing how our language developed to its present state and what its present structure is like.

Exercises—Seeing Through Words

I. Mark each of the examples below in one of the following ways: *C* (clear) if you have a firm and definite idea of what it means after the first reading; *R* (reachable) if you have a definite idea of what it means after looking up any words unclear to you; *U* (unreachable) if you don't know what it means even after you have looked up the unclear words.

1. An understanding of classroom fatigue among students in any grade must involve discovery of those students especially susceptible to it. Factors causing physical discomfort may be important, as may emotionally oriented causal situations.

2. The amounts deductible for medical and dental expenses for you and your wife, if either was 65 or over, are not restricted to the excess over 3 per cent of your adjusted gross income.

3. Unless a high level of patriotic endeavor is maintained, the greatest aims of the nation's finest spirits will be blunted, and the achievements of the centuries will be forsaken forever.

4. If the landing and take-off noises of jet aircraft can be reduced to no more than tolerable levels, greater community participation in constructive expansion plans for runway and terminal facilities may be anticipated.

5. The spectroscopic method of studying the sun's rotation, by comparing the Doppler shifts of the lines at opposite edges of the disk, is not applicable to the stars which show no disks, but can be applied to certain binary stars.

6. While it could hardly be said that Smedley was not handsome, not impeccable in dress and not without money, yet one found it difficult to avoid doubting his sincerity.

7. No action at law or in equity shall be brought to recover on this contract prior to the expiration of sixty days after written proof of loss has been furnished, nor shall any such action be brought after the expiration of three years after the time written proof of loss is required to be furnished.

8. If, when those who would belittle the dynamic interaction of harmonious entities have had their chance to speak, the whole of mankind would rise up to contradict them, surely peace and tranquillity will reign unhindered.

9. The insurer at his own expense shall have the right and opportunity to examine the person of the insured when and as often as said insurer may require during the pendency of a claim hereunder.

10. Whereas fleeting moments of joy may come out of an indifferent heart, it can be indisputably stated that permanent, lasting happiness must come from a soul flooded with true goodness and positive intent.

II. Rewrite each example you marked *C* into a single sentence which is more concise and clear to you. Avoid repetition or redundancy: "lasting" is not necessary after "permanent." Do not just substitute one word for another, but rearrange the ideas more tightly and clearly.

III. After class discussion, rewrite in the same way any other sentences originally marked *R* which now become clear to you.

IV. Mark each remaining sentence *MF* (my fault) if you think that the reason it was unreachable was that you did not know enough about the subject to understand it. Put *JW* (just words) if you think the author himself had no clear idea in mind when he wrote the sentence.

part

THE
LANGUAGE

I

DEVELOPMENT

OF THE LANGUAGE

I

If you looked at the French and Italian words for *hundred—cent* and *cento* respectively—you would easily guess that they are related, and they are. They both developed from the Latin word *centum*. And if you looked at the German word *hundert* you could recognize it as a close relative of the English word. You would be right again, but you could not prove it quite so easily, because we do not have any written records of the early form of Germanic from which modern English and German developed. We have to prove the relationship by other methods which are too complicated to go into here.

You would probably not guess that *hundred* and *centum* are also related; but if you happened to think of these two words along with *horn* and *corno, house* and *casa,* and various other pairs that begin with *h* in English and *c* in Italian, you might suspect that these resemblances were systematic, and that English is also related to Italian, although not nearly as closely as French is. Your suspicions would be justified. Experts can trace the relations among all four of these languages and a good many others. We can say roughly that French and Italian are sister languages, both born of Latin; that English and modern German are approximately second cousins; and that English and Italian are something like third cousins twice removed.

Nobody knows for sure how language began, or even whether it began just once or at a number of different times and places. What we do know is that some languages, as we have just seen, show evidence of a common origin, while others do not. If our written records went back a few thousand years further it is possible that we might find signs of resemblance between the languages that we have just mentioned and Chinese or Arabic or Navajo. But if such resemblances ever existed, they disappeared a long time ago, and it seems most unlikely that we will ever find any evidence to prove them. We must therefore study them as separate families, though they may have had a common ancestor about which we now know nothing.

Origin of English

English belongs, in a rather complicated way, to the Indo-European family, which includes most of the European languages and a few Asiatic ones. We do not know where the original speakers of the parent Indo-European language lived. Guesses about their homeland range all the way from northwestern Europe to central Asia. According to all the early records they were a tall, blond, and warlike people, with a good deal of energy and intelligence. In their native land they had developed neither writing nor cities, so there is not much evidence about how they lived when they were at home. But when they left home and went out in search of new lands—which they did in various waves from about 2500 B.C. to about 1000 B.C.—the Indo-Europeans seem to have been generally successful in conquering the countries they came to.

When a wave of them settled in a territory already crowded, they mixed with the original population. In time they lost their distinctive appearance by intermarrying with the earlier inhabitants, and sometimes they also gave up most of the features of their language. When a wave went to a more thinly settled territory, they naturally preserved their physical characteristics comparatively unchanged for a much longer time; and they were likely to preserve the distinctive features of their language also, though the two things did not always go together.

The Slavic and Celtic languages, as well as Indian, Persian, and some others, are of Indo-European origin, but the three branches with which English is most concerned are the Greek, Latin, and Germanic, particularly the last. All languages are changing to some extent all the time; and before the invention of writing they seem to have changed faster. Since the various waves left at different times, they were speaking noticeably different varieties of Indo-European at the times of their departures; and the further changes that took place after they left made their languages more and more unlike. As they split up and settled (more or less) in different regions, the differences became so great that the Greeks, for instance, could not possibly understand the Germans; and a little later some of the Germans could not understand the others.

Old Germanic split into North, East, and West Germanic. West Germanic split into High and Low German. And Low German split into further dialects, including those of the Angles, Saxons, and Jutes. There were differences in pronunciation, and even in word endings, between these last three; but most of the root words were enough alike to be recognizable, and the three tribes seem to have had no great difficulty in understanding each other. About 450 A.D. members of all three tribes moved into what is now called England (from Angle-land), and began to take it over. It is at this time that we usually say the English language, as such, began.

It is worth noticing that even at the very beginning of English as a separate language there was no one simple standard. The Jutes undoubtedly thought that the Angles "talked funny," and vice versa. Efforts have been made for centuries to develop a set of standard practices, and there is much to be said in their favor; but they have never been quite successful, and they never will be. There is just no way to make millions of people talk exactly alike.

These early English settlers do not seem to have made much of an effort to understand the language of the Britons who lived in England (then called Britain) before they came. The Britons also spoke an Indo-European language, but it belonged to the Celtic rather than the Germanic branch, and was by now completely unrecognizable to the newcomers. The English added only a handful of Celtic words to their language—not nearly as many as the Americans later picked up from the Indians.

We can only guess about how the language would have developed if the descendants of these three tribes had been left to themselves. The fact is that two great invasions and a missionary movement changed the language enormously. The total result of these and other influences was that the English vocabulary became the largest and most complex in the world, and the grammar changed its emphasis from inflections (changes in the forms of words) to word order.

The Scandinavian Influence

Some three hundred years after the West Germanic tribes had settled in England, there was another wave of invasions, this time by Scandinavians. In the history books these people are usually referred to as "Danes," but there were Swedes and Norwegians among them, and their speech was probably no more uniform than that of the first wave. The dialects they spoke belonged to the Northern rather than the Western division of Germanic. They differed rather more from the dialects of the Angles, Saxons, and Jutes than these differed from each other—roughly, about as much as Spanish differs from Italian. In spite of different habits of pronunciation, most of the root words were enough alike to be recognizable. The difficulty caused by differences in inflection was partly solved by dropping some of the inflections altogether and being broad-minded about the others. Spelling was not much of a problem, because most people could not read nor write, and those who could, spelled as they pleased. There were no dictionaries to prove them wrong.

Although these Danes moved in on the English, and for a time dominated them politically, their conquest was nothing like as thorough as that of the English over the Britons. After the early fighting the two peoples settled down together without much attention to their separate origins, and the languages mingled. On the whole, English rather than Danish characteristics won out; but many of the words were so much alike that it is impossible to say whether we owe our present forms to English or Danish origins, and occasionally the Danish forms drove out the English ones. Sometimes both forms remained, usually with a somewhat different meaning. Thus we have *shirt* and *skirt,* both of which originally meant a long, smock-like garment, although the English form has come to mean the upper part, and the Danish form the lower. Old English *rear* and Danish *raise* are another pair—sometimes interchangeable, sometimes not.

The Norman Conquest

In 1066 the Normans conquered England. They, like the Danes, had originally come from Scandinavia. But they had settled in northern France, and for some undiscoverable reason had given up their own language and learned to speak a dialect of French. For several centuries Normans, and other Frenchmen that they invited in later, held most of the important positions in England, and it seemed quite possible that French would become the standard language of the country. But the bulk of the population were still English, and they were stubborner than their rulers. Most of them never learned French, and eventually—though only after several centuries—all the nobles and officials were using English.

It was not, however, the English of the days before the conquest. A good many French words had gotten into the language; and most of the inflections that had survived the Danish pressure had dropped out, with a standard word-order making up for their loss. We need not go into the argument about whether the new word-order had to develop because the endings dropped out, or the endings disappeared because the new word-order made them unnecessary. The two changes took place together, and by the time of Chaucer (died 1400) the language had become enough like modern English to be recognizable. The pronunciation was quite different and the spelling was still catch-as-catch-can; but a modern student can get at least a general idea of Chaucer's meaning without special training, while he can no more read Old English than he can German or Latin, unless he has made a special study of it. Compare the two following passages:

1. Hwaet! We gardena   in geardagum
   Theodcyningas   thrym gefrunon

2. Whan that Aprille with his shoures soote
   The droghte of March hath perced to the roote

In the first two lines from *Beowulf* (about 700 A.D.), only *we* and *in* are readily recognizable; while in the first two from Chaucer's *Canterbury Tales,* only *soote* (sweet) offers much of a problem.

From Chaucer's time to our own the language has developed with no outside pressure comparable to that of the Danish and Norman invasions. Still more endings have disappeared, and there have been other changes; but the greatest development has been in the vocabulary. A considerable number of Chaucer's words have dropped out of use, and a much greater number of new words have been added. Some of these new words have been made by compounding or otherwise modifying old ones, but most of them have been borrowed from other languages, particularly Latin.

The Latin Influence

Even before they came to England our ancestors had picked up a few Latin words; and they learned others from the Christian missionaries who began to convert them in the sixth century. These early borrowings were taken directly into the spoken language, and most of them have now changed so that their Latin origins are not easy to recognize. *Street, wine, bishop, priest,* and *church* (the last three originally borrowed from Greek by the Romans) are examples.

After the Norman Conquest borrowings from Latin were enormously increased. French itself is directly descended from Latin, and we cannot always tell whether an English word came directly from Latin or through French. *Suspicion,* for instance, could have come into English by either route. But we do know that many words must have come straight from Latin, either because they don't occur in French or because their French forms are different. Scholars often could not find an English word for an idea they wished to express; and even if they could, they might think that a Latin word was more exact or more impressive.

English has also borrowed words from many other languages, particularly Greek, and is continuing to do so at present; but ever since the late Middle English period it has been a matter of helping ourselves, rather than yielding to pressure.

Development of a Literary Standard

The changes that took place in the language throughout the Old and Middle English periods were a natural development, unguided by any theory. Men talked more or less as their neighbors did, and anybody who wrote tried to indicate the sound of his speech on paper. There were no dictionaries, no grammars, and no printed books of any kind. As far as we know, very few people thought about the language at all; and most of those who did think about it seem to have considered it a crude and rather hopeless affair, unworthy of serious study. There were exceptions, of course, but they did not have much influence. Local differences were so great that a man trained in northern England would have serious difficulty reading a manuscript written in the southern part. However, the dialect of

London had a certain prestige throughout the country; and although this dialect itself was by no means uniform, and changed with shifts in city population, it gradually came to be accepted as the standard. By the latter half of the fifteenth century it was quite generally used in writing throughout the country except in the extreme north. The introduction of printing in 1476, with London as the publishing center, greatly strengthened the influence of the London dialect. Strong local differences in spoken English remain to this day, especially among the less educated classes. But throughout the modern period written (or at least published) English has been surprisingly uniform.

Eighteenth-Century Movement to Regularize the Language

Until the eighteenth century the uniformity was the result of social pressure rather than of educational theory. Early English grammars (the first appeared in 1586) had been written either to help foreigners learn English or to prepare English students for the study of Latin grammar. On the whole these books neither had nor were intended to have any influence on the use of English by native speakers. It was not until about 1750 that there was any general attempt to teach Englishmen systematically how to use their own language.

It is too bad that this attempt was not postponed for a few more generations. Since the really scientific study of various languages had not yet begun, the eighteenth century grammarians had to base their work on a set of theories that we now know are definitely wrong. For one thing, they thought that grammar had an absolute existence, and must therefore be the same in all languages. Since they believed that this grammar was well preserved in Latin and badly frayed in English, they often tried to reform a natural English expression on a Latin model.

For another thing, they thought that the simplifying of inflections, which had been going on for centuries, was decay instead of progress. They could not do anything about the ones that had already completely disappeared, but they did make a deliberate and fairly successful effort to preserve those that were just disappearing. We would not have so many irregular verbs today if they had just let nature take its course.

Perhaps the most dangerous of their ideas was that they could keep the language from ever changing any more. They argued that Latin had remained unchanged for centuries, and they saw no reason why English should not do the same. They failed to realize that the only reason classical Latin had remained unchanged was that the men who had written it had been dead for a long time. There were still scholars —there are a few even today—who could *imitate* classical Latin. But as a natural language for the people, Latin had developed, in different areas, into Italian, French, Spanish, and so forth. All of these languages, as well as English, are still changing, and we have every reason to believe that they will continue to change as long as they are used.

If these theories had merely been the bad guesses of a few scholars, they would not have done much harm. But they became the guiding principles in most schoolroom instruction just at the time when education was becoming general, and when the study of the English language was beginning to be recognized as an end in itself and not merely as a preliminary step to the study of Latin. As a result, during the two hundred years in which English has been seriously taught in our schools, it has been taught almost entirely on a set of theories which can now be proved unsatisfactory, so that a great part of the effort has been wasted.

Since most students find it hard enough to learn English grammar without making comparisons with other languages, we need not go into a detailed explanation of why the eighteenth-century theories were wrong. But the basic structural difference is easily grasped. Latin is a *synthetic* language. That is, it is highly inflected, and the relations between words are shown primarily by their endings. Old English was also synthetic, but modern English has become an *analytical* language. Most of the endings have dropped off, and even those that remain are much less important than they used to be, since the relations between words are now shown largely by word-order and *function words,* such as connectives and auxiliary verbs. It is now rather generally held that the shift from a synthetic to an analytical structure is an improvement, but most eighteenth-century grammarians considered it a calamity and tried to stop it.

One effect of this misdirected effort has been to interfere with the natural development of the language. By 1750 most of the Old English irregular verbs either had dropped out of use or had become regular: *help, holp* had become *help, helped; wash, wesh* had become

wash, washed, etc. A number of others were in the process of making the same change: *Blow, blew* to *blow, blowed; throw, threw* to *throw, throwed;* etc. We should probably still have some irregular verbs even if eighteenth-century grammarians had not deliberately resisted this development, but there would certainly not be so many. Most of us probably have a feeling that such forms as *blowed* and *throwed* are intrinsically wrong; but our acceptance of *helped* and *washed* as correct shows that this is purely a matter of habit.

At the same time, many of those troublesome verbs like *sing* and *take,* which have separate forms for the past participle, were simplifying to a single past form. This change also was resisted, on the theory that the small number of inflections was "the greatest defect in our language." The fact that only about forty of our verbs now have these separate forms proves conclusively that we don't need them, and most of them would probably have disappeared by now if they had been allowed to depart in peace. But after two centuries of insistence on the importance of these unfortunate survivals, we may never get rid of them.

After-Effects of Eighteenth-Century Grammatical Theories

Of course the language continued to change in spite of all objections; and if the grammarians had done no more than slow up the rate of change it could be argued (although not proved) that their efforts had on the whole been useful. But they did something much worse than this. By insisting on rules which often had no foundation in the speech habits of the people, they converted "grammar" into an artificial and generally distasteful subject. When a Frenchman studies French grammar, he is learning how educated Frenchmen actually talk and write; and in his later life he can practice what he has learned in school with a comfortable assurance. But a good deal of what an Englishman or an American learns under the name of grammar has nothing to do with the use of our language; and a good deal more is in direct conflict with the actual practices of most educated people.

The result is that many Americans go through life feeling inadequate, even guilty, about their language habits. Even if they actually speak English very well, they seldom have the comfort of realizing it. They have been taught to believe in a mysterious "perfect English" which does not exist, and to regard it as highly important; but they have never had the structure of the language explained to them.

American English

In the early part of the seventeenth century English settlers began to bring their language to America, and another series of changes began to take place. The settlers borrowed words from Indian languages for such strange trees as the hickory and persimmon, such unfamiliar animals as raccoons and woodchucks. Later they borrowed other words from settlers from other countries—for instance, *chowder* and *prairie* from the French, *scow* and *sleigh* from the Dutch. They made new combinations of English words, such as *backwoods* and *bullfrog,* or gave old English words entirely new meanings, such as *lumber* (which in British English means approximately *junk*) and *corn* (which in British means any grain, especially wheat). Some of the new terms were needed, because there were new and un-English things to talk about. Others can be explained only on the general theory that languages are always changing, and American English is no exception.

Aside from the new vocabulary, differences in pronunciation, in grammatical construction, and especially in intonation developed. If the colonization had taken place a few centuries earlier, American might have become as different from English as French is from Italian. But the settlement occurred after the invention of printing, and continued through a period when the idea of educating everybody was making rapid progress. For a long time most of the books read in America came from England, and a surprising number of Americans read those books, in or out of school. Moreover, most of the colonists seem to have felt strong ties with England. In this they were unlike their Anglo-Saxon ancestors, who apparently made a clean break with their continental homes.

A good many Englishmen and some Americans used to condemn every difference that did develop, and as recently as a generation ago it was not unusual to hear all "Americanisms" condemned, even in America. It is now generally recognized in this country that we are not bound to the Queen's English, but have a full right to work out our own habits. Even a good many of the English now concede this, though some of them object strongly to the fact that Americanisms are now having an influence on British usage.

There are thousands of differences in detail between British and American English, and occasionally they crowd together enough to make some difficulty. If you read that a man, having trouble with his *lorry,* got out his *spanner* and lifted the *bonnet* to see what was the matter, you might not realize that the driver of the *truck* had taken out his *wrench* and lifted the *hood.* It is amusing to play with such differences, but the theory that the American language is now essentially different from English does not hold up. It is often very difficult to decide whether a book was written by an American or an Englishman. Even in speech it would be hard to prove that national differences are greater than some local differences in either country. On the whole, it now seems probable that the language habits of the two countries will grow more, rather than less, alike, although some differences will undoubtedly remain and others may develop.

It also seems probable that there will be narrow-minded and snobbish people in both countries for some time to come. But generally speaking, anybody who learns to speak and write the standard English of his own country, and to regard that of the other country as a legitimate variety with certain interesting differences, will have little trouble wherever he goes.

Exercises—Chapter 1

Answer each of the following questions simply and briefly.

1. About how many years has the English language, as such, been in existence?
2. To what branch of the Indo-European family of languages does English belong?
3. Name three other modern languages of Indo-European origin.
4. Name three languages which have no known Indo-European origin.
5. What epic poem do we often associate with the beginnings of English?
6. What is the approximate date of the language of this poem as it has come down to us?
7. Should we associate the language of Chaucer's writing with *Modern English, Anglo-Saxon* or *Middle English?*
8. How far back does the period called *Modern English* extend?
9. Is the language of Shakespeare associated with *Old English, Middle English* or *Modern English?*
10. What *two* sets of circumstances may have brought Latin influence into English?
11. What happened in 1066 A.D. to change the nature of the English language?
12. Why didn't the Norman invaders bring to England a language more like that of their Scandinavian forebears?

13. What was the nature of the French influence on English?

14. Is it true that for a time the rulers of England spoke French?

15. What event in 1476 contributed to the growing uniformity of the English language?

16. At about what time were the first general attempts made to teach English systematically?

17. What language seemed to provide the early teachers with a model for English grammar to follow?

18. What was the attitude of eighteenth-century grammarians toward changes they saw taking place in the language?

19. Toward what end did the early grammarians direct their efforts regarding the changes that were underway in the language?

20. Whereas Latin and Old English may be called *synthetic* languages, what term more nearly describes Modern English?

21. Name two other languages in use today that might be called *synthetic*.

22. What grammatical devices are now employed in English to show relations between words which were once shown by inflections in Old English?

23. Besides the novelty of it, what other reason may have prompted American settlers to borrow words from the Indians?

24. What words are popular British equivalents of our words *subway, elevator, tavern* and *suspenders?* (Use dictionary if necessary.)

25. What are the American equivalents of the words *ironmonger, chemist, bobby* and *petrol?*

Suggestions for Discussion or Theme Writing—Chapter 1

1. Discuss the theory that languages change constantly with time, place and circumstance. Among the situations with which you illustrate your remarks, consider (a) the present differences between many languages having common Indo-European ancestry, (b) the difficulties that the 18th Century grammarians had with English, and (c) the contrast between the British *lorry, spanner, bonnet,* and the American *truck, wrench* and *hood.*

2. Suggest some analogies among *accepted* constructions which might explain why a child just learning to talk would suppose the following to be acceptable usage:

brang as the past tense of *bring*   *blowed* as the past tense of *blow*
slided as the past tense of *slide*   *taked* as the past tense of *take*

Might the *more* or the *less* intelligent beginners be the ones to make these mistakes, if all of them heard only standard English spoken? Explain.

A R E A S   O F   U S A G E   2

Standard English

Standard English is the kind of English that is, on the whole, used by people of education and standing in the community; and it is standard simply because such people use it. We will get along much faster if we can manage to get rid of the mysterious idea of "perfect English." There just isn't any such thing. Even our best speakers do not all use the language in the same way, and there are times when we can't possibly satisfy Jones without running into criticism from Smith. We simply have to accept this situation, and we ought to be able to survive it. But when Smith, Jones, and Robinson all agree that "I saw" is respectable and "I seen" is ignorant, we'll get along with them better if we adopt their practice.

Fifty years ago there was a general, though vague, belief that it was the duty of grammarians to lay down rules for the correct use of the language, and the duty of everybody else (except, perhaps, certain lovable characters who spoke in amusing dialects) to obey them. This belief has not entirely disappeared, but it is no longer respectable. Linguists now generally agree that "grammar is based on usage," and that a grammarian has no more right to say how people ought to talk than a chemist has to say how molecules ought to interact. The laws of grammar are like the laws of any other science, simply generalized statements about what does happen, not directives about what should—and they are subject to revision as soon as any new evidence comes in.

Since this new attitude sounds both scientific and democratic, it would take a bold man to call it wrong; but it takes only a reasonably careful man to say that it has to be analyzed rather thoughtfully before it can safely be adopted for general classroom use. Otherwise we will have no answer for Joe, who takes the logical view that if grammar is based on usage, usage obviously can't be based on grammar. Therefore anybody can talk exactly as he pleases, and if he is accused of violating the rules of grammar, he can answer: "Nonsense. If the grammarians don't recognize the way I talk it just shows that their rules are inaccurate or incomplete. I can't possibly be wrong, because I am a statistic."

Now, of course Joe can talk exactly as he pleases if he is willing to take the social and other consequences; and of course the grammarian's rules are incomplete. With hundreds of millions of people talking as much as they do, a grammarian cannot possibly analyze more than a very small sampling of the language. He realizes, of course, that there are many varieties of English, and he probably takes a very broad-minded view about them all, because he finds them all interesting. As a scientist he is not in the least inclined to say that standard English is *intrinsically* better than any of the other varieties; and he is certainly not inclined to tell the native speakers of standard that they should change any of their habits to conform to his private idea of what the language ought to be like. But he is in a position to say something like this:

These are the patterns of standard English. Anybody who is not sure that his own language is standard may use them as models. As a grammarian I can't say that they are better than any other patterns; but as an observer of American life I can say that they are generally believed to be better. When standard practice is divided I have tried to list all the widely used patterns; but I have not tried to list every variation that could possibly be called standard, because I would never have finished my book if I had.

Usage, Grammar, and Rhetoric

In the preceding section we mentioned the catchword, "grammar is based on usage." *Usage* is a very broad term used to cover the complete set of language habits of a person or a group—vocabulary, pronunciation, mechanics, and so forth as well as strictly grammatical matters. *Grammar* refers to those matters of word-form, word-order, "function words" (such as connectives and auxiliary verbs), and intonations which make up the general structural patterns of the language. Thus the difference between "We saw him" and "We seen him" is a matter of grammar, because it involves a structural principle that would apply to many other sentences; but the difference between "The youngsters interfered with the proceedings" and "The punks loused up the works" is one of usage. Grammatically these last two sentences are exactly parallel.

Obviously standard English involves more than grammar, but in this country grammar is particularly important. Anybody who has seen *My Fair Lady,* or seen or read Shaw's *Pygmalion,* on which it is based, will realize that in England pronunciation is the sacred thing. Eliza can safely use any words or constructions that she cares to, as long as she pronounces them acceptably. An American Eliza could speak with anything from a "southern drawl" to a "midwestern twang" without being suspected of imposture; but if she got tangled up with her verb and pronoun forms, the other ladies would be exchanging meaningful glances.

Rhetoric is concerned with *effective* rather than (or in addition to) "correct" communication. Such rules as "Avoid short, choppy sentences" and "Don't begin a sentence with *and*" are rhetorical rather than grammatical. They are reasonably good general advice, but may be disregarded at any time by a writer who knows what he is doing. Grammar is pretty much a matter of fact, while rhetoric is a matter of opinion. Since the effectiveness of a passage depends on the speaker, the audience, and the situation as well as the choice and arrangement of words, absolute rules about it are never reliable. This does *not* mean that rhetoric is unimportant. A moron can learn grammar by simple exposure if he is lucky enough to be brought up in the right surroundings. It is sound rhetoric that distinguishes a good writer or speaker from a bad one.

Communication and Etiquette

The rules of grammar may be divided roughly into two groups—those that make for clear communication, and those that deal with the etiquette of the language. When we are learning a foreign language we are particularly concerned with those of the first group. We want to be able to understand as accurately as possible things said in that language, and we want to be understood when we use it. If we manage to do these two things reasonably well, we are usually satisfied. Any minor errors we make will probably be forgiven us.

Our emphasis is quite different when we study English grammar. The rules we take most seriously deal with the forms of words; yet it is rather seldom that an incorrect English form really interferes with understanding. Two of the chief reasons for the study of grammar are that it can help us to talk and write in such a way as to gain the respect of those with whom we communicate, and that it can increase our self-confidence and peace of mind. Indirectly, this increases the probability of our being understood. Worrying about our grammar often distracts us from a clear presentation of our ideas; and if our uncertainty shows, or our usage is of a kind not generally admired, people may not listen to us as carefully as they otherwise would.

Shibboleths

Perhaps the best answer to the theory that etiquette is secondary to communication is a bit of Biblical history. When the ancient Hebrews were engaged in a civil war, one group, on a particularly dark night, had control of a ford. Members of both sides were trying to cross the river, and it was too dark to tell friend from foe. Somebody hit upon the idea of making everybody who wanted to cross pronounce the word *shibboleth,* because it happened that those of the "wrong" group had trouble with the *sh* sound. Anybody who pronounced the word "correctly" as *shibboleth* was allowed to cross. Anybody who pronounced it *sibboleth* was killed. Of course the pronunciation *sibboleth* did not prove anything against his virtue or intelligence; but it did prove that, for the purpose of immediate survival, he had been born on the wrong side of the tracks.

We do not usually act quite so drastically about modern shibboleths; but it is hardly necessary to argue that failure to conform to certain standards can seriously handicap a man's social and business career. We may feel very strongly that this should not be so; we cannot deny that at present it *is*.

Another thing we must realize is that some important grammatical habits have nothing whatever to do with logic. We know from experience that the man who says "I seen" or "them apples" is greeted with more raised eyebrows than the man who misplaces his modifiers or calls anything more complicated than a screwdriver a "doo-hickey." This is a simple matter of cause and effect. Since word-forms have little to do with making meaning clear, they are more often learned by unconscious imitation than by deliberate study. They indicate back-ground rather than ability, which makes them perfect shibboleths.

Now, a shibboleth is by its very nature completely unreasonable. If the other side had held the ford, a different pronunciation would have been the key to survival. The same principle holds true today. "It is me" may get you a low mark in an English class, but "It is I" may get you blackballed by the Elks. Which gives rise to the natural question, "Short of being a chameleon, what is a man sup-posed to do?"

Actually, the situation is not quite so bad as it sounds. We may find it advisable to shift gears occasionally, but a man who talks "standard English" comfortably and as a matter of course, without giving the impression that he is smug about his own language or overcritical about that of others, can usually get along as well in an Elks Club or a cow camp as at a meeting of a learned society. And the requirements of standard English are not nearly as numerous or as mysterious as many people seem to believe. We don't really have to worry about offending those precious souls who are upset by any-thing that a dictionary marks "colloquial." If we master the most important shibboleths, learn something about the structure of the language, and pay some attention to the speech and writing of people whose language habits we admire, most of us can get along very well.

Areas of Usage

As we have already seen, the variety of usage with which gram-marians usually deal, and to which educated people in general try to conform, is often called *standard*. The diagram below is intended to indicate the relations of standard to several other kinds of usage. It should be noticed that none of the lines are solid. Many of the words and expressions are common to several of the areas, and even the outer limits of the language cannot be exactly defined. There is also room for unlimited argument over exactly where the inner lines should be drawn. Nevertheless, the areas indicated are, in a general way, recognizable; and if we freely admit the existence of numerous borderline cases, the diagram may be of some use. At least it is more informative than one which indicates only "good" and "bad" English, or one which shows differences only as "levels." We should recognize

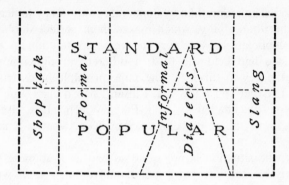

that one way of saying things may differ from another without necessarily being better or worse.

Formal and Informal Varieties of Standard English

In spite of a few minor differences, the general characteristics of standard English are surprisingly uniform throughout the country. If it is used naturally it will usually be respected in any sort of company. Of course, anybody who uses it with an air of showing off will arouse some resentment. And the man who regards it as a mysterious ceremony, and tries too hard to avoid ever making a mistake, is going to be consistently uncomfortable and occasionally ridiculous. Except for a few uses of verb and pronoun forms, the differences between standard and "popular" English are not nearly so great as is often supposed. They certainly do not justify the very widespread feeling that when there is the least cause for doubt, whatever sounds natural must be wrong.

The curious theory that standard English has to be formal has probably done more harm than any other idea connected with the language. Many of our best books and public speeches, to say nothing of letters and conversations, are definitely informal, and not a bit the worse for being so. The difference between formal and informal English is a matter of style and attitude, rather than of "level." Yet an amazing number of students have clearly been taught that only the formal variety of standard is truly legitimate, and that the term "colloquial" is practically equivalent to "illiterate."

It is impossible to draw an exact line between formal and informal English. In general, formal English is more impersonal. It does not emphasize the individuality of the speaker or writer, and it takes little account of the personal qualities of the audience. It is often rather bookish, and makes use of a larger and more exact vocabulary than we ordinarily meet in general conversation. It avoids short-cuts, such as contractions, abbreviations, and omissions. Its sentences tend to be longer, and their parts are more carefully fitted together. It is particularly appropriate to ceremonial occasions, and to serious communications addressed to comparatively expert audiences. Those who have been trained to respond to it may enjoy the precision and careful construction which are its best qualities.

On the other hand, formal English is likely to lack force and vividness. The very fact that it is formal implies that it depends more on arbitrary conventions than on natural speech habits, and it therefore demands more effort and concentration on the part of the audience. Some of them will find its longer and more complicated sentences confusing. Even people who are pleased by the sound often find it hard to get through to the sense; and frequently they fall asleep.

In choosing how formal to be on a given occasion, we should consider both the effect we want to produce and our ability to produce it. A speaker who attempts more formality than feels completely natural to him is likely to seem pompous to his audience. An exaggerated informality is equally likely to leave an impression of poor taste—or of sour grapes.

It seems reasonable to insist on standard usage in a classroom, but to let each student choose the degree of formality that suits his own temperament, so that he can talk to educated people without feeling either incompetent or unnatural. After all, the principal champions of strictly formal English today seem to be the writers of government bulletins and certain kinds of textbooks. If we are to take them as models, the world will become a gloomier place.

Popular English

If a man says "I don't have any more of those apples" he is talking standard English. If he says "I ain't got no more of them apples" he is talking something else, though it isn't easy to decide just what to call it. The terms *illiterate, vulgar,* and *substandard* have been used to describe this sort of speech. The term *popular* English now seems to be gaining ground, and will be used here. In this sense *popular* does not mean "generally liked" but "characteristic of the populace, or great mass of the people."

In spite of the general schoolroom attitude, there is nothing shameful about popular usage. It is the normal language of millions of intelligent and self-respecting people (as well as some others), and nobody has ever proved that it is essentially inferior to standard. None the less, a man who uses it is likely to be handicapped in both his business and his social career, simply because we generally associate it with the lower social and economic levels. Most people who have any interest in getting along in life would rather talk standard English if it were not made too hard or presented as too unnatural. About the only ones who make a deliberate effort to use popular seem to be certain politicians and salesmen who think they get along better by making a point of being "plain folks." The most common popular departures from standard usage are pointed out in the appropriate sections below.

Dialects

The word *dialect,* as used by a linguist, is not a term of reproach. It means simply the kind of language used by a limited group. Since English is not spoken uniformly over the enormous territory where it is used, everybody who speaks it must speak some dialect of it (or some mixture of dialects). Three major dialect areas have long been recognized in American English—New England, Western or General American, and Southern. Linguistic geographers now prefer the terms Northern, Midland, and Southern, and these may turn out to be more satisfactory when further studies have been completed. At any rate, the most obvious differences between the three are in pronunciation and intonation. We can often identify a man as a New Englander or a Southerner after hearing him say a few words, though we might read hundreds of pages of his writing without being able to guess where he came from.

There are people who regard General American as *the* language of the country, and believe that the other two should be conscientiously driven out. There are other people who believe that the New England variety is our only truly cultured form of speech, and that it should therefore be extended over the vastly greater areas where the other two varieties are normally spoken. And there are many Southerners who are quite sure that their way of speaking is best, though they usually show no particular desire to improve the habits of the rest of the country. On the whole, however, it is now rather generally accepted (at least by linguists) that the three major dialects are on an exactly equal footing. Possibly they will merge in the future, but we don't have to worry about it. Meanwhile, we may use the terms *standard* and *popular* English to extend across all three.

Within the three major dialectal areas, there are any number of minor dialects and subdialects, some of which are far from standard. Non-linguists ordinarily use the word *dialect* only in referring to these, and frequently imply that they are inferior to, as well as different from, the standard language. Some of these minor dialects, such as Pennsylvania Dutch, show a strong influence of the original language of the speakers or their ancestors. This may appear in vocabulary and construction as well as in pronunciation. These characteristics have been preserved by some sort of isolation, either physical, as in the Southern hill country, or social, as in many tightly knit national, religious, or occupational groups.

American dialects have never differed nearly as much as those in many countries, and during the past fifty years their differences have decreased in both number and degree. This is due partly to such influences as moving pictures, radio, TV, and more nearly universal education; partly to the fact that more people move around the country. Nevertheless, many regional variations remain. They are naturally more marked among people of limited education than among those who have had more experience, through reading, schooling, and association, with standard English; but to some extent they are found in all levels of speech.

A "dialectal" word or expression is therefore one of limited currency. Used in its own area, it is exactly as good as it is thought to be. *Goober,* for instance, is a perfectly good word for *peanut* in Georgia. But it may not be understood in Oregon.

Aside from the question of whether dialect will be understood, using it away from its natural range may have either of two opposite effects. Some people will tend to approve of it as strange and therefore fascinating; others will feel that it is strange and therefore inferior. The general effect probably depends more on the attitude of the speaker than on the proportion of dialectal expressions he uses. Either an aggressive insistence on dialect or an overanxious effort to avoid it is likely to create a bad impression.

Shop Talk or Technical Language

Both standard and popular English can be used over the whole range of our general interests. The term *shop talk* covers a large number of specialized sets of usages in which various groups talk about matters of particular concern to themselves. These range from the technical *jargon* of scholars and scientists to the *cant* of hobos and criminals.

Shop talk cannot be given a separate level from standard and popular English. It lies alongside them rather than above or below. Some varieties are used largely by people of considerable education and standing, and are quite as "good," within their narrower range, as standard. Others are clearly of no higher standing than popular.

The chief question about shop talk that arises in schools is whether it is permissible to carry it over into non-technical communications. Some people argue, for instance, that a bank can *loan* money, but that a friend can only *lend* a book. This is carrying a theory rather far. It is usually inadvisable to talk to people in terms that confuse them or give them a low opinion of us. But the standard language is always changing and growing, and shop talk is one of the natural sources of its growth. Each expression must be judged by the effect it apparently has, not by the one it theoretically should have.

Slang

If there is a man living who can explain satisfactorily why *bonehead* is a slang word and *blockhead* a respectable literary term, he would do a great service by making his explanation public. Until he does we shall have to agree that although "everybody knows" there is an area called slang, nobody can define it with any certainty.

Slang might be called a novelty language; and like most novelties, slang expressions are rather likely to be in doubtful taste at the beginning, and extremely likely to grow tiresome by too much repetition. It is impossible to estimate how many of them flicker and die out before the general public even becomes aware of them. Even those that sweep the country usually last only a short time. A few years after their vogue they may be completely unknown to the younger generation, and pathetic even to those who remember them. Yet many of them are so effective that much of the sparkle would die out of the language if all slang should come to an end.

At its best, slang is a vivid, cheerful, and often poetical way of speaking. It depends largely on metaphors, usually uncomplimentary ones. Such expressions as *brass hats, stuffed shirts,* and *sob sisters* would be hard to replace from the literary language. Brevity is another common characteristic. This may take the form of substitution of a short word for an unrelated long one (*crate* for *airplane*); by mangled abbreviation (*prexy* for *president*); or by simply shortening (*rep* for *reputation*).

Not all such shortenings are generally considered as slang, and it is impossible to draw a clear line. Perhaps the best test—admittedly not very definite—is whether the reason is simple economy of effort or space (*POW, f.o.b., phone*), or an attitude that is playful, disrespectful, or intended to confuse outsiders (*prof, pug, PDQ, BMOC*).

A slang expression may become so completely a part of the standard language that its origin is forgotten. A good many of our most respected polysyllables can only be explained on the theory that the ancient Romans had a pretty taste for slang—for instance, *recalcitrant* (kicking back), and *supercilious* (having eyebrows). On the other hand, if a slang expression happens to be particularly convenient, it may gain almost universal use in spite of continual opposition. *O.K.* has probably been attacked as unceasingly as any word in the language; and it is almost certainly now the most widely used term on earth.

Even if it does not win a permanent place in the language, a slang term may enjoy a high social standing during its lifetime. A desire to be in fashion is just as characteristic of hunt clubs as of pool rooms; and a phrase, like a hat, may seem delightful one year even though it is destined to be hopelessly out of date the next.

For these reasons the rather common schoolroom attitude that all slang is an evil to be opposed at all times seems silly as well as hopeless. If used with reasonable judgment, slang can be a valuable ingredient in any but the most formal language—and even there a dash of it is not always out of place. Roosevelt and Churchill both knew this—and even people who dislike their politics seldom deny their mastery of the language.

There are, however, a few tendencies that are worth avoiding:

1. *The lazy use.* Some speakers seem to feel that the plentiful use of slang terms will conceal the fact that they are not saying (or perhaps thinking) anything in particular. It may be no worse intellectually to call everything we approve *swell, slick, cool,* or whatever term happens to be in fashion, than to use such older words as *nice* or *fine* just as loosely; but the flashy character of the slang terms helps to deceive their users into the belief that they are communicating information.

2. *The show-off use.* Slang is often used to prove that the speaker is an up-to-the-minute insider. The latest phrases are rather worn like costume jewelry than used as language, and whoever can wear most and jangle them most often apparently gets the highest mark. This

form of amusement has a natural enough attraction for teen-agers, like the weird costumes and haircuts that sweep high schools; but if retained beyond adolescence it is likely to strike observers as pathetic, and it certainly should not be mistaken for a form of communication.

3. *The apologetic use.* A speaker is responsible for everything he says. If he chooses to use a slang term, he should do it firmly, and not apologize by putting it in quotation marks, either written or suggested by the tone of voice. (Since this is one of the very few places in this book where the writer takes a firm moral stand, it is hoped that readers will be suitably impressed.)

4. *The deliberately vulgar use.* Some people use slang not merely in the bubble-pricking fashion which is natural to it, but in a deliberate effort to reduce every statement to its lowest and ugliest terms. This does not necessarily indicate a naturally obscene mind. Often it appears to spring from a fear that the speaker will be considered a sucker if he does not continually demonstrate that he is a wise guy. Since the habit grows out of a feeling of personal uncertainty, it is not likely to impress anybody who does not share the feeling.

Exercises—Chapter 2

I. Answer each of the following questions simply and briefly.

1. Distinguish *usage* from *grammar* and *rhetoric*.
2. Cite a language rule which involves a *rhetorical* rather than a *grammatical* distinction.
3. What is the origin of the term *shibboleth?*
4. Suggest an expression (not already given in the chapter) that you would call a modern *shibboleth.*
5. Some rules of *grammar* make for clear communication; others don't. What characterizes the rules in the latter category?
6. In your own words, define *standard* and *popular* English, and write a statement two different ways to illustrate the distinction.
7. Distinguish between *formal* and *informal* usage and illustrate the difference with an example of each.
8. What is *dialect?*
9. Name the three major dialects generally recognized in American English.
10. Name four tendencies worth avoiding in the use of slang.
11. List three expressions which you think mark a speaker as poorly educated. In what area of popular usage does each expression fall?
12. List three expressions which you have been told are bad English, but which you think are in common use among people of edu-

cation and standing in your community. In what area of usage does each fall?

13. List three expressions which you think began as shop talk, but which you think are now coming into general usage. Is any shift between standard and popular usage accompanying the change?

14. Is there a difference between *slang* and the simple economy of space forced upon newspaper headline writers? Explain briefly.

15. Contractions, personal pronouns and an intimate tone may characterize what area of usage? Describe the opposite area.

II. Using your dictionary and a combination of logic and guesswork, categorize the following according to area of usage. (You may see fit to put some expressions in more than one category.) Some of the series suggest a common category; others may suggest a progression.

1. Devil, morgue, copyboy, galley, slug.
2. Dear Aunt Martha (Jones), Dear Mrs. Jones, Dear Madam (Martha Jones).
3. Draw, gully, ditch, holler, ravine.
4. Audio, video, teleprompter, compatible color, simulcast.
5. My father, my papa, pater, my dad, my old man.
6. Dogie (maverick), yearling, chuckwagon, round-up.
7. Carbonated beverage, fizz, soda, pop, soda pop, tonic.
8. Infantryman, G. I., soldier, doughboy, dog-face.
9. Climber, faller, powersaw, rigger, powdermonkey.
10. Pad, ignition, launch, lift-off, re-entry.

Suggestions for Discussion or Theme Writing—Chapter 2

1. Suggest some expressions you think the following speakers would use, and classify each expression according to the areas of usage shown on the chart on page 28:

    (a) An uneducated mechanic making a thank-you speech for a gift presented him during ceremonies marking his retirement.

    (b) An educated, practical-minded candidate for public office addressing a mass rally in (Boston) (Atlanta) (Omaha).

    (c) A world champion athlete addressing an eighth grade graduation class at a boys' school.

    (d) An uneducated person facing television cameras for the first time and answering a man-on-the-street reporter's question: "How can we achieve victory in the Cold War?"

2. (a) Write about a two-minute speech on "Why I Chose My Career" in completely formal, but not pompous, English.

    (b) Rewrite the same speech in a respectably informal style.

THE PATTERNS
OF GRAMMAR

3

The very popular statement that "grammar is a lot of nonsense" contains a great deal of truth, though not quite in the way that is usually intended. Let's look at some nonsense and see what we can learn from it:

The floog sirily mirlated naxes with a sool pern.

Since most of the words are strange we don't know exactly what this statement means, but we do know the following things:

1. Whatever happened, the *floog* did it.	Clue—position	
2. There was probably only one *floog*.	"	no -*s* ending
3. It was done to the *naxes*.	"	position
4. There was more than one *nax*.	"	-*es* ending
5. The action of *mirlating* is over.	"	-*ed* ending
6. *Sirily* tells something about how it was done.	"	-*ly* ending
7. *With a pern* tells more about how it was done.	"	word *with*
8. There was only one *pern*.	"	word *a*
9. *Sool* tells what kind of a pern it was.	"	position

We know these things because our language contains a system of patterns which convey what is called "structural meaning" almost without regard to the dictionary meanings of the particular words used. As the clues above indicate, the main elements in the patterns of written English are:

Word order, or relative *position*
Word form (usually, but not always, a matter of endings)
Function words like *a, the,* and *with,* which are more important for what they tell us about how other words are used than for exact meanings of their own.

In spoken English at least three other elements called *pitch, stress,* and *juncture* must be recognized. These are to some extent implied in writing, but cannot be indicated as explicitly as the first three. We will therefore postpone discussing them until we have seen how the more obvious elements work.

It used to be believed that a language was made up simply of words, which had only to be arranged according to the logical rules of "universal grammar" in order to make good sentences. It is now recognized that there is no such thing as universal grammar. Each language has its own patterns as well as its own words, and these patterns are matters of habit rather than logic. We have been exposed to our own particular patterns of word form, word order, and function words for so long that we now react to them automatically even when they are filled with nonsense words. If there were just one dialect of English we could use them automatically, too, and not have to think about them. But most of us have grown up in such a confusing mixture of dialects that simple imitation is not enough. In order to speak and write with accuracy and confidence we have to make some sort of study of the competing patterns; and we'd better make the study systematic so that we'll know when we have covered the ground.

Grammatical Position

In analyzing our nonsense sentence we gave only one clue for each bit of information, as if the three elements of position, word form, and function words could be completely separated. Actually they cannot. For instance, grammatical position is not merely numerical position in a sentence but relative position; and we recognize it by considering word form and function words as well as word order. Take another look at the first four words of our sentence:

The floog sirily mirlated

We know that the *floog* did the *mirlating*—that it is what we call the subject—not by the fact that it is the second word in the sentence, but by taking all the following facts together:

1. When we see a pattern like "The _____ _____ _____ed" we assume that the word ending in *-ed* is the verb, and that one of the two words between *the* and _____*ed* is the subject.
2. Since the word just before the verb ends in *-ly* it almost certainly

tells something about the verb and therefore cannot be the subject.

3. Therefore the other possible word—*floog*—is the subject. (Notice that if the sentence had begun "The floog *siliry*" instead of "The floog *sirily*" we would take *siliry* to be the subject and *floog* to be an adjective modifying it.)

It is obvious that the study of grammatical position could become a pretty complicated subject, but we don't have to go into it very deeply. To begin with we are interested only in the way it can help us to classify four important kinds of words.

The Kinds of Words

We have to classify words in order to discuss them in groups. Even in the last section we had to use the terms *verb* and *adjective,* though we have not yet had time to define these; and if we couldn't say things like "the possessive form of a noun is always written with an apostrophe" it would take quite a while to cover the language. Unfortunately, nobody has ever found a perfect way to classify words in English. The two most obvious ways are by form and by meaning. If we base our classes on either one of these we run into trouble with the other; if we try to use both at once we get a complicated mess; and if we decide to have two separate classifications we find that they overlap so much that it is very difficult to keep them separate.

As a compromise, not perfect but reasonably workable, we will use in this book a system based on three main principles:

1. We will use such familiar *single* terms as *noun* and *adjective* to designate the ways words and word-groups function in sentence patterns.

2. We will use such *double* terms as *inflected noun* or *regular noun* (which means "noun inflected in a certain way") to discuss forms and form changes.

3. We will not bother to classify a word at all unless we have a definite reason for doing so. And if a word happens to be both a noun (by use) and an inflected noun (by form) we will use whichever designation seems to be handiest at the time.

Classification by Position

We began this chapter by analyzing a sentence composed of three familiar words, *a, the,* and *with,* and six nonsense words, *floog, sirily, mirlated, naxes, sool,* and *pern.* We could of course make up any number of similar sentences; and if we made up, say, ten pages of them, we should discover the curious fact that all the nonsense words could be reasonably put into just four classes:

1. Words that pattern like *floog, naxes,* and *pern,* which can be called *nouns.*
2. Words that pattern like *mirlated,* which can be called *verbs.*
3. Words that pattern like *sool,* which can be called *adjectives.*
4. Words that pattern like *sirily,* which can be called *adverbs.*

The nucleus of an English sentence is a combination like *man is* or *girls sang* or *floog mirlated,* in which one word seems to name something and the other seems to say something about it—even if both words are nonsense or completely unknown. In such combinations we call the naming word the subject—and the kind of word that is or could easily be the subject we call a *noun.* The saying word we call the *verb.* Words that seem to describe nouns we call adjectives—*big* man, *young* girls, *sool* pern. And words that seem to describe verbs we call adverbs—*probably* was, *merrily* sang, *sirily* mirlated.

Far more than ninety-nine per cent of all the words in English fall into these four classes, and more are being added to them every year. They are therefore called open or unlimited classes. There is nothing surprising about seeing an unfamiliar word in a position that seems to indicate any one of these classes; and even if we are quite sure that the word has no real meaning we somehow feel that we know how it acts.

All the other kinds of words (which we will not classify just now) total only a few hundred all together, and no new ones are being added. We have to know these words individually to react to the patterns of our sentences; and if we replace them by nonsense words the patterns disappear. Let's try it:

Pra floog sirily mirlated naxes tran oc sool pern.

Possibly the successive endings *-ly, -ed,* and *-es* still suggest some meaning, but there is no longer a firm pattern for the sentence as a whole. Nonsense substitutes for *a, the,* and *with* won't work.

At first glance classification by position may seem a very roundabout way of getting at such familiar definitions as "a noun is a word used to name a person, place, thing, or idea," but it has its advantages. These familiar definitions work beautifully in selected sentences, but simply do not apply to the language as a whole unless we stretch them until they are practically meaningless. The reason is that we do not always use the same grammatical patterns to express the same ideas, and it is silly to pretend that we do. Look at the following sentences:

> Sometimes he works and sometimes he loafs.
> His industry and laziness alternate.
> He is alternately industrious and lazy.
> He acts industriously and lazily by spells.

Each of these conveys the same basic information; but the contrast between his working and his loafing is shown in the first sentence by verbs, in the second by nouns, in the third by adjectives, and in the fourth by adverbs. There just is no fixed relation between the meaning conveyed and the grammatical pattern used to convey it; and since we are discussing grammar, not philosophy, we'd better depend on the perceptible patterns.

The Forms of Words

The second element in our grammatical patterns is word form. Some words, like *always, into, must, tactics,* and *which,* have only one form; but most words have from two to five different forms called *inflections.* Inflected words fall into four groups, three of which may be divided into *regular* and *irregular* subgroups.

Inflected nouns
    Regular: boy, boy's, boys, boys'
    Irregular: man, man's, men, men's
Inflected pronouns
    All *irregular:* I, me, my, mine, myself

Inflected verbs
 Regular: save, saves, saved, saving
 Irregular: take, takes, took, taken, taking
Inflected adjectives
 Regular: big, bigger, biggest
 Irregular: good, better, best

These are the only kinds of inflection in English. Such endings as *-al, -dom, -hood, -ic, -ish, -ize, -ly, -ment,* and *-ness* are considered to make different words rather·than different forms of the same word. (It is much simpler to accept the fact that this is so than to try to decide whether it should be.) They are called derivational suffixes, and will not be discussed here.

There are many thousands of regular nouns and regular verbs, and both groups are still growing. Whenever we adopt a new noun like *sputnik* everybody seems to assume at once that the only reasonable plural is *sputniks,* not *sputnak* or *sputniki.* In other words, we automatically treat it as a regular noun. And if we adopt a new verb, or make a new verb out of an old noun, we treat *it* as regular. As soon as we read that sputniks *orbit* we know that we can also say that they *orbited* or have *orbited,* not that they *orbat* or have *orbiten.* It is therefore only the regular nouns and verbs that are "open." There are about six hundred regular adjectives, and this class might be called "open at one end." Nobody knows why, but whenever we adopt a new two-syllable adjective ending in *-y,* such as *newsy* or *corny,* we give it the regular *-er* and *-est* endings. All other new adjectives are unchanging, and show degrees by *more* and *most.*

Nobody has much trouble with the spoken forms of these three regular groups, and the spelling of the written forms follows rather simple rules which will be given later. The four irregular groups are more difficult, since each word has to be learned individually. Fortunately these groups are much smaller than the regular ones, and are shrinking rather than growing. They will be discussed in more detail in the next chapter.

Along with the four inflected groups we must consider one group of words that never change form but do have a characteristic form of their own—the *-ly* adverbs like *badly* and *wonderfully.* This is another open class; we feel free to add *-ly* to almost any adjective and thus make a new adverb, if we can find a use for it.

Function Words

Function words are words which are used to form grammatical patterns, and which cannot be changed without changing the patterns. Look at the following sentence:

The old man *had* cheerfully started *the* job *with a* sharp knife.

The words in ordinary type could be varied indefinitely without changing the pattern. We could find dozens of substitutes for *started* or *job,* and hundreds for each of the others. But if we change *the* to *an* or *had* to *has* or *with* to *on* we get a different pattern at once. *The* implies that you know which old man the sentence is about; *an* implies that you don't. *Has* puts the statement in a different time relation from *had.* And the things that you can reasonably do *on* a knife are quite different from those that you can do *with* it.

The difference between function words and others (sometimes called *content words*) is not absolutely sharp or reliable, and you can argue with the statements in the preceding paragraph if you care to. But if we consider the distinction as a matter of convenience rather than of desperate doctrine, we will find it useful. Function words are used principally to make up grammatical patterns; content words are used to fill those patterns and give them specific meanings. You have to know the meanings of the content words in a particular sentence to understand that sentence; but you have to know the ways most function words are used to understand English at all.

It is reasonably easy to divide content words into four classes— nouns, verbs, adjectives, and adverbs. A satisfactory classification of function words is a good deal more difficult. For the moment we will merely indicate three principal types:

1. Auxiliary verbs, like those italicized in the following verb-phrases: *will* go, *could* eat, *has* been, *is* going, *must have* seen.
2. Connectives, including all prepositions (*to, from, with,* etc.), conjunctions (*and, because,* etc.), and many words often called adverbs and pronouns (*there, when, which,* etc.).
3. Certain special modifiers of the kinds sometimes called determiners (*a, the, those,* etc.) and qualifiers (*very, quite,* etc.).

The Parts of Speech?

It may seem curious that we have discussed two different kinds of classification of words, one by function and one by form, without even mentioning the "parts of speech." But the fact is that the whole concept of parts of speech depends on a stable relation between form and function which has almost disappeared in our language. The concept can, of course, still be applied to modern English, but it no longer seems to be really useful; and those people who insist most strongly that there *are* parts of speech disagree about whether it is the function classes or the form classes that deserve this name. And those who take form as the basis disagree about whether it is simply the form of the words or the form of the patterns in which the words are used that must be considered.

Since there is no discoverable way of settling this argument (or of stopping it, either) we will simply disregard it. Anybody can call anything he wants to the parts of speech. Meanwhile we will try to make it clear whenever we are talking about form rather than function or function rather than form. When the two overlap (as they often do) we can use either set of terms safely as long as we don't over-generalize. Thus in the sentence "The best cost no more" we can say that *best* is an irregular adjective in form but a noun by function in this sentence; and we can call *cost* either an irregular verb or simply the verb without much danger of misleading anybody.

Conversion by Suffix

Earlier in the chapter we mentioned that endings other than inflections are called suffixes—for instance, *-dom, -ize, -ly,* and *-ment.* Suffixes are sometimes used to give words different meanings without changing their functional classification. Thus we have *gray* and *grayish,* both normally adjectives, and *man* and *manhood,* both normally nouns. More often suffixes convert words from one classification to another, as in the following examples:

> *Verbs to nouns:* appease—appeasement, serve—service
> *Adjectives to nouns:* free—freedom, happy—happiness
> *Nouns to verbs:* atom—atomize, gas—gasify
> *Adjectives to verbs:* dark—darken, tranquil—tranquilize

Nouns to adjectives: child—childish, man—manly
Adjectives to adverbs: glad—gladly, frantic—frantically

This kind of conversion is common in many languages, including Greek, Latin, and French, from which a great many English words come. It explains many of the related words in the language.

Functional Shift

Conversion of a word to a new function *without* the use of a suffix occurs much more often in English than in most other languages. This is known as *functional shift,* and it has gone so far as to make a single classification of words into parts of speech almost meaningless, as we have already suggested. The general tendency is to use any word in any way that is convenient and makes sense, without regard to its original classification. Thus we may use *work* as a noun (a *work* of art), a verb (they *work* hard), or an adjective (his *work* clothes). We cannot use it as a connective, not because of any grammatical rule, but simply because there is no way to do it. And nobody but a historian of the language has any reason to care about what its original part of speech may have been.

If a word shifts its function to that of a noun or a verb, it takes on the regular inflections of its new class. Thus the irregular noun *man* gives us the regular verb *to man,* with the forms *man, mans, manned, manning.* Likewise the irregular verb *to drink* gives us the regular noun *drink, drinks.* In other shifts of function no new inflections are needed.

Reason for Functional Shift

Quite obviously the underlying reason for functional shift is economy—either the use of a shorter word for a longer one or the use of a word instead of a phrase. Use of the plain form of a verb as a noun eliminates either the *-ing* inflectional ending (*talk* for *talking*) or a suffix (a *serve* for a *service* in tennis); and use of a noun as an adjective eliminates a suffix (*wool* clothes for *woolen* clothes, *atom* bomb for *atomic* bomb). On the other hand, use of an adjective as a noun often saves a word or more (*the poor* for *the poor people, the beautiful* for *that which is beautiful*). Verbs converted from nouns are particularly economical, though not always graceful. Thus *to requisition* stands for *to put in a requisition for, to contact* for *to get in touch with.*

When the two kinds of economy conflict, the one that makes the greater overall saving generally wins out—at least in circles where efficiency is more prized than grace. Thus *to certificate* is longer than *to certify,* but shorter than *to furnish with a certificate.* It is therefore often used when the certification consists of supplying a document rather than guaranteeing a statement.

Limits to Functional Shift

The fact remains that many functional shifts that might well have taken place have not done so. Sometimes this is because a familiar word that makes a shift unnecessary is already available. Thus the verb *to man* made it unnecessary to convert *boy, girl,* or *woman* into verbs. Juveniles or females can *man* a boat. Fifty years ago, when automobiles were still competing with carriages, we used *to auto* down to the beach, since *to drive* was not sufficiently specific, and any other available expression would have been longer. Now that carriages have practically disappeared the one-syllable verb *drive* clearly means to go by automobile. *To auto* is no longer economical, and there would not be enough saving in *to car* to make it worth while.

At other times we have simply failed to make a shift for no discoverable reason. Thus we say *to reward* and *a reward, to punish* but *a punishment.* A noun *punish* may develop in the future, but it has not yet done so. Moreover, some shifts that certainly have developed are often condemned. That is, although the general principle of functional shift is universally accepted, a few individual shifts have become shibboleths. We often hear that *like* must never be used as a conjunction, that *than* and *as* must never be used as prepositions, and that *loan* and *contact* must never be used as verbs.

To object to these uses on the basis of any grammatical theory is simply silly. Thousands of other words have extended their functions in exactly comparable ways, and there is not the slightest reason why this handful should not do the same. If we must condemn such expressions we should do so by making the honest statement that there is a certain amount of prejudice against them—just as there is now a prejudice against calling a man "a certain party" or a woman "an elegant female"—though there is no doubt whatever that *party* and *female* are, in other expressions, acceptable as nouns.

Intonation Patterns

So far we have dealt only with those elements of our grammatical patterns which are visible as well as audible. In spoken English at least three other elements would be perceptible (though not necessarily recognizable by people without some training). These can sometimes be suggested in writing, but cannot be indicated as explicitly as the first three. Compare the two following sentences:

Jack put salt in his coffee.
Jack put salt in his *coffee?*

Since these are identical in all three of the elements so far discussed, many people would call them "the same sentence punctuated in two different ways." But, intelligently read, they sound different and they mean different things—which should be enough to make them different sentences. The fact that the differences do not appear as clearly in writing as they do in speech proves only that our system of writing is imperfect—it indicates some differences less clearly than others. If you read both sentences aloud carefully and naturally you will see that they vary in three ways:

1. The first syllable of *coffee* is pronounced more strongly in the second sentence than in the first. This is a difference in *stress*.

2. This syllable is also pronounced on a lower musical tone, and the next one on a higher tone. These are differences in *pitch*.

3. At the end of the first sentence the voice comes down in pitch as it fades into silence. At the end of the second it does not. This is a difference in *juncture*. In order to make the comparison as simple as possible we have shown the difference in stress, pitch, and juncture only at the ends of the two sentences, but they occur throughout. Every syllable that is pronounced at all must be pronounced with some degree of stress and at some pitch; and whenever two successive words are not completely run together the transition between them can be called juncture. Thus *white house* has a kind of juncture not found in *Whitehouse;* the sort of pause often shown by a comma is a second kind; and the rising and falling tones as your voice fades off after different kinds of sentences are two others.

It is possible to indicate all these things consistently by a special system of writing—the stress by accent marks, the pitch by numbers, and the juncture by special symbols. Thus the second sentence might be written as follows:

$$^2\text{Jâck}+\text{pùt}+\text{sâlt}+\text{in}+\text{his}+^1\text{cóffee}^3\uparrow$$

(It might also be indicated in several other ways.) This more complete system of writing is very useful for experts who wish to make a detailed analysis of our sound patterns, but it is a little cumbersome for ordinary use. Most of us would rather get along with just a few hints, such as the italicizing of *coffee* and the question mark at the end. Moreover, experts are still disagreeing about such questions as how many degrees of stress and pitch are significant, and how regular and dependable are our uses of these elements. We are not therefore going into these matters in much detail. But we should realize that the experts are right in principle—these elements are quite as real as the first three, and at least some of the time they are quite as important. We shall see this when we come to consider the structure of sentences in Chapter 5.

Stress, pitch, and juncture together make up *intonation*. Every spoken sentence must have its pattern of intonation; and every good written sentence at least suggests one. If you don't believe intonation is as real or as important as the other sounds, perhaps you can remember a time when you were seriously misquoted by somebody who claimed to be repeating exactly what you had said, and who did repeat the same words in the same order—but who changed the intonation pattern so as to give an entirely different meaning.

Exercises—Chapter 3

Answer each of the following questions simply and briefly.

1. Name the main elements in the patterns of written English.
2. In discussing patterns of grammar, you may substitute the term *relative position* for what other term?
3. In forming grammatical patterns, what are words like *a, and, the, with* called?
4. We may divide *content* words rather easily into what *four* classes?
5. Where do auxiliary verbs and connectives fit into the patterns of grammar?
6. Name the four groups of words that are subject to inflection.
7. Three of these four groups (#6 above) inflect both regularly and irregularly. Which one does not? How does the fourth group inflect?
8. Word endings like *-dom, -hood, -ic, -ish,* and *-ize* are not to be confused with inflections. What are such endings called?
9. Roughly speaking, what percentage of all English words are included in the four categories, *nouns, verbs, adjectives* and *adverbs?*
10. Words that inflect *irregularly* are becoming increasingly outnumbered by those which inflect *regularly*. Why?

11. The words *simulcast* and *telemeter,* originally nouns, will probably come into general use as verbs (if they haven't already done so). How are they likely to inflect as verbs? Why?

12. The process of converting a word to a new functional class without the use of a suffix is referred to by what term?

13. Add a suffix to a noun without changing its functional classification. To another noun add a suffix which *does* change the word class.

14. Avoiding examples already given, illustrate the following conversions by suffix: a verb to a noun, an adjective to a noun, a noun to a verb, an adjective to a verb, a noun to an adjective, and an adjective to an adverb.

15. List three examples of functional shift not already used in the text.

16. Write two sentences (or three if possible) in which the same word is used in a different functional capacity (noun, verb, adjective, perhaps).

17. What is the underlying reason for functional shift?

18. What kind of patterns do *stress, pitch,* and *juncture* involve?

19. By what term do we refer to the degree of forcefulness with which a syllable is pronounced?

20. The intonational transition between any two spoken words that are not completely run together is referred to by what term?

21. Which of the following pairs of words change by inflection and which by the addition of suffixes: bone-bony, be-been, steal-stolen, song-songs?

22. Which of the following pairs change by inflection and which by the addition of suffixes: easy-easily, hardy-hardihood, pastor-pastoral, day-day's?

23. Is *chin* a noun, a verb, or an adjective? Explain and illustrate.

24. Is *toy* a noun, a verb, or an adjective? Explain and illustrate.

25. Is *rest* a noun, a verb, or an adjective? Explain and illustrate.

Suggestions for Discussion or Theme Writing—Chapter 3

1. Explain a number of different ways you can change the implication of the following sentence by changing the intonation pattern. (For a starter, try shifting the *stress* from one content word to another.):

Mother said she was unable to drive to the beach with you all today.

2. Discuss the effect of the concept of *functional shift* on the traditional concept of *parts of speech.* (You might wish to use the words *wrong, fast* and *outside* to illustrate your point.)

THE FORMS

OF WORDS

4

Inflections

In the last chapter we pointed out that words may be classified by either form or use, and that form and use overlap but do not perfectly coincide. For instance, *boy* has the forms *boy, boy's, boys,* and *boys'* which are typical of regular nouns; and it is used as a noun—that is, to name something being talked about—most of the time. But it may also be used as an adjective, as in the expression *boy baby.* On the other hand, *poor* has the forms of a regular adjective, *poor, poorer,* and *poorest,* and is generally used as an adjective; but it may also be used as a noun in such sentences as "The *poor* are suffering." There are times when the classification by use is important, but for the rest of this chapter we shall consider only the classification by form, since this is the only way we can lay out all the inflected words of the language in an arrangement that is both systematic and reasonably simple.

Inflected Nouns

Nouns may have as many as four forms, plain and possessive in the singular and plain and possessive in the plural:

	SINGULAR	PLURAL
Plain	A *boy* is here.	Three *boys* came.
	A *man* is here.	Three *men* came.
Possessive	A *boy's* dog.	The two *boys'* dogs.
	A *man's* dog.	The two *men's* dogs.

Many nouns do not have the possessive forms, and are thus inflected only for number. A few (mostly kinds of fish and game) do not have separate forms for their plurals (*salmon, trout, deer, elk*). Nouns which have neither a possessive nor a separate plural form are of course uninflected and will not be considered here.

Notice that the plain plural form *boys* has no apostrophe, but that all the possessive forms have one. If you are confused by possessive forms it is probably because there are several different systems in use. The following system, which is the simplest and most consistent, is at least as good as any of the others:

1. Write the appropriate plain form, singular or plural.
2. Add an apostrophe to indicate the possessive form.
3. Then add an -*s* unless you have already added one to form the plural.

Regular Noun Plurals

All nouns which add an /s/, /z/, or /iz/ sound (spelled -*s* or -*es*) to form the plural are considered *regular*, in spite of minor variations. Since most students can choose correctly between the three plural sounds more easily than they can learn rules about them, the following rules will deal only with the spelling of the written forms.

1. Most words form their plurals by adding simple -*s: bat-bats, place-places,* etc.
2. When -*s* alone would make an unpronounceable combination, -*es* is added: *box-boxes, match-matches, loss-losses,* etc.
3. Six common words ending in -*o* form their plurals in -*es: echoes, heroes, Negroes, potatoes, tomatoes,* and *torpedoes.* (So do eleven others which are much less common, at least in the plural, if you want to know: *bilboes, buboes, dadoes, dingoes, embargoes, goes, innuendoes, jingoes, mulattoes, noes,* and *vetoes.*) All other words ending in -*o* either may or must be written with -*s* plurals.
4. Words ending in -*y* preceded by a consonant take a plural in -*ies: copy-copies, lady-ladies,* etc.

When the -*y* is preceded by a vowel there is no such change: *boy-boys, monkey-monkeys,* etc.
5. Words ending in -*f* or -*fe* take a plural in -*ves* if the sound changes: *half-halves, wife-wives;* but *belief-beliefs, safe-safes.*

Irregular English Plurals

A few common native English words form their plurals in some other manner than by adding -*s* or -*es*. Fortunately, they are all so well known that they give little trouble. They are:

child-children	louse-lice	ox-oxen
foot-feet	man-men	tooth-teeth
goose-geese	mouse-mice	woman-women

Foreign Plurals

The English language has borrowed thousands of nouns from other languages, particularly Greek and Latin. It used to be the general practice to borrow both the singular and plural forms. Since the result was bewildering to those who knew only English, many people took a great deal of pride in their ability to handle such pairs as the following:

alumna-alumnae	dogma-dogmata
cactus-cacti	corpus-corpora

In the last fifty years or so, however, there have been two important changes:

1. New words have been introduced only in the singular, and have formed their plurals in the normal English way. Even the most learned people say *electrons* and *protons* instead of *electra* and *prota*.

2. Regular English plurals in -*s* or -*es* have developed alongside of the foreign plurals for most foreign words which are in reasonably common use, as the following list indicates:

SINGULAR	FOREIGN PLURAL	REGULAR PLURAL
appendix	appendices	appendixes
bureau	bureaux	bureaus
curriculum	curricula	curriculums
enema	enemata	enemas
focus	foci	focuses
ganglion	ganglia	ganglions

There are still some people who think the foreign plurals are better just because they are older; and there are others who apparently use them just to prove that they can. But the prevailing tendency is certainly in favor of regularity and simplicity. Foreign plurals tend to remain in use only under one of the following conditions:

a. The words are rather learned technical terms not in common use: *homunculus-homunculi; phylum-phyla.*

b. The plural forms occur much oftener than the singular: *datum-data; bacterium-bacteria.*

c. An -*s* would cause three *s* sounds in a row: *crisis-crises,* not *crisises.*

So much progress in this direction has been made that the following rules are now quite safe:

1. If you are used to hearing an -*s* plural, use it confidently.

2. If you are pretty sure that an -*s* plural is not correct, use the table below:

NOUNS ENDING IN	TAKE A PLURAL IN
-a (alumna)	-ae (alumnae—pronounced -*ay* or *ee*)
-us (alumnus)	-i (alumni—pronounced -*eye*)
-on (phenomenon)	-a (phenomena)
-um (bacterium)	-a (bacteria)
-sis (thesis)	-ses (theses—pronounced -*eez*)

Compound Nouns

Most compound nouns now regularly take the plural -*s* on the end, even if it did not originally belong there: *cupfuls, jack-in-the-boxes.* There are a few exceptions when the first part of the compound is the main word, and is described by what follows:

brothers-in-law	commanders-in-chief
courts-martial	passers-by

Even these words show a tendency to shift the -*s* to the end. All our good dictionaries now list *attorney generals* along with *attorneys general,* and the newest one (*Webster's New World Dictionary*) lists *court-martials* as well as *courts-martial.* If you are in doubt and can't look it up it is advisable to put the -*s* on the end, on the theory that natural ignorance is better than affectation.

To indicate possession, all compound nouns and groups of words that form a unit put the *'s* on the end: my *brother-in-law's* car; the *King of England's* doctor; *anybody else's* opinion.

Inflected Pronouns

There are eight simple inflected pronouns, listed below with all their forms.

SUBJECT FORMS	OBJECT FORMS	POSSESSIVE FORMS
I	me	my, mine
he	him	his
she	her	her, hers
it	it	its
we	us	our, ours
you	you	your, yours
they	them	their, theirs
who	whom	whose

Notice that:

1. Most of them have separate "subject" and "object" forms where nouns have one plain form.

2. Their possessive forms do *not* have an apostrophe, and some of them do not have an *-s*.

3. Most of them have two different possessive forms, one used when they are followed by the noun they modify (That is *my* book), the other when they stand alone (That book is *mine*).

The first seven pronouns are often called *personal pronouns*. The easiest thing to call the other one is simply *who*.

The Compound Personal Pronouns

The personal pronouns are combined with *self* and *selves* to form the following compound pronouns:

SINGULAR	PLURAL
myself	ourselves
yourself	yourselves
himself	themselves
herself	
itself	
ourself (reserved for kings, queens, and editors)	

Notice that some of these are based on the object forms of the simple pronouns, others on the possessive forms. It is important to get these straight, because such forms as "hisself" and "theirselves" are generally considered to be signs of great ignorance.

These words are used both to show "reflexive action" (he cut *himself*) and to show special emphasis (he did it *himself*). They are sometimes called "reflexive pronouns" in the first use and "intensive pronouns" or "intensive adjectives" in the second, but except in comparing English with a foreign language these terms are quite useless.

Compound Forms of *Who*

The compound pronoun *whoever* has the natural object form *whomever,* but the possessive form varies, appearing as *whosever, whose-ever, whose ever,* and even *whoever's.* With so much choice, it is hard to go definitely wrong.

Inflected Verbs

There are at most ten uninflected verbs in the standard language. *Must* and *ought* have only one form apiece, and on the whole it seems better to consider *could, might, should,* and *would* as now separate from *can, may, shall,* and *will* rather than as the past tenses of these verbs, though there are arguments for the opposite opinion. All other verbs except *to be* (see page 60) have from three to five inflected forms, and one phrase form that occurs so frequently it needs a name. These are:

	REGULAR	IRREGULAR
The plain form	walk	write
The singular form	walks	writes
The past tense	walked	wrote
The past participle	(walked)	written
The present participle	walking	writing
The infinitive	to walk	to write

Only about 45 verbs have a separate form for the past participle. The rest extend the use of the past tense form. However, it is convenient to call *walked* a past participle whenever it is used in a way parallel to *written.* Some grammarians call the plain form an infinitive whenever it comes directly after another verb (will *walk,* must *write*), but in this book the term infinitive always means the plain form preceded by *to.* Since the singular form and present participle are always (except in the verb *to be*) formed regularly from the plain form, the only difficulties are the past tenses of about 140 irregular verbs and the separate past participles of about 45 of these.

Strong and Weak Verbs

The division of English verbs into "strong" and "weak" classes, each containing subclasses, is useful in studying the earlier stages of the language, and is worth a few words of explanation here. The strong verbs originally formed their past tenses by a vowel change (*sing, sang*), while the weak verbs formed theirs by the addition of *-ede, -ode,* or *-de,* which later developed into *-d, -ed,* or *-t.* A thorough study of the laws of sound change shows that even such curious pairs as *bring-brought* have developed according to a regular process.

However, comparatively few people have time to make such a study; and a superficial approach to it merely causes unnecessary confusion (for instance, *bleed-bled* and *feed-fed,* which seem to meet the definition of strong verbs, are historically weak). Fortunately, this difficult subject is not in the least necessary in mastering the contemporary language. The important questions for a student of Modern English are simply whether a verb is regular or irregular; and, if it is irregular, how?

Regular Verbs

Most English verbs are now completely regular, so that if we see any one form we can be sure of what the others will be, even if we have never seen the verb before and have not the slightest idea what it means. The only things we have to watch in these verbs are certain general spelling principles discussed on pages 159-160.

Irregular Verbs

About 140 English verbs, most of them in very common use, are in some degree irregular. All but two of them (*begin* and *forsake*) are monosyllables, though some of them have compounds which follow the same pattern as the simple verbs (*get, forget; take, overtake*). There are a few other verbs which have both regular and irregular forms in good use, such as *thrive-thrived* (or *throve*). These are not included in the lists below unless the irregular forms are decidedly more usual.

Some optional irregular forms are as acceptable as the regular forms, but they are omitted here to simplify the picture. Anyone who finds that he uses an irregular form not listed here can easily check it in a dictionary to see whether it is in good standing. But if he masters the following lists he can be confident that he knows all the irregular forms *required* by standard usage. Even those verbs which are irregular only in spelling (*pay, paid*) are included.

Verbs with No Separate Past Tense

The following verbs ordinarily use the plain form for the past tense and past participle as well as the present. The forms *betted, quitted, ridded, wedded,* and *wetted* are common in British usage, but rare in American.

bet	hurt	shut
bid	let	slit
burst	put	split
cast	quit	spread
cost	rid	thrust
cut	set	wed
hit	shed	wet

Verbs that Add -d Irregularly

The following verbs form their past tenses with -*d,* but not in the regular way:

flee	fled	pay	paid
have	had	say	said
hear	heard	sell	sold
lay	laid	shoe	shod (also *shoed*)
make	made	tell	told

Verbs that Change -d to -t

The following verbs form their past tenses by changing -*d* to -*t:*

bend	bent	rend	rent
build	built	send	sent
lend	lent	spend	spent

Verbs that Add -t

The following verbs form their past tenses by adding -*t,* and making some other change, at least in sound:

bring	brought	leave	left
buy	bought	lose	lost
catch	caught	mean	meant
creep	crept	seek	sought
deal	dealt	sleep	slept
dwell	dwelt (also *dwelled*)	sweep	swept
		teach	taught
feel	felt	think	thought
keep	kept	weep	wept
kneel	knelt (also *kneeled*)		

Vowel-Change Verbs with No Separate Past Participle

The following verbs form their past tenses by a change in the vowel, at least in sound. They do not add -*d* or -*t,* although some of them end with these letters in both present and past:

bind	bound	meet	met
bleed	bled	read	read (pronounced *red*)
breed	bred	shine	shone (also *shined*)[2]
dig	dug	shoot	shot
feed	fed	sit	sat
fight	fought	slide	slid
find	found	spit	spat (also *spit*)
grind	ground	stand	stood
hang	hung (also *hanged*)[1]	stick	stuck
hold	held	strike	struck
lead	led	win	won
light	lit (also *lighted*)	wind	wound

[1] *Hanged* is used only in reference to death by hanging.
[2] "The sun *shone*," but "He *shined* the shoes."

The *-in-*, *-un-* and *-in-*, *-an-*, *-un-* Verbs

All of the following verbs have *-u* in the past participle, and all but five may unquestionably have it in the past tense as well. The simplest procedure is to learn to say *I began, I drank, I rang, I sang,* and *I swam,* and use the *u* form everywhere else. You can even find dictionary support for *I begun, I rung,* and *I sung,* but these three forms are now generally considered wrong.

begin	I began	I have begun
drink	I drank	I have drunk
ring	I rang	I have rung
sing	I sang	I have sung
swim	I swam	I have swum
shrink	I shrank *or* shrunk	I have shrunk
sink	I sank *or* sunk	I have sunk
spring	I sprang *or* sprung	I have sprung
stink	It stank *or* stunk	It has stunk
cling	I clung	I have clung
fling	I flung	I have flung
sling	I slung	I have slung
slink	I slunk	I have slunk
spin	I spun	I have spun
sting	I stung	I have stung
string	I strung	I have strung
swing	I swung	I have swung
wring	I wrung	I have wrung

Verbs Having *n* in the Past Participle

The following verbs have separate past participles containing *n*, sometimes preceded or followed by *e*. In standard English the forms with the *n* are never used in the simple past tense, but only in verb-phrases or as modifiers.

bear	I bore	I have borne
beat	I beat	I have beaten
bite	I bit	I have bitten (sometimes *bit*)
blow	I blew	I have blown
break	I broke	I have broken

choose	I chose	I have chosen
do	I did	I have done
draw	I drew	I have drawn
drive	I drove	I have driven
eat	I ate	I have eaten
fall	I fell	I have fallen
fly	I flew	I have flown
forsake	I forsook	I have forsaken
freeze	I froze	I have frozen
get	I got	I have gotten, got
give	I gave	I have given
go	I went	I have gone
grow	I grew	I have grown
hide	I hid	I have hidden (sometimes *hid*)
know	I knew	I have known
lie	I lay	I have lain
ride	I rode	I have ridden
rise	I rose	I have risen
see	I saw	I have seen
shake	I shook	I have shaken
slay	I slew	I have slain
smite	I smote	I have smitten
speak	I spoke	I have spoken
steal	I stole	I have stolen
stride	I strode	I have stridden
swear	I swore	I have sworn
take	I took	I have taken
tear	I tore	I have torn
throw	I threw	I have thrown
tread	I trod	I have trodden (sometimes *trod*)
wear	I wore	I have worn
weave	I wove	I have woven (sometimes *weaved*)[3]
write	I wrote	I have written

[3] Especially in such a use as "He *weaved* his way through the crowd."

Come and *Run*

These two verbs are exceptional in that their plain forms rather than their past tenses are used as past participles.

come	I came	I have come
run	I ran	I have run

The Verb *To Be*

The verb *to be* is a mixture of three old verbs (*aren, beon,* and *wesan*), which accounts for the wide differences in its forms. It is unique in having three present-tense forms (*am, are,* and *is*), none of which is identical with the plain form; and separate singular and plural forms (*was* and *were*) in the past tense. It also has the plain form (*be*), the present participle (*being*), and the past participle (*been*), for a total of eight forms, or three more than any other verb in the language.

Inflected Adjectives

Most adjectives of one syllable and many of two syllables (especially those ending in -*y*) are inflected to show degree: *hot, hotter, hottest; pretty, prettier, prettiest. Hot* is called the positive form, *hotter* the comparative, and *hottest* the superlative. This type of inflection is called comparison.

Adjectives of more than two syllables are not inflected in standard usage, but show degrees by *more* and *most* (*more beautiful, most beautiful,* etc.). Some adjectives of one and two syllables are treated in the same way, particularly those ending in -*ful* and -*ish*. There is no logical reason for this difference in treatment—it is simply a habit that has developed. When in doubt, it is safer to use *more* and *most*.

Some people have argued that such adjectives as *black, straight,* and *perfect* should not be compared in either way, because their meaning is absolute and not a matter of degree. According to this theory we should say "more nearly black," etc. However, *blacker, straightest, more perfect,* etc. are quite understandable, and are certainly in standard use.

Irregular Comparison

A few adjectives have irregular comparative and superlative forms. The most common of these are:

PLAIN FORM	COMPARATIVE FORM	SUPERLATIVE FORM
bad	worse	worst
far	farther	farthest
	further	furthest
good	better	best

little	less	least
	littler	littlest
	lesser	
many	more	most
much		
old	older	oldest
	elder	eldest

Elder, eldest, and *lesser* are not used much now except in a few set phrases, such as *elder statesman, eldest son,* and *lesser of two evils. Farther-farthest* and *further-furthest* are interchangeable as adjectives, though only *further* is used as a verb ("He *furthered* his brother's career"). *Littler* and *littlest* are generally used for physical size, *less* and *least* for all other purposes ("He found the *littlest* boy without the *least* trouble").

Such words as *utmost, topmost,* and *northmost* are often called irregular superlative forms, but it is simpler to consider them as separate words.

-ly Adverbs

Most of our adverbs are formed from adjectives by adding *-ly* (or *-ally* if the adjective ends in *-ic*). The fact that some adjectives such as *friendly* and *manly* also end in *-ly* causes some confusion. This can be avoided by remembering that *uninflected* words ending in *-ly* are all adverbs; *inflected* words with this ending may be adjectives, nouns (*jelly, tally*), or verbs (*to rely, to tally*).

Since the *-ly* ending is not considered an inflection, mention of adverbs may seem out of place here; but it is convenient to indicate that most of them are derived from and paired with adjectives.

Exercises—Chapter 4

1. Give a noun which does not have a separate form for its plural.
2. What is the maximum number of forms a noun can have in English? What are they called?
3. List the three steps given in the chapter for selecting the appropriate possessive form of a noun.
4. List the six common nouns ending in *-o* which form their plurals in *-es*.

5. The plural of *wife* is *wives,* while the plural of *belief* is *beliefs.* What distinction helps determine the pattern for the plural in words ending in *-f* or *-fe?*

6. What consideration is involved in determining the pattern for the plural of words ending in *-y?*

7. Which of the following nouns form their plurals irregularly: *blouse, goose, moose, mouse, louse, house?*

8. List both the *foreign* and the *accepted* English plurals of three foreign nouns in common use in English.

9. Under what conditions do foreign plurals tend to remain in use (in English)?

10. What form does the possessive take in all compound nouns and groups of words that form a unit?

11. List three ways the forms of the simple inflected *pronouns* differ from the general pattern of *noun* inflections.

12. With the exception of the word *who,* what label extends to the re- maining seven simple inflected pronouns?

13. In mastering English verbs, what simple classification is more es- sential than the knowledge that a given verb is *strong* or *weak?*

14. Give a regular verb (besides *walk*) and carry it through its various forms: the plain form, the singular, the past tense, the past participle, the present participle, and the infinitive.

15. While the *irregular* verbs consume a disproportionate amount of a student's time, there are relatively few of them—about how many in all?

16. *Put, rid* and *shut* have no separate past tense form. List two more such verbs.

17. List three verbs which form their past tense with *-d,* but not in the regular way.

18. *Bend* and *build* form their past tenses by changing *-d* to *-t.* List two other verbs which do the same.

19. Verbs like *feel* form their past tenses by adding *-t,* and making some other change, at least in sound. List three more.

20. What characterizes the change in form in such verbs as *bleed, fight,* and *hold?*

21. What is the past tense form of *sink, fling, swing,* and *swim?*

22. Two very common verbs form the past participles with the plain forms rather than their past tense forms. What are these two?

23. The words *aren, beon* and *wesan* are all old forms of what verb? How many forms does that verb *now* have?

24. List the positive, comparative, and superlative forms of these ad- jectives: *cold, elegant,* and *good.*

25. How are adverbs generally formed? Is this inflection?

Suggestions for Discussion or Theme Writing—Chapter 4

1. Using the noun *cat,* the verb *trade,* and the adjective *slow,* summarize the inflection patterns of regular nouns, verbs and adjectives in English.

2. Discuss the kinds of information which may be conveyed in writing through the variety of inflections (word forms) available to the writer.

THE STRUCTURE

OF STATEMENTS

5

Six Kinds of Sentences

There is a widespread superstition that (a) every legitimate unit of utterance is a sentence; and (b) every sentence must somehow have a subject and predicate, even though one or both of these may not be discoverable by ordinary ears or eyes, but must be "understood." If we want to get away from mind reading and talk ordinary sense we must give up either (a) or (b). We can say that such utterances as "Who?" and "Heads up!" and "Please pass the salt," which are certainly all right in their places, are legitimate nonsentences; or we can say that there are several kinds of sentences, only one of which must have a subject and predicate. One method would work about as well as the other, but since "legitimate nonsentences" seems to many people like a contradiction in terms, we will take the second choice.

We use at least six kinds of sentences, which may be called *questions, answers, commands* (including requests), *exclamations, comments,* and *statements.* Only the last of these must contain a *clause;* and it is the clause, not the sentence, which *must* have a subject and predicate. The first five have no structural requirements except that their intonation should be in keeping with their meaning. They may contain as little as a single word.

> *Question:* Where?
> *Answer:* Beyond that rosebush.
> *Command:* Forceps.
> *Exclamation:* Cheers!
> *Comment:* Not bad.

These are all completely standard in conversation, or in writing that is intended to give the flavor of conversation. We could of course expand each one to include a subject and predicate, but we would not necessarily improve them by doing so; and there is certainly no sound reason to pretend that they are abbreviations of longer expressions. The surgeon who says "Forceps" is not thinking "Please pass the forceps" or "Nurse, I need the forceps next." He thinks "Forceps" and he says "Forceps" and he gets forceps, which is language at its most efficient.

It is only the sixth kind of sentence, the *statement,* that must contain a subject and predicate—a noun-verb combination like *Alice says* or *everybody was* or *Finnegan pitched*. Except in plays, stories, and directions for do-it-yourself projects, the great majority of all written sentences are, or are intended to be, statements; and sentence fragments—generally regarded as the number one sin in student writing—are almost always unsuccessful attempts at statements.

The difference between statements and the other five types may be explained in this way: the other five types depend heavily on intonation patterns to indicate not only their specific meanings but the fact that they are intended as complete utterances. For instance, if somebody asked you what your brother was doing, you might answer "Working in the garden." If you did, you would use the same intonation pattern that you would use to finish the longer sentence "He is working in the garden." Your sentence would therefore *sound* complete; and since the words "He is" would not be in the least needed, it would *be* complete. But if you began a conversation with the same four words you would probably say "Working in the garden—" leaving your voice hanging in a way that indicated that you planned to add other words—as you probably would. Therefore the four words would neither sound like nor be a sentence. And in writing the four words will be a satisfactory sentence only if they are put in a setting that clearly indicates that they are to be pronounced with a final intonation pattern.

If you ask what *is* a final intonation pattern, you won't find the answer here. There are many of them, and the details are complicated. But you probably know of the difference between the way your voice sounds when you finish saying something definite, and the way it sounds when you simply break off in the middle of something. If you don't, this is the wrong book for you to be reading.

Of course statements also have intonation patterns, but they depend less on these and more on the readily visible elements of word order, word form, and function words. Our habit of writing largely in statements is therefore very sensible, for it leaves a reader less to guess at. Since it is the clause structure of statements that causes writers most trouble, we shall discuss this at some length before returning to a briefer consideration of the other kinds of sentences.

The Subject-Verb Combination

Any group of related words that contains a subject-verb combination is a clause, and every statement must contain at least one clause. Examples:

SUBJECT	VERB
It	is
I	have
My wristwatch	says

It doesn't do much good to memorize the definitions of these elements. The important thing is to learn to recognize them. For instance, a subject is often defined as something like "a noun about which the verb says something." But in the sentence "Stan gave Dick the money," the verb says something about three different nouns. Only one of them, *Stan,* is the subject; and it is recognizable simply by the way it is combined with *gave,* not by its meaning. If we reported the same transaction by saying "Dick was given the money by Stan" we'd have a different subject, *Dick;* and if we said "The money was given to Dick by Stan" we'd have still a third one.

The subject may be either a single word or a group of words, and it does not always come next to the verb.

SUBJECT	VERB
The *man* in the service station	*told* me so.
One of the players	*was* too anxious.
To drive a car like that	*takes* real nerve.

In each of these sentences we could call everything before the verb the *complete subject* and the italicized word or words the *simple subject*. Sometimes it is hard to decide just how much of the subject is *simple,* and it often makes no particular difference. But in such a sentence as the second it is important to notice that the simple subject is *one,* not *players,* and the verb is therefore *was* rather than *were.*

The verb may be either a single word like those in the sentences above or a verb-phrase such as *will go, must have been, ought to do,* or *might have been driving.* But it cannot be simply a participle or an infinitive, or a combination of these such as *having been* or *wanting to go.* Such phrases are useful in expanding clauses, but they do not take the place of the definite combinations *have been* or *wants to go.* A verb-phrase may be interrupted by negative words or other modifiers:

He *has gone.*   He *has* not *gone.*   He *has* already *gone.*

In each of these sentences the verb-phrase is simply *has gone.*

Independent and Subordinate Clauses

There is one other requirement for a statement. Its clause, or at least one of its clauses, must be independent. That is, it must not be introduced by a connective which shows that it is subordinate to something else. Any group of related words containing a subject-verb combination is a clause, but only an independent clause can stand alone as a statement.

INDEPENDENT CLAUSES	SUBORDINATE CLAUSES
He went there	Because she went
They will do it	If you want them to
We can leave it	When Andy comes

Each of these independent clauses could be used as a complete statement, or it could be joined to the subordinate clause at its right to make a longer one. But the subordinate clauses would not be complete statements if they were used alone. Other kinds of subordinate clauses, less likely to be mistaken for sentences, will be illustrated later.

Complements

Aside from the subject and verb a clause may contain one or two *complements.* A complement is a noun whose relation to the subject is shown simply by the verb. Thus in the sentence "Stan gave Dick the money," both *Dick* and *money* are complements. But in the sentence "Stan gave the money to Dick" only *money* is a complement, since *to* is used to connect *Dick* with the rest of the clause. In the sentence "He saw Dave, Al, Peter, and Charlie," there is only one complement in four parts.

In highly inflected languages like Latin, it is important to distinguish between various kinds of complements, because different ones require that the nouns be in different forms—or nouns in different forms indicate different relations when used as complements. Even in English people often talk about *direct objects, indirect objects, retained objects, objective complements, subjective complements,* and so forth, but on the whole this seems to be a waste of energy. Anybody who thinks it is important to insist on "It is I" instead of "It is me" can do so in a less complicated way; and aside from this construction all complements are in the same form. Certainly complements show a number of different relations. But unless you understand exactly what relations are shown in a given sentence you can't classify the complements; and if you do understand them you don't learn anything further by making the classification except some technical terms—and they won't last from one book to another because grammarians have disagreed so widely on what are the proper terms that one kind of complement has fourteen different names—and another has eighteen. But it *is* useful to see how complements function in clause patterns, because their functioning is one of our most important ways of indicating the connection of ideas.

The Basic Clause Patterns

Whether or not a clause is a complete sentence, it must contain a subject and verb, and it may also contain either one or two complements—not more. These are its only possible major elements; anything else it may contain must be a modifier of one of these or a connective.

The three basic clause patterns are illustrated by the three statements:

1. The *subject is* something.
2. The *subject does* something.
3. The *subject is affected* by something.

The first two are called *active,* the third *passive.*

"The Subject Is . . ."

In pattern *1* the verb acts rather like an *equals* sign, connecting two names for the same person or thing. It is usually some form of the verb *to be,* though a few other verbs are possible.

The man	is	a mechanic
	was	
	used to be	
	ought to have been	
	became	
	seemed to be	

These vary in detail, but in all of them the identity between the subject (*man*) and the complement (*mechanic*) could be symbolized (though of course not fully represented) by the formula:

$$\text{The man} = \text{a mechanic}$$

In this pattern there cannot be more than one complement, and there may be none. In such a sentence as "The man is busy" *busy* is not another noun renaming the subject, but an adjective modifying it; and in the sentence "The man is *in the next room*" the whole phrase *in the next room* is a modifier. In neither sentence could *is* be replaced by an *equals* sign without a considerable distortion of the meaning. On the other hand, "The man from the new garage on Fremont Street seems a much better mechanic than the one usually sent over by the Sloan garage" is just the simple *man = mechanic* pattern with a few trimmings.

"The Subject Does . . ."

In pattern *2* the subject and complement are different people or things, and the verb can be symbolized by an arrow rather than an *equals* sign, to show that the subject acts on the complement:

The man	needs	a mechanic
	hired	
	will have to get	
	had seen	
	might have injured	

All of these and a great many more could be symbolized by the formula:

The man → a mechanic

Like pattern *1,* pattern *2* can occur with no complement, as in "The man works hard" or "The man hunts a good deal." *Works* and *hunts* could be symbolized by arrows rather than *equals* signs; but there is nothing for the arrows to point to in these sentences. Unlike pattern *1,* pattern *2* can also occur with two complements (see page 71).

Is or Does?

Unfortunately patterns *1* and *2,* as patterns, look exactly alike. If you saw a sentence full of unfamiliar words, such as "The kleef plunned a veddle," you could not be sure whether to represent *plunned* by an *equals* sign or an arrow—though the arrow would be a much better bet on percentages. Sometimes even one unknown word could cause uncertainty.

A tyro became the star.
A tiara became the star.

The first requires an *equals* sign, because *tyro* means a beginner, and *became* must therefore mean "developed into." But the second requires an arrow, because *tiara* means a sort of crown, and therefore *became* must mean "looked well on."

This ambiguity of patterns actually causes very little trouble— much less than ambiguity of words does. We mention it only to show that it doesn't pay to be too dogmatic about the meaning of grammatical constructions. Both words and patterns convey meaning, but they do it simultaneously. Unless you are struggling with a particularly difficult passage you don't think first of the words and then of the patterns, or vice versa. You react to the words *in* the pattern. But if you have written a rather complicated sentence and are wondering whether it hangs together or not, some knowledge of the patterns may help you decide.

Verbs which can be represented by *equals* signs may be called *linking verbs,* and the complements that follow them *subjective complements.* Verbs which may be represented by arrows may be called *transitive verbs,* and their complements *direct objects.* Unfortunately a good many other names are also used for the same things. Rather than get into an argument about which names are better, we will try to avoid them all as far as possible. The two patterns can generally be recognized and understood even if you don't know what to call them.

Clauses with Two Complements

Verbs of the arrow kind may be followed by two complements, but not more. Look at the following sentences:

> The man gave the boy a dollar.
> The man called the boy a liar.

In the first the two complements refer to different things, and you may call *boy* the *indirect object* and *dollar* the *direct object.* In the second both complements refer to the same thing, and you may call *boy* the *direct object* and *liar* the *objective complement,* unless you happen to have been brought up under a different terminology. But the chances are pretty strong that you know what both sentences mean, and can make up other sentences on the same patterns, without calling any of the complements anything.

Once again the patterns are theoretically ambiguous. If you saw such a sentence as "The moof drissed the nule a flid" you could not tell which way to analyze it. Once in a great while even a sentence composed of familiar words, but without context, might be taken either way. Thus "He made the boy a soldier" might mean either that he turned the boy into a soldier or that he made a toy soldier for the boy to play with. But the chance of misinterpreting the patterns is again much smaller than that of misinterpreting the words. If we assume that the sentence deals with training, not toy making, there is still room for a good deal of difference of opinion about what qualities would have to be developed to justify the statement.

"The Subject Is Affected . . ."

The third basic clause pattern is the passive one. Here are three variations.

> The speaker was cheered by the large audience.
> The speaker was given a round of applause.
> The speaker was made the butt of many jokes.

The last two have a complement apiece—the limit for passive clauses. By a peculiar sort of perverted logic *round* and *butt* may be called "retained objects." Rather than explain why, we call them simply complements.

Why Talk About Complements?

Since we are not going to insist on calling the various kinds of complements anything in particular, or have any exercises in distinguishing one from another, you may very reasonably wonder if there is any good reason for talking about them at all. The answer is that they, along with subjects and verbs, are the major elements in clauses—they serve to form the framework. And it is sometimes very useful to be able to separate the skeleton from the padding in order to see how a sentence works. Actually, if there were any one set of terms in general use it would be worth while to go a little further in the analysis of complements; but with so many conflicting ones current it seems better to treat the whole subject as simply as possible.

Exercises—Chapter 5

I. Answer each of the following questions simply and briefly:

1. List the six kinds of sentences and give an example of each without repeating those already given in the text.
2. In what specific way may a *statement* differ markedly from the other five kinds of sentences?
3. How may the term *clause* be defined?
4. What distinguishes an *independent* from a *subordinate* clause?
5. Describe the three basic clause patterns.
6. Which of the basic clause patterns are called *active,* and which *passive?*
7. What are the *three* major elements in clauses (although some clauses may contain only two of them)?
8. In English all complements are in the same form, with the exception of what one situation?
9. Why are names for various *kinds* of complements more important in those languages which depend more on inflections than English does?
10. How many complements may each of the basic clause patterns contain?

II. Indicate after each of the expressions below whether it is a *question*, an *answer*, a *command*, an *exclamation*, a *comment* or a *statement*. Call any expression that fits none of these categories a *sentence fragment,* and don't lose sleep over borderline cases, but list all the possibilities. Isolate every clause, and note whether it is *independent* or *subordinate*. Label each according to its pattern, 1, 2 or 3, and circle all the complements.

1. Hey there!
2. On being a good sport.
3. What's the time?
4. Hardly ever wanting to, but having to anyway.
5. You men are all alike.
6. My cousin who works long hours.
7. Will you never get off the phone (?) (!)
8. Collies are easy dogs to train.
9. The prisoner sold his guard a painting.
10. The cake was eaten by persons unknown.
11. Hold the village at all cost.
12. At dawn, as near as I can tell.
13. The man thought the boy should take the money.
14. When all of a sudden.
15. The coyote and the wolf gave the doe and fawn a relentless chase.
16. Because I was supposed to meet him there.
17. The tired pitcher became a twenty-game winner.
18. Well, it's about time. (!)
19. Down the street came his brother.
20. He called his friends traitors and his brother a crook.

Suggestions for Discussion or Theme Writing—Chapter 5

1. Discuss the difference between a sentence fragment (an unsuccessful attempt at a *statement*) and the six kinds of *sentences* defined in the chapter. Illustrate the distinction with appropriate examples.

2. Listen to a casual conversation and recreate it on paper as accurately as you can. Label the sentences according to the categories listed in the chapter, then tabulate the results and compare the number of *statements* to the other kinds of sentences combined. Do the same for a piece of written English.

SIMPLE,
COMPOUND,
AND COMPLEX
SENTENCES

6

Before we go any further into the details of sentence structure, we should consider why it is that certain arrangements of words affect us as they do. We listen before we talk as, later, we read before we write. Long before we ever think about grammar or logic we come to realize that certain arrangements of words have fairly reliable meanings—quite as reliable as the words themselves. When we get to the point of making sentences of our own we naturally imitate the arrangement of sentences that we have already heard. Unless we imitate pretty accurately we are likely to be misunderstood and even more likely to be laughed at. Therefore we soon learn to be very accurate, at least with the simplest and most familiar patterns. Just how far we get with this automatic development depends on a number of things, which pure ignorance keeps me from analyzing here. Some children manage to make surprisingly complicated sentences quite young. Others, to put it mildly, don't.

By the time we get to school and begin to study language formally, we are already so used to the commonest patterns that we may feel that they are based on the laws of nature. Actually they are simply group habits that happened to develop. We might as well have developed a very different set of habits, but we had to develop *some* set and use them fairly uniformly or we could not communicate with much success. The proof of this statement is not hard to establish. Beyond the simplest patterns our habits are not nearly as uniform as they well might be—and a great many people have extreme difficulty in understanding what they hear or read, and in making their own ideas clear to others.

However, practically all of us get far enough so that when we read a sentence we automatically expect to find certain elements and to find them in a certain order. The first thing we look for is the subject; and we assume that the first word that can be the subject *is* the subject unless there is definite evidence that it is not. Thus if a sentence begins with *John* our first expectation is that it is going to tell us something about what John was or did, and we are usually right. But if it begins "John, Dick is . . ." the comma after *John* corrects the first impression. We now assume that the sentence is addressed to John but will tell about Dick. Or if the sentence begins "When John . . ." we can see at once that although some statement is going to be made about John, the main statement will be made about somebody or something else. We then keep our minds alert for the main subject.

Once we have found the subject, we expect a verb that makes a statement about it, and perhaps a complement to complete the statement. If these elements appear in their expected order, we accept the sentence as natural, and "understand" its structure— whether or not we know what the writer had in mind when he wrote the words. For instance, suppose you read that "The Calonians cultivated shaners." You can't possibly know who the Calonians were or what shaners look like, but you are likely to have a feeling that something definite has been said, just because the sentence follows a familiar pattern.

It is extremely useful to have a pattern so reliable that it automatically indicates the relation of words to each other, so that we don't have to guess about it or take the time to figure it out. Sometimes we could get along without it. For instance, we might understand such a sentence as "John pie ate" by realizing that very few pies are man-eaters. But we could only guess about the meaning of "John Tom hit." There are two obvious possibilities, and there is no pattern to help us decide which one is intended. For this reason we normally use a word-order that gives a clear indication of how the words are related to one another *no matter what words are used;* and we follow this order even when the particular words used are such that we do not actually need it.

Suppose we list five words in alphabetical order: *book, gave, Lucy, Pete, the.* These five words could be arranged in 120 different ways, but only *two* of the ways would make clear, normal sentences:

> Lucy gave Pete the book.
> Pete gave Lucy the book.

A few other combinations would be possible if we used commas, such as:

> Pete, Lucy gave the book.

Still others would be possible as parts of sentences, but would not make complete statements:

> The book Lucy gave Pete *is interesting.*

Most of the combinations, however, would be mere jumbles that would convey no information at all.

What we have to consider now is the area between those patterns that are learned automatically and those that have no meaning at all. Within this area there are a great many arrangements of words that skilled people can handle and respond to but that unskilled people can find it difficult to understand and even more difficult to use. Of course word order is not the only element in grammatical patterns, as we saw in Chapter 3; but it is probably the one that causes most trouble, and is certainly the one with which we shall be most concerned for the next few chapters.

Classification of Sentences

Sentences are classified according to their clause structure as follows:

1. *Simple* (containing a single independent clause):

One of his younger brothers works at the new cotton mill in Davis.

2. *Compound* (containing two or more independent clauses):

Eloise still lives in New York, but Pasquale has been in Oregon for years.

3. *Complex* (containing both independent and subordinate clauses):

When he has time, Milton likes to go fishing.

(If a complex sentence contains more than one independent clause, it may be called compound-complex.)

There is no particular value in merely learning to label the various types of sentences, but it is convenient to consider them separately to avoid having to face too many problems at once.

Expansion of Simple Sentences

The major elements of a clause are *formally* the most important ones, but they are not necessarily the ones that contribute the most information. You might describe a dog by saying "It is a dangerous and vicious animal, likely to bite anybody." You can guess which words would probably make the greatest impression on your audience. But in the structure of the clause *it—is—animal* are the major elements, and all the rest are secondary.

We may expand a simple sentence by adding modifying words or phrases to any or all of its major elements, or to the sentence as a whole. There is no theoretical limit to this expansion—it is quite easy to compose a technically simple sentence hundreds of words long and containing an indefinite number of related ideas. There is, however, a flexible practical limit. A sentence should not be so long or so complicated that the reader or listener will have trouble grasping it as a whole.

1. Perkins saw Eddie.
2. Yesterday afternoon old *Perkins,* the barber, definitely *saw* little *Eddie* getting on the bus.
3. Looking out the window yesterday afternoon during the rainstorm, old *Perkins,* the barber with the reputation of knowing everything about everybody in town, definitely *saw* little *Eddie,* the son of the new owner of the Elite Cafe, getting on the ancient bus driven by . . . etc.

All three sentences have the same three major elements in the same order. The first contains nothing else. The second contains a reasonable number of modifying elements which give it additional meaning. But the third is too much for one bite. There are so many modifying elements that the direct line of the statement is buried.

Modifiers are considered more thoroughly in the next chapter. Here we need notice only that while a simple sentence contains only one *formally complete statement,* a number of *implied statements* may be worked in by the addition of words and phrases. This use of implied statements (if not carried too far) greatly increases the efficiency and economy of our communication, as the following comparison shows:

> Perkins is old.
> Perkins is a barber.
> Perkins saw Eddie.
> Eddie is little.

Eddie was getting on the bus.
This definitely happened.
It happened yesterday afternoon.

Yesterday afternoon old Perkins, the barber, definitely saw little Eddie getting on the bus.

It is also possible to split any or all the elements in a simple sentence:

S	V	C¹	C²
The *man*	*gave*	the *boy*	a *dollar*
The *man*	*promised*	the *boy*	a *dollar*
and	and	and	and
the *woman*	*gave*	the *girl*	a *doughnut*

Each element of the clause is compound, but there is still only one clause.

Compound Sentences

A compound sentence consists of two or more independent clauses, each of which could be a simple sentence. It therefore offers no new problems in the internal structure of its clauses. In spoken English it is often quite impossible to tell whether a series of independent clauses is intended as one compound sentence or several simple ones. Except in prepared speeches, the speaker himself has usually given the matter no thought, and the listeners can only guess. In written English the distinction is made simply by punctuation. If the writer wants his independent clauses to be considered separately, he puts a period after each. If he wants to show that two or more statements are so closely connected that they should be taken as a single unit, he can do so by writing them as a single sentence. Frequently it makes little difference which he does.

We played tennis for a while, and then we went swimming.
I like Morris, but Doris bores me.
She went one way, he went the other.
The company was good; the food was awful.

We could split each of these sentences in two by substituting a period for the comma or semicolon. Whether or not this would be an improvement is a matter of individual judgment. If we split the sentences, we could drop the connectives *but* and *and* or keep them.

The clauses of a compound sentence should always be separated by punctuation, by some such connective as *and, but, or,* or *nor,* or by both. The reason is simply that the clauses *are* independent, and should not be allowed to run together. We need some indication of where one statement ends and the next begins. Elaborate rules stating when each of these separating devices should be used are not of much value. The writer should choose his means according to the effect he wishes to produce.

A comma indicates a slight break in the thought, and should be used only when the clauses are both very short and very closely related; otherwise it will result in a run-on sentence. A semicolon indicates a stronger break, and can be used with clauses of any length. A connective clearly indicates the intended relation between the two ideas; to omit the connective challenges the reader to find out the relation for himself, and this challenge is sometimes more effective than the ready-made indication. Further discussion of this problem will be found on pages 205-208.

There is no fixed limit to the number of clauses a compound sentence may contain; but it should not be so long that it is difficult to grasp as a unit.

Complex Sentences

A complex sentence contains at least one subordinate clause as well as at least one independent clause. So far we have mentioned only one kind of subordinate clause—the kind of adverbial clause which modifies the whole independent clause (see page 67). Subordinate clauses may also be used as subjects, complements, or modifiers of any of the elements in larger clauses. This interlocking makes it possible:

1. To split one clause by another.

1—	2	—1
The man	who discovered that	was a genius.

2. To run two clauses together, with no separation by punctuation or connective.

Mrs. Trimble said the train would be late.

Here the clause *the train would be late* is the complement in the main clause. It fits in directly after *said* exactly as *a few words* would.

3. To make one word serve a double function.

He knows who did it.

Here the whole clause *who did it* is the complement of *knows,* and within this clause *who* is the subject of *did.*

The possible variations in the structure of complex sentences are almost infinite. We can write modifiers of modifiers of modifiers and clauses within clauses within clauses as long as our ingenuity holds out—at the risk, of course, of losing our readers—not to mention ourselves. Some of the most troublesome problems in the use and structure of subordinate clauses are discussed in Chapter 8.

The Borderline Between Compound and Complex Sentences

By definition, a compound sentence contains only independent clauses, while a complex sentence contains at least one subordinate clause. This brings up three questions:

1. Can independent and subordinate clauses be reliably distinguished by their own structure?

Not always. Many clauses beginning with such words as *after, if, because, what, whom,* and *when* can immediately be recognized as performing a subordinate function; but a great many clauses cannot be classified without considering the sentences in which they appear. For example, almost any independent clause may be turned into a subordinate one by prefixing some such clause as "I know . . ."

2. Can independent and subordinate clauses be reliably distinguished by their functions in sentences?

The line between the two is so fine that it sometimes depends on the arbitrary classification of certain connectives as "coordinating conjunctions" and others as "subordinating conjunctions."

> *Independent:* Clem was interested, *but Dick was bored.*
> *Subordinate:* Clem was interested, *while Dick was bored.*
> *Independent:* He was tired, *for he had been up since dawn.*
> *Subordinate:* He was tired, *because he had been up since dawn.*

3. Is there any practical advantage in distinguishing between independent and subordinate clauses?

Not in borderline cases, such as those shown just above. However, *some* subordinate clauses bring up special problems that do not occur in independent clauses. If we don't push it too far, the classification can be useful in organizing these problems for study.

Exercises—Chapter 6

Classify the following sentences, *S* (one independent clause), *Cp* (two or more independent clauses), or *Cx* (one or more independent clauses and one or more subordinate clauses). Further indicate by numbering 1, 2 or 3, if the clauses in category *Cx* interlock with each other in one of the three ways the chapter suggests they might. If any of the sentences seem to you particularly bad, explain why.

1. The man thought the boy should accept the money.
2. These students realize why they are attending college; they have set certain goals for themselves.
3. Not wanting to hang around home, the boy asked to go to college.
4. Whoever told you that was a liar.
5. The parcel found in the street was my music teacher's tennis racket wrapped in an old piece of turkish toweling.
6. The nearest town was forty miles away, but we were in luck; my uncle was a mechanic, and we had plenty of tools and spare parts with us.
7. They fed the rabbit lettuce and carrots, but no grain.
8. He could, when he felt like it, make the tastiest salad I have ever eaten.
9. The waiter brought Duke what he asked for.
10. If there had been only one girl I could have talked myself out of the predicament, but with three girls it was a different matter.
11. She says she can drive in the race.
12. The young actor, preoccupied with learning his lines, gave his manager a curt reply.
13. Mother was a saintly woman, only five feet tall and weighing one hundred pounds.
14. What he wants is usually what he gets.
15. Socrates was an ancient Greek philosopher and he lived in the fifth century B.C. and the citizens of Athens condemned him to death and made him drink hemlock poison, and all for teaching men to think for themselves and not accept the mass opinions of the Athenian market place.
16. Fitzroy and at least two of the students will load and unload the truck.
17. Understanding the meaning of the words, Herbert passed the foreign-looking man the catsup.

18. Whether it is possible is what we want to know.

19. The pipes he smokes are all expensive.

20. Since he has what we want, we had better pay him the price he asks.

21. A shibboleth got its name from the Israelites in the Bible and they were camped at a river and feared a night attack by their foes and so made a password out of their word shibboleth and their enemies could not pronounce it and anyone who couldn't got killed and so today it means a password for certain kinds of social acceptance and to get you into a certain group or class or something.

22. George, running to catch the bus, and Alice, walking to the store, passed without speaking.

23. As a matter of fact, what you suggest is decidedly illegal.

24. The fact is that he wasn't even at the party.

25. You can tell whoever calls what I told you.

Suggestions for Discussion or Theme Writing—Chapter 6

1. Through the use of compounds, subordination, implied statements and general word economy, transform the following jumble of simple sentences into a reasonable paragraph: (Reorganize, if necessary.)

I have a farm. There are many animals. The animals do not get along very well together. There is a cat. There is a dog. There is a cow. Also there is a horse. And also there is a hog. The cow hates the dog. She attacked the dog yesterday and the day before and the day before that. The dog hates the cat. He chased the cat up a tree every day last week. The horse kicks the cow every chance he gets. The cat dropped on the horse's back, once. The horse kicked the side of the barn out at that time. Nothing bothers the hog. The hog does not bother anything. The cat is black. He is a Persian cat. His name is Hector. The dog is part collie and part shepherd and part beagle and part dachshund. He doesn't look like any of them. His name is Geronimo. The horse is a bay. He answers to the name of Lightning. The cow is a Jersey. I call her Mabel.

2. Choose one of the following clause patterns and expand it to twenty words or more *without* changing the basic pattern or the *simple sentence* structure. Then transfer the new bits of information you have supplied (implied statements) into as many separate statements (direct statements this time) as you can, and list them below the basic clause:

(a) cat was

(b) man lost money

(c) sheriff and deputy rode

(d) candidate drew applause and support

(e) child ate and drank

MODIFIERS 7

A modifier may be defined roughly as a word, phrase, or clause that supplies any kind of additional information (even negative information) about the element with which it is associated. A verb is not considered as modifying its subject. Thus in the sentence, "*Young* Lorenz worked *hard,* but made *no* progress," only the italicized words are called modifiers. If the modifier is a phrase or clause, it may itself contain secondary modifiers:

> He saw *a tall* man *in black clothes.*

Here the words *a* and *tall* and the phrase *in black clothes* modify *man;* and within the phrase, *black* modifies *clothes.* In discussing the structure of sentences we shall not usually have to bother about the internal structure of phrases.

We can avoid a good deal of trouble if we realize from the beginning that it is in human minds, not on printed pages, that modification takes place. No word automatically does anything at all to another word; but the relative positions of words stimulate us to make certain associations. When we see a combination like *tall man* we can be quite sure that the writer meant *tall* to refer to *man,* and that any normal reader will take it as he meant it. It is a convenient short-cut to express all this by saying "*tall* modifies *man.*" In dealing with this particular pattern—adjective plus noun—the statement is safe because our habits are so uniform that there is very little chance of either a misunderstanding or an argument.

But suppose we encounter a sentence like "He sent the man from Texas." The writer might mean "He sent the Texas man (somewhere or other)"; while a reader might take it to mean "He sent the (unidentified) man out of Texas." Are we justified in taking sides and saying what the phrase *from Texas* "really" modifies?

We could of course "make a rule" that in such sentences the final phrase must always be considered as referring to the word immediately before it, or a different rule that it must always be considered as referring back to the verb. But neither one of these rules would be an accurate description of good usage. The simple fact is that our habits of association are not as regular in this type of construction as in the *tall man* pattern, largely because there is less need for them to be. Let us look at some other examples, and illustrate the natural associations by simple diagrams:

1. He met a man from New York.

    He   met   a man
    _____
                        | from New York

Here the phrase clearly refers to the complement.

2. He knocked the glass from the table.

    He   knocked   the glass
    _____
              | from the table

Here the phrase clearly refers to the verb.

3. He sent a present from Paris.

    He   sent   a present
    _____
              | from Paris

                  or

    He   sent   a present
    _____
                        | from Paris

This might mean that he sent a present-from-London from Paris, or a present-from-Paris from New York; but the most probable guess is that both the present and the sending were from Paris. If this is true, one diagram would be as good as the other.

4. He shot the man from the bank.

    He   shot   the man
    _____
              | from the bank

    He   shot   the man
    _____
                        | from the bank

Here the two diagrams represent entirely different situations. Was the shooting done from the bank, or was the man shot an employee of the bank?

In the first two of the four sentences above the particular words used help the grammatical pattern to indicate clearly the intended association. The third sentence, about the present, is technically ambiguous, but there is not much chance of a serious misunderstanding. The fourth sentence, however, when printed alone, could mean either of two quite different things. It would probably be clear if spoken, because the speaker could show by his intonation pattern whether the man or the shooting was from the bank, and a listener would probably follow him. And it might be clear in writing if the context made one interpretation or the other automatic. But as a single written sentence it is completely ambiguous.

Thus we have four sentences containing the same grammatical pattern (as far as a reader can tell without knowing the exact meanings of the words) but indicating quite different relations of ideas. If we try to make a general rule to cover all four we may arrive at something like this:

The reader's natural tendency is to make the easiest association possible. Since the final phrase comes right next to the complement, the obvious first guess is that it refers to the complement. But if this association seems unreasonable, he will carry the phrase one position further back and try it with the verb. A writer should bear this tendency in mind, and arrange his sentence so that no misleading or ridiculous association is easily possible.

Of course we usually make our associations rapidly and subconsciously. It is only when we are puzzled by sentences, or when we deliberately analyze or diagram one, that we consciously consider such problems. We may do this quite informally by saying something like, "Oh yes, I see—*from the bank* goes with *shot,* not with *man.*" Or we may do it (usually at a teacher's request) formally and according to rule.

When we do attempt to analyze formally by rules, we have good reason to ask how sound the rules are. Let us look at another sentence that can be diagrammed in two ways:

John waved a greeting to the man.

    John   waved   a greeting
              to the man

    John   waved   a greeting
                         to the man

Here there is not the slightest doubt as to what the whole sentence means; yet we can make diagrams to indicate two quite different theories as to what the phrase modifies. And if we look for comparisons, we can find evidence on both sides:

John's greeting to the man was cordial.

John's	greeting	was	cordial
	to the man		

John threw the ball to the man.

John	threw	the ball
	to the man	

We may, of course, argue about which comparison is closer, and perhaps feel we have proved that one or the other of the diagrams is right. But this is merely playing a game with definitions. Association of *to the man* with *any* element in the sentence is neither as close nor as uniform as associations of the *tall man* type; and we can't make it so by drawing a picture.

Sometimes the question that arises is not which element a word modifies, but whether it modifies any one element or a combination of several:

Yesterday my brother went to town.

Here we could explain *yesterday* as modifying either the verb *went* or the whole clause *my brother went to town*. It makes a simpler diagram to relate the modifier to a single word; but the more natural thing to say is that it seems to modify the whole clause. Incidentally, this interpretation helps to explain why some modifiers can be put almost anywhere in a sentence, while others have a fixed position.

If there is any moral in all this, it is that a diagram may be a useful way of indicating a connection of ideas, but offers no convincing proof, since people who disagree about what the relations are will naturally draw different diagrams.

Position of Modifiers with Nouns

The obvious place to put a modifier is close to the word it modifies; and the two closest positions are immediately before and immediately after. Normally we put a single-word modifier of a noun before, and a phrase or clause modifier after. Thus we should say "A tall man," "The man in the street," and "The man who was here yesterday."

The habit of putting a phrase afterward is so strong that if for any reason we put it first we usually convert it into a single word by the use of hyphens. Thus we write *four-in-hand ties* and *off-the-cuff speeches*. The habit of putting a single word first is not quite so strong. Nobody would say *a man tall,* but we might say either *the only available man* or *the only man available*. The modifier comes first at least nine times out of ten. When it comes after the noun, it is usually because it introduces, or easily could introduce, a phrase. Thus we should say:

A broken bough	A bough broken by the wind
An appropriate sum	A sum appropriate for the purpose

The reason that such words as *appropriate, available,* and *possible* may be used after the noun even when they do not introduce a phrase is that they tend to suggest a phrase in a way that words like *tall* and *beautiful* do not. We should say "He is a possible winner" and not "He is a winner possible." But we might say either "The only possible explanation" or "The only explanation possible," because we are used to such expressions as "The only explanation possible under the circumstances."

Modifiers in Series

When two modifiers come before a noun, there are four possible relations:

1. Both may modify the noun independently. If so, the modifiers are usually "leveled" by *and, but, or,* or a comma.

Old, tired men   *Long* and *boring* books   *Air* or *sea* travel

2. The first may modify the second, while the second modifies the noun.

Dark green water   *Very old* men

3. The second may modify the noun, while the first modifies the combination.

A *long comic* book   The *old hired* man   A *new dollar* bill

4. The two may be taken as a unit modifying the noun.

A *high school* boy   The *land conservation* program
A *New Deal* politician

It is often a hair-splitting process to decide exactly which of these relations is intended (for instance, in *dark oak table*), and therefore unnecessary to indicate which one you have selected. When there is a chance of misunderstanding, the two more closely related words may be joined by a hyphen.

A *comic-book* salesman   *High-school* expenses
A *comic* book-salesman   *High* school-expenses

Many writers regularly use hyphens to indicate combinations of *modifiers* even when there is no danger of ambiguity.

A *high-school* team   The *high school* is new
A *New-Deal* politician   but   The *New Deal* brought changes.

Such combinations are not usually included in dictionaries as hyphenated words, but they are clearly established in standard usage. If a combination comes into very frequent use it is often written as a single word. Thus we may read *high school* texts, *high-school* texts, or *highschool* texts.

The series of modifiers preceding a noun may be considerably longer than two, whether they all modify the noun or some of them modify others.

A long, interesting, well-documented, and highly important book
The present Scottsdale High School athletic program committee

These longer series involve no further theoretical problems, but anybody with a sensitive ear will probably decide that the second one is at least a word too long.

Adverbial Modifiers

Modifiers of verbs can be placed more freely than modifiers of nouns. This is partly because there is usually only one verb in a clause, while there are likely to be several nouns; and partly because it often makes little difference whether we associate an adverbial modifier specifically with the verb or more generally with the clause as a whole. For instance we might find any of the following orders:

> *Slowly* Emmett walked down the street.
> Emmett *slowly* walked down the street.
> Emmett walked *slowly* down the street.
> Emmett walked down the street *slowly*.

Some readers might prefer one of these sentences to the others, or feel that they all showed some differences in emphasis. But there is no question that the same general information is conveyed by all four, and that a great many readers would consider them completely interchangeable.

Some modifiers are less flexible than others. If we substituted *fast* for *slowly,* we could not use the order "Fast Emmett walked," because a reader would probably think *fast* described Emmett, rather than the way he walked down the street. We should also be unlikely to say "Emmett fast walked," though we might have some trouble in explaining why. Other modifiers might have different numbers of possibilities, and it would make a definite difference where some of them were put.

The fact that there is no satisfactory general rule for such constructions need not trouble us. "Modification" is merely a matter of habitual association; and a position that seems natural to the writer will usually be satisfactory to the reader. There are, however, a few words about which an arbitrary theory has been developed. It is often said that the following pairs of sentences have different "real meanings," approximately as indicated:

> I *only* want ten cents. (I don't expect to get it)
> I want *only* ten cents. (That is all I want)
> I'll *just* see him for a minute. (Not talk to him)
> I'll see him for *just* a minute. (It won't take longer)
> He doesn't *even* have a dollar. (So he can't spend it)
> He doesn't have *even* a dollar. (He has less than a dollar)

The theory is that words like *only, just,* and *even* necessarily modify the words that immediately follow them. But the theory simply isn't true. It describes a habit that we might have developed, not one that we actually have developed. When we hear such sentences, the sensible thing to do is to try to figure out what the speaker actually means. If we want to express such ideas, and have any fear of being misunderstood, we can always say something like "All I want is ten cents" or "My desire for ten cents is merely a wish."

Successive Modifying Phrases

A phrase is usually placed immediately after the word it modifies. This ordinarily causes no trouble; but when two phrases are used, one of them must come first. There is then a possibility that the second may be taken as modifying the last word in the first phrase, instead of the word with which the writer associated it. This may result in an actual misunderstanding or in a ludicrous suggestion.

There is a man *from Kansas   in the car.*

Both phrases clearly refer to *man.*

There is a man *in the car   from Kansas.*

Either the man or the car may be from Kansas.

The car was identified *as the one stolen   by Jim Dodd.*

If Dodd merely identified the car, he might bring a libel suit on the basis of this sentence.

No general rule can be given on which type of phrase should be put first. A writer must remember that the reader will probably associate the second phrase with the nearest word to which it can reasonably apply, which is often the last word in the first phrase. If such an association would lead to misunderstanding, the writer may reverse the phrases. If the result is still unclear, he should completely rewrite the sentence.

General Principles of Modification

A comprehensive treatment of the problems of modification would require far more space than we can afford in this book; but careful attention to a few general principles will solve most of them.

1. Modification depends on association of ideas.

2. It's not enough for a writer to prove that his association is possible. Unless he makes it automatic for his readers, his sentence is ambiguous.

3. A written sentence gets no help from intonation. Word order is therefore doubly important.

Two common difficulties are discussed in the *Index to Usage* under the headings *Dangling Modifiers* and *Squinting Modifiers*.

Exercises—Chapter 7

I. Each of the following sentences is accompanied by a word or phrase to be used as a modifier. Insert the word or phrase in such a way that a reader will have no reasonable doubt about what association is intended. (There *may* be many satisfactory arrangements, of course.)

1. If you look closely you'll see the cuff-link I lost yesterday. *under the bed.*
2. From her bed she could see the mist from the water above the mountains in the distance. *rising.*
3. The table was sold to the stout man. *with a solid mahogany top.*
4. The stranger who had been running was arrested. *in the park.*
5. The bleachers were assembled and erected to serve the fans. *in the end zone.*
6. The coach had told him not to use that play. *many times.*
7. Drinking is a cause of marital discord. *frequently.*
8. He ran past the man. *panting and wheezing.*
9. He advised me to go to the police. *secretly.*
10. He shouted to ask if the man had seen the robber fleeing. *from his office.*
11. She asked me if I would treasure her photograph. *always.*
12. Leroy took a picture of the girl. *with the large camera.*
13. You cannot buy that watermelon for a dollar. *even.*
14. The plumber forced his assistant to carry the pipe. *loose-jointed.*
15. A bystander in a derby placed a large bill in the shirt pocket of the man on the sidewalk. *crumpled.*

II. Resolve the ambiguity in the following sentences by overhauling the present modification:

1. Fastened to the hatch with clamps and sealed tight with a rubber gasket the sailors can get into the diving bell and escape the sunken sub.
2. I worked for an old man who was a good friend of my father a few years after his death.
3. Will anyone perfect some amazing improvement on the modern automobile or airplane that has not had a college education?
4. The most common interest we have is horses, my mother especially.
5. After getting in the car and pulling away from the curb the traffic jam starts.

6. Bulging at every seam the woman carried her overloaded grocery bag to her car.

7. My dog is well trained having bought him from Mr. Dickason who is well known as a dog trainer and can stand on his hind legs.

8. Stewed to her complete satisfaction Marjorie served the chicken, but as she was carrying the platter to the table it cracked wide open.

9. Smoking blackly from every side the woman drove her car into the fire station.

10. Skidding around the corner on two wheels, the First Methodist Church came into view.

11. Having cut off his head with his pocketknife, Elmer remarked about what a fine trout he was.

12. After she had consumed a bale of hay my grandmother complained about keeping an elephant in the back yard.

13. Covered with new paint fore and aft Aunt Matilda took a fancy to the yacht after all.

14. Although the pack of hounds was at her heels, Mrs. Silverson ran to save the injured doe.

15. The rest of us love to watch the dogs run around the track after the rabbit but not Father.

Suggestions for Discussion or Theme Writing—Chapter 7

1. Prepare a unified paragraph in which you discuss the difference between (a) the positioning of modifiers of nouns and (b) the positioning of adverbial modifiers. Explain.

2. Prepare a 200-400 word presentation in which you elaborate upon the idea that modification depends on association of ideas. Illustrate with examples.

3. Explain how intonation can clarify modifiers which might be ambiguous in a written sentence. Illustrate.

SUBORDINATE
CLAUSES

8

In Chapter 6 we mentioned that subordinate clauses could be used as subjects, complements, or modifiers of any of the elements in larger clauses. Here are some examples:

Subject
His decision   is all right with me.
Whatever he decides

                                      Complement
He knows   my opinion.
                                      what I think of him.

                                      Modifier (adverbial)
He comes   often.
                                      whenever he can.

                                      Modifier (adjectival)
He hates   troublesome   people.
                    people   who cause trouble.

Another way of expressing approximately the same idea is to say that all subordinate clauses function as nouns, adjectives, or adverbs. There is no rule against using a clause as a preposition or a verb— but if you can think of a way to do it you will become famous (in a very limited circle, of course).

In classifying clauses by function we sometimes come across borderline cases, just as we do in classifying single words. We are not going to bother about such cases in this chapter, nor are we going to attempt a complete inventory. We are simply going to discuss those kinds which seem to cause trouble and confusion most often.

Relative Modifying Clauses

Adjective clauses are also called *relative clauses*. Some examples are given below:

> He is the man *who was here yesterday.*
> Her singing, *which was really beautiful,* drew a cheer from the crowd.
> This is the one *that I like best.*
> That is the house *where Jim used to live.*
> A boy *we know* has three horses of his own.

Notice that three of these clauses begin with *wh-* words, and the other two could be made to begin with such words. We could change the clause in the third sentence to "*which* I like best," and the one in the fifth sentence to "*whom* we know." These changes would not improve the sentences, but we *could* make them.

These *wh-* words are called *relatives* because they are said to relate the clauses in which they occur to the words that these clauses modify. When *that* is used in place of a *wh-* word (as in the third sentence) it is called a relative, too. Clauses like "we know" in the fifth sentence are sometimes called "relative clauses with the relative omitted," but if you want to be really fancy you can call them "asyndetic parataxis." It is all right to use them without calling them anything if the meaning is clear.

Identifying and Amplifying Clauses

Compare the two following sentences:

> The man *who was here yesterday* left that package for you.
> George Akers, *who was here yesterday,* left that package for you.

In the first sentence the italicized clause is called *identifying* because it is needed to tell you what man left the book. It is not set off by commas because it is so closely connected with the main statement that no commas are needed. But in the second sentence you already know who the man is—his name is George Akers. The clause is not used to identify him but to give you some additional information about him. It amplifies the statement and is therefore called an *amplifying* clause. And since this additional information interrupts the main statement (George Akers left that package for you), you set it off by commas. If you read the two sentences aloud naturally, you will probably find that your voice pattern tells you which one needs the commas.

Identifying clauses are often called *restrictive* or *essential,* and amplifying clauses *nonrestrictive, descriptive,* or *nonessential.* Any of these terms will do, but students seem to find *identifying* and *amplifying* easier to remember and keep straight.

When a relative clause comes at the end of a sentence instead of in the middle, it cannot be set off by two commas; but the choice between one and none follows the same principles as those explained above:

Identifying: There's the motel where we stayed last year.
Amplifying: There is the Vista Motel, where we stayed last year.

Variations in Identifying Clauses

In identifying clauses, *that* may always be substituted for *who, whom,* or *which;* and unless the relative word is the subject of the clause, it may be omitted entirely. Look at the following examples. You may have heard some of them called wrong by people who are sure there can be only one right way to do anything, but all are certainly in standard use.

1. A man *who* could help you with that is the ranger at McNary.
   A man *that* could help you with that is the ranger at McNary.

2. He is the one to *whom* you should send it.
   He is the one *that* you should send it to.
   He is the one you should send it to.

3. Here is a book *which* you might find interesting.
   Here is a book *that* you might find interesting.
   Here is a book you might find interesting.

The ideas that the relative should always be expressed, that *who* and *that* or *which* and *that* are never interchangeable, and that sentences should never end in prepositions may all be summed up in Churchill's famous note to an over-fussy editor: "This is the sort of nonsense up with which I will not for an instant put."

Restrictions on Amplifying Clauses

In amplifying clauses the relative word canot be omitted, and *that* should not be substituted for a *wh-* relative word. These restrictions cause no trouble with sentences like "Sally, *who* knows her best, says she isn't really sick at all." Few of us would be tempted to put the clause in any other form. But such sentences as the following do cause some confusion:

> Len Fogle, *whom* we met at the beach, is sending us some peaches.
> *Silas Marner, which* we read in high school, bores me to tears.

We can't simply leave out the *whom* and *which,* and neither *who* nor *that* is generally accepted here as standard. If *whom* and *which* do not seem natural, the best substitutes are *a man* and *a book*.

Relative Noun Clauses

Relative clauses may also be used in any construction in which a noun is possible. When so used, they begin with either the simple *wh-* relatives or with *whatever, whichever,* or *whoever*.

> He knows *who did it.*
> They will give it to *whoever comes first.*
> *Why he wants it* is a mystery.
> We don't know *when it happened.*
> This is *where they used to live.*

Only two troublesome questions arise:

1. There is a widespread prejudice against introducing *definitions* with *when* or *where,* as in:

> A debate is *when you argue a question.*
> A dead-end is *where you can't go any farther.*

The objection may not be logically sound (compare the standard "This is *where they used to live*"), but it is strong enough to be worth considering.

2. In choosing between *who* or *whoever* and *whom* or *whomever,* there is a theory that "the form of the relative pronoun is determined by its function in the clause in which it occurs, regardless of the function of this clause in the sentence." According to this theory the following uses are obligatory:

> I know *who* did it. (*Who* is the subject)
> I know *who* it was. (*Who* is the "subjective complement")
> I know *whom* you saw. (*Whom* is the "direct object")
> Tell me to *whom* you gave it. (*Whom* is the "object of a preposition")

Give it to *whoever* comes first. (*Whoever* is the subject)
Give it to *whomever* you see first. (*Whomever* is the "direct object")

If we take this theory seriously we shall have to recall a number of the concepts of Latin grammar which we have dismissed as inappropriate to English, simply to justify rules about one pronoun in its simple and compound forms. Luckily, all the available evidence indicates that, in spite of the objections of purists, the following sentences are in good standard usage:

> I know *who* you saw.
> Tell me *who* you gave it to.
> Give it to *whoever* you see first.

Some Practical Rules for Using *Who* and *Whom*

If you have learned to use *whom* naturally wherever the Latin-based theories call for it, you might as well continue to do so. If you find the choice between *who* and *whom* troublesome, follow these rules:

1. Use *whom* in such set phrases as "to *whom* it may concern" and "for *whom* the bell tolls."

2. Say "the man it belongs to" and "the boy we were talking about" rather than "the man to *who*(*m*) it belongs" and "the boy about *who*(*m*) we were talking."

3. Remember that *who*(*m*) can often be omitted or replaced by *that* or an explanatory noun.

4. Whenever you are in the slightest doubt, use *who*. "I don't know *who* it belongs to" is standard English, no matter what the rules say, simply because it fits in with the natural patterns of the language, and most standard speakers use it. But "John Dawson, *whom* I consider is a fine man" is slightly ridiculous as well as "incorrect." We get the impression that the speaker is trying awfully hard and still not making it.

5. Don't give *whomever* a thought. *Whoever* is unquestionably in standard use in all constructions.

Non-Relative *That* Clauses

On pages 94-96 we considered clauses in which *that* could be used as an alternate for *who, whom,* or *which.* In such clauses *that* serves as a structural part of the clause, either the subject or the complement. There are other subordinate clauses for which *that* serves simply as an introductory connective:

1. I know *that* he is coming.

Here *that* could be omitted. "I know he is coming" is also standard.

2. The idea *that* he is coming cheers me up.

When the *that* clause serves to explain a preceding noun, the *that* cannot be omitted.

3. *That he had worked hard* was proved by the results.

The use of *that* clauses as subjects is much less common than it used to be, and seems to many people rather stilted. However, the popular habit of simply leaving out the *that* ("He is tired is the whole trouble") is definitely not standard. This sentence could be revised in either of the following ways:

> The fact that he is tired is the whole trouble.
> The whole trouble is that he is tired.

If and Whether Clauses

Clauses beginning with *if* and *whether* cause no trouble when they are used as modifiers, since *if* and *whether or not* have quite different meanings, and *whether* alone is never used in a modifying clause.

> We are going at seven *if* you are here.
> We are going at seven *whether or not* you are here.

We simply would not say "We are going at seven *whether* you are here" without adding "or not" either after the *whether* or at the end of the sentence.

There is no good reason why these clauses should cause any more trouble when they are used as complements, but a number of arbitrary rules have been made by people who like to make distinctions even when they can prove no difference. All of the following variations are acceptable:

> I don't know *if he is coming.*
> *if he is coming or not.*
> *whether he is coming.*
> *whether he is coming or not.*
> *whether or not he is coming.*

If we used the clause as a subject rather than a complement, we should probably use one of the forms beginning with *whether:*

Whether (*or not*) he is coming hasn't been decided yet.

Sequence of Tenses

There are certain clauses in which the tense of the verb does not indicate actual time, but simply shows a grammatical relation to the main verb. Take such a sentence as "If I saw any, I would show you some." Here *saw* does not indicate past time, but rather implies that I *see* none now. This kind of adjustment is called *sequence of tenses,* and occurs in three types of clauses: (1) after verbs of saying, thinking, etc. (sometimes called "indirect discourse"); (2) in purpose clauses; (3) in certain conditional clauses.

In all three types the verb (or the first form in a verb-phrase) is *shifted from the present to the past.* There are some differences between the types, however, and these differences will be discussed in the next three sections.

Indirect Discourse

When a subordinate clause is introduced by a verb of saying or thinking in the *past tense,* the subordinate verb (or first auxiliary) is put in the past tense, regardless of the time indicated. This tendency is best illustrated by showing direct statements shifted to indirect discourse.

He *knows* you.	He said he *knew* you.
He *has* done it.	He told me he *had* done it.
He *will* come tomorrow.	He promised he *would come tomorrow*.
He *can* do it.	He thought he *could* do it.

This convention of sequence is almost invariably observed after verbs of *thinking*. We can hardly say "I *thought* I have" or "He *knew* we *are* there." But there is now a strong tendency to drop the convention after verbs of *saying*. Such sentences as the following are becoming very common, especially in newspapers:

He *said* he *believes* that it will work.
He *promised* he *will* take action tomorrow.

Such sentences amount to direct quotations in content, although they are indirect in form. They are sometimes distinctly clearer than the older type; for when sequence is observed, both "I *am* there" and "I *was* there" may appear in indirect discourse as "He *said* he *was* there." Theoretically, this ambiguity could be avoided by always shifting a direct *was* to an indirect *had been;* but actually this is seldom done.

Purpose Clauses

When the verbs *may, can, will,* and *shall* are used in subordinate clauses to indicate *purpose,* sequence of tenses is regularly observed:

> He *is* resting so he *can* play tomorrow.
> He *was* resting so he *could* play the next day.
> He *works* in order that he *may* be secure.
> He *worked* in order that he *might* be secure.
> He *has* been saving so he *will* have some spending money.
> He *had* been saving so he *would* have some spending money.

Sequence is not used in clauses indicating *result*:

> He worked Sunday so he *could* (purpose) rest today.
> He worked Sunday, so he *can* (result) rest today.

Conditional Sentences

Such sentences as the following, in which one statement depends on another introduced by *if,* are known as conditional sentences:

> If he *had* any money yesterday, he *will* still *have* it tomorrow.
> If he *had* any money, he *would* give you some.

Notice the difference between the two. In the first, the *condition* is an open question—we don't know whether he had any money or not. In such sentences the verbs are used independently, and any tense may be used in either clause. But in the second there is a clear indication that he does not have any money. *If* clauses of this type are called *contrary-to-fact* clauses. Sentences containing contrary-to-fact clauses follow a rather curious pattern. Fortunately, most of us use it automatically.

1. The main clause must have a verb-phrase beginning with *could, might, would,* or *should.* Present and future time are indicated

by *would go, might help,* etc. Past time is indicated by *would have gone, might have helped,* etc.

2. In the *if* clause, present and future time are indicated by the past tense, and past time by the past perfect.

> If we *had* the money, we *might buy* it.
> If you *tried* tomorrow, you *could* probably *find* one.
> If he *had known* the truth, he *would have acted* at once.

A special difficulty in conditional sentences is the choice between *was* and *were* when the *if* clause has a singular subject. The rule is that *was* is required to express actual doubt, and *were* to express a contrary-to-fact condition.

> If it *was* there yesterday, it must still be there.
> If I *was* rude, it was unintentional.
> If Morgan *were* here, he could tell us.
> If I *were* you, I wouldn't do that.

This left-over bit of the subjunctive mood is certainly unnecessary, since no other verb has preserved a special form; and recent studies indicate that even in standard usage *was* now appears about half the time in contrary-to-fact clauses. However, a good many speakers of standard still consider the use of *were* in such clauses a matter of great importance. Since people are actually losing chances for good jobs by saying "If I *was* you," *were* is obviously of much greater practical importance than, for instance, *whom.*

There are some clauses that lie between the extremes of contrary-to-fact conditions and definitely open questions:

> If anything *were* to happen to him, she would collapse.
> He looks as if he *were* unhappy.

In such clauses the usual alternative is not to substitute *was* for *were,* but to say "If anything should happen" or "If anything happened," and "He looks unhappy."

Inverted Contrary-to-Fact Clauses

It used to be fairly common to indicate that a condition was contrary to fact, or that a wish was unlikely to be fulfilled, by inverted clauses without the *if.*

> *Had it not been for the rain,* they would have gone.
> *Were he only to come,* we should be saved.

Such clauses are now going out of use.

Adverbial Clauses

Most subordinate clauses other than those discussed are adverbial.

He came *when she called.*
Frank finally got the car started, *after all the rest of us had failed.*
Warner and Betty, *although they were both tired,* kept on working.
He got up early *so he could see the eclipse.*
He has practiced regularly, *so he may have a chance.*

There is often an argument over whether such clauses modify only the main verb or the whole independent clause; and another argument about whether they are "temporal," "concessive," or what not. Neither argument seems to serve any useful purpose, since there is seldom any question of structure involved.

The "proper use" of connectives introducing such clauses has also received a great deal of attention; but most of the rules evolved are highly unreliable. For the most part we must simply depend on our ears to pick up the standard patterns of speech. When we are in serious doubt about the appropriateness of a particular connective, the specific information in a dictionary is usually more helpful than any general treatment in a grammar.

Exercises—Chapter 8

I. Mark the italicized clauses in the following sentences *A* (amplifying) or *I* (identifying). Set off the amplifying clauses with commas. Read the sentences aloud, with and without pauses for the commas, and see if you think the punctuation has any value.

1. Here is the book *you ordered.*
2. Everyone *who has experience in mountaineering* will be needed for the search.
3. We always buy our Christmas cards from Leroy Coulter *who lives in our block.*
4. This is the Mr. Smith *who wrote those letters to the editor.*
5. The only letter *that has not been opened* is addressed to you.
6. A small-caliber rifle *which is the only kind for me* would not fire this ammunition.

7. A stranger *whom we met on the train* told us about these jobs.

8. Charles Fisk *who is our congressman* attends that church.

9. The tramp *who worked for them last year* is now a rich oilman.

10. The girl you saw was Clara Evans *who used to go to dances with my brother*.

II. In some sentences below, the italicized word is unnecessary. Cross out the ones you think could be omitted.

1. The car *that* I wanted had already been sold.

2. Thomas Brothers, *where* I bought my first car, has gone out of business.

3. If he knows *that* I'm looking for him, he hasn't done anything about it.

4. Lisa Crane, *whom* I knew as a child, signed a Hollywood contract.

5. The dog *that* bit my brother has already been impounded.

6. He gave the piano to Elmer Binet, *who* plays "Chopsticks" on it in his memory.

7. Frank gave us the smaller twin *which* would have been abandoned by its mother.

8. No one told me *that* you knew my brother was in a bomb-disposal squad.

9. I never told anyone *that* Frank had such a risky job.

10. Frank, *who* faints at loud noises, finds the work quiet and absorbing.

III. Insert an acceptable relative word in each of the blanks below, unless you decide (that) none is needed to complete the meaning.

1. Someone is always borrowing the books _____ I have never read.

2. Hand me the dictionary _____ is on the table.

3. The doctor says I must give up coffee and tea, _____ are my favorite drinks.

4. Before we ran out of gas we passed a station _____ was closed for the night.

5. The very next station, _____ sells groceries, too, never closes.

6. The only teller _____ could vouch for me was out of the bank.

7. The next time I will not put my finger in the barrel of a gun _____ is loaded.

8. Mary Putnam, _____ is the only girl I liked, eloped last week.

9. His sports car _____ was very low-slung, could not navigate the ruts.

10. The toy _____ my uncle invented could never be patented.

Suggestions for Discussion or Theme Writing—Chapter 8

1. Rewrite the following paragraph, playing down the less-significant detail through subordinate clauses (and implied statements) and thus emphasizing the significant observations. (You may find some of the original information completely unusable.):

We went out for the evening and did various things. We took in a movie. It was called THE SUN ALSO RISES. It was a powerful show. Then we went to a diner to eat. Joe Shirpo owns the diner. We ate hamburgers. Then we went down to the beach. We took Mike's car. The grunion were running. There were many of them. But we stopped on the way to pick up pails for the grunion. They shone in the moonlight. That is, the grunion did. The water was cold. We got wet. But our pants were rolled up. After that we went uptown for cokes. But we stopped on the way to leave off our grunion. We left them at Carl's house. He was one of the boys with us. There were three others, too. All the others were brothers. There was Sam, Mike, and Leroy Schmidt. Leroy was the oldest. Mike was the one that got out of Reform School last year. Sam can be picked out easiest of all. He is white-haired. Mike's car is an Olds. We never did eat the grunion, though. Joe Shirpo has a way of fixing hamburgers. Movie stars come clear across town to eat Joe's hamburgers.

2. In a paragraph of a hundred words or more, use a subordinate clause as a subject, another as a complement and one each as adjective and adverbial modifiers. Identify the different uses.

NON-STATEMENT
SENTENCES
AND SENTENCE
FRAGMENTS

9

In Chapter 5 we listed six kinds of sentences—statements, questions, answers, commands and requests, comments, and exclamations. Since then we have been considering statements, which are the only kind with a definite structural requirement. It is now time to pay a little attention to the other kinds.

Noninformative "Statements"

Sentences with the clause structure of statements may be used as questions, commands, or exclamations (if they are used as answers or comments, they remain statements):

Question: He will be here tomorrow?
Exclamation: That's a shame!
Command: All members of the team will report here at four o'clock.

Questions and exclamations in such form should be short enough for the reader to see the end punctuation at the first glance. Otherwise he must either start to read them as statements and then reconsider, or (as often happens) simply disregard the final punctuation and so miss the point. Many people will pay some attention to punctuation if it strikes their attention before they have made up their minds about a sentence, but not afterward.

Questions

The question is the only kind of sentence in which clauses of different form from those used in statements appear. Such reversals as the following are typical:

STATEMENT	QUESTION
He is going there.	Is he going there?
They have finished.	Have they finished?
You could have done it.	Could you have done it?
He lives there.	Does he live there?
He finished it yesterday.	Did he finish it yesterday?

Since most students find it very much easier to use such séntences acceptably than to learn rules about them, no rules will be given.

It is also possible to convert statements into questions by adding such tags as *is he? didn't they?* and *won't you?* at the end. For sentences of more than a very few words these tags work much better than simple question marks, since they do not affect the normal intonation pattern of the main part of the sentence. Take such a sentence as "He'll be driving over from Los Angeles tomorrow if he can get away from the office in time, won't he?" If you leave out the *won't he* and depend entirely upon the question mark, the intonation becomes much more difficult.

These tags cause little trouble unless the verb is *am* and the pronoun *I.* Neither the Irish *Amn't I?* nor the British *Aren't I?* is generally accepted in this country; and *Am I not?* is at least as far astray on one side as *Ain't I?* is on the other. We don't have any handy general tag like the French *n'est-ce pas?* or the German *nicht wahr?,* and *Huh?* doesn't really sound elegant. Perhaps the best thing to do is to revise the whole sentence so that no tag will be needed.

Indirect Questions

When one speaker's question is quoted exactly by another, it remains a direct question and requires a question mark.

John asked, "How many gallons of oil will you need for the boat?"

But if it is merely reported by another speaker it becomes part of a statement and needs no question mark.

John asked how many gallons of oil you will need for the boat.

Answers

Answers may be in the form of statements, or they may be simply the words or phrases needed to supply the information requested. It is rather silly to supply a subject and verb just to make an answer conform to an overgeneralized definition of a sentence. However, very short answers sometimes seem curt to the point of rudeness, especially if there are several of them in a row. Adding a subject and verb (not necessarily the most obvious ones) is one way to pad them out to a more pleasing figure.

Q. What time is it?
A. It is ten.
Q. How do you know?
A. I know by the kitchen clock.
Q. Is the clock right?
A. Yes, the clock is right.

This sounds like either sarcasm or a quotation from a primer.

Q. What time is it?
A. Ten.
Q. How do you know?
A. Kitchen clock.
Q. Is the clock right?
A. Yes.

This sounds like a strong, silent man—of about ten years.

Q. What time is it?
A. Ten o'clock exactly.
Q. How do you know?
A. I can see the kitchen clock.
Q. Is the clock right?
A. It was by the radio at noon.

This sounds much more courteous—but notice that adding *exactly* is just as helpful as adding *I can see the*.

Exclamations

Exclamations, even more than questions, must be short to be effective. Don't write: "Isn't it wonderful that Molly gets a three-week vacation this year and is going to spend all but two days of it here with us!" Break it in two and say: "Molly gets a three-week vacation this year and is going to spend all but two days of it here with us. Isn't that wonderful!" The purpose of an exclamation point is to make a reader react with some excitement. He may do it for a few words, but not for too many at once—and he certainly is unlikely to go back several lines to get excited about what he has already taken in with complete calm.

Commands and Requests

Commands and requests may be in the form of statements, questions, "imperative sentences," or (when the situation makes them clear and courtesy does not forbid them) phrases or single words:

> *Statements:* You will report to the mess sergeant.
> I wish you'd get Mr. Adams on the phone.
> *Questions:* Will you kindly stop that noise?
> Would you pass the cream, please?
> *"Imperative sentences":* Don't drive so fast.
> Please wait just five minutes more.
> *Words and phrases:* Not so fast.
> Tickets, please.
> Careful.

In speech the intonation of commands and requests is particularly important. Polite phrasing makes an impatient or domineering tone sound worse rather than better. In writing there are no particular structural problems.

Comments

If you must know, "Comments" is an entirely new classification for sentences, invented in this book to supply a defense for the instructor who criticizes sentence fragments by writing in the margin "Not a sentence." However, it is a very useful type of sentence in its place (which is usually *not* in the middle of a student paper), and has been in use for a long time, even if it has lacked a name.

Clauseless Sentences in Writing

The five types of sentences we have just discussed may or may not have a clause (subject-predicate) structure. Even without clauses they are completely standard in conversation. Obviously they are needed in plays and fiction, where the only structural requirement is that the language should seem appropriate to the characters. They may also be used to give a conversational flavor to other types of writing. There is nothing wrong with addressing a reader directly—telling him to do this and asking him about that—if you think he'll stand for it. But on the whole clauseless sentences require a little more skill and judgment than statements; and if they are not successful they fall very flat indeed.

Sentence Fragments

Such expressions as those italicized below are called *sentence fragments.*

> I looked out. *John running down the street.* I called him.
> Suddenly I heard a noise. *Under the oak tree.*
> It must be a dismal life. *To have no friends at all.*
> We'll probably do it tomorrow. *If he comes.*

The first three lack complete verbs, and the fourth is a typical subordinate clause. All of them might be satisfactory in some settings, but when they occur in places where our training has led us to expect full sentences, they jar on many readers, and a teacher is almost certain to mark them wrong.

A student may argue quite correctly that the sentence fragments shown above are perfectly clear, and that many successful writers make very free use of similar fragments.

If we answer him honestly, we must admit that the sentence is not always the most effective unit. Compare the two following paragraphs, one written in sentences, the other in fragments:

> In summer the desert is blazing hot. The merciless heat of the sun is intensified by reflections from the bare, red rock of the hills. There seems to be no animal life, and even the few gaunt saguaros look as if they were at the end of their endurance.

> Blazing summer on the desert. Merciless heat of the sun. Heat pounded back by the bare red rock of the hills. Not an animal in sight. Only scattered, gaunt saguaros, waiting for the end.

The omission of any part of a familiar pattern naturally throws emphasis on what is left; and if we read without prejudice, we may well decide that the second treatment is more effective, because it presents the impression more vividly and leaves it up to the reader's imagination to supply the connections. But this very fact makes it more of a strain on the reader. Too much of it is tiring; and unless the material is unusually interesting, we are likely to turn to a writer who gives us ready-made connections that are easy to follow.

Anybody who has read much English has come to expect sentences as the normal units of expression. Consciously or subconsciously, he looks for a subject and predicate in each one. Any departure from the pattern jars his attention. If the departure is deliberate and skillful, it can be very effective. If it is merely careless, it is usually irritating and sometimes bewildering. A man who is confident of his writing and unconcerned about criticism may do as he pleases. Anybody who wants to avoid conventional criticism will do well to write in full statements except when he is clearly imitating conversation.

Exercises—Chapter 9

Indicate which of the following could be completed by (a) supplying a complete verb, (b) supplying a subject, (c) omitting a subordinating connective, (d) adding an independent clause, or (e) none of the above. (In some cases both c and d may apply.) After marking the entries, go back and make the appropriate adjustment.

1. At our house the day before Christmas.
2. Even though she was the best student in the class.
3. Never had it so good.
4. The boy, tired and sleepy, gone to bed.
5. Because the river is rising and the bridge weak.
6. Better to try it again.
7. The next child to be a boy.
8. How he could bring himself to do such a thing.
9. Thus trying to make amends for his conduct.
10. The rest of the company ready to come to the rescue of the lost platoon.
11. Complete chaos, especially during the time.
12. In the window, so all the neighbors could see the lights.
13. Was having a wonderful time.
14. A long and weary road that he must travel.
15. Wherever he had been climbing when the avalanche struck.
16. Because of the rain outside, putting on his raincoat.
17. After the skating party, the chestnuts roasted over the fire.

18. Because of his lack of education, was unsure of himself.
19. Than the old Ford could climb.
20. Whether he can get his vacation at that time.

Suggestions for Discussion or Theme Writing—Chapter 9

Construct fifteen *sentences* with the clause structure of *statements,* making five of them questions, five commands, and five exclamations. Looking back over what you have written, comment on the length that seems appropriate to the various types. Discuss the difference between (a) the intonation these sentences would require if spoken, and (b) the intonation of the same word patterns spoken as simple statements.

PROBLEMS IN WRITING

THE FIRST PAPER　　IO

Whatever else you do in freshman English, you will certainly have to write some papers. This means a considerable number of hours devoted to actual work. For a great many students it means even more hours given over to fussing, fuming, and general frustration. The work is unavoidable, but the wasted effort can be greatly reduced by following a sensible method.

How Not to Write a Paper

Joe Williams begins his paper by writing his first sentence, with the blind hope that it will somehow generate a second, which will in turn generate a third. Of course if this generating process does happen to go on long enough the paper will get written, but the process often stops pretty early. Joe writes his first sentence, and then looks at it. The second one somehow doesn't leap to his pen. He looks at it again, and then lights a cigarette and looks at it some more. After a while he crosses it out and writes another first sentence. This can go on for hours.

Eventually Joe gets five sentences written, and decides that they will pass for a paragraph. It is not quite as good a paragraph as he had hoped to write, and he is not very sure about where to go on from there. He decides that maybe he has selected the wrong topic. He tears up the paper, takes a drink of water, lights another cigarette, and makes a few remarks about English and English instructors. Then he starts all over again. He begins by writing his first sentence.

Joe is not really a fool. He wouldn't start building even a simple cowshed by driving a post in the ground, nailing a board to it, and then looking for a good place to put the next post. He would lay out his ground plan first, put all his posts where he had decided that they belonged, brace and connect them, and then begin to put on the sheathing. But it has never occurred to him that writing a paper is a construction job, a job most people can do much better by planning it in advance.

Selecting a Topic

The first step in planning a paper is selecting the topic. Let us consider all the possibilities.

(1) Your instructor assigns a specific topic, say "Why I came to State." Don't allow yourself more than a few seconds to think about what a silly subject this is. If you do, you'll not only be wasting time, you'll be making your job definitely harder by allowing your distaste to build up. If you have to, you have to, and you might as well start right in.

(2) Your instructor gives you a choice of two or three topics. If one of them appeals to you at once, take it and forget the others. Otherwise, give yourself not more than two or three minutes to decide, and don't change your mind. It is easier to write on any of them than to decide for sure which one is best.

(3) Your instructor gives you a free choice of topics. If this wild liberty tends to send you into hours of alternate doodling and daydreaming, you may find the following hints helpful:

(a) Do not try to find a subject that will allow you to dazzle your instructor with your brilliance. He'll settle for less.

(b) Do not expect to find a topic that immediately suggests the whole paper. You may be lucky enough to do this, but if you don't, there is a simple method of developing the subject that will be discussed later.

(c) Just let your mind run over some ideas until you come across a subject that you find interesting enough to talk about, and decide firmly to write about that. Do not worry about whether it is the best possible subject. Do not worry about whether it is sufficiently learned or important to write a paper about. And remember that no subject, in itself, is either interesting or uninteresting. But if a subject interests you, you have a fair chance of making it interesting to somebody else. Your instructor may not share your enthusiasm for working over hot-rods or planning a vacation wardrobe. But he is far more

likely to be interested in your honest opinions about such subjects as
these than in whatever you might find to say about something that you
merely think you *ought* to have ideas about.

Selecting Your Points

Once you have chosen your general topic, the next step is to decide
just what parts of it you want to treat. Remember that you can't
possibly tell all about it. There is *always* a great deal more that could
be said than you are going to have time to say. Even if you started
out with something as simple as a burnt match you could go on
indefinitely—what it is composed of, how it was made, how it was or
might have been used, what an improvement it is over earlier methods
of making fire, what changes matches have made in our everyday life,
and so on. The idea that you have said all that can possibly be said
and are still 150 words short of the assigned length is a common
source of discouragement—but it is *always* false.

The first step in developing a topic is to take a piece of paper and
list the first things that occur to you. They don't have to be in any
particular order—yet. Here are three subjects with possible preliminary listings:

BURNT MATCH	FOOTBALL GAME	MY ROOMMATE
looks useless	score	good guy
made of wood (pine)	opponent	funny hair
When was it invented?	Miller's run	tinkers with car
flint and steel	crowd	sings off key
be careful	excitement	does his share
forest fires	other good plays	comes from Payson
rubbing sticks together	weather	wants to be a doctor
different kinds	fumbles	doesn't talk much
pretty cheap	injuries	lent me his shirt
chemicals (sulphur)	condition	nice when I came in
	spirit	

Suppose you decide to go on about your roommate. Put the figure
1 before the first item, "good guy." Then go down the list and put
some more 1's before the other items that seem to be closely connected with the first. Your list now might look like this:

MY ROOMMATE

1   good guy
     funny hair

	tinkers with car
	sings off key
1	does his share
	comes from Payson
	wants to be a doctor
	doesn't talk much
1	lent me his shirt
1	nice when I came in

Now put a 2 before the next unmarked item, "funny hair." This tells you something about his appearance, and is the only one of the items that does. You'd better decide whether to leave it out or add some more. If you want to describe him, add at the bottom of the list something like this:

2	tall and lean
2	broad shoulders
2	big hands and feet
2	blue eyes
2	long nose and chin

Of course you could say a lot more if you wanted to give a complete catalog, but this is enough to give a general idea of his appearance.

Now put a 3 before the next item, "tinkers with car." Since this is one of his personal habits, you might group it with "sings off key" and "doesn't talk much." Now that you're on the subject of his personal habits, it may occur to you that he is a good listener, that he likes to bowl, and that he smokes an unusually foul-smelling pipe. So you add these items at the bottom of the list, with a 3 before each.

All the items but two now have numbers, and it begins to look as if you might have enough to say without using them, so you cross out "comes from Payson" and "wants to be a doctor." Your list now looks like this:

MY ROOMMATE

1	good guy
2	funny hair
3	tinkers with car
3	sings off key
1	does his share
3	doesn't talk much
1	lent me his shirt
1	nice when I came in
2	tall and lean

2	broad shoulders
2	big hands and feet
2	blue eyes
2	long nose and chin
3	good listener
3	bowls
3	vile pipe

The next step is to rearrange these items in something like the order you will use in your paper. Since you have three sets of numbers, it seems logical to divide the paper into three paragraphs: one on the "good guy" idea, one on his appearance, and one on his habits. There is no fixed rule that says which should come first, but you might decide to begin with his appearance, go on to his personal habits, and end by telling what a fine fellow he is. It will take a little time to rewrite the list, but not nearly as much as it would to keep on going up and down it to make sure you were not leaving anything out. You therefore rearrange the list as follows:

A.

funny hair
tall and lean
broad shoulders
big hands and feet
blue eyes
long nose and chin

B.

tinkers with car
sings off key
doesn't talk much
good listener
bowls
vile pipe

C.

good guy
does his share
lent me his shirt
nice when I came in

The next step is to decide in what order you are going to take up the points in each paragraph. Obviously, you don't want to begin with his hair and end with his chin, with his feet and shoulders in between. That would give a badly scrambled impression of his anatomy. You might begin with his hair and work down, or with his feet and work up, but perhaps it would be better to give a general outline impression first, and then get down to the details of his features. If you decide on this plan, you can number the items under A as follows:

A.

4	funny hair
1	tall and lean
2	broad shoulders
3	big hands and feet
5	blue eyes
6	long nose and chin

Now you could put all this information in a single sentence, running about as follows: "My roommate is tall and lean, with broad shoulders, big hands and feet, funny yellow hair, blue eyes, and a long nose and chin." This is all right as far as it goes, but it doesn't give a very definite impression. Your reader doesn't know whether your roommate is handsome or homely, clumsy or graceful—and besides, the sentence only contains 24 words, when you had hoped for maybe a hundred. Of course you could simply use more words to say the same thing, but the only satisfactory way to expand a sentence is to put in more ideas, and let the words take care of themselves. Working on this principle, you might come up with something like this:

My roommate is a tall, lean country boy, built something like Rock Hudson with broad shoulders and narrow hips. His hands and feet are so big you might think he'd be clumsy, but he seems to handle them all right. He has a lot of straw-colored hair that sticks out in all directions, no matter how hard he tries to keep it brushed down, and friendly looking blue eyes. He has a nose about six inches long, and a chin that makes me think of Fearless Fosdick. He's certainly not handsome, but once you get used to his face, you can stand it all right.

This isn't a startling literary effort, and isn't meant to be. It is simply an example of how you can expand a paragraph and make it a little more interesting, once you get the order of the main ideas satisfactorily arranged. If you worked over the items under B and C in the same way you would have a fairly well organized paper of reasonable length without too much strain.

At the first attempt, this may seem to be a rather complicated method of working out a paper, but a great many students have found that it saves a good deal of time in the long run. You know what you are doing, step by step, and you do your selecting and rearranging at the easiest time. You are not so likely to have to throw away whole pages that have taken a long time to write, or to find yourself tacking on at the end things that should have gone in much earlier.

Paper Is Cheaper than Time

If you write a paper by the process just described you will obviously have to use a sheet or two of paper that you could have saved if you had simply started with the first sentence—and if you had been lucky. Of course thrift is a virtue, and it may seem positively immoral to say that the more paper you throw away the better. But you can't save everything, and real thrift often consists of spending cheap things freely in order to save what is valuable—and *paper is cheaper than time.*

If your working time is worth a dollar an hour, it is false economy to lose an hour's work to save three cents worth of paper. Many a student has failed a course or even flunked out of college as a direct result of this kind of economy. Mow lawns or sit with babies for five hours to buy extra paper. Save yourself 50 hours by using the paper freely. Then let your conscience decide whether you should use the extra 45 hours to mow more lawns, improve your grades, or master ping pong. Any of these activities is more profitable than "economizing" at the rate of three cents an hour.

Do Your Rearranging the Easy Way

When you have written a paper out in sentences and paragraphs, it is hard to rearrange it without copying the whole thing. Moreover, you often fail to see the necessity of rearranging it. Each sentence may seem to have a reasonable relation to the sentences before and after it, and it is hard to get a bird's-eye view, to find out if some essential parts are missing, or if there is unnecessary back-tracking or repetition. But if you begin with an outline, the *structure* stands out clearly. For instance, if there are three steps in a process and you have headings for only two, you can immediately insert the third. If you have said the same thing twice (which often happens) you can cross out one entry or combine the two. Or if you have zig-zagged from one part of a subject to another, you can get all the related entries together. Then when you get down to the actual writing, you can put everything in reasonable order the first time.

So far we have considered only the simplest kind of outline—a mere jotting down of points to be discussed, followed by a rearrangement into satisfactory order. Later on we will see how a more systematic outline can be useful, especially in longer papers. But even the simplest outline requires a reasonable amount of space, so that you can make insertions and corrections until you get it into a satisfactory form. If you try to get it all into two square inches you lose much of the advantage of the method.

Don't Be Afraid to Copy

Nobody likes to waste time in unnecessary copying, but it is often quicker to write, examine, correct, and rewrite a sentence than it is to work it all out in your head before you put it down. You probably wouldn't do a problem in long division in your head if you had paper and pencil handy to help you. Getting your material down where you can see it makes it much easier to handle and rearrange. Unless you are either pretty good or very easily satisfied you will probably have to make a second copy anyhow. It saves both time and emotional strain to make up your mind at the beginning that your first draft will have to be copied. Then you will make every change that seems reasonable. Otherwise you will sit and wonder whether something that doesn't quite satisfy you will satisfy your instructor. It probably won't—and the seconds will be ticking away into minutes while you worry about it.

Never Crowd Your Writing

Students often think instructors are heartless to demand adequate margins, double spacing, wide-lined paper, and even a little blank space between words. All of these demands add to your total expenses —possibly as much as fifty cents a month. But the plain fact is that you cannot afford to crowd your writing, *even in your first drafts and your own notes.* Crowded writing is too hard to read. It not only takes you longer to pick out the words, it makes a much less vivid impression. You may have to read it several times as often, and even then you may learn less from it.

Suppose you are reviewing a set of notes before an examination. If they are adequately spaced, they stand out clearly, and you can get the picture as a whole. If they are too crowded, you have to look at each word too carefully, and you are very likely to lose the continuity. Moreover, they are almost impossible to change—there is no room to make a correction or to insert an additional point that you missed when you made them but now think should go in. You may get so discouraged that you give up the review and decide to trust to luck. Or you may try to find somebody else who has written notes that are fit to read.

Now consider a crowded first draft. It offers all the same difficulties and a few additional ones. You have to correct this before turning it in, but the mistakes are hard to see and still harder to correct in a way that will be easy to copy. There is no room to make an insertion, or to cross out a clumsy phrase and revise the word order. You may have to revise it twice when you could have managed with one revision if you had left yourself room to make clear and adequate corrections on the first draft. You actually waste more paper as well as time.

The advantages of adequate spacing on the final copy are even more obvious, though a good many students fail to see them. Most instructors will permit a few corrections if they are neat and legible. Leaving yourself room may mean the difference between inserting a phrase that you have somehow left out and having to recopy a whole page. Moreover, your instructor needs room to make comments and corrections, and the best place to make these is right at the point to which they apply. Some students seem to have a subconscious belief that if they don't leave the instructor room for corrections he can't mark them down. But he will have room to put a D or an E on the back. If he doesn't have room to show you why, it won't help much.

Another thing to consider is that crowded writing is certain to annoy your instructor. Probably he is a very fair-minded man and won't mark you down for it consciously. But wouldn't you just as soon have him in a good mood while he is deciding your fate?

A Few Recommended Practices

Your instructor may give you his own set of instructions about the mechanical rules to follow in writing a paper. If he does, you will be wise to do all your griping about his unreasonableness at one session. Then forget about it, clip the instructions in your notebook, and follow them religiously. It saves so much time. Save your wild, free spirit of independence for more important things. If he does not give you special instructions, those listed below will probably prove satisfactory. They include a few details beyond the liberal use of paper, but we can't have a separate chapter on everything.

(1) Always leave adequate margins—an inch and a half at the top and on the left, and an inch at the bottom and on the right is the general rule. Remember that the right-hand margin is the margin of error, especially on typed papers. You need room for an occasional word to go over without running clear off the page or requiring a hyphen where the rules don't permit it.

(2) Leave space between your lines. On a typewriter, double-space. In longhand, use wide-lined paper. If you have only narrow-lined paper, write on every other line.

(3) Don't write too many words on a line. Even when very compact writing is legible, it has an irritating effect. We become used to reading at a certain rate of speed. If we find we are taking twice as long as usual to read a page, we are likely to feel resentful.

(4) Don't make your writing deliberately difficult to read on the theory that it will be hard for your instructor to prove you are wrong. You may arouse his combative instinct.

(5) Use a legible writing instrument. If your instructor says that he will accept papers written in pencil, he means about a number 2 lead. Very soft pencils smudge. Very hard ones are practically unreadable by artificial light. Don't use a worn-out typewriter ribbon. It is even harder on you than on your instructor. You won't notice half your mistakes. He may get annoyed and concentrate on looking for them.

(6) Proofread carefully, and make neat corrections. Particularly with typed material, many students seem to proofread as fast as possible and hope they will find nothing wrong, on the theory that any correction will spoil the neat appearance of the page. Your instructor is interested in your *writing,* not your *typing.* Not one student in a hundred can type a paper without averaging one or two mistakes to a page, and instructors know this. When a paper comes in without a single sign of correction, your instructor does not auto-

matically congratulate you for neatness. He is much more likely to suspect you of carelessness, and to read it with the idea that he can find mistakes even if you can't. And he is not at all likely to consider that a typing error is a "mere" typing error. It is an error, the same as in longhand. And he is almost certain to feel that if it isn't worth your while
to check a paper carefully before handing it in, it certainly isn't worth
his while to spend much time on it. He may simply give it an E
without bothering to make detailed criticisms. Even if he marks all
the mechanical errors—most of which you could have found yourself
if you had really looked for them instead of subconsciously trying to
miss them—he may not bother to make the kind of suggestions that
would be helpful to you in writing your next paper.

Exercises—Chapter 10

Divide the entries below as you think they might comprise the parts of
a paper entitled "Frontier Stereotypes." Indicate your groupings by number, and arrange the numbers within the groups to indicate order of
presentation. Next to the entries you consider most appropriate for opening, closing, and so forth, write a sentence justifying your choice for that
position. (Of course there may be some entries that you just can't make
fit.)

1. Vigilantes.
2. Water rights.
3. Meanwhile, back at the ranch.
4. One calf grows into the world's largest herd.
5. Girl kisses horse.
6. One man against the town.
7. The lost mine.
8. Six-shooters that fire indefinitely.
9. Nine times around the same rock.
10. The bad guy sneers.
11. Rustlers.
12. Head them off at the pass.
13. Hero kisses girl when there is no alternative.
14. The honest bartender.
15. The hidden loot.
16. Hero marries rancher's daughter.
17. Bad guys return to rescue jailed cohort.

18. No saddle-tramp is going to marry my daughter.
19. The ghost town.
20. Lost in the desert.
21. The sophisticated gambler.
22. Hero kisses horse.
23. Homesteaders (squatters) (sodbusters).
24. Sheepmen.
25. Take the shortcut.
26. Hero rides off into the sunset.
27. The gold strike.
28. Bad guy fires first shot point-blank—misses.
29. Good guy never sneers.
30. You'll just have to trust me.
31. Good guy fires second shot from galloping horse—never misses.
32. Don't shoot, or you'll hit the old man (the kid) (the girl).
33. The stagecoach (payroll) robbery.
34. Where is your bill-of-sale for these cattle?
35. Villainous father (mother) and four equally villainous sons.
36. The reluctant avenger.
37. The mysterious drifter.
38. Circling vultures.
39. You'll never get away with this.
40. My boys'll tear this town apart, piece by piece.

Suggestions for Discussion or Theme Writing—Chapter 10

1. Choose either "Burnt Match," or "Football Game," (p. 117) and expand, rearrange, and organize the list as the author has done with "My Roommate." Then expand *one* of your final groupings into a unified paragraph.

2. Briefly summarize the steps of the theme-writing process as it is discussed in the chapter.

3. List twenty points that might be included in a paper on some topic of your choosing. Divide the list into three or four reasonable groups, adding or deleting to fit the general divisions as they take shape. Rearrange the points within the groups according to their most effective order of presentation, and expand one or more of the groups into complete paragraph form.

PEOPLE,
LANGUAGE,
AND THINGS

II

Many people have said that language is the most important of all human activities. Some of them have added that learning to talk is the most remarkable intellectual achievement that most people ever manage. We could devote a number of pages to discussing each of these statements, but maybe you'd just as soon save the time. We will therefore settle for the simple statement that language is both very important and extremely complicated. We can then examine at our leisure a rather less obvious statement: Although almost everybody learns to use language after a fashion, most people don't do it very well, at least partly because they take it so much for granted that they never give any real thought to how it works.

To put the matter as simply as possible, people use language to talk about things—if we use "things" as broadly as possible, to include relations, actions, and other people as well as objects. Language is therefore a *way of connecting* people and things. But it can connect them effectively only if it fits reasonably well at both ends. And since the general structure of our language was worked out thousands of years before our present ideas of the human nervous system and the structure of matter were developed, we can hardly expect that a good fit will be automatic.

Suppose you were a medieval sailor who came across a lemon for the first time, and later you wanted to describe it to a friend. You could tell him how big it was, and what shape, and what color. You could describe the skin and the segments and the seeds. You might even give him some idea of how it tasted by comparing it to other fruits you both already knew. But you could not tell him about its cell structure or its vitamin content, because you would have no way of perceiving these things, or even guessing about them. Naturally there would be no word for vitamin in your language, and the word for cell could not yet be applied to a tiny unit of living matter of a kind which nobody had yet seen through a microscope, or even imagined. Our language is always *limited by what we know*. And at their best our statements describe not things as they are but things *as we perceive them*.

When Iron Was Solid and the Earth Was Flat

When our remote ancestors developed the language from which ours is descended, they were necessarily trying to describe the world *as they knew it;* and they could examine it only with their unaided senses. Their reasoning may have been every bit as good as ours is today, but their data were inadequate. Consider a man of the iron age, looking at a bar of the iron for which we have named his period. When he called it solid he meant solid, because as far as he could tell it was a simple, continuous, uniform substance. It was *solid* as a child means the word—and as most of us do, too, when we are not really thinking about it.

Some of the Greeks later figured out that it couldn't really be that solid, because if it were it would be totally indestructible. Democritus said that it must be composed of tiny, invisible particles, which might be rubbed off by enough force, or between which a cold chisel might be forced. But he thought of the particles as *tightly packed, uniform,* and *at rest*. What made the bar iron rather than lead was simply that it was composed of iron particles rather than lead particles. Iron was one substance and lead was another. He had no reason to suppose that the bar would change in the slightest degree, if it was protected from rust and other outside damage. And he had no reason to suppose that it was not exactly the same as another bar.

Compare this with our current knowledge of iron. *Our* bar is composed of moving molecules, which are an arrangement of moving atoms, which are an arrangement of moving protons and electrons and we don't know how many other kinds of wave-particles, all moving at various speeds, some of them practically as fast as light. In this whole rush of activity not a single thing stays still for an instant. In other words, the iron is changing all the time, and as it changes it acts in different ways. If the molecules are made to move faster, the iron will burn you at a touch. If they are rearranged magnetically, the bar will attract other pieces of iron. If they are re-arranged in another way the bar will crystallize, and may break un-expectedly. But whether or not the changes in the iron affect it in a way we can notice, they are taking place all the time and at enormous speed. We may still call a piece of iron solid, but we now know—or ought to know—that this means only that it *acts* in certain ways because the particles of which it is composed are comparatively dense, and their movements are confined to certain patterns in a restricted space. The iron *is happening.* If you think this is too academic to be important, try shielding yourself from radiation be-hind a "solid" sheet of iron. Make your will first.

Because we know more about the structure and activity of metals than our ancestors did, we can make even simple objects such as hammers and knives of a much better quality than they could man-age, to say nothing of electronic gadgets and nuclear reactors. And because we have learned something about the way the earth rotates while it revolves around the sun, while the whole solar system is doing something or other in the Milky Way, which in turn—but perhaps we had better stop here. Anyhow, what we have learned about the complicated movements of the earth in relation to other bodies is being used every day in navigation, farming, and many other fields, not to mention long-range missiles and satellites.

Now let's turn for a moment from things to people. Our ancestors thought of thinking as a *non-physical* process that operated by its own mysterious laws in a vacuum called the mind. Or if the mind was not precisely a vacuum, at least it was a perfectly uniform substance of which each of us somehow had a little part, and which did not affect what passed through it. The speed of thought was supposed to be infinite, and the "laws of thought" were supposed to be absolute and unvarying. If we learned these laws we had only to consider the universe and *think,* and the truth about it would come to us. This theory ran into a few snags, but it was pretty generally believed for centuries, and it has by no means died out today, even among people who ought to know better.

In a world where people and things are as simple as this it is easy to believe in "perfect communication." I see something happen. I frame in my mind a pattern of symbols that exactly and completely reflect this happening, and pass them on to you. Since your mind is essentially exactly like mine, you receive the symbols with no distortion and understand them exactly as I do. If you don't, you must be either stupid or wicked; and since I am a teacher I may ridicule you or pray for you or beat you, all the while exhorting you to think, *think,* THINK. And if you never do get the pattern quite straight it is all your fault, because I know more and better established alibis than you do.

The modern theory of thinking is a little different from this. There is a good deal that we don't yet understand about the process, but we have some pretty reliable evidence about parts of it. For one thing, it takes place not in a mysterious, standardized "mind," but in individual and physical brains, no two of which are alike. Each one of these brains seems to operate rather like an electronic computing machine, though in a far more complicated fashion. It contains millions of short nerve-lengths, comparable to wires, and millions of nerve-connections, comparable to switches. But the cell structure is such that electrical impulses pass through the circuits at not more than about 400 feet per second; and it is the passage of these impulses that constitutes our thinking. Far from being instantaneous, thought is less than half the speed of sound, and very slow indeed compared with the speed of an electric current passing over ordinary wires (186,000 *miles* per second). That is why electronic brains can solve in a few hours problems that would keep mathematicians busy for many years.

Even the simplest thought requires a current to pass over a complicated circuit containing innumerable switches. When an impulse starts, it might follow any one of an enormous number of routes, depending on how the switches click. But once a route has been selected, there is some tendency for the switches to set, so that a second impulse starting from the same point as the first can more easily follow the same route than pick out a new one of its own. It is by this setting of the switches that memory and habits develop. Sometimes it takes many repetitions to make the switches set.

A switch may be set so firmly that a possible connection is blocked out temporarily, or even permanently. For instance, most of us have had the experience of doing a complicated problem of arithmetic, in the midst of which we have made a very obvious mistake, such as multiplying two by two and getting two as the result. We have then checked it over several times without finding the error—two times two still seems to give us two. One of our switches has temporarily been jammed in the wrong position. Fortunately, not every passage of a nerve impulse jams a switch; most merely make it easier for the switch to turn one way than another.

There are always a number of impulses passing through different circuits, and these affect each other. The way we think at a given time is therefore guided largely by our earlier experiences—not only the things we have encountered, but the particular paths that our nerve impulses have followed as a result of encountering them. NO TWO OF US STARTED OUT WITH EXACTLY THE SAME WIRING SYSTEM, AND THE ORIGINAL DIFFERENCES HAVE BEEN INCREASED BY LATER ACTIVITY.

Now let's consider how language can be used to connect people as we know them now with things as we know them now. A word can no longer stand directly for a thing, because the thing won't stand still for it to stand for. A while ago we mentioned the "laws of thought" which for centuries were regarded as beyond question. The first of these is that "Everything is identical with itself," which may be expressed symbolically as "A = A." This may seem so obvious that it is hardly worth saying—but think again. Our piece of solid iron is really an enormous number of particles moving so fast that it is *not* identical with itself long enough to talk about it, and neither is anything else. The first law of thought is a very useful convention when we are dealing with mathematics, or any problem about abstractions, but it is simply not true about anything in the physical universe.

It will be easier to accept this if we recognize at once that the word *identical* (along with its common equivalent *same*) is used to express two quite different ideas which we often fail to keep separate. If you take a bite out of an apple, then leave the apple on your desk for a week and take another bite, it is useless to argue about whether it is the same apple. In the sense of continuity it is the same apple; in the same sense of identity of structure it is *not,* as your nose and tongue will tell you at once.

Our language-makers saw no reason for making such a distinction, because they thought in terms of "substances" rather than of structure. Since *their* bar of iron was uniform and inert, *continuity implied identity of structure*, and the word *same* covered both things at once. If the bar got to be somehow different—for instance if it got hot and burned their hands—they would explain that the substance was still the same, but that an *accident* called heat had been added. Of course they knew that many things quite obviously change—for instance, apples mature and decay. But since they did not know *what happened* to bring about these changes, they could not discuss them very accurately. They thought of the world as basically static, with only bits of movement here and there, and they devised their language to describe that kind of a world. We *know* that the world has nothing static in it, but we don't usually *think* of it in this way, because we think largely in their language.

The Bang That Changed Our Thinking

Most of us are not very happy about the atomic bomb, but it has had one good effect—it has made millions of people accept, and accept as important, the discoveries of modern physics about the nature of the physical universe. As long as only a few specialists played with cyclotrons in laboratories, J. Q. Public could ignore their theories, and he had some excuse for retaining the old "common-sense" attitude of "I believe what I see." The bomb convinced him instantaneously of what he might not otherwise have learned to appreciate for generations—that the nature of the world in which we live is very different from what it seems to be, and that this difference is not merely a matter of academic theory, but a matter of actual life and death.

Most literate people, since Hiroshima, have learned to accept the statement that all matter is composed of particles in constant and enormously fast motion. Einstein's relativity, which used to be something between a mystery and a joke, has now been shown to be both true and important. But most of these same people have not really modified their habits of thinking and talking to conform with these important facts. They are rather like many of the contemporaries of Columbus—once he had discovered America, they "believed" that the earth was round (which a number of people had known for thousands of years), but they certainly didn't *realize* it. They still thought of the sun as rising and setting, rather than of the earth as spinning, and they had an uneasy feeling that if they went to the other side—which of course was the "bottom"—they would be in imminent danger of falling off. Many of them were very much upset by the idea. When a feeling of solid certainty was taken from them, life seemed much more dangerous.

Actually, it was all the safer. The better we understand the forces at work on earth, the better we can prepare for them. There is no record that anybody has fallen off the earth because it has been discovered to be a whirling ball; but there is plenty of evidence that knowledge of its shape and motion has made for more safety and efficiency in navigation, farming, and a large number of other activities.

The idea that not only all knowledge, but all motion and position, are "merely" relative seems to upset many people in much the same way that their ancestors were upset by Columbus's discovery. They feel that they are asked to give up all their old certainties, with nothing equally stable to take their place. It takes a while for them to realize that their old certainties were merely delusions, and that the new theories not only take nothing away but actually supply useful corrective information.

Our ancestors thought in terms of "substance" rather than of molecular and atomic structure and activity, and the language they invented is full of expressions like "identical objects," "the same thing," and "these are exactly alike." They not only used these phrases, they believed in them, and got into trouble accordingly. We may still use them for convenience, but we should know that we are talking loosely when we do. It is accurate to say that two triangles are exactly alike, because triangles are *pure abstractions,* with nothing physical about them to cause a variation. But if we say that two ball bearings are exactly alike we can mean only that they are so nearly alike that we can *probably* afford to neglect their differences.

Some readers may think it is splitting hairs to insist upon making a distinction between indistinguishable or negligible differences and no differences at all. They are likely to say that for all practical purposes the two things are exactly alike. But the fact is that we can never be sure in advance what all practical purposes will be. If a ball bearing cracks, the difference between it and one that would not crack is obviously important. Possibly we could have avoided the poor choice by a more careful examination. Perhaps we had to take the chance; but it is at least well to know when we are taking such chances, and to bring a few spares along.

There are times when it is useful to *pretend* that things remain identical with themselves (so that they will hold still while we talk about them) and even that they are identical with each other. If you have a problem that begins "Farmer Schwartz has ten cows, each of which gives eleven quarts of milk a day," and so on down to "How much does he get for the butter?" you have to assume a number of identities or you'll never get the answer. It often pays to neglect minor differences in order to simplify a calculation. But it usually does not pay to believe that the differences are not there because you have neglected them. If Farmer Schwartz, for instance, did not recognize that differences in care, feed, and sanitation affected both the quantity and quality of his milk, he would probably not remain in the dairy business very long.

One result of our ancestors' inadequate knowledge of the structure of the physical universe was that it gave them no reason to suspect that *physical things* and *mathematical conceptions* cannot be treated exactly alike.

Compare the two following:

1. A equals B.
   C equals B.

Therefore

A equals C.

In mathematics or logic the conclusion is indisputably true.

2. A is an apple.
   C is an apple.

Therefore

A equals C.

The form of these statements is very much like that of those above, but we are now dealing with physical things—and the truth of the conclusion is not quite so convincing. If we were dealing only with imaginary apples in a school problem, where the only thing definitely said about apples is that "an apple is worth five cents" or "an apple weighs six ounces," the statement that A equals C is just as solid in the second problem as in the first. But if we are dealing with actual physical apples, we know that no two of them are in all respects exactly alike.

But although we actually know this, our language leads us to forget it, and we continually say such things as "an apple is an apple," "all Germans are alike," and "Fords are better than Chevrolets" without paying any real attention to the differences between individual apples, Germans, Fords, and Chevrolets, and with the subconscious assumption that two things wouldn't both *be* apples or Fords unless they were "essentially" alike.

A good many of the words our ancestors invented describe things and conditions that do not exist. Unless we use these words with great care we are likely to make the mistake of thinking that the things they seem to point to are really there. I can still remember the time my baby sister got an "unbreakable" doll for Christmas. She happily tossed it out of a sixth-floor window, and wept bitterly when it smashed on the concrete below. It was her first lesson in the actual relativity of words that sound absolute.

Few of us would make that particular mistake after we had cut our second teeth, but we—or at least some grown-up people that we know—make others that are directly comparable, and perhaps more serious in their consequences. You hear them saying with perfect seriousness that coffee is better than tea. If they mean by this merely that they usually like coffee better than tea, we can hardly argue. But some of them will drink without protest anything called coffee, no matter how weak or strong or stale, and scorn anything called tea in contrast. They often view tea drinkers with dark suspicion. Or they will argue for hours about whether "the dog" really is or isn't "Man's best friend." With one part of their brain they know perfectly well that no two dogs are alike; but with the other—the part conditioned by their inherited language—they feel that any animal that can justly be called a dog must be essentially composed of a sort of doggy substance, so that he is somehow like the others.

Our ancestors did not think they knew all about everything; but they did think: (1) that they knew all about some things; (2) that they could express this *all* exactly in language; (3) that by using language they could transfer information complete and unchanged from one mind to another.

On the other hand we can now see: (1) that nobody knows all about even the simplest thing; (2) that we can indicate what we do know only *approximately* in language; (3) that since no two brains work exactly alike, we can never get a bit of information complete and unchanged from one brain to another. It is true that the change may be so small that it does not matter *in a given situation,* but there is always a little loss and change, and it is important to bear this in mind. For one thing, it will save you a shock when a situation comes up where the change does make a difference. For another, it will keep you from beating your brains out attempting the impossible. An engineer who realizes that there is always a little loss from friction will not waste his life and talents attempting to construct a perpetual motion machine.

In later chapters we will see in detail how some of our traditional ideas about language get us into trouble. The object of this chapter is simply to help us to realize that the language habits developed to describe *the world as our ancestors knew it* have to be adjusted considerably to describe *the world as we know it.*

Exercises—Chapter 11

I. Answer the following questions briefly and simply:

1. What was the "bang" that changed our thinking? Explain briefly.
2. What implications about the nature of thoughts (at least two) follow our acceptance of thinking as a *physical* activity?
3. Words do not describe things as they are, but things in what other light?
4. How can a bar of iron be said to be happening? Explain briefly.
5. If given unlimited thought on a problem, will not all rational minds inevitably reach the same conclusion?
6. If two men saw the same thing but gave two different accounts of it, would one of them have to be lying?
7. What is to be gained by distinguishing between
   (a) indistinguishable or negligible differences and
   (b) no differences at all?
8. How well oriented to the relationship between words, himself and the physical universe is the man who says "I believe only what I see?"
9. Suggest a word you might find in a manufacturer's guarantee which may sound absolute, but have only relative significance.
10. Which generally lasts longer, a *temporary* filling in your tooth, or a *permanent* wave in your hair?

II. Mark each of the following sentences *N* (new) or *O* (old), depending on whether you think it reflects a recent or a more ancient idea about people, language or things:

1. I know exactly what you mean.
2. Anybody who really tries can learn to do this in half an hour.
3. Words in themselves have no meaning at all.
4. A poet should not stop revising until he has found the exact words that convey the thoughts in his head.
5. *Nice* is often misused in the sense of *agreeable;* it really means *precise.*
6. I will tell you once and for all what that line of the poem means.
7. I wouldn't have another Ford; my last one fell apart after ten thousand miles.
8. With these new shock absorbers on your car, you're perfectly safe.
9. A glass of good, pure milk never hurt anybody.
10. The dog is man's best friend.
11. Whatever your senses tell you about an object is likely wrong.
12. Of course I can wear the dress; Mabel says it's a perfect fit on her, and we're the exact same size.
13. Beyond our solar system are the fixed stars.
14. The relative solidity of air raises re-entry problems for space-craft designers.
15. Structural defects deep within a steel casting may be detected by X-ray.

Suggestions for Discussion or Theme Writing—Chapter 11

1. Discuss the idea that ". . . the nature of the world in which we live is very different from what it *seems* to be . . ." and propose a half-dozen illustrations of the idea from your own experience. (For instance, the space inside an "empty" room generally *seems* to be a vacuum, but the fact that we can breathe and remain conscious in such a room suggests that it contains oxygen, at least.)

2. Discuss (a) identity of structure, and (b) continuity of process as they would influence whatever observations you wished to make about your car or your cat.

WORDS
AND MEANINGS

12

What Does a Word Stand For?

Most of us think we know what "meaning" means. We may say, for instance, that the word "stool" *means* a chair with no back. If anybody asks us what we mean by "means," we probably say that the word stands for the piece of furniture. In a way this is true, but it needs more examination. Just how is the word connected with the thing?

What happens when you look at a stool? Light waves reflected from it strike your eyes and stimulate a flow of electrical currents over nerve-paths leading to your brain. It is in the brain, not in the eye itself, that the effective seeing takes place. If your optical nerve is cut, your eye becomes completely useless. And what you see in your brain is a *partial and not particularly accurate image of the stool*. The people who developed our language did not know this. They "believed what they saw," and they had good reason to, because the human eye was the keenest instrument of perception available. Anything that it could not see could only be guessed at, not measured. But you know that at best your eyes have missed the cell structure, not to mention the spacing and motion of the particles of which the cells are composed. How much else they have missed depends partly on the accuracy of your vision and partly on the *influence of your previous experiences*.

Suppose, for example, that a carpenter and a typist, both with 20-20 vision, look at a stool in a lunchroom. The carpenter may notice the grain of the wood and the way the rungs are joined to the legs—details of which the typist is completely unconscious. But she

may notice a roughness that would be likely to snag her stockings—
a different detail that the carpenter might not see at all. There is no
use saying that they both *saw* it all but only *noticed* parts. We have a
phrase for that: certain details "failed to register." We can talk and
act only about what does register, accurately or inaccurately. If you
don't think this is important, consider the hunters who have shot
cows and even wives after clearly "seeing" bucks complete with
spreading antlers.

Even the bare act of seeing is not as simple as the passing of a
current through an electric circuit. *Secondary* nerve circuits are
brought into the action, and these inevitably affect the mental picture
that is formed. *Which* secondary circuits are brought in depends on
previous experience—that is why the carpenter and the typist see
different stools. When you speak of the stool you may think, and
even insist, that you mean "the whole stool," but you cannot mean
more than you are conscious of meaning (though what you say may
mean more to somebody else than it does to you). If you sit on the
stool without noticing that the paint is wet, you are not likely to
admit that the stickiness of the surface was included in your meaning.
The "object" that you see and talk about is a *unique abstraction,*
created by a reaction between your nervous system and the physical
process.

You may find it hard to grasp the idea in the last sentence, because
you have almost certainly been trained to believe that objects have a
reality of their own, independent of observers. But the reality of
objects is a theory that will not hold in the light of modern science.
What exists is a *process*—an arrangement of dancing particles. The
object that the carpenter sees and feels and calls a stool is derived
from this process by the impressions made on his senses and modified by his previous experiences. The object that the typist sees is at
least slightly different because her senses and her previous experiences are different. Naturally there are similarities as well as differences in our nervous systems; and if our backgrounds are also similar,
we may derive objects that are very much alike. But no two of us
ever see quite the same things.

The stool you talk about, then, is an abstraction—that is, a selection of some of the characteristics of the underlying process. When
you speak the word "stool" you almost certainly use it to refer to even

less than you have seen. You may, for instance, have noticed a knot in the grain of the seat, a small crack in one leg, a smear of grease on another. But when you say "hand me that stool," you have no idea of calling your companion's attention to any of these details. In fact you may already have dismissed them from your own mind. You use the word merely to indicate those characteristics which you assume that he has also noticed and is likely to connect with the word. The word "stool" is therefore a second-level abstraction from the object already abstracted by your senses.

If you use the word to refer to a number of different objects, as in "I don't like to sit on a *stool*," you are using a third level of abstraction; and if you use other words like "seats" or "furniture" or "property," you go higher still—you include more and more different objects with less and less in common. Every time you go up a level you leave out more of the characteristics of the individual object. As a result, the higher you go, the less chance you have of getting your hearer to duplicate the impression in your own mind. If you say "Hand me that stool," you will probably be adequately understood. If you say "Get me a stool," he may bring one half or twice as high as you wanted. And if you give him some money and ask him to buy some "attractive furniture," it may mean the end of a friendship.

You may be used to thinking of words as divided into two classes, abstract and concrete; but the evidence shows that all words are abstract on one level or another. Moreover, the difference in levels is not a permanent characteristic of the words, but varies with the way they are used. Thus *wealth* is likely to represent a higher level of abstraction than *dollar*. But if I reach in my pocket, pull out a few coins, and say "Here is my entire *wealth* at the moment," I am using *wealth* on the lowest possible verbal level. On the other hand, if I say "He is always anxious to pick up an honest *dollar*," I am using *dollar* on a fairly high level. Nevertheless, since *dollar* is usually a low-level word, it will probably make a more direct and forceful impression on your hearer in most circumstances than *wealth* would.

Thinking of *levels of abstraction* may seem much more complicated than the simple division into abstract and concrete words. But it is a great deal more accurate; and once you get used to it, you will find that it straightens out a good many difficulties.

Three Kinds of Meaning

As we have just seen, when a man speaks, he uses words as symbols to indicate something that is going on *in his own mind*. His words are directly connected not with the processes in the outer world, but with his own abstractions from those processes. It is this private mental activity that the words mean to *him,* and we may call it *meaning 1*.

When another man listens, the words stimulate some activity in *his* mind. We may call this activity *meaning 2*. If it is very similar to that of the speaker, we say he understands—in other words, *meaning 1* and *meaning 2* are so similar that no noticeable difference appears; but the two meanings can never be absolutely identical.

When there is an obvious difference between the two meanings it is rather silly to argue about which is the "right" one, but it may be useful to consider which is closer to our *general habits of association,* which we may call *meaning 3*. For instance, if you ask a child for a chisel and he hands you a screwdriver, you may explain the difference between the two kinds of tools, and tell him which label is usually applied to each. He will probably accept your explanation; and since you now use these labels in very similar ways, you may avoid future misunderstandings. You have not, however, established the "real" meaning of the word, because *words in themselves have no meanings at all*. It takes a mind to develop a meaning by associating a symbol with something else, and no two minds work in quite the same way.

If you ask for a stool you can expect other people to know *roughly* what you mean. They are not likely to associate the word with a bed or a cat or a chisel. Our habits are enough alike so that a given word *limits* the possible associations within a certain range. But we must be prepared for borderline cases; a low-backed seat, for example, might be called either a chair or a stool. And we must realize that even when there is a complete *verbal* agreement there is still a little misunderstanding, because no two of us see exactly the same stool.

It is also important to realize that *meaning 3* or the "dictionary meaning" is merely a generalization derived from the *meanings 1* and *meanings 2* that occur in everyday communication. If you find a puzzling word in a sentence and look it up, a dictionary can tell you something about *how other people have used this word in the past.*

This information may give you a definite impression (*meaning 2*) about what the writer means by the word in this sentence (*meaning 1*). You may therefore learn something from the writer that you might otherwise have missed. But you cannot find the true and permanent meaning of the word, because there is no such thing.

Public and Private Meanings

The idea that we can all learn to speak exactly alike and use all words with only their universally agreed "correct" meanings is therefore a delusion that we might as well abandon. But we can profitably try to learn: (1) to speak more nearly alike; (2) to become conscious of the probable differences in our meanings.

If you say that a stone weighs ten pounds, a friend may argue with you or want to bet with you. Such an argument or bet may be settled by weighing the stone. When you read the scales you will probably agree about what the stone weighs. On the other hand, if you argue about which of two girls is prettier, there is no way to settle the question satisfactorily.

There is nothing mysterious about this. Some matters affect all of us so frequently that we have had to develop standards of measurement that are as impersonal as possible. We recognize that no scale and no measuring stick is absolutely perfect, and that it is possible to measure inaccurately either by cheating or by carelessness. However, both our commonest measuring devices and our methods of using them are so nearly uniform that most of us will ordinarily accept their readings without protest. Moreover, we are generally conscious of these standards. Consequently, when we say that a stone weighs ten pounds, or that a man is six feet tall, the information conveyed to all our hearers will be remarkably similar. Such statements as these may be said to have public meanings. Anybody knows how to test them; and anybody who does test them will get very similar results. *All statements that have public meanings involve some kind of measurement by generally accepted standards.* The standards need not be universally known, but they must be agreed upon by an appropriate group. Thus the statement that "Roberts suffered second-degree burns" has a public meaning. Anybody with much medical training will know that Roberts had blisters resulting from heat. And anybody who does *not* understand the statement will probably accept the explanation of those who do.

At the other extreme there are meanings which are purely private, because there are no acceptable ways of measuring them. You don't know how cauliflower tastes to your brother, and you won't get very far by explaining that it is "really delicious" if he finds it nauseating.

In between these extremes lies the area of most of our difficulties. You cannot prove that one girl is prettier than another as easily or as definitely as you can prove that she is taller; but there is likely to be a good deal of similarity in the opinions of a given group of people who have lived in the same atmosphere and have interchanged ideas. If we don't exaggerate the permanence or the "universality" of our local and temporary standards of measurement, they can be very useful for communication. Find an illustrated magazine of forty years ago and admire the glamorous beauties—those streamlined girls with the fascinating helmet-liner hats, their waistlines artfully arranged below their hips. It may be hard to believe it now, but they were beautiful once (I was there); and they may be beautiful again.

Some people cannot believe that their relative standards are less than absolute. Others feel that if they are not absolute they are no standards at all. But we must use what we have. We can now measure rather accurately many things at which our fathers could only guess; and as time goes on we may learn to do even better.

If we consider the question of meaning in this light, we arrive at the conclusion that *a meaningful statement should suggest a measurement,* considering "measurement" in its widest sense. If somebody says "It's cold outside," you may want to know what the thermometer reads, or you may simply ask "Should I wear my heavy coat?" The thermometer reading is a more public type of measurement, but you may not be skilled in interpreting it. Besides, it covers only the factor of temperature, and leaves out wind and humidity. You may find a less precise measurement more useful—for example, an estimate of how thick your clothing should be to keep you comfortable.

There is a widespread belief that some things are subject to measurement and others are not. It seems more accurate to say that some things are more *accessible* to measurement than others. We have been able to measure height and weight for a long time. Only recently have we begun to find ways of measuring the strength of brainwaves and the secretions of the ductless glands. Some of the measurements we should like to make are so complicated and difficult that we may never arrive at a satisfactory method of making them, or reach general agreement about a scale. But unless we can measure a thing—by at least a rough estimate—well, we can make noises about it, but how are we to say anything that has a discoverable meaning?

Alfred Korzybski has compared our statements about things to maps of territories. A good map is drawn to scale: that is, the structure of the map corresponds to the structure of the territory. And a meaningful statement should also correspond in structure to the territory that it describes. This is a very useful comparison, because on the whole we deal with maps rather more sensibly than we do with words. We know, for instance, that a man cannot draw a map of a place he has not measured, whether accurately with surveying instruments or roughly with his eye, and whether directly or by using somebody's else's map. And before we depend on a map we want to have some idea of how it came to be made and what kind of measurements were used in making it. Of course we might be deceived by an inaccurate or dishonest map, but we wouldn't believe one that showed rivers running uphill or palm trees growing out of a glacier. When it comes to verbal maps, however, some of us are ready to believe almost anything, because we have never thought of applying the structural test.

For instance, a politician promises to act "in the best interests of all the people," and thereby attracts a number of votes. This sounds like a fine way to act; and it would be, too, if water could run uphill. Unfortunately, some people would gain by having the income tax raised so the sales tax could be eliminated; others would be better off with the sales tax raised and the income tax reduced. If we want to know what the candidate actually plans to do about this issue, we'd better try to get him to talk in map language, so we can examine the structure of the events for which his words stand. He may be unwilling to do this, because as soon as he indicates what things and activities his words refer to he will probably lose some votes; but until he does, his words have no measurable meaning.

Sometimes the relation of a good verbal map to the territory it represents is direct and obvious—for instance, "John is six foot two and weighs over two hundred pounds." Sometimes it is less direct, but still possible to follow with confidence if you know something about the territory. "Murphy sparks the Panthers" might not convey much to some people, but almost any follower of baseball would read it as meaning not only that Murphy fields well and gets his hits when they count most, but that his teammates play better when he is in there. This is a very slight sketch of a complicated situation, but it is map language because the words stand for things that happen.

But when language is related *only to other language,* it has no value as a map of events, no matter how impressive it sounds. A faculty does not get anywhere by defining "liberal education" as "the kind of education that develops a broad cultural background." Neither phrase has any map value until the speaker decides what activities it represents. You can't just study "culture." You have to make up your mind whether to learn French verbs or differential equations or appropriate remarks to make after listening to Beethoven's quartets. It is sometimes convenient to have ambiguous map language, so that we may "agree in principle" and then make whatever interpretations we please. But when we want to convey or receive information, we'd better examine the relation between the words and the events they represent.

Writing to Somebody

We must remember, however, that this relation between words and events is not something that can be transferred whole from one mind to another. It can only be suggested, though sometimes (when all the measurements involved are public) very directly. At other times it has to be done indirectly or even with considerable distortion of details in order to make the main points clear to somebody with a very different background of experience. A young chauffeur once summed up a Conference on Communication so compactly that he left the experts who had been holding it wondering if they hadn't been wasting their time. "As I see it," he remarked, "what all this adds up to is: if you want to get a message across to somebody, you'd better tune in on his wavelength, and not just broadcast."

A great many people never do anything but broadcast. This is partly because they are too self-centered to think about adjusting to the other fellow's wavelength; but perhaps it is also partly because they have never been taught about wavelengths. In most of our schools no mention is made of *meaning 1* and *meaning 2* (see pages 141-142 above). Students are taught to find the "true meaning" of words, to use them "correctly and accurately," and to "say exactly what they mean." There is a clear assumption that if they do these things, everybody will understand them—or at least that everybody ought to.

Of course they are taught some other things too, such as "using language appropriate to the occasion" and even "establishing rapport with the audience." But the two sets of theories are in conflict, and they usually hear much more about the first set. They should not be blamed too much if, especially in writing, they tend to work on what they assume is a universal broadcast band.

A radio message conveys nothing unless both sender and receiver are tuned in, and it is useless to argue about which has the "primary responsibility" for the tuning. It may seem unfair to ask you to tune in to the writer when you read, and then tune in to the reader when you write—the other fellows ought to do some of the work. But if you think a little more about it you will probably decide that the writers that give you the most satisfaction are the ones that have managed to find your wavelength. It is not entirely one-sided. Besides, even from a purely selfish standpoint there are more important things than dividing the work into exactly even parts. If you want to learn something from a book that is already written, you have to make the adjustment or you will miss the message. And if you think it is at all important for your own writing to be understood and appreciated, you'd better tune your transmitter too. It may be extra work, but you will learn a lot more and exert a good deal more influence than your lazy neighbor.

It takes some imagination to adjust a paper to an audience. You must figure out not only what words they are likely to know, but what experiences they have probably had. You can't expect your estimates to be perfect, especially if you are writing for a number of different people, but you should make them carefully. You begin by thinking of what you and your audience have in common. When you go beyond this area, try to make your explanations in terms of these common holdings.

This may seem perfectly obvious, but a great many writers, not all of them freshmen, either never think of it or deliberately disregard it. The haughty ones take the attitude that people who don't know what *they* know are not worth considering. The overhumble ones assume that anything they know must be known to everybody else.

In between are the people who are not really attempting to communicate—they are just running off at the mouth.

It is very helpful to pick a specific audience for every paper you write. This audience may be either real or imaginary, and it may be either a single person or a fairly uniform group. But don't try to write to everybody at once. It can't be done, and any attempt to do it is likely to be either very dull or ridiculously inconsistent. Jimmy Brown writes an explanation of baseball. In the first paragraph he explains carefully that there are nine men on a team. But in the third paragraph he uses such terms as "squeeze play" and "drag bunt" with no explanation at all. It is rather hard to imagine anybody who would need the information in the first paragraph and at the same time understand the terms in the third.

Of course you may say that your real audience is your instructor, who is the only reason you are writing the paper. It is perfectly legitimate to aim your paper at him if you take the trouble actually to aim it—to figure out what he probably knows about the subject and how his mind works—and to hold steady throughout the paper. But don't expect to make a hit by displaying your ignorance on his favorite subject. And don't treat him like a specialist in Animal Husbandry in one paragraph and an idiot boy in the next. In any case, he is not likely to insist that you aim directly at him. He won't even insist that you tell him exactly who you are aiming at. But he will probably notice it if you are trying to aim in all directions at once.

Perhaps the easiest way to aim a paper is to imagine that you are writing it for a particular friend. You have some idea of what he already knows, not only about your subject, but about other subjects that you can relate it to. You therefore have a basis for deciding what you can reasonably leave out, as well as what you should put in. If you want other people to read it too, you can make a few explanations that he might not need; but keep him in mind as a guide to the general direction.

Exercises—Chapter 12

I. Mark the following sentences *Public* if you think they involve some kind of measurement by generally accepted standards, *Private* if you think they do not. Those you can't make up your mind about, mark *Controversial,* and add a sentence to justify your indecision:

1. I would like my steak medium rare.
2. Give me a pair of men's 32-32 jeans in 11-oz. denim.
3. Not only was my steak tough, but I had to slice the gravy.
4. You'll be pleased with the blind date I lined up for you; she's the prettiest girl you ever saw.
5. He's a stocky black gelding who stands about sixteen hands.
6. Shakespeare's writings have a deep spiritual and emotional quality.
7. This may hurt a little.
8. Iambic meter produces a solemn tone in any poem where it is employed.
9. He is one of the most interesting men I have ever met.
10. June temperatures were about four degrees above normal, but the humidity was down.
11. He's a triple-threat player, especially good on option plays.
12. Basketball is a more interesting game to watch than football.
13. Buzzard's Roost Road has some chuckholes, but my T-bird didn't hang up on any of them.
14. *Porgy and Bess* is the only true American folk opera.
15. The Grand Canyon of the Colorado is one of the wonders of the modern world.

II. The following statements are questionable as verbal maps of territories because no clear-cut *structure of events* for which the words stand is presented in them. You will prove this to yourself by presenting two widely differing sets of circumstances (structures of events) for which the statement could easily stand:

Example: He takes a deep interest in his fellow men.

(a) He went to a lot of trouble to help his neighbors get settled.

(b) He is always trying to poke his nose into others' business.

1. His remarks to the duchess were quite different from those she expected.
2. For the way you managed my campaign you will get everything that is coming to you.
3. All of her furniture was very old.
4. The natives decided to have the visiting missionaries for dinner.
5. I expect you to do a reasonable amount of outside reading.
6. All I ever did was to try to get ahead in the world.
7. I don't have a man on my payroll who will look me in the eye and say he wants to belong to a union.
8. A government should do for its citizens what they cannot do for themselves.

9. Let's all go down to the Malt Shop and live a little.

10. The national emergency will call for many domestic sacrifices.

11. We must have total victory in the impending struggle.

12. One average serving of parrot tongues, spiced, contains 99 calories.

13. My aim during my term of office will be to give the people what they want.

14. Our only object is to keep objectionable materials off the newsstands.

15. I train my boys to play clean and to play to win.

Suggestions for Discussion or Theme Writing—Chapter 12

1. Give a brief straightforward account of something (real or imaginary) that you have recently done which might arouse quite different reactions in different people. Then rewrite the account as it might be retold by:

(a) a sympathetic classmate

(b) a disapproving aunt

2. Consider that area of the United States we shall call the *Northwest*. Specifically, where is it? What is its climate? Its topography? Its products? Discuss the area in the light of the past (The Northwest Ordinance of 1784 and the Northwest Territory), the present (the Pacific Northwest?), and the possible future concept (now that Alaska is one of the United States).

BUILDING
A VOCABULARY

13

At least nine students out of ten are eager to increase their vocabularies; and at least eight of the nine apparently still believe in Santa Claus. It is painful to admit that nothing in this chapter will enable you to double your "word power" overnight, or even by the end of next month. At best it takes a number of years to develop a good vocabulary. There are certain techniques that help to speed up the process, and some of these will be discussed; but there are positively no magic tricks that will enable you to sprout new polysyllables without a long period of active effort.

The reason a large vocabulary is so important is that it is *symptomatic* of a wide knowledge and the ability to make accurate distinctions. If you are interested in fabrics and know a good deal about them, you will probably pick up the names you need to discuss them; but merely memorizing such names as *chambray, gingham,* and *sharkskin* will not make you an expert. Most good basketball players are tall; but nobody ever grew to six foot seven by playing basketball.

Nevertheless, a direct attempt at vocabulary building can be very profitable. In the first place, it will help you to *look for and recognize differences.* If you call every color between scarlet and magenta simply "red," the chances are that you pay little attention to the various shades. You take a girl on a picnic and compliment her on her beautiful "red" sweater. Three hours later she asks you to get that sweater from the car. It seems a simple errand, but when you get to the car there are three sweaters there, all different colors, but all "red" to you. Carefully saying "Eeny, meeny, miny, moe," you select one and give it to the girl. She says, "Oh, men! Here, Helen, you probably want yours too."

It won't do you much good to add *crimson, cardinal, tomato,* and whatever else the ladies have thought up recently to your vocabulary if you think of them as mere synonyms for red; but if you actually learn to associate each word with a different shade, you'll know more about colors from then on.

Another advantage of working directly on your vocabulary is that it *increases the number of stimuli* that your mind receives—and increases it in far more than direct proportion. If you read a ten-word sentence and react accurately to all ten words, you may learn something. But if you react accurately to only eight of the ten words, you don't necessarily get 80 per cent of the message; you may miss it completely. Most of us fool ourselves about this. We say, "Oh, I may have missed a few of the details, but I got the general idea." Unfortunately, the "details" that we missed may be the most significant parts. You wouldn't get much from a set of directions that ended with "Turn —— at the next corner and go —— blocks. You can't miss it." Yet there are plenty of people who would listen to a sentence like "The complete infeasibility of Governor Brown's program should be patent to all intelligent citizens," and go out to vote for Brown with renewed enthusiasm.

Learning New Words—One at a Time

The most obvious ways to learn a new word are to ask somebody what it means when we happen to come across it, or to look it up in a dictionary. Most of us use both these methods on occasion; but we often use them so inefficiently that they do us comparatively little good. We learn too little about the new word to keep a firm grasp on it, and a week (or even an hour) later it has slipped away again. The best way to keep it permanently is to try to learn not only what it means, but why it means that. Suppose you come across the word *fractious,* realize that it doesn't seem to have anything to do with arithmetic, and decide to look it up. If you turn to *Webster's New Collegiate Dictionary* you will find that it is defined as "apt to break out into a passion; cross; unruly." The easiest thing is to decide that *fractious* is simply a fancy synonym for *cross;* but if you do this you will probably forget all about your new word before you encounter it again.

On the other hand, suppose you decide to give it a minute of your time. It does look rather like *fraction,* and there may be a connection. You look a little higher on the page and find:

> fraction (frăk′shŭn), *n.* [OF., fr. L. *fractio* a breaking . . .]
> 1. *Now rare.* A breaking. 2. A piece broken off. . . .

Now you see that *fraction* comes from a word for *breaking,* which seems reasonable when you consider *fracture;* and *fractious* is "apt to *break* out." We all know people who break out into a bad temper at the slightest excuse. *Fractious* now seems like a pretty good word to describe them—and you will probably remember it for the rest of your life, because it fits in with what you already know.

It is not always necessary to analyze a word to remember it; and sometimes an attempt to analyze it will not prove helpful. But if you have come to the conclusion that it is not much good looking up words because you always forget them anyhow, you might try the above method.

Learning New Words—in Groups

Let us imagine that you know the following three words only by the definitions that appear beside them:

> *geometry*—a branch of mathematics
> *biology*—the science of plants and animals
> *autograph*—signature
> *Question:* What do *graphology, biometry,* and *autobiography* mean?
> *Answer:*   How should I know?

From the evidence given, there is no reason you should. But if, instead of being satisfied with the definitions listed above, you decide to analyze the words into their component parts, you may get a better result.

> *geo*—earth   *metry*—measurement

Geometry began as a method of surveying or "earth measurement." Both geometry and surveying have changed a good deal since that time, but the old word remains.

> *bio*—life   *logy*—science

Naturally, a life science must deal with plants and animals, but knowing that *bio* originally meant life will help you to find its significance in other connections.

auto—self   *graph*—write

A signature should be written by the man himself—otherwise there may be a sentence for forgery.

If we now take another look at *graphology, biometry,* and *autobiography,* we can make a pretty good guess about what they mean.

> *graphology*—writing science
> *biometry*—life measurement
> *autobiography*—self life writing

We might not be sure exactly how to interpret these combinations, but at least we have some definite clues to what they probably mean. If we run across them in context we may understand them without further trouble. Even if we have to look them up to find out that graphology is the science (or at least the study) of handwriting rather than of literary composition, we are more likely to remember them than we would be if their parts suggested no particular meaning.

If you take the trouble to learn as many as a hundred Greek and Latin roots, prefixes, and endings, you will be prepared to analyze *thousands* of words that you have never encountered individually—and very often you will be able to understand them just as well as if you had looked them up in the dictionary. This is a technique that can really pay big dividends.

Unfortunately, the method is not fully automatic. A great many instructors have tried using workbooks full of exercises on vocabulary building. When the first assignment is made, almost everybody is pleased and excited. This really looks like "the secret," and for a few days everybody makes rapid progress. But pretty soon only a few—the ones who do *not* believe in Santa Claus—are keeping it up. The rest have been discouraged by running into a few snags, and by discovering that even the "magic" method requires a continuous effort. They say, "Oh, it's a beautiful theory, but it only works about one time out of ten." Then they borrow somebody else's workbook, from which they can copy without thinking. After a while the instructor stops using the workbooks because he is tired of grading and regrading a student who graduated four years ago.

There *are* quite a few snags. If *com* means "with" or "together," you can understand *compose* and *compress,* but how about *command* and *commit?* The *hom's* in *homicide* and *homogeneous* have nothing to do with each other. And if *pent* means "five" in *pentagon,* how does *repent* come to mean "be sorry"? All the same, the method works a good deal more often than one time out of ten, especially if you do a little work too. Even the most automatic washing machine won't collect the clothes or separate the nylons from the denims; but it will save a good deal of time.

One exercise on building a vocabulary by analyzing the make-up of Greek and Latin words is given at the end of this chapter. If you want more, your instructor can recommend a workbook at a reasonable price. But you can continue to follow the method without using prepared exercises. Here are a few suggestions:

1. Remember that long words are built from short parts. See how many short parts you can isolate by comparing the long words you already know. In other words, find the common elements in words like *telegraph, telephone, telescope, phonetics, phonograph,* and *autograph.*

2. Remember that long words give you more clues than short words. Develop the habit of analyzing each new long word you learn, to see why its particular parts (most of which you have probably met in other words) were put together. This will make it easier not only to remember, but to pronounce and spell.

3. Don't expect your progress to be too rapid at first. It takes time and patience to get a good start; then the momentum picks up.

4. Don't waste time swearing when the method doesn't work. It carries no written guarantee. But a trawling net with quite a few holes in it will sweep up more fish than you'd have time to catch by hand.

What You Can Learn from a Dictionary

Most students have used a dictionary to look up the spelling, the pronunciation, or "the meaning" of a word—by which last they usually mean *a* definition or a synonym. To use a dictionary even in this way has some value; but it is seldom an inspiring process, and a good deal of the information picked up by such hasty dips is likely to be forgotten sooner than it need be. If you select a good dictionary and use it with some care, it will take you a little longer to look up each word;

but you won't have to go back so often, and what you learn will be more interesting, more valuable, and more likely to stick in your memory.

The first step is to discard the common superstition that "the" dictionary was dictated just after the Ten Commandments (presumably by the same author) and that it tells you exactly how you *should* *use* words. A dictionary is a record—never complete and always a little out of date—of how other people *have used* words. It presents a great deal of valuable information very concisely; and if you use the information intelligently, you can not only "avoid errors" but improve your ability to communicate. Let us consider some of the kinds of information that it is well to look for.

1. *Spelling.* Most English words have only one recognized spelling, but a rather surprising number have two or more. Some dictionaries list all of these separately; others list only the most usual one, and under it mention the others as variants. Find out which practice your dictionary follows. Such an entry as "*calory. A calorie*" indicates that *calorie* is considered the usual spelling. Notice that the division into syllables indicates where a word should be divided if it comes at the end of a line. Notice also that a dot merely indicates the division, while a hyphen indicates a compound word that should actually be hyphenated when written.

You will often find that you can remember a spelling more easily if you take the trouble to look at a related word just above or below the one that you are looking up. For instance, if you are not sure you will remember whether the second vowel in *sympathize* is *a, e,* or *o,* glance at *sympathetic.* This suggests *pathetic,* which you probably already know is spelled with an *a.*

2. *Pronunciation.* A great many words have several recognized pronunciations, not to mention the personal variations. Good modern dictionaries try to record all those that are widely used among educated people. They do not claim that the first one recorded is "preferred." It may be either the one that the editors consider most usual or the one that developed earliest.

The fact that many words are not normally pronounced in context as clearly as they would be if read from a list is recognized in all good dictionaries, but not always clearly indicated. This is perhaps just as well. Noticing the full pronunciation makes it easier to remember both the spelling and the meaning. However, over-careful pronunciation is as disagreeable as too much slurring.

The respelling of words to indicate pronunciation varies in different dictionaries. A key is usually given either on the inside of the front cover, or at the bottom of the pages throughout the book. You don't have to memorize the key, but you should find out where it is, study it carefully, and refer to it whenever necessary.

3. *Meanings.* Some students feel so virtuous about having taken the trouble to look up a word that they accept the first definition or synonym given, shrug their shoulders, and go on to the next thing. It is not their fault if the word doesn't make sense in the passage where they found it. That's what the dictionary said—and who's going to waste time going through all that fine print?

Of course you can hardly be expected to read every word in every long entry every time you turn to the dictionary. However, a few points are worth considering:

a. You can't understand a sentence by finding out "what the words mean." You have to find out what the writer means by the words.

b. A word may have several widely different meanings. It is wise to read at least far enough to find one that seems reasonable for the sentence you have in mind.

c. Meanings may be listed in either the order of frequency or the order of development. Find out which practice your dictionary follows.

d. Special technical meanings are usually signaled by italicized abbreviations, such as *Chem.* for chemistry and *Geom.* for geometry. Since these special meanings are usually listed after the more general meanings, it often saves time to begin at the bottom and look up for italics.

e. If you take the time to consider several different meanings, and try to understand their relations, you are much more likely to remember something about the word.

4. *Origin.* You may not care whether a word came from *Gk.* (Greek) or *OHG* (Old High German). However, a glance at the information given about the *etymology* often makes the word seem considerably more interesting, and therefore easier to remember. Moreover, if you form the habit of examining the etymology of every

word that interests you, you will soon begin to recognize parts of words, and will thus be able to analyze many of them without using the dictionary at all. In the long run this will prove even more useful than faithfully filling out all the exercises in a workbook.

Some of the Better Dictionaries

The three dictionaries generally recommended for students are *Webster's New Collegiate Dictionary* (G. and C. Merriam Company), *The American College Dictionary* (Harper and Brothers), and *Webster's New World Dictionary* (The World Publishing Company). The last of these seems to me quite definitely the best, but each has certain advantages and disadvantages, and each has its supporters and critics. The most satisfactory way to choose one is to look up a few dozen words in all three and see which you find most helpful. If you are not willing to go so far, your interest in building a vocabulary might be described as a wish rather than a plan. There are a few other portable dictionaries worth using; but if you don't have one of the three just mentioned, you had better ask your instructor about the one you have. Some dictionaries are almost useless. (And if you don't have *any* dictionary, it is to be hoped that you get your money's worth from your college's extracurricular activities.)

Every student who is seriously interested in the language should also become familiar with the big reference dictionaries, particularly the *Oxford English Dictionary,* the *Dictionary of American English,* and the *New International Dictionary of the English Language.* They will not be described here because you have to see them to believe them. Also, you can lead a horse to water, but it doesn't do much good to force a small sip down his throat. They are fascinating books for anybody who is interested in words.

Spelling

There are some students who can't remember how to spell a word even after they have looked it up in a dictionary. There are others who don't have much luck looking words up in a dictionary because they can't come close enough to guessing the spelling to have much chance of finding the words. Both kinds of students deserve a very limited amount of sympathy—especially from themselves. It is true that the

English spelling system is the worst in the world, but it really wasn't invented out of pure malice; and the rules are the same for everybody. Resentment and alibis make the job of learning to spell enormously more difficult. The job does not require unusual intelligence, but it does require close attention and a long and patient effort. You may not think it is worth the effort, but on the whole the country does. Some kinds of ignorance can be concealed for years, but bad spelling can show up every time you write a sentence; and it can cost jobs and promotions as well as bad marks on English papers. Few people can afford not to learn to spell at least reasonably well.

If you are a really poor speller, the first step is to find out what method of learning a new word works best for you. Some people do best by spelling a word out loud a number of times; others by writing it down repeatedly; and still others by tracing it with a pencil after it has been correctly written. Find out whether your eyes, your ears, or your muscles help you most in this particular job. As you try each method, be sure you give your full attention to what you are doing. It is a pure waste of time to use any of them while you are thinking about something else. Five minutes of *real* work on spelling is worth much more than an hour of semiconscious droning or purely mechanical copying.

The next step is the critical one. Learn three new words a day every day for the next month—just everyday words that have been giving you trouble. Anybody bright enough to be in college can do this if he wants to. Most poor spellers give it up and find a new alibi before the first week is over. At first the results are slow and don't seem worth the effort; and if you figure that at this rate it would take you the rest of your life to learn a third of the words in your dictionary, the whole prospect seems pretty gloomy. But if you really work at the problem consistently and *alertly* for a month you will find that you have made real progress, and the ninety new words you know will be the smallest part of it. For one thing, you will find that you are seeing words more clearly, and new ones are easier to learn. For another, you'll have something to build on. You'll be ready to learn a good many words in groups instead of individually. This group method is so attractive that many people want to begin with it; but it seldom works well until a good foundation has been laid by the simple but unpopular one-at-a-time method.

The third step is to make sure that you know enough about the alphabet to understand general spelling rules. If you are still confused by such terms as *consonants, digraphs, diphthongs, long vowels,* and *short vowels,* study the entries in the INDEX TO USAGE under VOWELS AND CONSONANTS and DIPHTHONG, DIGRAPH, AND LIGATURE. There is very little profit in memorizing rules that you don't understand.

Adding Endings

Two of the most frequent questions that occur in spelling are when to double a final consonant and when to drop a final *e* when adding an ending to a word. Look at the following examples:

	Long	*Short*
a	fate, fated	fat, fatten
e	recede, receding	pet, petted
i	dine, dined	din, dinned
o	robe, robed	rob, robbed
u	fume, fumed	glum, glummer

Rules:

1. A final *e* shows that the preceding vowel is "long"—that is, that it is pronounced as it is in reciting the alphabet. This *e* is dropped when an ending beginning with a vowel is added.

$$\text{fate} + \text{ed} = \text{fated} \qquad \text{dine} + \text{ing} = \text{dining}$$
$$\text{quote} + \text{able} = \text{quotable}$$

2. When a word ends in a *single* vowel followed by a single consonant, the vowel is short. If the final syllable is stressed, the consonant is doubled when any ending beginning with a vowel is added.

$$\text{bat} + \text{ing} = \text{batting} \qquad \text{acquit} + \text{ed} = \text{acquitted}$$

3. If the final syllable is *not* stressed, the final consonant is not doubled before an ending beginning with a vowel.

$$\text{benefit} + \text{ed} = \text{benefited}$$

4. When two successive vowels precede the final syllable, the syllable is long, and the consonant is not doubled when an ending beginning with a vowel is added.

$$\text{green} + \text{est} = \text{greenest} \qquad \text{gain} + \text{ing} = \text{gaining}$$

You may find it easier to remember a few typical words and use them as patterns than to memorize these rules. There are a very few exceptions, but they will not be mentioned here, since anybody who needs to study this section would do better to concentrate on the regularities.

Words Ending in -y

1. Words ending in a vowel plus *y* keep the *y* before any ending.

day, days   employ, employing

2. Words ending in a consonant plus *y* keep the *y* before *-ing,* to avoid the *-ii-* combination, but change it to *i* before other endings.

dry, drying, dried, drier, drily   baby, babies

Notice that *-ed* and *-es,* not simply *-d* and *-s* are added to the *i.*

3. Two things should be noticed about *-ly* endings.

a. When the original word ends in *l,* the *-ly* ending results in a double *l.*

fatal, fatally   casual, casually

b. Adverbs formed from words ending in *-ic* add *-ally* instead of simply *-ly.*

romantic, romantically   electric, electrically

-ei- and -ie- Words

There is a famous rule that goes:

> *I* before *e*
> Except after *c*
> Or when sounded as *a*
> As in *neighbor* and *weigh.*

This is interesting, and the last part of it is reasonably sound; but the first two lines rather suggest that somebody once tried to generalize from *relieve* and *receive* without bothering to check in a dictionary. Actually, the combination *c-e-i* occurs in the word *ceiling* and in derivatives of the Latin *capio*—*deceive* and *deceit, receive* and *receipt,* and so forth—and almost nowhere else. In endings the combination is always *c-i-e—fancy, fancier, finance, financier,* etc. After letters other than *c, i-e* is a better bet if you don't know and don't have a dictionary handy; but there are many exceptions.

Additional Spelling Rules

The rules given above cover only a few points, but they are about the only ones that are simple enough, reliable enough, and applicable to enough words to be generally useful to people who have serious trouble with spelling. Such students usually seem to find a more extensive set of rules confusing rather than helpful. Better spellers who feel they could profit by a more detailed set of rules will find the section on "Orthography" in *Webster's New Collegiate Dictionary* as sound and compact as anything readily available. If you use this, don't try to swallow it all at once. Read the first rule and make sure you understand it. Try it out on a few words you already know how to spell. Look up a few others and see how well it works with them. Don't balk if you find one or two exceptions—it is still much better than a plain guess. Then put the book away and let the rule soak in for a few days—trying it out every time an appropriate word comes up in your reading. Do *not* try to learn several new rules at once. You will almost certainly either get them jumbled together or forget them all. When you have completely absorbed the first you can go back for a second helping.

Exercises—Chapter 13

I. With the aid of your dictionary, define the root syllables and prefixes in the words below. Suggest if you can a logical *sense* in which the two original words might have become united to form the single word. Then list two other words, each containing one of the root syllables or prefixes:

Examples: loco/motion, re/tract

Root or prefix	Definition	Sense in which the two are combined	Another word with the root or prefix
loco-	place	locomotion suggests	*loca*tion
-motion	movement	movement from place to place	*moti*vity

| re- | again, back | to *draw back,* in the sense of retracting a | *re*turn |
| -tract | draw | statement by taking it back | con*tract* |

astro/nomy	hypo/dermic	post/pone	stereo/type
contra/dict	in/clude	pre/scribe	sub/vert
dis/miss	micro/scope	pro/gress	syn/thetic
ex/pel	mono/gram	psycho/therapy	tele/meter
hydro/plane	non/sense	pyro/mania	thermo/stat
hyper/sonic	philo/sophy	re/voke	trans/mit
			ultra/marine

II. To each word in the first column below, add the *-ing* ending. To each word in the second column, add the *-ed* ending. To each word in the third column add the *-s* ending. In adding these endings, follow the spelling rules given in this chapter.

1	2	3
bid	appeal	berry
bribe	applaud	brandy
compel	bully	cater
complete	cherish	comply
conceal	clot	convert
concede	confide	cry
deify	curtsy	display
dine	defray	ditty
display	dispute	donkey
guess	drag	enjoy
incite	dread	flurry
knot	hug	gypsy
note	lop	holiday
refine	lope	jockey
refuse	persever	levy
remit	play	liberty
ride	prefer	malady
rip	rebut	marry
rope	recede	pantry
set	revile	parody
sin	rival	play
slip	specify	prey
slope	staple	proxy
span	steer	scurry
spar	strap	sky
spare	tour	society

Suggestions for Discussion or Theme Writing—Chapter 13

1. Discuss the value of vocabulary building, its relationship to acquired knowledge, its value as a key to wealth and executive leadership (as promised by the *word power* promoters), and its value as a key to understanding.

2. Discuss the usefulness of a good dictionary, in the light of its being ". . . a record—never complete and always a little out of date—of how other people *have used* words."

SEVERAL KINDS OF TRUTH

14

For a good many centuries "the search for truth" has been considered the noblest activity of the human mind, but the seekers after truth have come to such different conclusions that it often seems that very little progress has been made. In fact, there are many people who feel that we are actually going backward. They admit, often contemptuously, that we have accumulated more "knowledge" than our ancestors, but they think we are farther from the truth than ever, or even that we have lost the truth that we once possessed.

If people look for anything long enough without finding it, the question naturally arises whether the thing is really there to find. It is one thing to look for the lode from which visible gold nuggets must have come. It is quite another thing to search for the pot of gold said to be hidden at the end of the rainbow.

The idea that there is no such thing as truth seems pretty discouraging, so let us try a less disturbing one. You have seen a picture of a chimera, a mythical animal with a lion's head, a goat's body, and a serpent's tail—and maybe an eagle's wings for good measure. There is plenty of evidence that each part of this animal exists—but there is no reliable evidence that the parts ever occur in this combination. It is at least conceivable that the seekers after "truth" have made a similar mistake and invented an imaginary combination.

It is enlightening to consider that the noun *truth* comes from the adjective *true,* and that the Latin word for truth, *veritas,* also comes from an adjective, *verus.* In both languages the notion of *true*—accurate, conforming to facts—seems to have developed before the notion of *truth.* We cannot definitely prove this, since even older words meaning "truth" may have been forgotten, but it seems reasonable. If you want to find out whether a man has told the truth, you compare his words with the facts. If they fit, you decide that his statement was true. You may then say either that his words were true or that he spoke the truth—but the second statement is merely a grammatical variation of the first. You cannot simply examine his words to find out whether there is something called truth in them. For one thing, the same set of words may be true or false under different circumstances. If two boys both say "He hit me first," one of them is probably lying. Of course you may accept words as being true without even thinking of the facts for which they stand—but if you do, you don't know what you are accepting.

The next thing to consider is whether all true statements are true in the same way—whether they are all part of the same animal. Let us look at a few:

1. She really loves me.
2. Washington crossed the Delaware.
3. Two times two is four.
4. Water boils at 212 degrees Fahrenheit.

Intuitional Truth

If you "know" that she loves you, you couldn't prove it by testimony, even hers—some people are such liars. You couldn't prove it by anything she does, because there are always possibilities of different motives for the same acts. And unless you are unusually conceited you would probably not try to prove it by logic. It is simply a personal feeling of certainty. Such feelings are very important, and occur on a wide variety of subjects. Philosophers call them *intuition,* theologians call them *revelation,* and gamblers call them *hunches.* No disrespect is intended by coupling the three terms. Taken together, they indicate that people of very different backgrounds have independently developed a belief that some kinds of "truth" cannot be discovered by ordinary mental processes, but are perceived in a direct personal flash.

There is a great deal of difference of opinion over the value of this kind of truth. To take it on the lowest level first, one gambler will say "Always play your hunches" and another will say "always play the percentages." Observation seems to indicate that neither man will always follow his own advice. A man who never plays a hunch is not likely to have the temperament to gamble very much; and a man who never considers the percentages is not likely to have the money to gamble very long.

On the philosophical level we find a very similar situation. Plato, for example, says that intuition is the direct contact of the purified soul with the mind of God, and that it is the only reliable basis for important truths. It is *personal* and it is above ordinary mental processes. But Plato also tries to prove things by such other methods as logic and evidence. Opposed to him are other philosophers who completely deny the validity of intuition, and try to prove everything by purely logical methods. But they have to start somewhere, with things they think—or feel—they know. And a Platonist might reasonably say that only intuition could explain these initial "certainties."

Most religions depend, at least in part, on revelation. In some, each member is expected to experience a personal direct contact. In others, a revelation to a prophet must thereafter be accepted on faith by others. In either case, the revelation is believed to be a flash of truth that cannot be tested by ordinary means. It must simply be accepted.

Almost any gambler will tell you that not all of his hunches have proved trustworthy. And almost any theologian will tell you that not every experience that *feels* like a revelation actually comes from God. The devil may have misled you, or there may be a glandular disturbance. "False prophets"—many of them obviously sincere— have been known from very early times.

Suppose we now group all three terms under the first heading, *intuition,* and see whether we can come to any conclusion about its usefulness. It is impossible to prove that such a thing does not occur, and it is impracticable to find out its exact frequency or reliability. But it seems reasonable to say that it should not be overworked. We can respect a man who prays for guidance—a flash of intuition—in making an important decision. But he wouldn't impress us if he sat in a mathematics examination and simply prayed for the right answers to be flashed into his mind. These answers are accessible by ordinary methods, and we should expect him to work them out for himself. There is certainly nothing irreligious about the statement that heaven helps those who help themselves.

We simply cannot get along without intuition. If we think a sunset is beautiful, it *is* beautiful to us, and there is not much to be gained by arguing about it. Even an oyster has an elementary set of values.

When he touches one particle he will recoil and reject it. When he touches another he will absorb and digest it—all, so far as we know, without conscious thought. A man is somewhat more complicated than an oyster, and so is his life. We must make innumerable intuitive decisions every day. Sometimes we do this because there is not time to examine the logical or experimental evidence, sometimes because we distrust such evidence even if we do not know how to argue against it. And there are times when our intuition is a sounder guide than either logic, which may be accurate but not quite applicable, or experiment, which is never quite conclusive.

But it is possible to respect and follow our intuition without insisting that it is absolute or infallible; and it is useful to remember that our intuition is to some extent molded by the society and traditions in which we live. A reaction to Shakespeare, for instance, is not an isolated event; it is set in the whole background of our other experiences. Obviously a man who knew no English could not appreciate Shakespeare; and neither could one who had grown up with an almost entirely different set of social, moral, and aesthetic values. A convinced prohibitionist is not likely to appreciate Toby Belch. And a contemporary Russian, trained from birth to regard women primarily as stalwart producers of quotas, could hardly be expected to know what Comrade Romeo and Comrade Juliet were talking about. Even the best dictionary would give him very little help.

A little modesty about our "intuitive" or "instinctive" certainties is therefore often appropriate. We can appreciate Shakespeare just as much without insisting that the quality of his genius is a universal truth. Suppose that you genuinely enjoy Shakespeare. You intuitively feel that he is great, and you have the comforting support of a good deal of respectable testimony to back your intuition. But if the boy next door prefers Zane Grey, it would be rather silly to tell him dogmatically that Shakespeare *is* great, and that Grey *is* trash. He has his own intuition, and he could bring in some testimony, too—especially on a secret ballot. But it is not at all silly to explain that while Shakespeare may be a little discouraging at the first reading, millions of people for hundreds of years have found him extremely rewarding; and that those people who have taken the trouble to read both writers well enough to understand them seem to give Shakespeare a tremendous preference.

Even in religious matters we can act according to our own beliefs without taking the arrogant attitude that everybody who disagrees with us must be wrong. To admit the possibility of error is not treason to our faith, as some people seem to think; it is simply a touch of modesty about our own knowledge and intelligence.

Testimonial Truth

We accept the statement that Washington crossed the Delaware simply on *testimony*. We can't prove it logically, we can't observe it for ourselves, and we probably have no deep inner feeling that convinces us. But a number of people in a position to know have said that he did; nobody has given any good evidence that he didn't; and nothing else that we know makes the statement particularly improbable. Therefore most of us accept it without question, and the chance of our being mistaken is extremely small. Testimony can never give absolute proof. The people who make it may be mistaken or lying, or both. But we have to rely on a good deal of testimony, or we would lose all the advantages of cooperation. And we are certainly in the habit of saying that statements based on generally accepted testimony are true. Of course we often disagree about the value of a particular testimonial statement.

During the Middle Ages testimony was generally considered the most certain basis for truth, and a man who was bold enough to question "the authorities" was taking his chances. If he proved by experiment that they were wrong he might be burned as a heretic before he was hailed (by later generations) as an intellectual hero. The theory was, roughly, that man was incapable of finding the truth by his own unaided intellect; and a man who believed his own experiments against a long tradition, based on ancient revelation, was guilty of impiety. Moreover, the fact that "truth" was regarded as a simple thing led to the idea that anybody who attacked "a truth" was attacking "truth itself."

The doctrine of modern scholarship is that we should respect an authority's statements, but be ready to revise them whenever new evidence indicates clearly that they were not accurate. The technique of using authorities critically rather than following them blindly is discussed at some length in Chapter 24. The widespread use of this technique is one of the reasons that we have increased the scope of our knowledge enormously in the last few centuries. We might increase it still faster if we realized more clearly that even "scientific truth" is not a simple thing, but composed of at least two very different strands.

Mathematical Truth

In dealing with the physical universe, scientists try to rely on testimony and intuition as little as possible, and to use mathematical and experimental methods as much as possible. This procedure seems to be sound, and has resulted in a great advance in the scope and accuracy of our knowledge. But although the two methods can profitably be used together, they are far from being the same thing. The very general tendency to jumble them together as "scientific truth" is a dangerous error that leads to all sorts of misunderstandings.

The example of mathematical truth we gave earlier was the familiar statement "Two times two is four." This is certainly true so long as we are concerned with *numbers alone.* But as soon as we use the numbers to represent anything physical, our certainty is reduced (as it always is when we deal with the physical universe) to a matter of approximation and probability.

Suppose, for instance, that you buy two cows from Mr. Callahan on Monday and two cows from Mr. Thorpe on Tuesday. Since you have bought two cows two times, you should now have exactly two times two cows, or four cows; and if all you want to do with your cows is to count them, you do have exactly that. But if you want to milk them or breed them or resell them, you may have either more or less than you bargained for. No two cows are alike, and the most accurate use of mathematics will not eliminate their differences.

There is no use saying, "The number of cows is exact, even if the milk production is uncertain." We have already admitted that the *number* is exact—you do get exact numbers in mathematics. But what the number stands for is not exact, though we sometimes find it useful to pretend that it is. For instance, you may agree to buy so many cows at so much a head, in the expectation that they will "average out." In other words, you and the seller agree to disregard some actual differences because you can save a good deal of trouble by so doing. It is only by making such arbitrary agreements that we can pretend that mathematics ever describes physical things exactly.

If we turn from counting to measurement, the approximate relation of mathematics to physical things becomes so obvious that even mathematicians admit it. A theoretical rectangle, ten feet by twenty, must contain exactly 200 square feet. But if we are interested in the floor of a room said to be ten feet by twenty, we can only know that it will contain approximately 200 square feet. We may be sure that the approximation is very close, perhaps that the possible error is a very small fraction of a square inch. We can measure more closely with modern instruments than with an ordinary foot-rule; but we cannot measure exactly, and there is no reason to suppose that we ever will. We must therefore come to the conclusion that while mathematics is an excellent way of describing many physical things and relations, its statements about them are only approximate (though the approximation may be very close) and probable (though the probability may be very high).

This is by no means an attack on the value of mathematics. A modern airplane, for instance, simply could not be built without a great deal of mathematical calculation. We can't afford to guess how strong this part will be or how fast that one will turn. We must calculate very carefully, and we may be confident that the actual performance of the machine will be very close to what we have calculated. But we are always prepared for at least a small margin of error.

A famous mathematician once remarked that insofar as mathematics is perfectly true and accurate, it deals with nothing whatever— as soon as it describes anything physical it is no longer quite accurate or quite true. Our ordinary life is full of *apparent* exceptions to this statement. You may be quite sure that you have exactly five fingers on each hand, unless you stop and wonder whether the thumb is "really" a finger, or whether the other four are equally useful in pounding a typewriter or measuring a drink. Then you are forced to conclude that mathematics permits us to deal exactly with numbers, but only approximately with the things they can be made to stand for.

Experimental Truth

The statement that water boils at 212 degrees involves a mathematical term, but it cannot be proved by mathematical means. It is based simply on a large number of observations which have given results so uniform that we can be sure as we are of anything that *under certain conditions* a pot of water will boil at this temperature, as nearly as we can measure it. But if the conditions vary significantly, the boiling point will also vary.

Let us suppose that the first few hundred observations of the boiling point of water were all made in one small area at very nearly sea level. The results would all be so nearly alike that the tiny differences could be attributed to slight inaccuracies in the instruments, and it would be reasonable to suppose that water always boiled at exactly the same temperature.

But then suppose a scientist happened to vacation in the Alps, taking his teakettle and thermometer along. He would be amazed to discover that his water boiled at a much lower temperature than usual. He might think his thermometer had gone wrong and send for another. But when that gave a similar reading he would see that what he had taken for a reliable general rule did not always work.

He could not possibly know at first why the result was different. He might guess that it was because of the composition of the water, or the latitude or longitude, or some other reason. But it would probably occur to him before long that the altitude might be a factor, and he could easily check this by trying experiments at different altitudes. The result would be quite satisfactory, for he would find that the boiling point varied quite regularly with the altitude, and he might come to the conclusion that change in altitude was a direct cause of change in boiling point—and publish a paper to prove it.

Now suppose another scientist reads this paper and is impressed but not convinced. He makes similar experiments and gets very similar results, but two things continue to bother him. One is that the results are not quite as consistent as they should be, considering the accuracy of his instruments and his care in using them. The other is that he can see no reason why altitude *in itself* should have any effect at all. He therefore wonders whether the cause may not be the altitude, but some other factor which tends to vary with the altitude. It occurs to him almost at once that one such factor is air pressure; and perhaps he has an intuitive feeling that a connection between air pressure and boiling point is more reasonable than one between altitude and boiling point. He therefore tries a new experiment by creating a slight partial vacuum at sea level and boiling water in that. When he finds that even at sea level his water boils at a lower temperature when the air pressure is reduced, his theory is confirmed. Other scientists follow his lead, and use a barometer as well as a thermometer whenever they experiment. Now the slight but disturbing irregularities in the reports are all but wiped out. What seemed at first like erratic differences are now seen to be regular consequences of changes in conditions. Science has progressed.

If our scientist has learned the full lesson from his new experiments, he will realize that even his improved results are not necessarily final. He has shown that the boiling point varies with one previously unsuspected factor. May it also vary with others, such as the amount of light, the strength of a magnetic field, or an electrical current passing through the water? Will it be the same in a moving train as it is in a house? He may guess that none of these factors will be significant, but the only way he can be sure is to try them out.

Of course a scientist must frequently combine the mathematical and the experimental approach, and so must an engineer or a housewife. Let's consider a group of engineers designing a new airplane. They want it to go so far, so fast, carry such a load, and cost so much a mile to operate. Starting with highly (but not perfectly) reliable data gathered by their predecessors, they begin their calculations. Thousands of factors have to be taken into account, from the tensile strength of metals to the pilot's nervous reactions. Thousands of pages of calculations will be necessary, all of which must be performed with the greatest possible accuracy. When these are finished and checked, they know how the plane *should* perform. But they don't know how it *will* perform until they have actually tested it.

Some parts of the testing can be performed early, with sub-assemblies or small models, in a laboratory, in a wind tunnel, or elsewhere. But when all possible preliminary work has been done and the completed plane is ready for its first flight, there is still much that they have to learn. How close to the estimated speed will the actual speed be? What factors that they have failed to consider will affect performance? (Remember the sound barrier?) In general, what "bugs" will develop? Without the certainties of mathematics their plane would be a hopelessly wild guess. But in applying their mathematics to physical materials and conditions, they have left certainty behind for approximation and probability. Now they are ready to observe and correct; and when they have finished they will have a plane on which passengers will cheerfully bet their lives.

The housewife's problems are different only in degree. She has a 13-pound turkey, and the cookbook says to roast it 25 minutes per pound. Unless she (or her husband) can multiply accurately, the turkey may turn out to be anything from crude rubber to a cinder. But if she takes it out after exactly five hours and 25 minutes it may still be a long way from perfect. She is not cooking *the* turkey in *the* oven, but *a* turkey in *her* oven; and mathematics needs a little help from experiment if the bird is to be fit to eat.

Exercises—Chapter 14

Mark the following statements *I* (intuition), *T* (testimony), *M* (mathematics), or *E* (experimentation), to indicate the principal basis you think accounts for whatever truth the statement contains. (Use *two* or more letters where you feel you must spread the responsibility.) In addition to the above, mark with *X* those statements you personally think are debatable or untrue, and defend your position in a brief comment.

1. Corned beef is better than bacon.
2. The space around us usually contains oxygen.
3. For a time the rulers of England spoke a kind of French.
4. I paid more income tax last year than anyone who told me how much he paid.
5. My four cows gave a daily average of three gallons of milk for the first half of this year.
6. They tell me Number 5 has never lost a race, and Number 9 holds the world record for the distance, but really Number 7 is going to win.
7. Ernie Pyle was killed by a sniper, near the end of WW II.
8. In most instances, vaccination prevents one from contracting polio.
9. Lardo feels better against the roof of your mouth than the high-priced spread does.
10. Joe Louis could have beaten Jack Dempsey.
11. Rockets can escape the earth's gravitational pull.
12. Phoenix has higher relative humidity than Tucson because there is more irrigation of crops carried on around Phoenix.
13. It will take forty thousand gallons of water to fill a pool that size.
14. The Chinese invented gunpowder.
15. Table salt is a combination of sodium and chlorine.
16. Cancel my reservation; I've got this strange feeling that Flight 53 is not going to reach Cincinnati.
17. I wouldn't marry you if you were the last man on earth.
18. Bicarbonate of soda generally neutralizes many acids.
19. Maybe if you'd tap that gadget there a few times with the pliers the engine would start.
20. Coronado explored the Southwest several hundred years ago.
21. My wheat land produced twenty bushels to the acre this year.
22. I get 24 miles per gallon on a fifty-fifty mixture of white and regular gas.
23. Whoever it was that said I was a name-caller is a dirty, contemptible liar.
24. The cake should be done after forty minutes in a 425-degree oven.
25. This last quarter is bound to hit the jackpot.

Suggestions for Discussion or Theme Writing—Chapter 14

1. Give four reasonably important questions, each of which could best be answered by appeal to a different kind of truth.

2. Discuss a more complicated problem which could be effectively solved only by using (but not indiscriminately mixing) several different kinds of truth.

OUTLINING
AND PARAGRAPHING

15

In Chapter 10 we discussed the use of a very simple type of outline as a way of organizing the material for a paper. Most students seem to feel that to require a more systematic and elaborate outline is utterly unreasonable—the sort of thing that might be expected from an English instructor, but certainly *not* the sort of thing that a sensible student should take seriously, or learn any more about than he can help. But the fact is that a really sound outline, written in complete sentences and carefully checked for consistency, is one of the best labor-saving devices ever devised. Very few students can afford to neglect it.

The Thesis Sentence

Before the word *thesis* meant a long paper with lots of quotations and footnotes, it meant the argument or intellectual position that such a paper sets forth. In other words, if you write a paper involving any thought, your thesis is the main idea that you develop, and you should be able to express it in a *thesis sentence*. Some people write mostly by accident, and can construct such a sentence only after they find out what they have said; but it really saves a good deal of trouble to write it first.

Suppose you decide to write a paper about required as against elective courses. There is obviously a good deal that could be said on this subject, and you might wander around indefinitely if you just plunged in with no particular plan. Just writing *about* a subject isn't enough. You have to decide definitely the main things you are going to say; and about the best way to decide whether these things add up and stick together is to put them into one sentence and examine it for direction, consistency, and completeness. Then work the sentence over until it satisfies you. Not until you feel that it is a satisfactory summary of your whole argument can you really call it a thesis sentence.

Here are three possible *preliminary* thesis sentences for a paper on required courses, indicating the three most probable general attitudes:

1. There are three reasons why required courses are almost worthless to most students.
2. Although many students object, a well-rounded set of required courses provides a much better framework for an education than a patchwork of electives.
3. The arguments for elective and required courses are so nearly even that I can't make up my mind which I prefer.

Each one of these at least indicates a direction, and might pass for a thesis sentence in a pinch; but not one of them is detailed enough to give you much help in the next step. Remember, an outline, intelligently used, is not an extra task, to be skimped as far as possible; it is a preliminary step designed to make the whole job easier and more efficient. A good outline is worth two rough drafts; and if yours is good enough you won't have to do much more than copy to get your final paper. Suppose you decide that the first of the three preliminary thesis sentences expresses your attitude. You have three reasons in mind now; an hour from now you don't want to be scratching your head and saying desperately, "Now what in the world was that third reason?" Moreover, now is as good a time as any to decide the order in which you are going to consider the reasons. You might therefore expand the sentence to something like this:

Required courses are almost worthless to most students because: (1) they resent taking them and won't do their best work; (2) the class attitude is not likely to be stimulating; (3) the instructors don't even have to try to be interesting, because they have a guaranteed supply of victims.

Possibly there is something to be said on the other side, but at least you have a thesis that can be developed.

The Main Headings

In its revised form this thesis sentence indicates pretty clearly both the line you are going to take and the main divisions of your paper.

Let's assume that the paper is supposed to run from three to five hundred words. Then three paragraphs will be about right, and the three numbered clauses can be used as a basis for the three main sentences in your outline. Of course you might have an introductory paragraph and a closing paragraph, or one of your main divisions might be long enough to break into parts; but the obvious division is into three paragraphs, and you might as well start out with that in mind.

You may be tempted to put down topic headings instead of sentences, perhaps something like this:

    I. Student resentment
    II. Class attitude
    III. Instructors not interesting

All right, you have put them down, and thereby saved a few minutes, but what is the next step? These headings don't seem very helpful. Maybe it would be better to take a little longer and write definite sentences, something like this:

I. The first objection to required courses is that students resent them and won't do their best work.

II. You are not stimulated when the other students are obviously bored.

III. Since we are automatic victims, the instructors don't even have to try to be interesting.

These sentences are more likely to suggest further subdivisions than the mere headings; but before you go any further you had better see how they fit with each other. If you have any experience with outlines, it will take you only a glance to see that they do *not* fit. The first sentence talks about "students," the second talks about "you," and the third talks about "we." The viewpoint is shifting around for no apparent reason, and your instructor won't stand for it. Writing your actual paragraphs this way would mean either a complete revision or a poor grade. But if you can catch the shifting viewpoint in the outline you can straighten it out in a couple of minutes. This is the first great advantage of efficient outlining. Suppose you decide to eliminate the "you" and "we," and stick to the third person throughout. And while you are at it, it might be a good idea to pick up "the first objection" with "the second" and "the third." Your outline might now look like this:

I. The first objection to required courses is that students resent them and won't do their best work.

II. ~~You are not stimulated when the other students are obviously bored.~~ The second is that the general boredom makes the classes far from stimulating.

The third is that
III. ~~Since we are automatic victims,~~ the instructors don't even have to try to be interesting, since they have a guaranteed supply of victims.

Developing the Outline

You are now ready to put in the subdivisions—still in sentence form. You might come up with something like this:

I. The first objection to required courses is that students resent them and won't do their best work.
    A. Students must take courses in fields in which they have no interest.
        1. Agriculture students must take a course in art.
        2. English majors must take Introduction to Mathematics.
    B. Even if a student has a potential interest in a required course, he is likely to loaf just because it was forced on him.
    C. The instructors are often very dull in required courses.

II. ~~You are not stimulated when the other students are obviously bored.~~ The second is that general boredom makes the classes far from interesting.
    A. In a good class the other students often contribute as much as the instructor.
    B. Students in required courses are so bored that they contribute very little.
    C. The two dullest classes I have are the required ones in economics and physics.

The third is that

III. ~~Since we are automatic victims,~~ the instructors don't even have to try to be interesting, since they have a guaranteed supply of victims.
   A. The best classes are those that offer a challenge to the instructor as well as the student.
   B. The instructor in an elective course knows he has to be interesting enough to attract students.
   C. Instructors in required courses have no such challenge, and often become very dull.
      1. Professor Tanner hasn't changed his lecture notes in 23 years.
      2. Nobody knows whether Dr. Schoonmaker has changed his notes or not, because his voice puts everybody to sleep.

Checking the Outline

By now your outline has grown to the point where you could use it to write a paper of the required length—but you'd better not. It is just at this point that its real value is available. The ideas are now set down in skeleton form, where they can easily be checked for possible omissions, repetitions, or inconsistencies. Moreover, there is still some blank space between the lines. Changes in the content and organization can be made without recopying, and additional points can be inserted where they clearly belong. Your outline is actually better than a solidly written first draft—but only because it is written in complete sentences. Phrase headings simply wouldn't show those inconsistencies and shifts in viewpoint that ruin so many papers. Let's check it over and see what we find.

Sentence I,C has nothing to do with the main heading for I; it would fit better under III. In fact it is included in III,C. Leave it there, and cross it out under I. Sentence II,C has to be considered carefully. The shift to an "I" subject may be justified if you simply give an illustration and remember to get back on the main track; but why are these two classes dull—because of the other students or because of the instructors? If the trouble is with the instructors, save this for III. If these are the two classes taught by Professor Tanner and Dr. Schoonmaker, you don't want to discuss them twice. But if the trouble is with the other students, rewrite II,C to make it clear right in the outline; otherwise you may go off in the wrong direction later.

Once you have made these changes, you might be ready to go ahead and write your paper; or you might decide to make the outline even more complete. Some students find it wise to put practically every detail in the outline, because the skeleton form makes it easy to check. By writing one good outline they can save themselves a couple of drafts. Others find they can get along with no more than what is shown above. You will have to find your own level. But remember that complete sentences give you both a check on the general structure and a guide to the final form that is much more reliable than you would get from words or phrases that might be pointed in any of several directions.

What Is a Paragraph?

One way of describing a paragraph is to say that it is composed of a group of sentences so related that they make up a larger unit. Another is to say that it is a division of a longer paper. We will discuss the first approach in Chapter 19. Since we are now considering the development of a paper from an outline, it is the second that concerns us here.

In the outline we have just considered there were three main headings. A paper written from this outline might consist of one long paragraph; but if we decided to divide it, the most reasonable division would probably be into three paragraphs, one for each of the main ideas treated. This is not an absolute certainty. If one of the divisions turned out to be considerably longer and more complicated than the others, it might be further subdivided; but three is the best preliminary guess for a paper of the assigned length (300 to 500 words). If you treated the subject in 5000 words instead of 500, you would need a good many more paragraphs—perhaps one for each sub-heading. In any case, you should make your division by balancing two principles:

1. Each paragraph should be of a "reasonable length."
2. The divisions should come at "natural breaks" in the thought.

"Reasonable Length"

The idea that "correct paragraphing" is an exact science is pure superstition. If you set any book in solid type and gave it to a dozen editors to break into paragraphs, you would get a remarkable variety of results. But although it is impossible to prove that any division into paragraphs is perfect, it is entirely possible to prove that many divisions are ineffective, misleading, or ridiculous. Reasonable paragraphing is a skill which can be developed with a little intelligent practice.

In representing dialog it is usual to start a new paragraph with every change of speaker. Otherwise there are no generally accepted limits, though some stylebooks contain arbitrary rules. However, since the basic purpose of paragraphing is to assist the reader in grasping the relation of ideas, it is usually wise to make the paragraphs of a convenient size, and to keep most of them within fairly uniform limits. An occasional very short paragraph may be dramatic, but this device will not stand much repetition. Any very long paragraph is likely to irritate many readers. Newspapers, which are very careful not to strain their readers, often have an average length of less than fifty words, and rarely permit paragraphs to go over a hundred. Thus nobody can choke on too big a bite. On the other hand, a scientist or philosopher may average two or three hundred words to a paragraph, and occasionally reach three times this length. He can reasonably assume that his audience is capable of digesting larger helpings, and perhaps he is capable of handling larger units than the reporter could control. But his paragraphs are not necessarily better just because they are longer. An editor who broke them up, either by a very slight rewording or by a simple change in typesetting, might make them easier to read and understand.

You will therefore have to find your own "reasonable length" by considering both your own method of writing and the probable reactions of your readers. As a rough guide, an average length of somewhere in the neighborhood of 100 words is usually satisfactory for student writing. If you find that most of your paragraphs are much shorter than this, you are probably breaking your writing into too many pieces and failing to show how your ideas fit together. If you find any paragraph much over 150 words, take a second look at it. It may be all right; but if you are not sure it all sticks together, you had better break it up.

"Natural Breaks"

When you write from a good outline, you have a prepared guide for the approximate divisions. If you have written several sentences about Section I and are now going to cover Section II, it is time to start a new paragraph. About the only cause for hesitation is a sentence used to link the two paragraphs together. Should it be placed at the end of the first paragraph or at the beginning of the second? If you find it hard to decide, it may be a good idea to change the wording slightly, so that one division or the other seems more reasonable. When you make your final copy, indent as your corrections indicate.

If you are writing without an outline, don't worry too much about the paragraphing in the first draft; but before making the final copy, examine your draft carefully and see if you can find where the natural breaks in the thought are. Perhaps the best method is to imagine that you are writing a much shorter summary of your paper. You might find that you could summarize your first five sentences in one sentence, your next seven in a second, and your last four in a third. You would then insert a ¶ mark after your fifth sentence and another after your twelfth. If you have already indented anywhere else, put a "no ¶" at each indentation. Then (on the final copy), indent as indicated.

Exercises—Chapter 15

Assume that you listed the topics below as possible subjects of discussion in a paper on College Life. Realizing the topics cover too wide a range for your purpose, you decided to divide the original subject and make three separate papers: I, *The Campus as a Place to Live;* II, *The Campus as a Place to Learn;* III, *The Campus as a Place to Take Part in Social Activity.*

(a) Mark each of the topics below I, II, or III, according to the division in which you think it most appropriate. (Some may be marked for more than one paper, others not at all. Or you may wish to fill in with topics missing from this list but necessary for the development of the paper as you envision it.)

(b) Rewrite the *topics* for one of the three papers as *complete sentences,* according to your particular slant on that aspect of the subject and the use you wish to make of it.

(c) Group together those which make logical subdivisions of the whole.

(d) Arrange the groups of sentences into logical outline form.

(e) Compose one or more of the actual paragraphs as directed by your instructor.

1. Initiation of freshmen.
2. The nightmare of registration.
3. The number of hours a person should take.
4. Sorority-fraternity exchanges.
5. The friends a person makes in his classes.
6. The uncertainty of membership in fraternity or sorority.
7. Snap courses.
8. Dating.
9. Outside-of-class help from instructors.
10. The campus hang-out.
11. The teachers you get.
12. The need to get along.
13. Free movies on some evenings.
14. Problems that come up if you want to change your program.
15. Blind dates.
16. Plain old studying.
17. College-sponsored dances.
18. Athletic events.
19. Finding study time.
20. Prestige in housing.
21. The cost of membership.
22. The need to share.
23. College dormitory.
24. Fraternity or sorority house.
25. Cultural affairs.
26. Bull sessions.
27. Library facilities.
28. Getting an adviser.
29. Examinations.
30. Chaperons and sponsors.
31. Polishing the apple.
32. A word about cribbing.
33. Time spent on organizational affairs.
34. The feeling of belonging.
35. House rules.
36. Library hours.
37. Room rent.
38. Grading system.
39. Cost of food.
40. The intellectual atmosphere.

Suggestions for Discussion or Theme Writing—Chapter 15

1. For five of the following subjects construct a thesis sentence which narrows the topic, if possible, and sets forth an intellectual position (attitude) close to your own. Compose *three* thesis sentences for the remaining subject, covering a wide range of attitudes, if possible. Defend or explain your choices briefly.

(a) honor halls
(b) athletic scholarships
(c) plagiarism
(d) queen contests
(e) selection of cheerleaders
(f) outspoken teachers

2. Develop a *sentence* outline (through the first main divisions and subdivisions) from one of the following topic sentences. (Since all the possible attitudes are not included, you might have to pretend agreement with one of these, just for this exercise.)

(a) Campus parking lots should operate on a space-rent basis so the cost of providing them can be borne by those who use them.

(b) Campus parking lots should be free and open to all because they are provided by public funds.

(c) Campus parking lots should operate on a space-rent basis because there are more student cars than can be accommodated and the charge will force some of the cars off the campus.

(d) Campus parking lots should be free and open because in Russia freedom is restricted, and we don't want to be like the Communists.

DEFINITION, CLASSIFICATION, AND GENERALIZATION

16

The way we learn about anything new is to find out how it resembles things that we already know, and how it differs from them. If a child asked you what a zebra was, you might say something like: "It's a wild animal that lives in Africa, a good deal like a horse, but chunkier and with black and white stripes, and I hear it's much harder to tame." A zoologist would give a more precise, and perhaps a more elaborate explanation, but he would use the same general method—comparison with the known to explain the unknown.

Since we don't have time to make a separate investigation of everything, we soon develop the habit of grouping things that are sufficiently similar, calling them by the same name, and reacting to them in the same general way. This habit is absolutely necessary. It wouldn't really be practical to make a new examination of every potato before deciding whether it was edible, not to mention peas. But since the habit emphasizes the similarities of things called by the same name and tends to conceal their differences, it can be dangerous if not practiced with some care. It is therefore worth our while to give a little thought to three closely related processes that the habit involves—definition, classification, and generalization.

Formal Definition

A formal definition must explain two things—the *genus* or kind to which something belongs, and the *differentiae,* or differences from other members of that kind. As you can see, this is quite in line with the first sentence in this chapter—since it tells us what the thing is like and how it differs; but the formal definition must be precise and absolute. Informally, you might explain a regular pentagon by saying that it is like a square except that it has five sides instead of four. Formally, you would have to say that it was a five-sided regular polygon. The word *polygon* puts it in the genus of figures bounded by straight lines connected by angles; the word *regular* differentiates it from all those figures whose lines and angles are not exactly equal; and the word *five-sided* completes the differentiation by excluding all hexagons, octagons, and so forth. A good formal definition leaves nothing to guess about. It says that the thing defined *is* a member of a class, *with* certain differences from other members—and it says so directly and definitely. There are no *likes* or *kind ofs* or *is whens*. And a noun is defined by other nouns, a verb by other verbs, and so forth.

Mathematical Definition

Formal definitions are indispensable in mathematics and logic. A mathematician can define a square or a circle or an equilateral triangle *completely,* and his definitions will apply exactly to all squares, circles, and equilateral triangles, future as well as past. Suppose, for instance, he defines a square as a plane figure consisting of four equal lines connected by four equal angles. He does not have to worry about whether the angles will be exactly equal in the next square he encounters. They must be, or it will not be a square.

The reason for this certainty and regularity is simple. Since mathematical concepts have *no physical content,* there is no reason for them to vary. A "square" on the blackboard is merely a representation of a true square. And every square is exactly like every other square in its "essential characteristics"—that is, the characteristics covered by the definition (size and position, for instance, are usually left out). *The definition controls the class.*

Of course other mathematicians may refuse to accept their colleague's definitions, and make new ones of their own. But if they find his definitions satisfactory they can accept them and use them exactly and uniformly. They may find that a definition implies additional consequences unsuspected by its originator—for instance, that every square can be divided into two equal triangles. But they will not find any irregularities because *there is nothing physical to change or vary.* Consequently, they can talk about "all squares" or "all circles" with complete confidence.

Physical Definition

When it comes to defining things that do have a physical content we have an entirely different problem. Suppose a zoologist attempts to define a dog. Whatever definition he gives must be based on not quite complete observation of some dogs. No two dogs are the same; no one dog stays the same; and nothing he says about dogs will make them more uniform than they actually are. His definition does not control the class. If he chooses to talk about "all dogs" he is certainly going beyond the boundaries of his knowledge, and very possibly making a fool of himself.

A zoologist is very likely to know this, and to act accordingly. Students of some other branches of knowledge frequently fail to realize it. The completeness and regularity of mathematical definitions are so effective and satisfactory that they are tempted to use them even when they are dealing with things that do have physical content. So they define "democracy" or "the psychopathic personality" or "the progressive school" with impressive formality, and then get so impressed by their definitions that they never again take a clear look at the things their definitions are supposed to be about. In a way they lead a very happy life. I know people whose faith in progressive schools is absolutely unshakable, because any school that has faults open to the public view is not "really progressive."

Of course there are times when it is useful to define classes of physical things, and there is nothing wrong with doing this formally, as long as you realize that what you are doing is simply *explaining how you are using words.* If you are going to write a paper about sports cars you'd better let your readers know whether or not you include hot-rods on one side and low-slung family cars on the other. But you will simplify things for everybody concerned if you make it clear that you are simply explaining what *you* mean when *you* use the word. If you make the rather common mistake of insisting that your meaning is the only true one, you are wasting time and probably losing friends.

In this connection there are two important things to remember.

The first is that it is often better to let the context explain a term than it is to define it. Look at the following paragraph:

He received his formal education in the public schools of Cleveland and at the University of Michigan, where he majored in economics. But the really valuable part of his education was gained in other institutions— Durfee's Pool Hall, the West Side Democratic Club, and Larkin's Meat Packing Company, where he worked in the summers.

Here the word *education* is used in two quite different ways, and is not defined in either use. But most readers will grasp what is meant by "formal education" and will have a pretty good idea that the "valuable part" of his other education was what he learned about different sorts of people. A definition of terms would be unlikely to make the paragraph any clearer—and it would be very likely to make it dull, pompous, and generally ineffective. You have to give your readers credit for knowing something.

The other thing to remember about definitions is that your readers are not completely at your orders, and have formed their own opinions on some things long ago. There is a very good chance that they are going to continue to interpret words according to their own habits, no matter what you say they mean. If you want to use the term *American* for any inhabitant of North or South America, and *U. S. Citizen* for a U.S. citizen, you have all sorts of good reasons on your side. But no matter how carefully you explain what you are doing, most of your readers will probably think of U.S. citizens every time they see *American,* and react to your paper accordingly. It isn't wise to think too much about what they ought to do. Think about what they will do.

Social Definition

Of course the fact that definitions of physical things do not control classes is horribly inconvenient. Consider the difficulties of lawmakers. They define crimes, property rights, and all sorts of other things, and then lay down rules of procedure based on their definitions. Moreover, these rules are workable a good proportion of the time. If a man steals some money in one way, we can call it theft and send him to jail for six months; if he steals in a different way, we can call it burglary and send him up for three years; and if he steals in still a third way, we can call it robbery and send him up for twenty. But no matter how carefully the definitions are framed, some criminal will come along whose actions are not clearly in any of the classes, and there may be a long and expensive trial to decide whether what he did was "really" one crime or another.

Now consider the case of a man who is convicted of robbery— unjustly, he believes—and sent to prison for twenty years. He admits that he picked up a wallet which he saw fall out of another man's pocket, and walked away with it. But he believes that this is simple theft, and that he shouldn't get more than a year in prison. Unfortunately, he happened to be carrying a hunting rifle at the time, and the jury decides that this made the crime armed robbery instead of simple theft. Our criminal argues that this was simply a coincidence, and that he didn't even threaten the victim. But the victim says that he saw the gun and assumed that the criminal would use it; otherwise he would have taken the wallet back. The case might have been decided either way, but it was in fact called robbery, and the criminal is in for a long term. After some years of meditation he may come to the conclusion that in his case the definition *did* control the class.

But the fact is that the definition had no effect on the crime itself. What he did was simply what he did—an action on the borderline between two different things that the lawmakers were thinking of. What the definition controlled was the court's later *action* about the crime.

In our everyday affairs we must let our actions be controlled by definitions to some extent, because we haven't got time to investigate every new incident from scratch. Even as simple an action as buying a can marked "Tomato Soup" depends on accepting a definition and making a small investment in the belief that it is probably satisfactorily accurate. But the soup *may* have a peculiar taste, or even give us ptomaine poisoning; and the manufacturer cannot eliminate either of these possibilities by the precision of his definition. All he can do is to be very careful about his materials and processes in order to make his product as nearly uniform as possible.

Definitions and Classifications

A definition is appropriate only when we are talking about a *class* of things. There is no necessity for defining a unique thing—we simply describe it. For instance, if we think of the earth all by itself as the place where we live, no definition is necessary. But if we think of it as part of a set including Mars, Venus, etc., we *classify* it as a planet, and *define* planets in such a way as to show *how they resemble each other* and *how they differ from members of other classes,* such as stars.

If we remember that in the physical universe no two things are exactly alike, we are led to see some interesting things about classification:

1. Classification of physical things can never be as exact (and complete) as classification of mathematical abstractions, because there is always the possibility of borderline cases. We may be quite sure that a rose is a plant and that a cow is an animal, but we can't find the exact line between plants and animals. In some of the simpler forms of life, botanists and zoologists disagree. When we realize that classifications are often useful but never perfect, we save a good deal of misdirected energy.

2. There are always a number of different ways of classifying anything, and no one of them is the one right way. Different ways are useful for different purposes. For instance, Mary Pemberton may be classified as a human being, a female, an American citizen, a blonde, a minor, a freshman, a resident of Arizona, and a member of Blue Cross, not to mention a few dozen other things. Our first impression may be that some of these classifications are "real" and others "arbitrary," or that some are important and others trivial. But the fact is that they are all quite real, and any one of them may be important at a given time. If Mary wants to cast a vote or buy a drink, the fact that she is a minor becomes for the occasion more important than the fact that she is female; and if she needs an emergency operation the fact that she is a member of the Blue Cross may save her life when neither her sex nor her citizenship would do her any good. Naturally, some of the classifications that can be applied to her are more likely to be permanent than others, and are important on more different occasions. But they are all based on certain similarities with *some* people and differences from *other* people. Even the fact that she is human is not always the most important thing about her. In a war we may be trying to preserve our people and equipment and to destroy the enemy's people and equipment. In a very practical way we classify her with our tanks rather than with their women. She

may not think the classification is flattering; but if it means that she goes on living she can hardly deny that it is real.

3. Classifications are *invented by observers,* and are based on the similarities and differences that we recognize, not on the ones that "really" exist. It is all very well to define a fair ball in baseball as one that lands between the foul lines; but in practice it is and has to be one that the umpire *says* lands between the foul lines. Of course if it lands in center field there is not much chance of an argument; but if it lands within inches of a foul line it has to be called one way or the other, and it is what it is called by the umpire that counts.

If this illustration seems trivial, consider the case of Alvin Spivak, who was born in the United States of parents who were both citizens, but who was brought up in a foreign country and did not return to the United States until he was twenty. Theoretically we may argue that Alvin is a citizen; but suppose he has no way of proving, or even of suspecting, this fact. If he never gets the privileges of a citizen it doesn't mean much to say that he is one. Or consider Toni Frandl, a native of Switzerland who takes out naturalization papers in the United States. We say he is now an American citizen, but the Swiss say he is still a Swiss one. Neither country recognizes that the citizenship in the other is real; but Toni might suspect that there was some reality in both if he were jailed by one country for evading military service, and later extradited and hanged by the other for treason.

We may summarize the whole business of classification by the two following statements:

1. When a thing is classified in any given way, it presumably has some similarities to other things in the same classification. When we call it by a class name we *emphasize these similarities.*

2. But since no two members of a class are exactly alike (unless we are dealing with pure abstractions), there must also be some differences. And when we call a thing by its class name we *neglect these differences.*

In other words, to call anything by a class name tells only *half the story.* Our laziness, our vanity, and our emotions all tend to obscure this fact. We find it convenient and agreeable to say "All those Micks are alike," or "A German is a German—I don't care what you say."

But all Irishmen are not alike, and the statement that a German is a German, conclusive as it sounds, doesn't really tell us anything.

Alfred Korzybski devised a convenient technique for indicating the *other half* of the story. He says, in effect: "There is no such thing in nature as *the German*—there are only German$_1$, German$_2$, German$_3$, and so forth. The fact that they have some things in common is indicated by the word *German;* but we need the index numbers 1, 2, 3, and so forth to remind us that there are also differences between them. Moreover, even German$_1$ does not stay the same. We should learn to distinguish between German$_{1_{1939}}$ and German$_{1_{1952}}$."

It is not likely that you will add much to your popularity if you go around talking about "German$_{1_{1952}}$" on every possible occasion. But if you get into the habit of thinking in terms of dates and index numbers, you may avoid not only some unsound conclusions but some unfortunate events. It is all very well to say that "a cow is a gentle animal" if you realize that you are merely talking in terms of probabilities, based on a limited experience. And your statement may seem satisfactory enough as applied to the next seven cows that you happen to meet. But if cow$_8$ gores you, you can't stop the bleeding by explaining that she is not a real cow.

Generalizations

The fact that generalizations often have exceptions is, of course, widely realized. In fact, many of us have been specifically taught to "avoid generalizations" completely. It is quite impossible to do this, and we should be of no use to ourselves or anybody else if we seriously tried to. Tiger$_8$, for instance, may be as gentle as cow$_8$ is rough; but until you are perfectly sure of this you had better act on the firm generalization that tigers are dangerous. But we should try to understand the nature of generalizations so that we won't be completely at their mercy.

All generalizations are based on the *assumption of regularity,* and we need such an assumption to guide our lives. If we could not take it for granted that water is usually wet, the year about twelve months long, and our mothers' meals reasonably free from poison, living would be something of a strain. But in order to act efficiently, we have to know when we can assume that the regularity is complete and certain, and when we must assume that it is only approximate and probable.

It is only when we are dealing with such concepts as triangles and circles that we have complete and certain regularity. What is true of one circle must be true of all, because they are all alike by the definition which created them. Consequently, if we have learned anything about circles by studying a few of them, we can generalize confidently about all the others. In fact, if the ratio between diameter and circumference of even one circle is *pi,* the same ratio must hold for all others.

But when we deal with physical things we are in a much more complicated situation. Physicists assume that the "forces of nature" operate regularly—or at least that they "tend" to. For instance, the speed of light is said to be a constant, with a value of approximately 186,000 miles per second. They therefore use this figure in all sorts of equations and it works out very well, but two things must be noted.

One is that the figure is not quite exact. We can measure accurately enough to determine that the figure is a little over 186,000 miles, which is close enough for most practical purposes, but we cannot find the exact number of odd feet—our instruments are not fine enough. Consequently there is always a little margin of error in our calculations.

The other is that the exact figure would represent not the actual speed of light, but the speed at which light would travel in a perfect vacuum if such a thing existed. The actual speed of a given ray of light, even in outer space, is always at least a tiny bit slower.

Any generalization about physical things is therefore at best a matter of approximation and probability. All our observations show that light *tends* to travel at about a certain speed. Since we assume regularity, we expect that light will always *tend* to travel at this speed (we cannot get quite the exact figure). When we can figure the interfering factors—glass, mist, or cosmic dust—we can correct the theoretical speed and come very close to the actual speed. But we can never be sure we have recognized all the interfering factors, or figured them correctly.

When we have to generalize about a more complex situation, such as the chemical effects of apples or the habits of a group of people, we have many more variables to consider, and the chance of making mistakes about some of them is much greater.

A child who has one apple tree in his back yard may come to the conclusion that red apples taste sweet and are safe to eat, while green apples taste sour and sometimes lead to cramps. He reaches these conclusions by approved scientific processes; but his generalizations have a rather small base. When he encounters other apple trees he may find that some green apples are sweet, and some red ones are sour. He will have to revise his original idea that color is a reliable index of taste. It is still evidence, but it must be considered along with other things.

Perhaps he will find that the color of the seeds is a more reliable guide than the color of the skin, but he won't find this or anything else a perfect guide. Apples vary enormously, and so do the people who eat them. This is not because the forces that make up an apple or a person are more erratic than those that make up a beam of light. It is because there are more of them, and they are more likely to modify each other's behavior. If we want to make a generalization about apples that will be useful and reasonably reliable, we'd better limit it.

This limitation on the usefulness of generalizations as applied to physical things was not understood in the Middle Ages. It was assumed, for instance, that iron was "essentially" iron, and "naturally" uniform. If something that seemed to be iron happened to act in a peculiar way, it simply wasn't "really" pure iron, and there you were —a little flustered, perhaps, but with your definitions and generalizations "essentially" undisturbed. It was therefore quite generally assumed that mathematical or logical statements about physical things could be exact and rigorous. Since the complete and exact truth could apparently be expressed in words, it seemed that the correct definitions would hold good for all members of a class, and that universal generalizations could be perfectly sound.

Such ideas are not respectable today. Almost any scientist will now tell you that his "knowledge" is only tentative. It consists only of what he has learned from observation and experiment (his own or others'); and it is subject to correction or revision whenever new or more accurate observation suggests the necessity. But the old habits persist, and a good many people who follow the "scientific method" very carefully in their own special fields forget about it when they move into others.

Prejudices

One of the most harmful kinds of generalization is the kind that results in a prejudice against a group—racial, religious, occupational, or of some other kind. The fact that such prejudices are harmful is now widely recognized, and a good deal of progress has been made in overcoming them; but we might move even faster if we supported our humanitarian efforts with an analysis of the mechanics of the situation.

In the first place, we should recognize that not all generalized disapprovals are prejudices. Some of them might be called "postjudices," because the judgment is reached after a reasonable examination of the evidence instead of before. If you happen to know a gang of fifty Corsican thugs who spend their time robbing stores, setting fire to hospitals, and cutting up passing citizens with pocket knives, there is no prejudice involved in disliking them for what you know they have done. But if you assume that all other Corsicans are naturally inclined to act in the same way because they are Corsicans, then you are prejudging people before they have acted. That is a prejudice. A reasonable (though not entirely accurate) opinion of a small group has been unreasonably extended to cover a much larger group.

The Purple-Eyed Corsicans

The next thing to notice is that a prejudice usually involves the assumption that there is an invariable relation between two characteristics—one readily perceptible, but not in itself significant; the other difficult to perceive, but definitely vicious. Suppose we notice that all Corsicans have purple eyes. We should not at first dislike them for that; purple eyes in themselves can do no harm. But they make it easy to recognize Corsicans—so whenever we see a man with purple eyes we know that he is certain to be handy with a match box and a pocket knife. You can't tell us that Corsicans aren't different from other people—look at their eyes.

This would be very sound reasoning if there were really an invariable association between knife-wielding and any kind of pigmentation. Nobody has yet proved that there is. However, it is easy to understand why some people think they have.

Let's assume that there actually is a town called Eastport where all the thugs are purple-eyed Corsicans, and where practically all the Corsicans are highly undesirable citizens. It is natural enough for the other inhabitants of this town to react to purple eyes as they would to a rattle on a snake's tail—not dangerous in itself, but a fair warning of poison in the fangs. The association is there, and only a fool would disregard it. But the assumption that the association is one of cause and effect requires investigation. All the evidence we have shows that people—regardless of the color of their eyes—can be badly warped by the pressures of an unfavorable environment. If it happens that the Corsicans in this town live under especially severe pressures, there may be some reason other than their nationality that makes them so unpleasant.

Possibly they came to the town late, when blue-eyed and brown-eyed citizens had already taken up the available land, opened the necessary stores, and so forth. The Corsicans could find jobs only as day laborers, at low pay; and they could find shelter only in run-down houses and cheap shacks. Even these places were expensive, considering the wages they earned, and they crowded together to save rent. It is hard to heat enough water on one stove to bathe three families, and the shacks began to take on a characteristic odor. The rather limited diet that they could afford helped the odor along, and the word began to get around that Corsicans smelled. These Corsicans certainly did.

Those of the children that went to school did not have a very happy time. Naturally, their language was something of a handicap. Moreover, the other children made fun of them—of their accent, of their "stupidity," of their shabby clothes, of their unpleasant odor, and of their purple eyes. The other children would have done most of this by themselves; but they were encouraged by their parents to be even more unkind. They were warned not to sit next to the Corsicans, who were dirty and probably diseased, and not to play with them too much. Pretty soon the Corsicans learned to keep to themselves—whereupon they were accused of being clannish and un-American.

All of the young Corsicans were made to feel inferior. Some of them accepted their status despondently. Others made rather pathetic efforts to improve it. Still others grew bitterly resentful and tried to fight back. They couldn't do much at school where they were out-numbered; but if three or four of them happened to find a brown-eyed boy alone in an alley, they would beat him up. This was not at all sportsmanlike of them, but then they were not very nice people by now. In fact, practically all of the things that the older inhabitants said of them were beginning to be true. It was rather too bad that their parents had chosen to move to Eastport rather than Westport; for in Westport many of the earliest settlers had been Corsicans. Many of their descendants now owned businesses and fine homes and belonged to the country club. Nobody thought there was anything funny about their purple eyes. Curiously enough, they didn't even smell bad. But in Westport you must learn to be wary of the Maltese. They were brought in as construction hands, and it was a great mistake. . . . You can't trust a yellow-eyed man. They use knives. There is even an odor about them.

Revising Prejudiced Generalizations

Naturally, we have to make generalizations based on our experience. A man who has lived all his life in Eastport shouldn't be blamed if he thinks he "knows Corsicans." But if he says "You can't tell me anything about Corsicans" we may suspect that he is afraid to examine new evidence because it might shake his confidence in his own wisdom. If he moved to Westport with a fairly open mind, he might discover that the Maltese there were surprisingly like the Corsicans in Eastport, once you looked past the purple and yellow eyes. He might even come to the conclusion that what made both groups so unpleasant was a combination of slum conditions and social disapproval, rather than national origin. But the chances of his having an open mind might be rather small. So many of us give more weight to one early impression than to a dozen later ones.

I once had a student who cherished a very strong prejudice against Texans, about which we talked at some length. It developed that he had known four loud-mouthed, narrow-minded, arrogant Texans, whom he disliked for what seemed to me very good reasons. He came to consider them as "typical Texans"—a rather small base for a generalization. He then met one or two "non-typical" Texans, and was broad-minded enough to like them as exceptions. Later he met a number of other likable Texans. Since his "non-typical" Texans now outnumbered his "typical" ones, you might think that he would now revise his generalization, but it apparently never occurred to him to do so. It wasn't that he couldn't count, but he thought of "typical" Texans as Texans, and of agreeable Texans simply as people, so that the comparison never suggested itself. Moreover, he had meanwhile met a number of other arrogant and loud-mouthed people; and since they fitted in with his picture of Texans, he thought of them as Texans, too—although he didn't really know whether they came from Texas, Oklahoma, or Missouri. They might even have moved from New Jersey to become he-men. He had never given the matter any thought. When he put all his facts together, he found that they added up something like this: (1) four unpleasant people known to be from Texas; (2) 17 pleasant people known to be from Texas but never counted as Texans; (3) about 30 unpleasant people *assumed* to be from Texas with no real evidence. The student managed to revise his generalization.

This is not an incident invented to prove a point. The conversation actually occurred, and I have no reason to believe that the student was not telling the truth—he looked sheepish enough. Probably most prejudices do not involve as wild a distortion of the evidence as this one; but there is a general tendency: (1) not to count the Corsicans who don't fit the picture; (2) to count everybody who does fit the picture as a Corsican, whether or not he really is one.

It is perhaps worth mentioning that a prejudice may be harmful to the holder as well as to the object. If you move to Westport and insist on hiring a "nice" Maltese girl instead of a "nasty" Corsican as a baby sitter, you may come home early some day and find your little darling smoking marijuana.

Exercises—Chapter 16

Indicate whether you find the definitions and generalizations below *generally acceptable* (mark *A*) or *generally unacceptable* (mark *U*). Also indicate beside each entry what per cent of your friends and acquaintances you think would find the statement acceptable.

1. Water is a liquid.
2. Bullies are cowards.
3. A *major* college is one that encourages big-time football.
4. No man who is willing to work needs to be out of a job more than a week.
5. Hitchhikers are potential robbers and murderers.
6. American women are younger—thanks to advertising.

7. A square is a plane figure with four equal sides and four right angles.

8. A liberal in politics is a person who openly admits that the U.S. Post Office is not a private enterprise.

9. Public schools are those schools open to everybody.

10. A tricycle is a three-wheeled vehicle operated by foot pedals.

11. A bureaucrat is an official of a bureau.

12. Approximately one half of the married persons in the U.S. are women.

13. America is weak because we Americans have lost respect for the flag.

14. A gila monster is a large orange-and-black venomous lizard of the Southwest.

15. The dog is man's best friend.

16. Poor people are happier than rich people.

17. A loyal teacher is any teacher who signs a loyalty oath without protest.

18. *Modern conveniences* means a flush toilet, hot and cold running water, and either a bathtub or a shower.

19. A politician is anyone who has been a candidate for an elective public office.

20. A labor boss is a man who holds a supervisory position in a labor union.

21. Poor people are happy with their way of life and wouldn't want to change it.

22. An atheist is a person who has no religion.

23. Most Americans deplore sex and violence in their TV shows.

24. If a person gets material things without having to work for them, his moral fiber will be destroyed.

25. The Grand Canyon of the Colorado is one of the seven wonders of the modern world.

26. Money can't buy happiness.

27. Arizona is a land of health and sunshine.

28. What the majority prefers in music, art, literature and drama must be the best.

29. Coffee in the system causes sleeplessness.

30. Working wives are poor mothers.

31. The best things in life are free.

32. An appeaser is a person who favors reconciliation of international differences by means short of war.

33. Most people brush their teeth after every meal.

34. Red Cross workers are unpaid volunteers.

35. Hospitals never refuse a patient.

36. There is no proven link between cigarette smoking and lung cancer.

37. Anybody who really wants to work hard can become financially successful.

38. A pedagogue is a teacher of children or youth.

39. A Marxist is any person whose ideas you disagree with strongly.

40. Since teachers punch neither a till nor a time-clock, they live in ivory towers and are therefore out of touch with the world.

Suggestions for Discussion or Theme Writing—Chapter 16

1. Classify yourself in at least twenty different ways (for example, American, male, left-hander), each of which might be important in the way you would act or be treated under certain circumstances. Then classify a close friend and a person you dislike under the same categories (Canadian, female, right-hander). Discuss some of those possible situations where any one classification might be tremendously important— even a life-or-death matter.

2. Write down one of your own generalized attitudes, and then describe the steps you would have to take to test and (if necessary) revise it, according to the suggestions in the chapter. If you can't think of a generalization of your own, try one of these:

   (a) Athletes are poor scholars.

   (b) Red-headed persons are quick-tempered.

   (c) Teenagers are poor drivers.

   (d) Old persons are wise birds.

3. Imagine that you are the only person ever to have visited another planet, one you found composed of and inhabited by things clearly animal, vegetable, and mineral, but otherwise unlike anything you know on Earth. Would your attempts to describe what you saw involve definition? Classification? Generalization? Or all three? Explain.

CHECKING

SENTENCE

STRUCTURE

17

The most obvious errors in grammar are those that involve incorrect word-forms; but the errors that interfere most seriously with communication are those that have to do with the structure of sentences. Unless you can make your clauses fit together and put your modifiers where they belong, your readers are likely to be either completely bewildered or so contemptuous that they won't care what you are trying to say. Many instructors will mark a paper all the way down from A to E if they find a single sentence fragment or run-on sentence. They are also likely to feel very strongly about ambiguous modifiers and shifted constructions. There are some things you are supposed to know for sure.

The basic patterns of English sentences have already been discussed in Part I—complete with enough exercises for most tastes. Unfortunately, many students do such exercises as guessing games, without really trying to master the principles involved. This is natural enough: exercises are usually aimed at a few specific points, and the sentences in them can often be analyzed or corrected almost mechanically. But when it comes to checking over your own sentences the problem is more complicated. Similar mistakes are not conveniently grouped together; you have to check every sentence for everything. The following sections contain suggestions for a reasonably systematic examination. If you find that you are making some kinds of mistakes frequently, you may feel it advisable to go over some of the earlier exercises again, not to win points from your instructor but to help yourself.

Examining a First Draft

Take the first draft of a paper you have not yet turned in. If you don't have one ready, write it before going any further. You can't work in a vacuum, and the only way you can examine your own sentences is to have some of them in front of your eyes, before anybody else has made any suggestions about them.

Now read the first paragraph at a normal speed, and see whether you are *clearly and automatically aware* of the sentences as units. Some people, particularly those who have never paid much attention to punctuation, are not. If you have any trouble grasping the sentences as units, make a second draft of the paper, *indenting each sentence* as if it were a separate paragraph, and showing the real paragraph divisions by extra spacing. This is using a crutch—but a crutch is sometimes a handy thing to use, and some students have found this one extremely helpful.

Now examine your sentences one at a time. Make sure that each one contains a subject-verb combination that makes a definite statement. It it does, and if the whole sentence strikes you as clear and sensible, put a check mark after it. If it doesn't, and you can see what is wrong with it, make the necessary change and then put the check mark. But if you have any doubt that the sentence hangs together effectively, put an X after it. It needs revising. We are not concerned just now with the fine points of style or even of grammar, but simply with the basic structure of your statements. If they are not completely clear to you, you can't expect them to satisfy your reader. When you have your doubtful sentences marked you can study the following sections for possible reasons for trouble.

Are Your Sentences Too Long?

A good many freshmen have failed their English course primarily because their high school teachers had insisted on their writing long sentences before they were ready to do it. As a result, the students strained to throw in extra phrases, and hoped that they would somehow jell—which they often failed to do. This can be very discouraging.

Remember that there is no one best length for a sentence. There are advantages in fitting several ideas into a single unit, but you shouldn't make the unit so complicated that it will be a strain on the reader. Even more important, be sure that you don't make it too complicated for yourself. You must find out how much of a sentence you can control. If the best you can do is a "short, choppy sentence," that is too bad, and you ought to learn to lengthen your span—but not all at once. Don't play too safe, or you'll never learn anything; but keep your sentences short and simple enough so that you can feel reasonably confident that their structure is sound—and notice what you are doing. In this way you can develop both your confidence and your structure, and work up the length and variety of your sentences gradually, without getting lost.

Sentence Fragments

It was explained in Chapter 9 that there is no clear line between some clauseless sentences and sentence fragments. The same group of words may be a sentence in one place and a fragment in another. In fact, the same group of words may be admired in a book by Hemingway and marked wrong in a paper by you, even when it is used in the same kind of situation. This is very sad, but life is like that. However, most instructors will let you use clauseless sentences if they are sure you are doing it consciously. The usual arrangement is for the student to put an asterisk (*) before each intentional clauseless sentence. The instructor may still criticize it, but he won't mark your paper down for it nearly as much as if he thought you were doing it by mistake. You might ask your instructor if he is willing to accept such an arrangement. Meanwhile, we will consider only unintentional sentence fragments.

There are two requirements for a full sentence. It must have both a subject and a verb, and the main statement made must not be overshadowed by a connective such as *although, before, if, since,* or *when.* A simple example is:

John has gone away.

If we omit *John,* or *has gone,* or even *has* there is not enough left to be a full sentence. And if we substitute *having* for *has* the sentence is still defective. Even a compound participle like *having gone* does not make the kind of definite statement that *has gone, goes,* or *went* makes. If you have been getting marked down for fragments, check every sentence and see if the necessary parts are all there.

In a sentence as short as the example, you are not likely to have any trouble if you actually *look at what you have written.* This seems simple enough, but some students find it very hard to do. They focus their eyes on the sentence, but instead of seeing what they *have* written, they remember what they *meant to* write. They look, for instance, at "John gone away" and pronounce with complete sincerity "John *has* gone away." If you have any trouble of this kind, it will help to leave a considerable time between the writing and the checking—you are less likely to be misled by echoes. And when you do check, read aloud if possible, or at least with a complete consciousness of the *sound* of the words. Next, try to find the right pace to get your eyes and ears working together. If you read too fast you may insert words without noticing that they are not actually there. If you read too slowly you will simply repeat the words individually and not notice the ones that are not there, because you will lose all feeling for the sentence. Some students find that beginning with the last sentence and reading up makes it easier to see the words that are actually there.

If a fragmentary sentence is fairly long, it may be a little more difficult to find a missing element, but the approach is the same. Look at the following example:

> Under the influence of Senator Roberson, Chairman of the Armed Services Committee, and for years an advocate of greater air power, voted to increase the appropriation.

Here there is a satisfactory verb, *voted,* and several nouns, any of which could be used as a subject; but none of them is used as a subject here. Unless you can find a clear-cut *subject-verb nucleus,* you have no sentence.

If you can see at a glance that the sentence about Senator Roberson is incomplete, you can easily change it so that it means something definite; there are a number of ways to do this. But if you have to puzzle over it, you had better break it into at least two parts. You might come up with something like this:

> Senator Roberson, Chairman of the Armed Services Committee, has for years been an advocate of greater air power. Under his influence *the Senate* (or *the committee*) voted to increase the appropriation.

Of course you don't want to carry this process too far. Look at the next version:

Senator Roberson is Chairman of the Armed Services Committee. For years he has been an advocate of greater air power. He influenced the Senate. The Senate voted to increase the appropriation.

This (especially the last two sentences) is almost childish. But it is at least better than the long fragment.

In the other type of sentence fragment, there *is* a subject-verb nucleus, but the statement it makes is overshadowed by a connective.

> *When* he was living in New Jersey.
> *Although* they were very tired.
> *Because* Mr. Jones asked me to.

We could make sentences of each of these either by omitting the first word or by adding an independent clause; or we could use two of them as legitimate non-sentences in answers to questions. But as they stand they do not make definite statements, and if you use them as sentences you are almost certain to be marked wrong.

Run-on Sentences

You are expected not only to write complete sentences, but to write them one at a time. Two sentences that could stand separately may often be joined by a connective or a semicolon, but it isn't safe to use anything less. If you do, you will have written a *run-on sentence,* and a good many instructors feel that a single run-on is reason enough for an E on the whole paper. If you use only a comma to join the two independent clauses (which could be separate sentences) your instructor may call the result a *comma fault* or *comma splice.* If you use nothing at all to join them, he may call it a *fused sentence.* The term *run-on sentence* covers both types. Almost anybody can see that a fused sentence is unsatisfactory, but many people do not understand the objection to comma splices. It may therefore be worth while to study the construction rather carefully.

Let's start off with two independent statements:

You wouldn't have much chance of making the team at State. There are too many lettermen coming back.

This is satisfactory. Although there is nothing but position to tie the two statements together, most readers would have no trouble making the connection. You might, however, emphasize the connection by using a semicolon instead of a period:

You wouldn't have much chance of making the team at State; there are too many lettermen coming back.

This punctuation makes it a little clearer that the two ideas are to be taken together as parts of a larger whole. If you want to make the relation even more obvious, you could substitute a connective (with or without a comma) for the semicolon:

You wouldn't have much chance of making the team at State(,) *because* there are too many lettermen coming back.

Since all three versions are equally correct, you may choose whichever you happen to prefer. In this particular example it certainly makes little difference. But notice the following points:

1. A connective indicates the relation between the two ideas most definitely. It is therefore a trifle easier for the reader, and probably a little more natural for most writers.

2. A semicolon indicates that the two ideas should be considered together, but leaves the reader to find the exact connection. It is thus half visual aid and half mild challenge. This may sound a little complicated, especially if you feel that you are never either aided or challenged by a semicolon. If so, you may be relieved to know that semicolons are becoming comparatively rare except in rather academic writing. A sentence consisting of two clauses separated by a semicolon may always be repunctuated as two separate sentences.

3. A period is the most distinct indication of separation. It is therefore the normal way of separating two independent clauses unless you want to indicate that they are closely related.

It is possible that you may be rude enough to say that you don't see what's wrong with putting just a comma between the two clauses and writing it this way:

You wouldn't have much chance of making the team at State, there are too many lettermen coming back.

A really satisfactory answer to this objection is not easy to make. The sentence is as clear with a comma as with a semicolon, and some capable writers would punctuate it that way. But most English instructors would mark it wrong, and they would have a sound reason, which we can best show by making the sentence a little longer:

In spite of your size, speed, and ferocious determination, you wouldn't have much chance of making the team, according to Davis in the *Morning Post,* there are too many lettermen coming back.

In this version there are commas in both the clauses, and we need something stronger than a comma to set the clauses apart and show where the principal break should be. We might put a semicolon either after *team* or after *Post,* depending on what we wanted "according to Davis in the *Morning Post*" to modify (did he say that you couldn't make the team, or that many lettermen were returning?).

Since a comma splice is often ambiguous, most instructors feel that it should never be used—or at least that it should be used only by experts under special circumstances. The following examples might pass without criticism:

> He took one side, she took the other.
> He was cold, he was tired, he was hungry.

The sentences are short, they don't need connectives, and semicolons would only slow them up. However, using comma splices even in such sentences as these is rather like swinging on a three-and-nothing count —you'd better get a sign from the coach before you try it.

If you are not yet convinced, consider the two following sentences:

> When he was in New York last year he stayed with his brother.
> He was in the east last year he stayed with his brother.

The first contains only one independent statement, "he stayed with his brother." The subordinate statement "When he was in New York last year" is obviously a mere qualifying remark that is closely related to the main statement. Since the nature of the relation is shown by the word *when,* there is no need for a connective between the two clauses. And since the relation is close, there is no need for strong punctuation between the clauses. You could put a comma after *year* if you felt that a pause was appropriate, or you could leave it out; but a period or a semicolon would be worse than useless.

The second sentence, however, contains two independent statements. Since that is enough for two sentences, you should either punctuate it as two sentences or show that the two statements are so closely related that they can reasonably be considered as parts of a larger whole. One way to do this would be to insert a connective. Another way would be to use a semicolon, which would indicate that the two statements are separate, but are to be considered together.

Suppose, for instance, that somebody has asked why "he" seemed to be annoyed with his family. You might write (with that dry wit that makes you so popular) "He was in New York last year; he stayed with his brother." If you don't have that dry wit, or fear that your reader won't appreciate it, maybe you'd better be more explicit.

With this comparison in mind, you might consider the following statements:

1. The relation between two independent clauses is not usually as close or as obvious as the relation between an independent and a subordinate clause.

2. The relation between two independent clauses should therefore be either explained by a connective or suggested by a semicolon. A comma is usually not enough.

3. Since the relation between an independent and a subordinate clause is close, there is often no need for any punctuation between them. If you would naturally pause between the two, insert a comma.

Shifted Constructions

Another type of serious structural error is the *shifted construction* —a sentence started in one way and finished in another. For instance:

He had spent his vacations for nearly twenty years along the trout streams of the eastern slope of the Rockies were his favorite fishing waters.

We could improve this attempt at a sentence by inserting a comma and a *which* after *Rockies;* but it would probably be inaccurate to say that the writer forgot to put these items in. More probably he started out with the intention of stopping the sentence at *Rockies;* but by the time he had written that much, he had forgotten that he had written *streams* as part of a modifying phrase, "along . . . the trout streams . . ." He therefore went on as if *streams* were the subject. The result is a fusing of two possible sentences:

He had spent his vacations for nearly twenty years along *the trout streams of the eastern slope of the Rockies* were his favorite fishing waters.

The italicized part could be the end of one of the sentences or the beginning of the other; but the writer should have made up his mind which sentence he was writing. Here are some other examples:

He came here because of *the reputation of the Law School* was what attracted him.

She is a great admirer of *Henry Fonda, Laurence Olivier, and Spencer Tracy* are among her favorite actors.

Faulty Parallelism

A special type of shift is illustrated in the following sentence:

I thought I would go up to Roosevelt Lake and trying to get some bass.

When the writer started on this one, he had two reasonable possibilities:

1. I thought I would   go
                        try

2. I thought of   going
                        trying

Both of these are what are called *parallel constructions,* as the diagrams indicate. They are obviously economical and effective, since they eliminate useless repetition. Without them we would have to say "I thought of going and I thought of trying," or "I thought I would go and I thought I would try." But they have to be consistent to be effective. In the sentence under consideration, the writer apparently forgot which way he had chosen to start, and finished the other way. In this particular sentence, the intention of the writer is still clear, but the effect is definitely clumsy. Here are some additional examples.

It's really easier to do the work yourself than if you have to supervise somebody else.

They called just when the phone was ringing and somebody at the back door.

It is possible to be too particular about parallel structure, but the following principle is a good one to keep in mind:

Whenever a statement *branches into parts,* keep the parts parallel. Balance a clause by a clause, a phrase by a phrase, a participle by a participle, an infinitive by an infinitive, and so forth. If you do this, your reader can follow your ideas readily. If you don't, he may have to go back over your sentence and guess about the connections you intended. Even if he guesses right, he won't admire the construction.

There are so many possible ways of shifting constructions that it would be confusing rather than helpful to try to list them all. But there is one great underlying commandment that is worth remembering: *Make sure that you have finished your sentence the same way you started it.*

Ambiguous Modifiers

If a reader doesn't associate your modifiers with the words you meant them to modify, the result may be anything from a laugh at your expense to complete misunderstanding. The main thing to bear in mind is that a reader cannot hear the writer's intonation pattern, which often is enough to show a listener which words go with which. A writer must therefore be careful to use relative position and punctuation as helpfully as possible. The general theory of effective modification has been discussed in Chapter 7. Two particularly troublesome errors are *dangling* and *squinting modifiers,* discussed under those headings in the INDEX TO USAGE.

Exercises—Chapter 17

Mark *OK* those sentences below which you think are satisfactory. Mark the others *F* (fragment), *R* (run-on), *S* (shifted constructions), *P* (faulty parallelism), *A* (ambiguous modifier), and *O* (other—for any that don't seem to fit any of the categories). Correct by punctuation or rewriting, all but the ones marked *OK.*

1. The forward shot a basket would mean a win.
2. Looking south the view is wonderful it is on the edge of a hill.
3. One could easily write a book about Odysseus, Homer proved that.
4. I can proudly say each incident has been one enlightening experience after another.
5. Scarcely ever knowing which way she went, or caring.
6. I found I knew no one, my training in school to be of little help, and the job simple.
7. For years I have been playing in a dance band and enjoyed every minute of it.
8. While she sits around, I did the washing.
9. When he happens to stumble across the huge tracks, a thrill runs up and down your spine and the hunter gets a desire to get this deer.
10. A job that isn't dirty or one that anyone can do.
11. He likes fishing and hunting are two of his favorite sports.
12. That's all right his father has plenty of money to pay for the party.
13. I put the rifle to my shoulder and fired, much to my surprise the wildcat tumbled to the ground.

14. The policeman never turned around because traffic was too heavy which saved me from getting a ticket.

15. The hall was narrow and low-ceilinged, but it was large enough not to bump each other going down it.

16. I washed my hands and face in the Colorado River, riding to the bottom on mule-back.

17. Some reasons for low grades in college might be taking part in athletics, a wife or husband, hours spent on a job or some people worry too much.

18. Blood counts were easy, having done them many times in training.

19. I had to run naturally after all that hurrying the bus was late.

20. I usually discourage overgeneralization, yet my students continue to try to explain the universe between one capital letter and the ensuing period.

21. I believe knowledge is a wonderful thing to have to make life richer by understanding things better.

22. Mary enrolled for painting, harmony, music appreciation, and to study art history.

23. In answer to your letter I have bought a farm with 400 laying hens.

24. My sister was pretty, intelligent, generous, and every characteristic of a likable person.

25. Howard Tymes, the big man at all the parties and dances, and the man who ran for congress that year the Little Red flooded out the business district.

Suggestions for Discussion or Theme Writing—Chapter 17

1. Write down the opening sentence of five novels. (Try for a range of times and talents, Hemingway, Faulkner, James, Melville, and Wolfe, for instance.) It seems reasonable to assume that each of these sentences was allowed to stand only after considerable deliberation and, perhaps, revision. Discuss the sentence structure of the five. Which ones do you find effective? Which not? Explain.

2. As quickly as you can move pen over paper, write a hundred words or so on the first subject that comes to your mind. Then go back and rate yourself on clarity of thought, as well as the length, variety, and structure of the sentences. Rewrite any sentence whose structure or clarity may be questioned.

THE USES
AND LIMITATIONS
OF LOGIC

18

The kind of reasoning used in the formation of generalizations, discussed in Chapter 16, is called *inductive*. Properly used, it begins with careful observations of physical phenomena and works up to a systematic explanation of them. This explanation is called a hypothesis. It may be anything from a bare guess to a firm and well tested belief, but it is always subject to reexamination and possible revision when new evidence comes in. For example, many of the hypotheses of Isaac Newton, which for centuries seemed to be absolutely solid, have had to be modified in the light of Einstein's theory of relativity. Newton's system has not been destroyed, it has been refined. For most purposes it still works well enough, but when we are dealing with the great distances found in outer space or the tiny distances found within the atom we find that Einstein's system works better. And of course the time may come when we know enough to modify that.

The inductive method is the one primarily used in the experimental approach to knowledge, as we saw in the section on experimental truth. The mathematical or logical approach begins from the other end. Whether logic is a branch of mathematics or mathematics is a branch of logic is a question I do not feel competent to settle. At any rate, both mathematicians and logicians proceed by *deductive reasoning*. That is, they begin with general statements assumed to be true and work down from these to more particular statements which must be true if the general ones are.

It is silly to argue about which of these methods is better. They are appropriate for different purposes. A scientist usually forms his hypotheses by a combination of induction and hunches, and he may test them the same way (if he doesn't have any hunches, he may be a good technician, but he'll never get very far except by pure luck).

But once he is satisfied with a hypothesis he will say, "All right, let's assume this is true. Now what follows?" It is now time for a stage of deductive reasoning, to open new possibilities. Of course his conclusions must again be checked by observation, and then—and so forth, and so forth. Science moves forward by steps, and it takes two legs to walk.

We have already looked at two examples of inductive reasoning— the investigation of the boiling point of water under different conditions (pages 170-172) and the generalization about apples (page 194). On this subject I will say no more, simply because I can think of nothing else useful to say. Anybody can reason inductively up to a point; but the ability to do it well seems to depend rather on mental make-up than on a special method. *Deductive reasoning,* on the other hand, follows a method that can be usefully explained. It is often called *formal logic,* or simply *logic,* the term which will be used for the rest of this chapter.

Logic may be defined roughly as a systematic method of *comparing statements* in such a way that they will produce reliable additional statements. Suppose, for instance, that somebody asks you whether a German-born friend of yours has become a naturalized citizen of the United States. Since you have never heard the matter discussed, you do not immediately know; but you decide to see whether anything you do know will lead you to the correct answer. Is there anything about him that is *characteristic* of either citizens or non-citizens? Among other things, you know that he is employed as an engineer in the State Highway Department, and you remember that in your state only citizens are eligible to hold such jobs. You therefore conclude that he *must be* a citizen. Two bits of information which apparently had nothing to do with each other when you picked them up have been made to produce a third bit of information.

Everybody of even moderate intelligence compares statements in some such way as this; but a good many people do not know how to *test the connections* to see whether the results they get are reliable. Suppose we compare two attempts to prove the same thing:

    1. All Communists read Marx.
       Jones reads Marx.
         Therefore Jones is a Communist.
    2. Only Communists read Marx.
       Jones reads Marx.
         Therefore Jones is a Communist.

Perhaps you see at a glance that the first argument proves nothing at all, while the second is quite sound. However, if you read the newspapers you must realize that millions of people are actually convinced by arguments like the first, so it may be just as well to study the structure of the two arguments. The easiest way to do this is to change the form of the statements so that they can be readily diagramed, and then see what the diagrams indicate.

1. All Communists are readers of Marx.

This can be diagramed as follows, with the circle marked C standing for Communists, and the circle marked R standing for readers of Marx:

Jones is a reader of Marx.

If we want to add the information in this statement to the diagram we already have, we must put a little circle J for Jones somewhere within the circle marked R for readers. But there is nothing to tell us *where* in the circle it goes—whether it should be within or without the circle marked C for Communists.

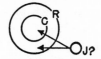

We therefore have no basis for deciding whether Jones is a Communist or not.

2. Only Communists are readers of Marx.
This has to be diagramed with the circles in a different relation:

Jones is a reader of Marx.

If we add the information in this statement to the diagram we have just drawn, we must put the little circle for Jones in the medium-sized circle marked R; and if we do this we *inevitably* put it also within the larger circle marked C.

We are therefore justified in drawing the conclusion that Jones is a Communist. If the first two statements are true, the conclusion *must* be true.

Syllogisms

The kind of argument we have been considering is called a *syllogism*. It is the principal device of traditional logic, and very useful if you know how to handle it. There are various types of syllogisms, and it is possible to discuss them at great length and in highly technical terms. But the basic principles are simple, and by using our three circles we can get at these principles much more rapidly and directly than we could with words alone.

A syllogism consists of two statements *assumed to be true,* from which a third statement follows inevitably *if* the first two are true. The first two statements are usually called the *premises,* and the third the *conclusion.* Thus if we say (1) that all college students are intelligent and (2) that Dick is a college student, we can draw the conclusion that Dick is intelligent. Of course if the statements are not true, the conclusion may not be true either; but it is *logically sound.*

The First Statement

The first statement must show the relation between *two classes.* Typical statements of this kind are:

> All Frenchmen are Europeans.
> Some Irishmen are policemen.
> No Bolivians are Europeans.

Some Irishmen are not policemen.
Casey is an Irishman.
Casey is not a policeman.
The Spartans were Greeks.

Notice three things about these statements: (1) we may talk of all or part of a class; (2) an individual (Casey) is considered a class by himself; (3) the verb in the statement is always some form of the verb *to be*.

If you have a statement like "John *eats* pie," you have to change it to "John *is* a pie eater" before you can use it in a syllogism. It is then easy to show the relation between the two classes by drawing two circles. There are only a limited number of possible relations. The most obvious are these three:

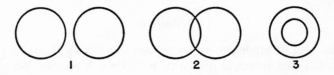

The first of these is simple, reliable, and reversible. It indicates definitely that the two classes do not coincide at all. If the two circles stand for Bolivians and Europeans, this diagram shows not only that no Bolivians are Europeans, but that no Europeans are Bolivians.

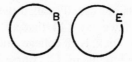

The second is also reversible, but it is not as simple as the first. Suppose we use it to diagram the statement that some Irishmen are policemen.

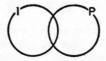

Does it also indicate that some policemen are Irishmen? A glance shows that it does. Since the two classes overlap, some members of each must also be in the other. But this diagram fails to give us any reliable information about the parts of the two circles that do *not* overlap. If we want to be really careful, we had better draw it this way:

The solid parts of the two circles indicate our definite information; the dotted parts indicate mere possibilities. Thus the diagram indicates that certainly some *and possibly all* Irishmen are policemen; and that certainly some *and possibly all* policemen are Irishmen. We cannot be sure *from our premise* that either circle actually extends beyond the overlap. Of course we may know as a matter of general information that there are Irishmen who are not policemen and policemen that are not Irishmen; but neither fact follows logically from the statement that some Irishmen are policemen.

We might also draw overlapping circles to indicate that some Irishmen are *not* policemen. To do this accurately we would need a diagram like this:

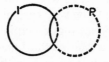

The area within the solid curves indicates the Irishmen who are not policemen. But we cannot tell either whether there are Irishmen who are policemen (in the overlapping area) or policemen who are not Irishmen. In other words, a really accurate diagram might show the circles overlapping, separate, or with the P inside the I. But on the basis of our statement, the only diagram we can draw is one that shows that *at least some* Irishmen are not included in the class of policemen.

The third diagram also has to be considered with care. Suppose we use it to indicate that all Frenchmen are Europeans:

This seems to indicate that there are some Europeans who are *not* Frenchmen. This is true enough, but it is not contained in the statement which our diagram is supposed to illustrate. Therefore we might draw a more careful diagram this way:

This shows that the inner circle *cannot* extend beyond the outer circle; but, as the arrows indicate, it may completely fill the larger one.

For most ordinary purposes we do not have to be as careful as all this; we can draw our circles with solid lines and without arrows. But we should remember to be very careful not to make any assumptions from the parts of circles that could be drawn differently.

There is another thing about the third diagram that deserves special emphasis, because failure to realize it is the most common cause of faulty logic. It can represent either of the following statements.

> *All* Frenchmen are Europeans.
> *Only* Europeans are Frenchmen.

But it does not imply the statement that all Europeans are Frenchmen or that only Frenchmen are Europeans. Remember: (1) the class described by *all* must be represented by the *smaller* circle; (2) the class described by *only* must be represented by the *larger* circle.

The Second Statement

The second statement in a syllogism must show the relation between *one* of the classes in the first statement and a *third* class. The information contained in this statement may then be added to the diagram representing the first statement. We gave examples of this in the two syllogisms, one valid and one invalid, that attempted to show that Jones was a Communist. Other examples will be found in the next paragraph.

The Conclusion

If the diagram representing the first two statements now shows definitely the relation between the third class and the class *not* mentioned in the second statement, a valid conclusion may be drawn. Otherwise the syllogism proves nothing at all.

1. All Norwegians are blonds.
   John is a blond.

   No conclusion possible.

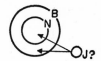

2. All blonds are Norwegians.
   John is a blond.

   Conclusion: John is a Norwegian.

3. No marines are cowards.
   Dave is a marine.

Conclusion: Dave is not a coward.

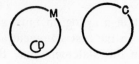

4. Some of his friends are sailors.
   All of his friends are clever people.

   Conclusion: Some sailors are
   clever people.

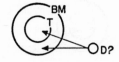

5. Only big men are tackles.
   Dick is a big man.

   No conclusion possible.

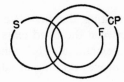

Of course you may be quite capable of testing a syllogism for validity without drawing a picture of it; but if you have to check one it is much easier to do it with the three circles than by learning a large number of rules about *universal negatives, particular affirmatives,* the *laws of conversion,* and the *fallacy of unwarranted distribution.* All you have to do is to draw the first two circles in such a way as to indicate the information contained in the first statement, add the information contained in the second statement, and see whether the combined diagram proves anything or not.

There is, of course, a good deal more to logic than the study of syllogisms; and I hope I have not given the impression that the whole subject can be condensed into one neat little capsule for handy absorption. But the basic principles of the logical method are illustrated in the material we have examined, and the importance of this method should be obvious. A man who thinks illogically is like one who pays no attention to the difference between the signs for multiplication and division, or addition and subtraction. When he attempts to work out a problem for himself he is completely unreliable. And when he receives information he is likely to be at the mercy of the man who hands it out.

Truth and Validity

If you learn the method shown in the preceding pages you can avoid *illogical conclusions,* because you will have found out a reliable way of tracing the connections between *statements assumed to be true.* But you must resist the temptation to believe that when a conclusion is logically sound or "valid" it is inevitably true. The conclusion is certainly true *only* if the basic statements are certainly true. And this is *never* possible when the statements deal with physical things. This does not mean that logic is useless in dealing with physical things, but only that it must be used with appropriate caution.

A True Syllogism

Examine the following syllogism:

> All squares are rectangles.
> ABCD is a square.
>
> Therefore ABCD is a rectangle.

This is not only a sound syllogism but a perfectly true one, because both squares and rectangles are *pure abstractions created by definition,* and the definition of a rectangle includes the definition of a square. All squares have the same properties *by definition.* It is therefore unnecessary to examine every square that has been conceived or that may be conceived in the future to see if its sides and angles are equal; if they are not equal, it is not a square. The same is true of "all rectangles." Remember, *no square has ever been drawn.* The *figure* ABCD that you see on a blackboard or in a book is not a square, but merely the representation of a square. If you should measure it with very accurate instruments and find that two of the angles were 89 degrees and the other two 91 degrees, you would not have found an exceptional square that violated the rule. You would merely have found a slightly inaccurate *representation* of a square, which is nothing to get excited about.

An Approximately True Syllogism

On the other hand, let us consider the following syllogism:

> All Englishmen are tea-drinkers.
> Derek is an Englishman.
>
> Therefore Derek is a tea-drinker.

This follows the same form as the syllogism about squares and rectangles, and is equally sound from a logical point of view. We may therefore say that *if* the first two statements are true, the conclusion is equally true. But if we examine the argument closely we notice an important difference. Englishmen are *not* created by definition, but by cohabitation. We cannot, therefore, be certain in advance that they are all alike. We are not justified in making a statement about all Englishmen until we have examined them all. If Derek is an Englishman, we have to find out that he is a tea-drinker before we are justified in making the statement that all Englishmen are tea-drinkers. In other words, we have to know that he is a tea-drinker before we can prove that he is a tea-drinker. Our logic does not seem to be getting us very far.

This does not mean that logic is useless when applied to physical things, but only that it never produces hundred per cent certainties in this field as it does when applied to mathematical abstractions. With physical things, logic can give us only probabilities and approximations—but so can measurements. Let us rephrase our syllogism about Derek in such a way as to make it useful.

> A very high proportion of Englishmen are known to be tea-drinkers.
> It is very nearly certain that Derek is an Englishman.
>
> Therefore it is extremely probable that Derek is a tea-drinker.

If we are expecting to have Derek as a guest, this more elastic syllogism will be useful. In the first place it suggests that we have some tea on hand when Derek comes. It also suggests that we ask him about his taste before we start forcing tea down his possibly unwilling throat. If it turns out that he is an unusual Englishman, we are spared a shock—and maybe we can get a refund on the unopened tea.

The Limitations of Logic

The reason that logic cannot be used rigidly with physical things may be explained quite simply. In a class of abstractions *created* by definition, all members are exactly alike, and some characteristics are *inevitably* associated with others. If you prove that something is a circle, you know that the relation of its diameter to its circumference is exactly *pi,* because that's the way circles are. But when we turn to the physical world we find:

1. That the members of a class are never exactly alike. Even if the class has only one member, that one is constantly changing.
2. That the association of characteristics is merely a matter of probability.

Consequently, when a man says "All Syrians (or women or college professors or Fords) are alike," he is not telling the truth, though he may be perfectly sincere. And when he says "Anybody that would do that would steal sheep," he is treating a probability (possibly a pretty good one) as if it were a fact.

There are two obvious temptations to say (and think) things like these. First, it is flattering to the ego to pretend that we know "all about" something. Second, it saves a lot of trouble. If you "know" in advance that all Mexicans are lazy, all Scotsmen stingy, and all politicians dishonest, you are spared the task of finding out about them one by one. Before yielding to these temptations, however, it might be a good idea to consider whether you can afford to yield to them.

It is often said that many fanatics and certain types of lunatics are among the most logical people in the world. You can't find fault with their chains of reasoning, and even their facts are often approximately right. But because they treat approximations and probabilities as absolute certainties, their conclusions are wildly wrong.

The Communist Theory

Perhaps the most terrifying example of logic run wild is the development and spread of communistic theories. Marx's theories are collectively known as dialectical materialism. *Dialectical* is another word for logical, and *materialism* indicates that physical things are to be taken as the basis of all thinking. In other words, Marx believed: (1) that logic can be applied directly and exactly to physical things; (2) that by *defining* such things as capitalists and proletarians he somehow exerted such control over them as to make them all exactly, or at least "essentially" alike. He would probably have denied this, but it is implicit in his whole theory. He states very definitely that if people own property and employ labor they *must* act in certain ways, and their actions will *inevitably* bring about certain results. Moreover, he asserts that the interests of capitalists and proletarians are inevitably opposed.

Now, whatever else he was, Marx was a well-educated and highly intelligent man. His logic is sound throughout. If you take his assumptions as true, you simply cannot avoid his conclusions. And the fact that a great many people do take his assumptions as absolutely true is causing an enormous amount of trouble in the world today.

The basic fallacy of dialectical materialism is not that the assumptions—the things stated to be true—did not happen to be true. It is that they could not *possibly* have been true in a world composed of evermoving and changing arrangements of particles. Marx examined a certain number of specimens which he classified as capitalists and proletarians, and observed their activities. Up to this point he was acting like a respectable scientist. But then he lost his scientific modesty. He did not say:

This is the way these specimens have been observed to act. We may reasonably expect similar specimens under similar conditions to act in similar ways in the future. But of course if conditions change or new evidence is discovered we shall have to revise our tentative conclusions.

Instead he said in effect:

I have examined these specimens and found out all about them. They are exactly alike in all significant characteristics, and all their successors will be exactly like them. Any minor differences we may disregard as nonessential. No further observations are necessary, because this is the permanent truth. And if further observations seem to contradict my results, or changed conditions seem to modify the actions of later specimens slightly, we must explain the differences away. For instance, if you find a capitalist who does not seem to act like my capitalists, it is merely because he is clever in concealing his nature.

In other words, Marx thought that a definition of a capitalist, like a definition of a circle, could be effectively made to cover unobserved and future specimens. Instead of realizing that definitions of physical things are merely general statements based on past observations, he treated them exactly like° definitions of mathematical abstractions. This was not an isolated mistake by Karl Marx; it was a typical example of an attitude which had been widely accepted among educated people from Aristotle's time to his own, *but which has now been demonstrated to be completely unsound.* Of course this attitude has by no means disappeared. We are still plagued with plenty of learned people who think that by "defining their terms" they can somehow keep the changing universe in tidy order. But at least we have discovered how to disprove their arguments.

As we have already said, Marx himself was both well-educated and intelligent. If he had lived a century later and been exposed to modern knowledge of the physical universe, his theories might have taken a very different form. But today he has millions of followers who accept his theories quite uncritically as a matter of faith. They are led by thousands who have been trained to follow the kind of logical argument he used—and used extremely well—but who have not been trained to recognize the *limitations of logic.*

The fact is that the whole economic set-up of the twentieth century, especially in America, is quite different from the set-up in nineteenth-century England that Marx observed. His capitalists and proletarians were not quite so uniform as he thought they were, but at least they were on the whole fairly distinct groups, with interests that were often sharply opposed. Our economic classes are about as scrambled as our national blood lines. The workers at the Acme Knitting Mills may be sharply opposed to the owners in a given dispute, but they can hardly be opposed to all capitalists. Between their bank accounts and their insurance policies and a few stocks and bonds salted away here and there, almost all of them are to some extent capitalists themselves. Marx simply hadn't figured on this (how could he—it hardly occurred in his time), and Marx's followers are very much annoyed about the whole situation. They have spent years and years building a bridge across a raging torrent, preparing to lead their people over it and into the promised land. But they haven't noticed that the water has gone down and that people from both sides have been wading across it, fraternizing, intermarrying, and even settling down on islands that have appeared in the middle. It is all very confusing.

Logic—Handle with Care

It is easy for most of us to accept the statement that the rigid application of Marxist logic to economic facts is a delusion, because we are opposed to Communism anyhow, and will believe almost anything that shows it up. But Communists do not have a monopoly on this type of confusion. There are plenty of capitalists, soldiers, educators, and all sorts of other people who are perfectly certain that anything that was "logically proved" some generations ago must still be true today, no matter how much things have changed in the meantime.

There are perhaps even more people who take statements that are actually statistical summaries, only roughly true, and treat them as if they were absolutely reliable. They argue, for instance, that since fresh air is healthy, everybody should sleep with a window open. Their logic is beyond criticism, and perhaps their first premise is ninety per cent accurate; but their conclusion is sometimes unfortunate for children with sinus trouble or hay fever. You can undoubtedly find other examples.

Using sound logic on any practical problem is like using sound mathematics on an engineering problem—if you don't do it, you may go hopelessly astray. But when a good engineer has made his exact calculations, he always allows a reasonable margin of safety, because he realizes two things. There *may* be a factor or so he has not allowed for; and a part that *should* stand a thousand pounds of strain *may* break at five hundred. When we are dealing with the physical universe we never know *all* about anything. And no matter how carefully we define our classes, we can't make their members exactly alike.

Imitation Logic

It is possible to make honest mistakes in our reasoning, just as it is possible to make honest mistakes in arithmetic. But it is also possible to short-change people logically. In fact it is a good deal more than possible—it is a very widespread habit indeed, and it gets far more toleration than it deserves. Pillars of society who wouldn't think of sneaking a quarter out of the change for a ten dollar bill seem to feel no guilt at all as they talk their customers out of millions—of dollars or votes or whatever it is that they happen to need. The general attitude seems to be that outright and provable lies are bad, but that tricking people into reaching the wrong conclusions is quite legitimate.

Consider advertisements, for instance. Some of them give real evidence in favor of their products. When you read that a big trucking company has saved twenty per cent on their tire bills by switching to Rollright Tires, you may well be looking at a sound argument. If you have trucks of your own you'll want to check further before buying. Maybe they switched from an off brand that's only half as good as some of the others, in which case a twenty per cent improvement isn't enough. Maybe there are other concealed tricks. But when a company uses advertisements of this sort, which invite factual checking, and which would boomerang if the facts weren't accurate, there is a pretty good chance that the facts will stand up.

A second kind of advertisement doesn't bother with evidence at all, but simply tries to get you to react without thinking. If you have heard about Sticko Gum often enough and long enough, you may come to feel (not think) that Sticko *means* gum, and it would be rather far-fetched to ask for any other kind. The gum may or may not be good, but there's no use arguing with this kind of advertising, because there is nothing to argue about.

It is a third kind of advertising with which we are concerned—a kind that pretends to appeal to your reasoning powers, but actually tries to short-circuit them. There are various subtypes, but they all have one thing in common: they try to tempt you to accept some sort of loose association as a substitute for an accurate connection. Are you worried about your waistline, your skin tone, or your gas mileage? Okay, do something about them—but is there any real reason to think that the product that brought them to your attention is the best cure? The people in the picture certainly look happy with their Butterfly motorboat. But (even if they are not paid for doing so) are there enough of them to make a convincing sample? The Purple Streak may well be the only car that has all seven of those features—but are they the most important features? And do you really know for sure that twisty-bar suspension is any better than curly-spring?

Of course advertisers aren't the only ones that try to make you accept their arguments rather than examine them. Politicians, charitable organizations, governments, even religious bodies, may do the same. The motives are often excellent, and there are times when it may pay you to yield without a struggle. But when you act emotionally you might as well know what you're doing, and not pretend that you are guided by pure reason.

There have been various analyses of the kinds of tricks used to make you think you're thinking. Twenty-odd years ago the Institute for Propaganda Analysis gave a good deal of publicity to "the seven" common propaganda devices.

1. The Name Calling Device.
2. The Glittering Generalities Device.
3. The Transfer Device.
4. The Testimonial Device.
5. The Plain Folks Device.
6. The Card Stacking Device.
7. The Band Wagon Device.

It became a popular classroom game, complete with objective tests and statistical analyses, to classify all suspicious statements under these headings.

We are not going to try to play the whole game here because it has a tendency to shift the emphasis from "Is this statement sound?" to "What shall we call this unsound statement?" and often winds up in hairsplitting arguments. But we must take time for a few words about one of them, because The Testimonial Device seems to have become a national disease.

Under appropriate circumstances testimony is perfectly reasonable grounds for belief. We don't have time to study everything, and the obvious way to get a sound opinion on a subject about which we don't know much is to ask a man who does. But if the answer is important to us, we ought to make sure of at least three things:

1. That the man's expert knowledge really covers the question. Maybe a low earned-run average qualifies a man to judge razor blades, but the connection seems remote.

2. That the opinion is really unbiased. The fact that endorsements have a cash value, and that "celebrities" often switch, for a consideration, from one brand to another, is well known—but it doesn't seem to interfere with advertising effectiveness.

3. That most other experts would accept his opinion. This doesn't mean that the majority of experts is always right. But if you believe a man *against* most other experts, you shouldn't do it simply on the grounds that he *is* an expert. You ought to understand his reasoning, or be in love with him, or have some other sound grounds.

This third point deserves special attention. It is amazing how many people will seriously argue that spiritualism, for instance, simply must be true because three well-known scientists have said that they believed in it. "And if men like that, with trained minds and international reputations, believe in it there simply *must* be something in it." The fact that hundreds of equally well-known scientists have said they don't believe in it is left out of account.

Exercises—Chapter 18

I. Answer each of the following questions briefly and simply.

1. Which kind of reasoning is the one primarily used in the experimental approach to knowledge?
2. How does the chapter define *logic?*
3. How many statements are involved in a syllogism?
4. What must the first statement of a syllogism show?
5. What circumstances must prevail before a *valid* syllogism can also be assumed a *true* one?
6. What two qualifying considerations must be applied to logical arguments about *physical* things?
7. Are the members of a class of physical things ever exactly alike? Explain briefly.
8. What degree of stability did Karl Marx apparently see in such classifications as *capitalists, proletarians,* and so forth?
9. When testing validity with the circle-drawing method, what part of the syllogism is illustrated by the first *two* circles?
10. When testing validity with the circles, what is indicated when the final circle can readily fall in *two* different places?

II. Construct a syllogism from each of the arguments below, and mark it *V* (valid) or *I* (invalid). If you have to add an implied premise, indicate it by enclosing it in parentheses. Indicate beside every *valid* syllogism whether or not you think the conclusion is also generally true.

1. As soon as Jim started bragging I knew he was from Texas.
2. You can't believe anything Leroy tells you. Doesn't he always go fishing on his days off?
3. You won't have any trouble selling door-to-door in this building; these are all *bachelor* apartments.
4. Of course she owns a cat. Didn't I see her with four cans of cat food in her shopping cart last week?
5. Premier Khrushchev is not a Blue Cross member, but 57 million freedom-loving Americans are.
6. Certainly this is the better pen. It's priced at $2.95, and the other is a 98-center marked down to $.69.
7. It's apparent Archibald is a virile man. Note the anchor tattooed on his hand.
8. Brand X candy is good for you because it contains no sugar.
9. Brand X soap is obviously pure because it floats in water.
10. It's plain that Jones hasn't violated the law. Jones is very successful, financially, and no lawbreaker could achieve financial success.
11. The Slaughterhouse Gang is honest; that's sure. Isn't its worst enemy the Scarface Mob that everybody knows is full of thugs?
12. Could the defendant be guilty of felony as charged? Of course not; what you see before you is a mother of three children.
13. Since Sam Smith, height 5'5", was chosen to the All-American team, it follows that small men are just as good as big men in basketball.
14. *Sweet Sally Brown* was the best novel of that year, as anyone knows. Can you name a single book that outsold it?
15. Brand X detergent cannot be surpassed for washing mustache cups, since it is the *only* detergent that is made exclusively for that purpose.

Suggestions for Discussion or Theme Writing—Chapter 18

1. Differentiate between *inductive* and *deductive* reasoning, supplying sufficient examples of each to make the distinction clear.
2. Discuss the difference between truth and validity in syllogisms. When do they occur together? What limits *truth* in syllogisms whose statements deal with *physical* things?

PARAGRAPH

DEVELOPMENT

19

In Chapter 15 we discussed paragraphs as divisions of a larger unit. In this chapter we will examine them as combinations of smaller units —sentences. Of course single sentences, or even single words, may be used as paragraphs; but since these offer no problems of combination, we need not consider them here.

The first requirement of a good paragraph is that it should consist of a group of *related* sentences, and that the relations should be clear to the reader as well as the writer. To take a very simple example, you might write one sentence describing a man's face, another describing his build, and a third describing his clothes. Since each of these deals with his appearance, it would be easy and natural to put them into a single paragraph. If you added a fourth sentence saying that he was scared, it might seem decidedly out of place. But if you said that he *looked* scared, it would be connected with the rest of the paragraph in a way that any reader could understand.

The problem is not always as simple as this. Look at the following paragraph:

Forrester's technical preparation for the job is excellent. He has a B.S. in electrical engineering from M.I.T. and an M.S. in physics from Caltech. His military service was spent largely in the Signal Corps laboratories at Fort Monmouth, but he also spent some time as assistant personnel officer of his battalion, and later as acting company commander—two assignments that indicate both a recognizable talent for handling men and experience in doing it. After his release from the service he spent three years in the Special Tubes Research division of Northern Electric Company, where he received three promotions and two special bonuses for original contributions.

It seems natural enough to put all his Signal Corps assignments together, but the last two have nothing to do with his technical preparation. They may be just as important as the others, and they may be closely related to his laboratory assignment at Fort Monmouth; but not in the way that the writer says he is organizing his paragraph. Of course he might cross out *technical* and say that he was using a chronological organization; but that's not the way he started, and it's probably not the best way. If he wants to make Forrester's qualifications really clear, he'd better put all the technical ones together and then use a separate paragraph to discuss his executive ability. If he concentrates on one main idea at a time he is much less likely to leave something out—as he apparently has done here. If Forrester received three promotions—not mere salary raises—at Northern Electric, it seems likely that he was handling men there, too, and doing well at it; but this point is pretty well buried.

Another requirement of a good paragraph is that it must be arranged in some recognizable order. If it is narrative, it may follow the time sequence of events. If it is descriptive, it should follow some kind of space arrangement—right to left, top to bottom, center to circumference, or perhaps the most striking features first, then the less obvious ones. You can take your choice, but you should stick to it. If you shift from one to another your reader is likely to get lost. When there is no such handy guide as time or space you may proceed from cause to effect, from evidence to conclusion, or in any other reasonable way; but you must pick out some definite line of progress.

A generation ago, when our classifications seemed to be more permanent and reliable than they do now, it was usual to drill students on at least six guaranteed methods of constructing paragraphs. They were not always the same six, but the following list is reasonably typical: (1) by definition; (2) by particulars and details; (3) by comparison and contrast; (4) by illustrations and examples; (5) by analogy; (6) by effective repetition. These are still perfectly good methods, and you may find the list helpful if you don't worry about mixing them a little; but too much drill of this sort often gave students the idea that a paragraph was a hopeless technical mystery instead of merely a reasonable grouping of related sentences. The fact is that a good many people with orderly minds often develop most of their paragraphs quite well almost without thinking of them. However, most of us can profit by learning a few general principles.

Topic Sentences—Actual or Possible

When we were discussing division into paragraphs (page 182) we mentioned that one of the best ways to decide how to break up a paper was to see how many successive sentences could reasonably be summarized in a single sentence. The sentence which gives the gist of a whole paragraph may be called the *topic sentence*. The topic sentence may or may not actually appear in the paper, but it should always be easy to write in making a summary. Any time you find it hard to summarize a paragraph in a sentence, there is probably something wrong with the paragraph. Let's look at a few examples, with the topic sentences in italics.

1. *During the past three days Shirley had been having a pretty strenuous time.* On Monday her mother had driven off to attend the PTA convention in Denver, leaving her in charge of the housekeeping. That afternoon her father had come home early with a bad cough and a temperature, which meant that his meals had to be served in bed. On Tuesday the hot-water heater had developed a leak and the service porch had to be mopped up twice—once for the water and once after the plumber. And on Wednesday Aunt Junie had stopped by so late that she just had to be asked to dinner, and had stayed till nearly eleven. Meanwhile classes went on as usual, with midterms due next week.

2. Seventeen of last year's lettermen are returning, including nine of the starters. Medigovich and Tietjens, both of whom were slowed by injuries last year, are back in top condition. There are at least seven really promising junior college transfers, and three former lettermen are back from the service. Then there is last year's undefeated freshman team, generally considered the best in the school's history, coming up. *Altogether, the football picture is so bright that even Coach Nickerson finds it a little hard to weep steadily.*

3. The next morning Hal got up before daylight, put the coffee pot on to perk while he shaved and showered, and was just backing out of the garage when the edge of the sun peeped over the horizon. He had covered a hundred miles before he came to a restaurant that seemed to be open. There he had ham, eggs, and toast, along with more coffee, and returned to the wheel feeling decidedly more cheerful. It was still too early for much traffic, and he averaged well over seventy until nearly eight o'clock. Thereafter he had to slow down, but he had built up a comfortable margin, and had no trouble reaching the bank by opening time. [*Hal drove to the bank in a hurry.*]

In the first of these examples the topic sentence comes first. The rest of the paragraph expands it with detail. In the second example the details come first and the topic sentence summarizes them. The third example contains no topic sentence in the paragraph itself, but the one added in brackets contains the gist of the paragraph. Expressed topic sentences usually come first or last, but they may appear anywhere.

There are people who believe firmly that every sound paragraph must have an expressed topic sentence. (This idea may be connected with the popular superstition that the way to mark a textbook is to find the topic sentence in each paragraph and underline it. Then you can forget everything else even faster with a clear conscience.) Certainly it is often appropriate to state the main idea clearly before going into details, or to show how the details you have given add up. to form a coherent whole. But very often an expressed topic sentence would mean needless repetition and a waste of time. This is particularly probable in narratives, as in the third specimen paragraph above; but it is likely to be true in other kinds of writing whenever the material is fairly simple and a reader can be expected to absorb it without being prodded by special emphasis.

If you write from a good outline—and follow it—you should not have much trouble with paragraph structure. You can see whether what you have put down for a given paragraph belongs together, and whether the order of ideas is satisfactory; and you can add, delete, or rearrange before going any further. But if you use a very sketchy outline or none at all, you will probably do your paragraphing by instinct or guess work on the first draft; and unless your instinct is remarkably sound you will have to do some revising before the final copy. As you examine each paragraph you can check it in the following steps.

First, see if it contains anything that looks like a topic sentence. If it does, see whether this sentence gives a fair indication of the contents of the whole paragraph. If the two don't jibe, one or the other should be changed. If the sentence is clear it is usually wise to let it stand and modify the paragraph to conform, even if this means more work. The very fact that the paragraph is longer and more complicated than the sentence means that it has given you more opportunity to get off the track.

If the paragraph contains no topic sentence, write one down on a separate piece of paper. With a good paragraph this should be easy. If you find the sentence difficult to compose, the paragraph is probably confused. It is then wise to write a good sentence to indicate what you should have said, and change the paragraph to conform. You can now decide whether the sentence should actually appear in the paragraph or not. If you think it should, find a good place and put it in.

This process sounds rather more cumbersome than it actually is. A freshman paper seldom contains more than half a dozen paragraphs. If you pay any attention at all to the structure of one, the obvious first step is to see whether each paragraph develops one reasonably clear-cut idea. If it does, a topic sentence should not be hard to find. If it doesn't, find a topic sentence that tells what you *meant* to say in that paragraph. Then say it.

When you use this method, the most important thing to remember is that you have nothing at all to gain by fooling yourself. If you have left out something that you know should go in, or gone off on a side-track that really gets you nowhere, there is always a temptation to justify it; and it is often possible to modify the topic sentence in a way that looks quite reasonable (as long as you are being sympathetic with yourself), and then say: "There! that's the way I meant to do it all the time." Your instructor will almost certainly take a different view. The fact that a topic sentence has been twisted until it fits a bad paragraph won't impress him at all. What he wants is a good paragraph.

Remedial Outlines

We have already mentioned several times that a good outline can save a lot of trouble. Many students learn this lesson early and use outlines consistently. There are others, however, who feel that the very act of writing generates ideas, and that they can do better by starting out with no more than a rough mental outline, and filling in as they go along. Sometimes this feeling is merely a cover-up for laziness, but there are times when it is justified. Students with a combination of fluency and a good sense of proportion can often get along very well without written outlines; and such a combination can be developed, at least to some extent, by practice.

However, nobody ever reaches the point where all his paragraphs come out right in the first draft, and most of us occasionally write one that is very hard to straighten out. It meets the topic sentence test all right—everything in it is on the subject. And each sentence seems to lead logically enough to the next. Nevertheless the whole effect is not as clear as it should be, and no change that occurs to us seems to improve matters.

One of the best ways to proceed at this point is to make an outline of what you have written, as short as possible, but covering every structural relation. It should follow the exact order of the paragraph. Then you can examine the bare bones and see how they fit together and what kind of rearrangement they need. Sometimes the trouble will stand out at once. Sometimes you may have to analyze the outline very carefully before you find what is wrong. But structural mistakes are almost always easier to spot in an outline than in a complete paragraph. Here is an example:

Unsatisfactory paragraph

My second reason for wanting to be a certified public accountant is that I like the kind of life they lead. My uncle gets to travel to all sorts of interesting places. He also gets to see how many different businesses are run. He has to work very hard sometimes, but in slack periods he can manage to take a number of short vacations. Of course not every accountant manages to do this. Some of them work just as regularly as file clerks, except that they put in longer hours at rush seasons. But my uncle can pretty well call his shots. He always seems to have a job in the trout country about the time the fishing season opens, and one in the deer country during hunting season. I suppose he pays his own expenses when he is actually hunting or fishing, but he can always charge getting there and back off to business. He says the secret is to specialize in the kinds of problems they have in the places that you like to go. I like his method much better than Mr. Radek's, even if Mr. Radek does make more money. If you are going to do all your business right in the same city you might as well be a banker.

Outline of paragraph as written

If you decide (as you should) that this paragraph is *not* satisfactory, you won't need to write a complete sentence outline of it, but you do need a topic sentence to show what you are trying to say, and an outline detailed enough to show the framework. You might come up with something like this:

Topic sentence: My second reason for wanting to be a CPA is the kind of life they lead.

    A. Uncle travels to interesting places
    B. Sees how many businesses are run

C. Hard work but many vacations
D. Some CPA's like file clerks, but work harder
E. Uncle calls shots:

    1. Fishing season
    2. Hunting season
    3. Free transportation to fun

F. Specialize in problems in places you like
G. Method better than Radek's even if less profitable
H. Might as well be banker as like Radek

It doesn't take much thought to tell you that you should get all the material about your uncle's methods together, and the material about people like Radek together. Then you have to decide which should come first. If you want a strong positive effect, you had better save the part you like till last. And to make sure that it all fits together neatly you'd better use a complete sentence outline as your next step.

Revised outline.
Topic sentence:

My second reason for wanting to be a CPA is the kind of life some of them lead.

A. There are some, like Radek, whose lives are as dull as file clerks', except they work even harder in rush seasons.

    1. They make lots of money, but don't get much out of it.
    2. You might as well be a banker as do all your accounting in one city.

B. But some accountants lead varied and interesting lives.

    1. My uncle picks his spots.
        a. He always is in a position for
           i. Fishing when the season opens.
           ii. Hunting during the deer season.
        b. He pays actual vacation expenses, but gets his travel free.
        c. He specializes in problems of places where he wants to go.
    2. I want to follow his lead.
        a. You get to see many businesses.
        b. You lead a well rounded life.

Revised paragraph

My second reason for wanting to be a certified public accountant is that I like the kind of life that they—or at least some of them—lead. Mr. Radek, who lives near us, is enough to discourage anybody from the profession. He makes a lot of money, but I don't see what he gets out of it. He does all his work right in the city, and his life is just about like a file clerk's or a banker's, except that he has to do more overtime work at rush seasons. But my uncle, even if he doesn't make quite as much money, really leads an interesting life. Sure, he works hard sometimes; but when times are slack he gets off—and he gets off in the right places. He always seems to have a job in trout country about the time the fishing season opens, and one in the deer country during hunting season. I suppose he pays his own expenses when he is actually hunting or fishing, but getting there and back he can always charge off to business. He says the secret is to specialize in the kinds of problems they have in the places you like to go. That's what I want to do; and actually there is a little more to it than getting free vacations. You get to see how a lot of different businesses are run, and to take part in them. If you pick ones that interest you it makes for an interesting and well rounded life.

You may think there is a little more in this than there was in the first, unsatisfactory paragraph. There is, and it is perfectly natural. When you improve the organization of a paragraph you are very likely to open logical spots for additional ideas to make it more interesting.

You may think that this is a very laborious way to revise a poor paragraph, but it's hard to find a better one. Almost any writer can tell you that revising an unsatisfactory paragraph is much harder than writing a good one in the first place. The moral seems to be that it is a sound principle to figure out in advance what you are going to do; then you won't have so much trouble figuring out what you should have done.

Exercises—Chapter 19

By number, assemble the sentences below into groups as their subject matter seems to suggest, then arrange the entries within each group in some logical order to form some semblance of a paragraph. (You may have to fill in with transitions or an occasional sentence of your own, and you may wish to ignore some of the offerings below.) If one of the sentences in a group can be called the *topic* sentence, indicate which it is.

1. And in almost every case the victim has exhausted his resources before he turns for the better.
2. Charlie hadn't worn a necktie—or cared how he looked, for that matter—since the dedication ceremony at the dam, and that was thirty years past.
3. Charlie Nevins was old.
4. And the town he talked about had not been seen for forty years.
5. By midnight the air was chilly and very clear, and the neons cut sharp, colored lines in the black sky.

6. He hadn't eaten peanuts since he acquired dental plates, during World War I.

7. Gambling might be called a sickness.

8. The middays were hot, but the nights still very cool.

9. Those who engage in it sometimes develop a fever-like flush.

10. He couldn't remember how long he had carried the knot of pain in the lower part of his back.

11. It was getting on toward summer in Las Vegas.

12. But above all, Charlie looked up and down the street for buildings long turned to ashes and crumbled masonry.

13. As the illness runs its course, delusions and hallucinations sometimes accompany it.

14. On that particular day there had been some dust, early in the evening, and a brief spatter of rain to settle it.

15. In some cases, precautions may be taken to prevent it, but once the germ gets into the bloodstream, the victim is almost powerless to fight it.

16. He even discovered that it was easier not to know what was going on in the world than it was to puzzle over newspaper type through his bifocals.

17. Nor could he remember when he hadn't had a cough or hadn't smoked a pipe.

18. The disease is highly contagious, but rarely fatal.

Suggestions for Discussion or Theme Writing—Chapter 19

1. Suggest a plausible set of details to accompany each of the following sentences:

(a) Except for Miss Forbes, the night supervisor, everyone around the hospital tried to make my convalescence as pleasant as possible.

(b) Opening night was just twenty-four hours away, and too many things still had to be done before curtain time.

(c) The drive back to civilization was hot and seemingly endless.

(d) In all circumstances Leroy Humperdinkle was a man who could not be hurried.

2. Construct a remedial outline for the following paragraph, and rewrite it according to the process suggested in the chapter. Then follow the same procedure with one of the least successful paragraphs from one of your recent themes:

You can educate yourself without attending a college. Most of us lack the self-discipline such a life demands, however. You need to be in good health, and you should not have family responsibilities. You must be willing to support yourself with a job and spend long hours at study. Wide reading is the key to self-education. But you will lack guidance. You will not have anyone to help you select the right things to read. Reading lists will help. Yet you will never know whether or not you understand the reading, since there is no one to test you over it. You can't be wanting a degree to get a specific job, either. And many jobs specify that a degree is necessary. These employers do not take into account whether or not you are educated, just as long as you hold a degree. Besides, social pressure makes many young persons attend college. When all the other high school graduates go away to college, the student who vowed he would never go—and who responded accordingly to his high school assignments—feels the pressure to conform, and often decides at the last minute to attend. And while college expands one's social life, self-education offers no time for socializing.

REPORTS,

INFERENCES,

AND VALUE

JUDGMENTS

20

Two boys were talking. There was a blow, and one of the boys fell to the ground. Three girls standing nearby were asked to describe what had happened.

Irene said: "Tom and Max were talking. Then Tom hit Max in the face and Max fell down."

This is a report. Irene's words tell nothing that she hadn't seen and heard. She draws no conclusions and offers no opinions—simply recounts the facts that she has observed.

Jane said: "Tom and Max were arguing about something. Then Tom got mad and knocked Max down."

This is not a pure report, because Jane's words go beyond what she had seen and heard. She tries to guess at the reason. We could easily make several other guesses. "Getting mad" is a complicated chemical process not visible to the naked eye. Maybe the boys were putting on an act. Tom might have been trying to kill a mosquito—a big, dangerous one. Or maybe he knocked Max down rather sorrowfully, to prevent him from committing a crime. All these explanations are unlikely. Jane's guess is probably quite right; but it is still a guess, and the chances are she doesn't know it. Very few people have been trained to separate their inferences from what they have actually observed.

If you think that the moral of all this is that reports are better than inferences, you are wrong. They are simply different. We really need a flourish of trumpets here to emphasize the point. There are times when you should simply report the facts and let somebody else decide what they mean. There are times when you should decide yourself. But you should *always* know which you are doing. People who can't distinguish between observable facts and their inferences from those facts cause a lot of trouble—particularly for themselves. However, before we go into this any further we'd better listen to the third girl.

Ann said: "Max and Tom were talking, and without any warning at all that big bully Tom hit poor Max when he wasn't looking and knocked him down."

This is a judgment. Ann has gone a step further than Jane. Not only has she guessed about things she couldn't see, but she has weighed the whole incident (including the part she has guessed) on her scale of values.

Here again we must emphasize that there is nothing wrong about what she has done. True, she would probably not go unchallenged if she talked that way as a witness in a lawsuit. There the jury is supposed to do the evaluating, and the witness is supposed to give a report as nearly factual as is humanly possible. But if she told her friends the simple, observed facts and made no comment at all on the values, they would probably think she was either cold-blooded or feeble-minded. A person who has no values, or who is unwilling to bring them out, is not of much use to society (and there is *my* value judgment for today). But even when we are sure enough of our judgments to fight for them, we shouldn't mistake them for observable facts.

Let's consider the matter from the other side for a moment. What do *you* want when you ask a question? If you ask a friend about a movie or a new restaurant, you probably want a value judgment. You want to decide whether or not to go, and you have some respect for his judgment or you wouldn't bother to ask him. You may want him to report a few details—is it a mystery or a romance or do they specialize in chicken or steaks—but your main question is simply is it good enough to be worth your while? If he gives you a forty minute report on the details and then tells you to form your own opinion, you'll probably never ask him again. Or suppose your car is making funny noises and you call in the hot-rod expert from next door to listen to it. He can observe only the same noises that you can, but he has learned to draw better inferences from them. Maybe he can tell you what's making the noise and how important it is. You want his inferences, his value judgments, and perhaps a little free labor to boot.

On the other hand, suppose your little sister and brother have been squabbling and you are trying to bring peace back into the family.

The more you hear about who was mean and who was unfair and who really started it the more confused you get. Their inferences and judgments don't help you a bit. What you'd like to get is a simple report on what happened. Then you could do your own inferring and judging, and decide what action to take.

We cannot draw an absolute and permanent line between observations and inferences, or between inferences and judgments. Ordinarily we will accept the statement that a man saw a deer as a simple report of his observations. But if he shoots the deer, and it then turns out to have been a cow, we have to revise our estimate. We may then say that he saw a shape, inferred that it was a deer, and will now have to pay two hundred dollars for confusing an inference with an observation. Perhaps the difference between inferences and value judgments is even harder to define rigorously. However, if we are not fanatical about it, we can make reasonably reliable distinctions. We might define an inference as the result of examining observed facts in the light of past experience. We may have to hurry over "observed facts" a little, but so does everybody else. Then we can define a judgment as an evaluation of either facts or inferences. And finally (to return to the title of our chapter) we can insist that a report must confine itself to a record of observations, with no inferences and no judgments—or at least with no statements that can be proved to be either of these things. However we define them, we will certainly find that many people firmly believe that *their* inferences and *their* judgments are reports of observable facts. Let's assume that a student has written the following paragraph:

Mrs. Smith is one of the most disagreeable women I have ever met. She is completely selfish, has very bad manners, and flies into a temper at the slightest excuse. She is mean to all her family, and I pity anybody who has to associate with her.

Now suppose the instructor says, "That is all right for a judgment, but I would like you to write a report to back the judgment up. Tell me some of the things that you have seen Mrs. Smith do that led you to make this judgment." He is likely to get another paragraph that looks something like this:

I have frequently seen Mrs. Smith do very selfish things. She insists on monopolizing the family car, even when her husband and children need it much more than she does, and she spends far more on clothes than she can afford, while her husband goes around practically in rags. I have seen her get perfectly furious just because her husband suggested going to a different movie from the one she wanted to see. She expects him to wait on her all the time, but she doesn't even thank him when he holds her chair or gets up to bring her a book which she could have easily reached. She scolds her children in a very unpleasant voice, and doesn't take the slightest interest in their plans or even in their welfare.

This paragraph contains a good deal more information than the first one, but it is *not* a report of observable fact. Such words and phrases as the following indicate inferences or judgments or both: *very selfish; insists on monopolizing; even when her husband and children need it more than she does; practically in rags; perfectly furious; just; expects; doesn't even thank.*

It is possible that some of these inferences and judgments are wrong. She may, for instance, be devoted to her children but afraid of spoiling them. But let us assume that Mrs. Smith *is* a thoroughly unpleasant woman, and that all the inferences and judgments are quite sound. They are still inferences and judgments, and they have no place in a factual report. They would not, for instance, be admitted as testimony in a lawsuit. Let us see if we can write a clean report on what the student had actually observed. It might go something like this:

One rainy morning I heard Mr. Smith ask his wife if he could take the car that day. She said that that was ridiculous, since she had a lot of shopping to do. Mr. Smith then walked to the bus station, four blocks away. About an hour later, after the rain had stopped, I saw Mrs. Smith drive to the grocery store, two blocks away. She was gone about ten minutes. The car stayed in the garage for the rest of the day. I have never seen Mr. Smith drive to work.

Mrs. Smith has a new fur coat every two years, and more hats and shoes than any woman I know. In the last four years I have seen Mr. Smith wear only two suits. Both are now very shiny at the elbows.

One evening they stopped at our house and borrowed the paper to see what movies were showing. Mrs. Smith said, "There is nothing much good—I suppose we might as well see Doris Day." Mr. Smith said, "I hear *The Outsider* is very good—why don't we see that?" Mrs. Smith threw the paper down on the table and said, in a much louder voice than she had been using, "I should think a man who can't afford to take his wife to a night club would at least let her choose the movie." She then walked out of the house without saying another word to anybody. Mr. Smith thanked us, said goodnight, and followed.

Another evening when they visited us Mrs. Smith sat down, then reached over and put her cigarettes and matches on a table about two feet away. A few minutes later she interrupted her own conversation to say, "Cigarette, Harry." Mr. Smith got up, crossed the room, took a cigarette from her package, handed it to her, and lit it. She did not thank him.

Although her house is two doors away from ours, I often hear her telling her children that they are lazy, stupid, clumsy, and selfish. I cannot hear their answers. Late one afternoon she was sitting on our porch when her boy came over and asked if they could have dinner early that night so he could get to scout meeting on time. She told him that they would have dinner when she was ready. She continued to sit and look at a magazine for half an hour after my mother had excused herself and gone in to prepare our dinner. Both of her children have a great many colds. My mother once suggested that she give them vitamin pills. Mrs. Smith said that they were too expensive and that she had no faith in them.

There are several things to notice about this report. It may or may not be unbiased. We simply can't tell whether the writer has left out all the nice things that he has seen Mrs. Smith do, or whether he has never seen her do anything nice. But as far as it goes the report does tell what Mrs. Smith did without making any guesses, no matter how reasonable, about why she did it. In the second place it leaves out all words that indicate judgment. There is a difference between saying "She did not thank him," which is a simple observation, and "She did not *even* thank him," which would certainly suggest that she should have. Maybe she should, but a report is no place to say so. And in the third place, since the reader is allowed to form his own reactions, they will probably be much stronger than if we had tried to force ours on him. Anybody reading the judgment is likely to think "The writer certainly has got it in for Mrs. Smith. I wonder how much of that is true and how much is prejudice." But anybody reading the report is almost certain to feel that Mrs. Smith is a thoroughly unpleasant woman. Even if he suspects that some evidence on her side has been left out—that she can't really be quite *that* bad—she will seem bad enough.

The technique works just as well in the other direction. If you want to describe your favorite character you will probably arouse more enthusiasm by showing him in action at his best than by telling how good you think he is.

Now if you will just glance back at the various accounts of Mrs. Smith you will notice that the report is very much longer than the judgment. This is not an accident. You simply cannot give the evidence on which a judgment is based in as few words as you can give the judgment itself. It takes only three words to say "Mary is wonderful," but it takes a good many more to report things about Mary that lead reasonably to such a conclusion. This is something that may be worth remembering the next time you discover, after writing fifty or a hundred words, that "there is nothing more to say." There is at least a strong possibility that what you have said is a judgment—your own brief summary of a lot of evidence. If so, the best way to expand your material is to get back to the facts or events on which the judgment is based, and report on them.

Naturally a good many papers call for opinions—inferences and judgments—as well as facts. But even in such papers it is usually a good idea to give a reasonable selection of the facts first. Your reader is much more likely to be interested in your opinions if he can see some of the evidence on which they are based.

Exercises—Chapter 20

Mark the following sentences *R* (report), if you think they could have been made strictly on the basis of observable facts; *I* (inference), if you think they involve any guesswork, no matter how reasonable, and *J* (judgment), if you think they involve a personal evaluation. A sentence may be marked both *I* and *J,* but not *R* and *I* or *R* and *J.*

1. In Pleasanton the rain stopped at 9:34 P.M. and started again sometime after 10:50 P.M.
2. I sell the Harold family two pounds of T-bones every day.
3. He gets his height from his mother's side of the family.
4. Jim was a good boy until he started running with a gang.
5. The dirty thief had two of the stolen bills in his possession.
6. Anybody who could afford the car I saw him driving last night would have to be rich.
7. Ralph is the only one of those boys who won't steal at every opportunity.
8. One look at the way you spell, and it's clear you never went to college.
9. The bathroom scales registered 193 under Uncle Herbert, and Uncle Charlie went 206 on the same scales a moment later.
10. You look a little nearer to the weight you really ought to carry.
11. After all Stevens had done for him, he gave the appointment to Dudley.
12. The dam broke last night sure; that's the fourth house that's gone by here this morning.

13. I wouldn't call him a liar, but I wouldn't trust him very far with the truth, either.

14. She must have some income aside from her salary to dress like that.

15. The hero's eyes glinted with good-humor as he was presented with the boss's daughter and the vice-presidency of the bank.

16. Fans, it is eating Brand X cracklings that enables me to pole-vault over fifteen feet.

17. By accepting an out-of-state campaign contribution, Candidate Jones made it very clear he wants outsiders muscling in.

18. The business is now priced at $10,000.00, and from licensed contractors I have three bids averaging $4500.00 each, for minimum repairs.

19. Calling the cop a blind bureaucrat is what made him get angry and write the ticket.

20. Police records indicate that a man answering his description has four arrests, two convictions and one confinement in prison.

21. You won't go wrong buying that brand; I got one when they first came out, and it has given me a year's trouble-free service.

22. Any teacher who smokes in the boiler room on the sly would certainly poison the minds of our nation's youth.

23. Somebody in the family is squandering the money, or they could dress better than they do on his salary.

24. He said there was a politician and an honest man in the car, but I could see only one silhouette against the light.

25. After you pass the junky Adams place, turn right, across that makeshift WPA bridge, and go exactly four miles north to the ramshackle Burroughs residence.

Suggestions for Discussion or Theme Writing—Chapter 20

1. Write a brief *report* of observations which might have led the writer to make the judgments below:

(a) Wilfong is a hopeless romantic. He sees the world through rose-colored glasses. He opens his eyes only to what he wants to see around him, and that is always the positive, the hopeful, and the fortunate.

(b) You'll never find a steakhouse to compare with The Wagon Wheel. It's fabulous. Al, the chef, is out of this world. The salads are known from coast to coast, and the steaks are the living end.

2. Write a paragraph presenting an appropriate selection of the following information, with inferences and judgments favorable to one view-

point in the dispute. Then write a paragraph favorable to the opposite point of view. Conclude with a brief statement of your final attitude.

MIDDLEBURG, IDAHO—Middleburg College today dismissed football team captain Tom Hathaway, 19, for what it called "lack of academic interest," while attorneys for the fleet fullback charged that the college dropped him because he had failed to "produce on the gridiron."

Hathaway, who led the nation in total yardage last year, could not be reached for comment. In four games of the current season he has gained 143 yards. He has failed to complete a pass this year, although two attempts have fallen into enemy hands for 69 yards and two touchdowns.

In their statement, the player's attorneys contended that so much pressure had been put on Hathaway to succeed on the field that not only his football playing but his studies had suffered as well. "They had the boy so worked up that he couldn't do anything right," the lawyers reported.

Two of the student's instructors told reporters they were satisfied with the boy's work. They said he turned in his completed make-up work for Friday and Monday when he appeared each Wednesday. Hathaway's English instructor reported that he had not seen the student all year, and his math teacher said that the football captain had failed every test he had appeared for, excusing himself on the grounds that he hadn't yet bought a textbook for the course.

On the campus the president of his fraternity, Bill Jenks, called Hathaway "the most active frat man we ever had." And Miss Diane Shultz, 19, a friend of the young fullback, told reporters, "School officials kept pestering Tom until he got so shook up he would even forget our dates several times each week."

Meanwhile, Mrs. Gilbert Hathaway, 4431 Broad Street, the star's mother said, "Tom was a good boy at home, but something happened to him down at that college."

INDIRECT

USES OF LANGUAGE

21

So far we have been considering language mostly as a direct method of communicating information. We have seen that the communication is never quite perfect, but that it is often adequate; and we have been interested in ways of increasing its efficiency. We may now consider some of the other uses of language. There will not be time to go into all of them, or to go very deeply into any of them. But there are a few points that cause such widespread misunderstanding that even a very hasty treatment may be of some value.

Aside from exchanging information, we may speak to arouse emotion or to quiet it, to relieve our own tensions, to get something done, or for any of a number of other reasons. Sometimes our purpose is so obvious that no misunderstanding is likely to result:

Wipe your shoes.
Now, now, honey.
Ouch!
With ,an *A!* With an *A!* With an *A-R-I-Z-O-N-A!*

It would be possible to discourse on the historical background, internal structure, and psychological and sociological implications of each of these expressions; but if we simply take them all for granted we won't lose much.

On the other hand, there is a curiously widespread superstition that whenever an expression sounds like a bit of information, that information is its *real* meaning, regardless of the intention of the speaker or the effect on the listener; and that whoever takes this information most literally has justice on his side. We have all heard conversations like this:

Jim: I'm afraid I'm out of matches.
Bob: Is that so?

Jim: Yes. Have you got any?
Bob: Yes.
Jim: Well, what about giving me a light?
Bob: Oh, is that what you want? Why didn't you say so?

Of course Bob may merely have a retarded sense of humor; but there are plenty of Bobs who act like this seriously, and even with a feeling of virtue. They know what words mean—and let anyone who trifles with the meaning beware.

Equivocation

In the example just given, the listener used the supposed "real" meaning against the speaker. It is just as easy, and probably a good deal more usual, for the speaker to use it against the listener.

Little Brother: Owwww! Owwwwwwww!
Father: Pete! Did you hurt Danny?
Pete (to Father): Gee, Dad, I never even touched him. I don't know why he's crying. (To himself): Well, I *didn't* touch him—I just touched the baseball bat. And I don't *know* that he's crying because the bat happened to bump into his head. Dad didn't ask me to guess.

Equivocation is the deliberate use of ambiguous language in the hope that the hearer will make one interpretation and proceed accordingly while the speaker holds another one in reserve, either to soothe his conscience or to keep a hidden control over future events. No sermon on the moral aspects of equivocation will be delivered here; but it is worth mentioning that legally equivocation is not as respectable as it used to be. There was a time when courts of law generally held that a sentence could have only one real meaning, and that anybody was entitled to take advantage of this if he could. Courts now usually hold that decisions should be based on the *intent* of the lawmakers or contracting parties. They recognize the possibility of several reasonable interpretations of the same words, but treat deliberate ambiguity as an act of bad faith that weighs against the party responsible for it. There are, however, a good many Petes left in the world.

Denotation and Connotation

It may seem that the quibbling and equivocation considered in the two preceding sections are such obvious abuses of language that they hardly call for serious discussion. But there aren't many of us who haven't indulged in something like them at one time or another; and we may have justified ourselves by the peculiar but popular theory that a speaker is bound to be honest only about the *denotation* of a sentence—its literal and formal content. Whatever is implied is merely the *connotation* and if a listener allows himself to be misled by that, it's his own fault. (As technical terms in logic, *denotation* and *connotation* have entirely different meanings, which need not concern us here.)

Up to a point the distinction between denotation and connotation is useful, but it must be taken with at least two grains of salt. In the first place, the line between the two is not absolute; and in the second place, the connotation is not always the minor element. What is implied can be both as real and as important as what is stated. Consider the following three sentences:

Channing worked steadily all day and spoke to nobody.
Channing concentrated on his job all day, and would not be distracted by idle conversation.
Channing hadn't a pleasant word for anybody else, but buried himself all day long in his own job.

If you take these as units, they are clearly quite different sentences. Yet there are people who would say that all three have the same denotation, and the first contains nothing else; that the second carries the connotation that Channing was an earnest person who took his job seriously; and that the third carries the connotation that he was a rather sulky person who took his troubles and perhaps himself too seriously.

It is certainly true that the three sentences indicate a common core of information, and that some of their differences are suggested rather than directly stated. But the idea that the denotation and connotation can be completely separated simply won't hold up. We know from experience that even the first sentence, supposedly free from connotation, might affect various readers in quite different ways. Channing's boss, for instance, might think "How admirable," while the boss's daughter might sigh "How dull." And both of them might consider the inferences they drew about Channing's character more important than the specifically stated facts about his behavior.

The three sentences about Channing make a rather crude set of contrasts, deliberately chosen so that the chance of uniform reactions is pretty high. Let's look at a slightly less obvious set:

> The next day Peters did nothing.
> The next day Peters loafed.
> The next day Peters relaxed.

You might feel that "did nothing" is neutral, that "loafed" suggests that he neglected what he should have been doing, and that "relaxed" suggests that he was taking a well earned rest. But if a friend disagreed you would have some trouble proving your point. There are people who are just as dogmatic about connotations as about denotations, insisting that certain words automatically arouse pleasant or romantic or terrifying associations; but the fact is that associations are individual matters, depending on temperament and past experiences. When we want to enrich our direct statements with suggestions, the best we can do is use our judgment and play the percentages. There is no use telling a man that Carcassonne is a hauntingly beautiful name, evocative of all the pageantry of medieval life, if the only thing it suggests to him is a pack mule coming back from a deer hunt—with the carcass on.

But it is even sillier to minimize the importance of connotations. The fact that we can't be quite sure of what the effect of a word on a particular mind will be doesn't make the effect any less real. If Lincoln had begun his Gettysburg Address "Eighty-seven years ago," instead of "Four score and seven years ago," you might never have heard of it. The denotation of the two expressions may be the same, but the meaning is not; and any paraphrase of the speech comes about as near the original as a clumsy bus boy's attempt to make a substitute for a great chef's masterpiece. You can call them "essentially" the same if you want to; but if you do, you'd better eat the bus boy's food, and leave the chef's for somebody who knows better.

After all, connotation is mainly a technique of implication, and what is implied may be even more important than what is directly stated. Suppose a friend asks you if you have seen anything of your new neighbors, and you answer "Yes, we called on them—*once*." You haven't been guilty of anything that could be called slander, but you have certainly *implied* that you don't think much of them; and your friend will undoubtedly *infer* that that's what you mean. If he comes back with the remark "I saw them both cold sober one day last week," you can turn your kind attention to some other friends—without ever saying a nasty word, of course.

Slanted Language

As we have just seen, it is impossible to avoid "connotation" completely; but we can make a rough practical distinction between the "impartial" language of an unbiased speaker and the "slanted" language of a speaker with a definitely one-sided attitude. We should recognize, of course, that slanting may be entirely unconscious. A Frenchman who thinks of the Germans as "Boches" may use the term even when he has no idea of influencing anybody. We should also recognize that slanted language is not necessarily vicious. It may be used to inspire generosity or heroic efforts as well as to sell worthless goods or to gain votes for incompetent politicians. If everybody always spoke with complete impartiality, a great many things would never get done.

The ideal of "hearing the evidence on both sides and then making up our own minds" is attractive, but probably no human being has ever quite reached it. We live in an atmosphere of words, and we cannot be entirely immune to their effects. We might as well face the fact that none of us analyze every statement we hear. We haven't the time. If we hear a statement often enough, or hear it under particularly impressive circumstances, we are likely to assume that it must be true without even stopping to think what "true" means as applied to this particular statement. There is probably no way of curing us completely. But if we want to retain even a reasonable degree of independence, there are a few things we should consider when we do analyze a statement.

1. Is the speaker primarily interested in accuracy, or does he have some other purpose?

2. Does he know enough to justify his statement?

3. Is he loading the dice by using emotional words? (This is a hard one, because if he is clever enough to use *our* favorites we may not notice that they are loaded.)

4. Is he stacking the cards by taking all his material from one side and pretending that it is typical of the whole?

5. If he does, has he really examined the evidence, or merely swallowed it?

If we decide that the speaker is merely trying to sell us something he is paid to sell, or to persuade us to do something that is to his advantage rather than ours, we may be able to reject his statement without much difficulty. We may even wonder how anybody could be fooled; but the records—expressed in sales, in votes, and in countless other ways—show that millions of people *are* fooled every day. It is probably wise to assume that even we are taken in occasionally.

Practice in analyzing slanted language is both fascinating and valuable. It is well to recognize, however, that such analysis is not an exact science. All words have varying connotations. We should try to make reasonable judgments about the writer's intentions (conscious or subconscious), without hoping for complete accuracy in our own interpretations.

Directive Language—Open and Concealed

If a teacher says to a boy "Never use the word *ain't*," the command is perfectly clear. We all recognize that one of the uses of language is to get other people to do things or to refrain from doing them. In this case the boy knows he has received an order, and we may leave it up to him to decide whether or not he will obey it. But if the teacher tells him "Nice people never say *ain't*," the situation is a little more complicated. Her statement may or may not be accurate, and she may or may not believe it is accurate. But we may reasonably suppose that her primary purpose is not to convey information but to influence the boy's conduct.

All of us encounter thousands of such concealed directives. "Loyal Americans do this," "Society leaders wear that," and "Only the chosen few will appreciate such-and-such." No matter how flimsy the concealment, some people are likely to be fooled. They are believers in the primitive magic of words. If they smoke the same cigarettes as Sophia Loren, they will be "like" Sophia Loren. And if they are "like" her, think of what it will do for their chest development. They wouldn't put it quite as plainly as this—but they do buy the cigarettes.

Sometimes the directive nature of a statement is so well concealed that even intelligent people may be deceived. We read that "Four out of Five Doctors Use Premium Brand." This may be true, and it may be significant—but why is the man telling us? Does he simply want to educate us about the habits of doctors, or does he want us to buy his product? If we suspect that he is trying to influence us, we had better look all around the question before deciding. How many doctors is he counting? And is it possible that doctors get a special discount that may affect their choice?

As some of the examples above indicate, concealed directives may be used by people with admirable motives as well as by those who simply want to trick us into doing something to their advantage; and the users may be quite unaware that they are doing anything but telling the simple truth. Moreover, we may find it profitable to obey a directive even though it is offered from purely selfish motives. Premium Brand may be the best one for us. It would therefore be silly to reject all such directives on principle. But whenever we encounter a statement that seems to offer a reason for us to do something, we can evaluate it intelligently only if we consider the purpose of the man who made it as well as the direct information contained in it.

Literal and Figurative Language

There are people who think that all statements should be not only true, but true in the most literal possible way. They condemn all such expressions as "He died laughing" and "Her blood boiled," not because they are overworked, but on the theory that they are not quite honest. Such high regard for truth is praiseworthy, but a little simple. It is rooted in the fallacy that there is only one kind of truth, and that it can be expressed exactly and rigidly in words.

Fortunately, such people are a very small minority; but unfortunately, a good many students seem to think that a discussion of the ideas considered in this and the preceding chapter is in effect an invitation to join the group. They get suspicious of all inferences and judgments, even when they are reasonable and appropriate; and they make such a strained effort to avoid any slanting that their writing loses not only its color but much of its content. There are many things that can be conveyed so much more effectively by suggestion than by direct statement that if we avoid suggestion we simply leave the things out.

In communicating, we do not convey information unchanged— we attempt to stimulate activity in another mind. Sometimes a bare, factual statement will do this satisfactorily. At other times such a statement might fail, while a somewhat distorted statement might have the desired effect. No dishonesty is necessarily involved in the distortion. You rely on your listener to correct the distortion; and if you have caught his attention and suggested some helpful associations for him to make, you may give him a more accurate picture than you could have conveyed by trying to be literal.

Notice that "trying to be." It is simply impossible actually to be completely literal for more than a very few minutes at a time. The last sentence of the preceding paragraph was written without the slightest idea of using figurative language. Yet a moment's thought will show that *caught* and *picture* have been somewhat twisted from their earlier meanings; and a few minutes with a dictionary will show that even such precise-looking words as *accurately, associations,* and *attention* are not as literal as they seem. They were simply twisted earlier and more completely. *Accurately,* for instance, could be analyzed as something like "having-been-cared-for-shaped." You can find out about the others for yourself.

It is well to avoid overstrained figurative language, and to be careful about expressions that have been used often enough to lose their freshness, and not often enough to become completely natural in their figurative meanings. But if you want to avoid figurative language entirely, you might just as well stop talking.

Exercises—Chapter 21

Mark each of the following sentences *E* (equivocation), *C* (concealed directive), or *O* (other), according to the particular variety of indirection you think the speaker had in mind. If you recognize a clear-cut case of *connotation, slanting,* or *figurative language* among those marked *O*, specify which you think it is. In every case write a blunt statement of the sentiment you think the speaker was trying to mask with the subtlety he has attempted.

1. If the captain isn't pleased with your police-up job, nobody gets a pass this weekend.
2. You're the only girl in the world for me.
3. The salesman may have called it inexpensive, but I'd say it's cheap.
4. As your husband's physician I can tell you he's doing about as well as can be expected after this sort of operation on a person in his condition.
5. Quitters never win, and winners never quit.
6. In one instance, the judge made it very unpleasant for the teacher for not having obtained the jury-duty exemption in advance.

7. Don't let the other kids complete their sets of Droopy Flakes trading cards before you do.

8. Please, Gertrude, let's not call it the *dirty clothes basket;* it's really the *soiled clothes hamper.*

9. Smart folks eat at Joe's.

10. Everybody who is anybody will read *War and Peace.*

11. Anytime the champ can't lick that Mick, he ought to hang up his gloves.

12. When she told me I should reduce, I practically died laughing.

13. I wouldn't dream of trying to talk my way out of a ticket, officer —my uncle, the mayor, says the police force never shows favoritism.

14. None of us believes for a moment that the inaccuracies of the last speaker's statements were intentional.

15. You can live in a house, a residence, a domicile, an abode or a habitat, but there's really no place like home.

16. Just as I was about to propose to her, Sally blurted that she just loved Keats and Shelley.

17. I didn't say my political opponent should be in Alcatraz; while speaking in San Francisco I merely suggested that there was a nearby island he ought to visit.

18. A recent editorial says that conservative students are no longer afraid to stand up to collectivist professors.

19. Some say that the eggheads of the United States are not living up to their responsibilities.

20. I like neither hillbilly nor long-hair music, but prefer good popular songs.

21. My product spreads like glue and tastes like roofing cement, but it costs less than the low-priced spread *and* the high-priced spread.

22. It's time patriotic Americans stopped knuckling down to a bearded foreigner.

23. Audience reaction in the foregoing program was technically augmented.

24. In this Western movie the good women of the town tell the heroine that she should be on the stage—then they put her on the next one out of town.

25. Such a lovely dress, my dear—what a shame they didn't have it in your size.

Suggestions for Discussion or Theme Writing—Chapter 21

1. Choose a word for which there are many approximate synonyms, and arrange a list of them so that there will be a progression of connota-

tions which are (from your point of view) favorable, neutral and unfavorable. Thus, describing the place where you live, you might have a list as follows:

home	lodging
residence	quarters
house	place
abode	pad
domicile	shack
dwelling	

Discuss the more interesting connotations in detail (other things besides *favor* or the lack of it may be suggested; "quarters" may connote military life to a veteran, for instance).

2. After studying the dictionary definition of the word "euphemism," select a word such as *death, dying, janitor, sick,* and write as many words or phrases that *stand for* about the same thing but are considered less offensive or less distasteful. Discuss euphemisms in the light of their denotative and connotative significance.

FINDING A STYLE 22

In Chapter 17 we discussed a rather systematic method for finding and repairing sentences which were definitely bad because of structural flaws. Since almost anybody with much experience in using English carefully would agree that the sentences criticized *were* bad, we were on reasonably firm ground. Unfortunately, when we move up from avoiding bad sentences to writing good sentences we must leave much of our certainty behind. It is easy enough to say that good sentences should be clear, well organized, and forceful; but even after we have agreed on these adjectives there is room for a good deal of difference of opinion about what sentences deserve them. When we read a textbook full of "awkward" and "improved" sentences it often strikes us that the supposed improvement is pretty dubious. And when we examine our own sentences it is sometimes hard to decide whether we should be praised for using effective repetition and parallel constructions or condemned for using unnecessary repetition and monotonous sentence structure.

The fact that only the lowest steps in the composition process can be taught with much uniformity and certainty is disturbing to tidy minds, but there is nothing surprising about it. Musicians, tennis players, and insurance salesmen can get only so far by drilling on "fundamentals." To get any farther they must learn to work with their own particular abilities and limitations, and so find their own ways of doing things. They are still subject to criticism, and they may still be able to learn from others (as the best ones usually realize), but hard-and-fast rules won't help them much from now on. They have to see how things work, and make up their minds about what they can use.

This chapter will therefore not consist of absolute *do*'s and *don't*s, but of some points to be considered in learning to write your own kind of effective sentences. It would be silly to pretend that all the points are presented impartially. They are presented as the writer sees them, on the basis of his experience. Anybody whose experience leads him to different conclusions has a right to disagree.

Words Are Not Clothes

"I have often thought exactly the same thing, but I could never express it so well." Millions of people have used that sentence, and every one of them has been fooling himself. The idea that words are the clothes in which thoughts are dressed is a pure, though popular delusion. If a man knows both English and Spanish well, he doesn't think in "brainish" and then decide to clothe his thoughts in English or Spanish. He thinks in one language or the other, and his thoughts will vary a little according to the language he chooses. This is partly because some distinctions are easier to make in English, others in Spanish; and partly because his own previous experiences with the two languages have not been quite the same.

If English is the only language you can think in, the difference is merely one of degree. A particular thought is formed (not clothed) in a certain selection and arrangement of words, and you can't change or rearrange the words without modifying the thought. Let's consider a specific example:

> *Dick:* I guess he's a nice fellow, but I'm never quite comfortable with him. He's so kind of far away. I mean he's so—
> *Bob:* You mean he's thinking about himself so hard that he hasn't got much attention left to give to you?
> *Dick:* That's it exactly!

Now "that" may be "it"—but it is not a mere rephrasing of Dick's thought, nor is it *the* thought that Dick was groping for. It is *a* thought that Dick is willing to adopt once it is suggested to him. Now for the first time he sees, or at least guesses, what was happening that made him uncomfortable.

What Is Style?

If you are used to thinking of style as a technique for playing wonderful tricks with words, you may feel that we are approaching the subject from a peculiar angle. But technique, though important, is secondary. Think of the thousands of extremely skillful painters whose pictures are of no interest or value whatever. They handle their brushes so well that they can paint anything that they can see —but they can't really see anything for themselves. In writing as in painting, a man's style can only be a reflection of the man. He can express only what he perceives—his sense impressions filtered through his nervous system, and modified by comparison with his previous experiences. If he can't see the funny side of things, he will never develop a humorous style, no matter how earnestly he drags in jokes. And if he is only interested in sweeping general effects, he will never be able to show his readers delicate shadings.

Good styles, therefore, vary considerably, and anybody who wants to write effectively must find his own. It need not be an especially remarkable one, but it must be personal—an expression of the way the writer sees things. Train yourself to see; keep the picture in mind when you talk; and make the words fit the picture. Success is not guaranteed—but this is a more promising approach than memorizing a dictionary and a rhetoric, and hoping that you will eventually have something to say.

It is only an approach, of course. Even if you perceive things clearly and independently, there is still the problem of developing sufficient skill with words to convey your impressions to your readers forcefully, vividly, and without too much change. But this is a technique that cannot be developed first—it must grow out of your perceptions; and there is no one technique that suits everybody. That is why those books that pretend to expound "the secret" of a good style are, for most readers, such dismal failures.

If you have a good ear for tones and rhythms, you can learn to get certain effects—but what kinds of effects interest you? Do you like Bach, bop, or both? If you have a good ear for dialog you can make people come alive on your pages, even if you bring in only an occasional remark to illustrate a point. If your ear is dull but your eye is keen, you will have to work in a different way. Whatever your make-up, you have to find methods you can use, rather than simply good methods.

Your instructor probably has anywhere from twenty to fifty C students who are passively waiting for him to pour a dose of guaranteed style down their ready but not particularly eager throats. If you join them he can't do much more for you than go through the motions. But if he finds that you are taking the trouble to sharpen and clarify your perceptions and looking for ways to get them over to a reader, he may be able to give you some real help.

Get the Picture Straight

As we said earlier in the chapter, we don't think first and then put our thoughts into words—we think in a certain selection and arrangement of words. If we accept the very reasonable assumption that no two arrangements of words can have exactly the same meaning, it follows that whenever we improve one of our sentences we are improving one of our thoughts—which can probably stand it. Notice that it is clearly impossible to improve a thought simply by reconsidering the words themselves; we have to consider how well the words represent the *things, relations,* and *processes* that they stand for. Let's think again about the map-territory relation that was discussed in Chapter 12. You can "pretty up" a map by using colored inks, more careful lettering, and so forth. But the only way you can improve its accuracy is to get the lines and symbols into a more exact relation to the features of the territory that they are supposed to represent.

A vague, weak, or poorly constructed sentence may mean either that you have not seen the territory clearly, or that you have not represented accurately what you have seen. In either case, another careful look at the territory may help you to straighten out the map. For the moment we need not worry about whether this is a method that always works. In the next few sections there will be examples of how it does work, and you can decide for yourself how useful it is.

Maps of No Territory

There is no use trying to understand a sentence like "His works have that indefinable quality of universality which all critics agree is the very essence of poetic genius." It makes a reasonably agreeable noise, but it does not stand for anything on this earth. There is nothing that all critics agree about—some of them think that *Hamlet* is a very poor play. And whether we define "universality" or agree to accept it as indefinable, it doesn't stand for anything that we can point out as actually existing. Notice the difference between this term and "genius." The latter term may be hard to describe exactly, or to agree about; but Shakespeare did have the power of writing in such a way as to move many people deeply—and we might as well call this power "genius" as anything else.

Or take the happy compromiser who says "we must find the solution that will serve the best interests of all concerned." There is nothing wrong with that set of words, but they are meaningful only if there really is such a solution. Very often the interests are so opposed that what will serve some will inevitably injure others. If you want the new school on the east side where it will raise the value of your property, and I want it on the west side where it will raise the value of mine, how can we both win—by putting it in the center where it will raise somebody else's and leave us both out in the cold?

A man may be forgiven if he personally sees a mirage and mistakes it for a real territory, or even if he accepts somebody else's *reasonable* mirage in good faith. But he cannot write intelligently unless he considers the structure of what he is writing about; and if the thing has no conceivable structure, he can't write a very satisfactory sentence about it. Students (and others) who think of language as an isolated process having nothing to do with people or events often write about nothing at considerable length. Of course you may write intelligently about Centaurs or Utopias—but then you are deliberately distorting the known structure of events for a special purpose. That is quite a different thing from neglecting structure entirely.

Inflated Sentences

An honest student who is having trouble stretching his paper to three hundred words is likely to be annoyed if a quarter of the words he *has* managed to find are crossed out, to the tune of such comments as "deadwood," "padding," and "unnecessary verbiage." The student may honestly believe that the "secret" of writing ability is the knack of finding more and bigger words to express a given idea. This is a very unfruitful delusion. Compare the three following sentences:

> The majority of the individuals in attendance at the meeting gave evidence of an inclination to return to their domiciles.
> Most of the people at the meeting seemed to want to go home.
> The yawns, sighs, and frequent glances at watches showed that most of the people at the meeting wanted to go home.

The second sentence is better than the first because it says just as much in fewer and simpler words. The third sentence is about as long as the first; but it justifies its length by adding additional information. It also contains a clue to how to find some useful extra words if you really need them.

Let's start with the phrase "seemed to want." If you blow it up to "gave evidence of an inclination," you have five words instead of three, and 27 letters instead of 12. Your friends may say "Boy, he can sure sling the old lingo!" But if you slung it that way very often, they might shorten their comment to "What a windbag!" Would they be wrong? There must be a better way.

Take another look at the phrase. What does "seemed to want" stand for? What do people do when they seem to want? Different things, depending on circumstances. A very vague phrase, then. What did the people at the meeting do? They yawned, they sighed, they looked at their watches. Why not tell your readers this? It is more definite and more interesting, as well as longer, than "seemed to want." A more careful look at your territory has enabled you to improve your map by adding significant details—something quite different from messing it up with fancy curlicues.

There is nothing wrong with big words or long phrases as such. We sometimes need them to convey exact information. But you can't make a river any deeper by drawing it in dark blue ink.

Show the Proportions

Consider the following sentence:

He was a big man and he was very tired and he decided to finish one more row.

We might criticize this on the grounds of "faulty coordination" and "excessive predication"; but perhaps it would be simpler to say that it is like a map showing three separate hills of exactly the same height, when the actual territory is a ridge consisting of one fairly high peak, a lower one, and a little knob. A more accurate map might be something like this:

Although he was very tired, the big man decided to finish one more row.

Here the taller peak, or main statement, is indicated by the independent clause "the . . . man decided to finish one more row." The lower peak is indicated by the subordinate clause "Although he was very tired." And the little knob is reduced to the adjective "big"—it is not worth a whole clause of its own.

The difference between the two sentences is not primarily a matter of rhetoric. If you can't *see* the relative importance of ideas, you can't show it in a sentence. A student who writes sentences like the first one may improve with practice, but he won't make much progress if he thinks only of the writing. His first effort should be to get a clearer picture of what he is writing about. When he does this he will find it rather natural to put his main ideas into independent clauses and indicate his minor ones by subordinate clauses, phrases, or simple modifiers.

The process of subordinating minor ideas should not be carried too far. Don't try to put more in any one sentence than you can fit together without strain. But make sure that what you do put in is shown in proportion.

Get Down to Earth

Try to form a mental picture of "a domestic animal." You can't very well do it without selecting some type of domestic animal, say a horse. Now try to form a mental picture of a horse. If the picture is to be at all vivid, it must be of a particular horse, perhaps a young bay gelding with a white star on his forehead. Now try to give somebody else an idea of what you see. Which expression would you use —"domestic animal," "horse," or "bay gelding"?

Suppose you have written the sentence, "Alex has an unpleasant disposition." This shows that you don't like Alex, but it doesn't show why. Does Alex kick dogs, sulk at parties, or make nasty remarks about his friends? "Unpleasant disposition" cannot mean *anything* to your reader until he makes some kind of guess about how Alex acts. Why not toss your information directly to the reader, instead of throwing it up in the air and letting him worry about getting it down? There are so many things floating through the air, and he may get hold of the wrong one entirely.

One reason for using words on a high level of abstraction is laziness. It is much easier to draw a picture of "a" mountain than to work out the contours of a particular mountain. But if you take the trouble to find out the actual shape of Old Baldy, you will probably be able to tell your readers what it looks like.

Another reason for roaming the high levels is that it often makes the writer feel important. When a student writes "Participation in extracurricular activities has a beneficial effect on my morale," he feels that he is walking hand-in-hand with the philosophers. If he is forced to translate his sentence into something like "I feel better when I play tennis and go to a few dances," he may be considerably deflated. It is not only that he misses the lovely polysyllables—he has been reduced from Great Thoughts to everyday observations. But observations are the basis of most sound thinking—and everyday observations, if we can make them clearly and accurately, are likely to be the most important of all.

Clichés

Now let's consider clichés, also known as *trite, hackneyed,* or *stereotyped* expressions. Such phrases as *brown as a berry, fast and furious, guardian of the law,* and *sweet sixteen* have been used so often that they could just as well be put in with a set of rubber stamps—and many readers feel that the stamps are about worn out. However, the principal thing about them is not simply the number of times that they have been used; it is rather that they are seldom used to describe a direct impression. The color of a tanned face might remind you of a cigar or a saddle or a chestnut. If you said it was as brown as any of these things you would be making a map of the territory as you saw it. But if you said "brown as a berry" you would be simply borrowing a piece of a familiar old map because you were too lazy to make a new one of your own. You can't map a river accurately by taking "typical curves" from other rivers. You have to see how your river actually runs.

A great many phrases do not become trite no matter how often they are used—*his only son, must have been, one of the few,* and so forth. The principal reason is that these phrases accurately represent recurrent relations, and can be used just as directly the millionth time as the first. It is a good idea to be suspicious of a phrase that you have heard hundreds of times, but the real test is not how often it has been used, but whether you are using it to describe your own impressions or picking it up because it is handy and hoping that it will fit. If you use too many clichés you are likely to start thinking in them, which is dangerous because it discourages analysis. Sixteen, for instance, *may* be a particularly sweet age—but there seem to be a lot of parents who would just as soon skip it.

A second reason why phrases like *his only son* and so forth do not become trite is that there is nothing tricky or strained about them. They stand up well because they are simple. On the other hand, the alliteration in *brown as a berry* and *fast and furious* probably made them seem clever when they first occurred, but it wore thin some centuries ago.

Unfortunately there is no one definite point at which a word becomes a cliché. A student who has read very little may come across a phrase that seems to him new and vivid. He uses it in his next paper with pride and pleasure. But his instructor, who has read a hundred or a thousand times as much, is already bored with it and marks it "trite." The student cannot understand this, especially if he notices that other phrases in his paper, which even he has seen hundreds of times, are passed without such criticism.

The fact is that a given phrase (such as "the fact is") often seems for a time quite vigorous and effective, and a large number of people use it with general satisfaction all around. Then some of those who have heard it a lot begin to regard it as trite. It seems to them that the people who still use it are trying to be sparkling and not doing very well. The phrase is now a cliché. But sometimes it continues to be so common that it loses the effect of being an unsuccessful effort, and becomes merely a useful idiom, no more noticeable or objectionable than "must have been" or "one or the other."

Some instructors undoubtedly "carry to extremes" their "relentless opposition" to "overworked phrases," and "reduce their students to a state bordering on complete frustration." Their students will probably have to "grin and bear it"—at any rate, "no satisfactory solution is offered here." But "one or two suggestions are made for what they are worth":

1. When you are checking a paper, see whether you have used any rubber-stamp phrases.

2. When you find one, decide whether it strikes you as accurate and sensible, or whether you have really wanted only part of it and used the rest without thinking.

3. If it looks fancy, throw it out. You don't want any second-hand fanciness.

4. If you can easily say about the same thing in fewer words, shorten it.

5. Try not to swear at your instructor for marking things "trite." His principle is sound, even if he overdoes it.

Too Many Nouns

One of the easiest ways to write dull and often tangled sentences is to use too many nouns. Compare the following statements.

His surprise was the result of his lack of comprehension of the senti-
ments of the audience.

He was surprised because he did not understand how the audience felt.

The result of the adoption by the instructor of an attitude of excessive
dogmatism is the development among the students of an atmosphere
of inattention.

If the instructor gets too dogmatic, the students stop listening.

You may think the last comparison is exaggerated, but the fact is that whole books—and far too many of them—are written in a style that uses nine nouns where two would do. Excessive length is only one of the faults. Read the longer sentence aloud and see how it bumps and pounds along. You will understand why it is sometimes called "cobblestone style." Then think what must happen to the mind of the man who habitually allows himself to think in such phrasing as this. Nouns are comparatively rigid and static words which tend to conceal activity. We have to use some of them, and there are times when even the high-level ones like *adoption* and *dogmatism* and *inattention* may be useful. But you have to be careful to think through them to the activities for which they stand; and if you string too many of them together you are likely to treat your frozen generalizations as real things. Many a counsellor would get further if he would only think "Now what's eating Pete?" instead of "Which of the aberrations of adolescence is the causative factor in this antisocial behavior?"

Whenever you get tangled in a series of nouns, try to think of what actually happened, and use verbs and modifiers to show it happening. This method may sound suspiciously simple, but it very often works.

Let Your Ear Help Your Eye

Most linguists will tell you that spoken words are the primary symbols with which we communicate, and that written words are merely secondary—they stand for the sounds that stand for the things. This seems reasonable. On the other hand some of the people who write books on how to read are quite sure that this indirect representation is most inefficient. They say that the written symbol should suggest the thing directly, and that to read efficiently you should be completely unconscious of how the word sounds. This seems reasonable, too—until you begin to check. Then you find out that a good many people who have been trained to read in this way don't seem to read at all well. You may even suspect that the writers who advocate this theory do so in self-defense—anybody who thought of how *their* sentences sounded would soon give up, and there would go the royalties.

We haven't time to analyze this argument completely, and (if you must know) I am not qualified to do it. If you can read and understand somebody else's writing without noticing how it sounds, maybe you escape more pain than you miss pleasure—it depends a good deal on what writers you read. But if you inflict your *own* writing on other people without even noticing how it sounds to you, you deserve whatever happens. If what you have written is not worth your time to listen to—and listen carefully—it is not likely to be worth anybody else's. In most matters our sight is our master sense, but not in language. If a sentence is confused or clumsy or just too dull to be worth reading, your ear will tell you so sooner than your eye will. Good and bad sentences look a good deal alike, if you read them fast enough; but they don't sound alike to anybody who takes the trouble to listen.

We can't give any fixed rules for how they ought to sound; tastes as well as styles vary, and you can't expect to please everybody, no matter what you do. But there is good sense in the common complaint "I can't hear myself think." If there is any thought behind your writing, you'd better listen to that, too.

Exercises—Chapter 22

Mark the following sentences according to their principal faults as you see them. *A* (abstractions where less abstract terms would suffice), *I* (inflated, or burdened with deadwood), *P* (proportion—failure to distinguish major and minor details), *C* (clichés), or *N* (too much reliance on nouns). Rewrite each sentence to eliminate its faults, if possible.

1. I lost my job, my wife ran away, the kids fell sick and the Yankees lost to Kansas City, by one run in the ninth.

2. This will provide me with a background which will prove to be a very important period in my life.

3. True to his word the noble Redman vaulted into the saddle and rode off into the sunset.

4. With pail in hand, Jack, in the company of Jill undertook the climb to the summit of the rising ground.

5. Through strategy we can achieve total victory.

6. She was fair of skin and her eyes were blue in color.

7. When something fatal happens to a friend it might just be a comfort from all the burden.

8. Something of interest to me in the browsing room is the little room for music playing where I get a chance to sit and enjoy listening to old-fashioned music because I don't get an opportunity like that very often, so I enjoy this part very much, just being able to sit back and listen to good music just for pure pleasure.

9. I believe that knowledge is a wonderful substance to make life richer by helping people understand things and know things.

10. I feel I have gained an experience through that situation.

11. The lack of the need for air in running electric motors caused the engineers to turn to electricity for power because submarines often run in a submerged position without much air.

12. My uncle was awarded a citation because he performed brave acts outside of the regular duties he was supposed to do in working toward the termination of the second global holocaust of the twentieth century.

13. The planes were out of formation, one man's parachute failed to open, and the trucks that were to take the soldiers back to the barracks were twenty minutes late.

14. The torrential downpour was a boon to our feathered friends, but it played havoc with all the people except Noah's kith and kin.

15. The charge against me is nothing more nor less than an accumulation, nay rather a superabundance, of terminological inexactitudes.

16. Your duties as a soldier are: to keep yourself fit, to train yourself

well, to be killed in battle if called upon to do so and to salute all commissioned officers.

17. The inability to read a road map or a timetable with optimum accuracy has been the cause of many a ruined weekend trip or vacation on the part of families or individuals on vacation.

18. The circles of diplomacy at times afford little reliability or sound indication as to the feelings and desires of the individual citizens whose representatives they are.

19. We had spread out a veritable bonanza of goodies when the pesky mosquitoes launched a dastardly attack and put us to flight.

20. The inavailability of scientific measuring devices notwithstanding, the officials of the local constabulary could discern by olfactory observation of the automobile operator's exhalations that he was definitely under the influence of alcoholic intoxicants.

21. When a person is self-conscious of himself he cannot do his best work for anybody or anything.

22. From my experience, the process of counting the total number of words in a theme written for English causes more consumption of time than the actual writing of the aforesaid theme itself.

23. Unless we renew the patriotism of our founding fathers, this bountiful country of ours will bow before the yoke of tyranny.

24. Reaching into her handbag, she pushed aside a Red Death lipstick, an embroidered handkerchief, a 22-caliber pistol and thirty-eight cents change and took out her comb.

25. It has often been said that neither check, coin nor currency is adequate legal tender to purchase those things which will redound to our everlasting joy.

Suggestions for Discussion or Theme Writing—Chapter 22

1. Another man at another time and place might have said, "If I can't be free, I'd just as soon be dead," or "Death is the only honorable alternative if liberty is lost," or "If a man can't have liberty, he's better off dead." But Patrick Henry made a much stronger impression by saying "Give me liberty, or give me death!"

Suggest more literal alternatives for the expressions below, and compare them to the originals:

(a) How sharper than a serpent's tooth it is to have a thankless child.

(b) The wicked flee when no man pursueth: but the righteous are bold as a lion.

(c) The race is not to the swift, nor the battle to the strong. . . .

(d) When the gods wish to punish us they answer our prayers.

2. Take from your college catalog a paragraph that seems to you rather cloudy. See if you can improve it by substituting specifics for generalities.

LETTERS

23

Personal Letters

Most people like to get letters, but a great many people dislike writing them, not only because of the time and effort they take, but because the writers (or potential writers) feel embarrassed and uncertain about how to go about the job. The suggestions below are not guaranteed to eliminate such feelings, but they may help. We can begin by analyzing the form in a very simple example.

327 E. Davison St.
Portland 3, Oregon
July 20, 1959

Dear Bob,

We have been here for two weeks now, and it looks like a good summer. There are some tennis courts only about five minutes away, and next weekend two of the boys at the plant and I are going to try the trout fishing on the McKenzie. The job is fairly tough, but interesting, and I'm off at four thirty. Can't complain.

I ordered a lumberjack shirt for you. They were out of your size, but said they could get it to you in about two weeks.

How do you like your job with Fenner? Can't say I envy you, but maybe I'm wrong. Drop me a line some time if you're not too exhausted.

Yours,
Dick

The Form

No detail of the form used above is sacred, but here are a few things to notice:

1. *The address.* If you want an answer, you'd better put the address on every letter. Not everybody keeps an address book, and some

people throw envelopes away as soon as they have opened them (possibly so they'll have an excuse for not answering). You could put it at the end of the letter; but if you put it down first you won't forget it, or leave it out because you have come to the end of the page.

2. *The date.* You could use "Tuesday" instead of "July 20," or leave out the date entirely. But if your letter refers to any event that your friend might want to pin down later, a point of reference might be helpful. If he begins to worry about whether his shirt has gone astray, "Tuesday" won't help him much.

3. *The salutation.* You can say just "Bob" if you want to; but there is nothing either effeminate or presumptuous about addressing any-body as "Dear" in a letter, even if you wouldn't do it in person. Also, it saves time and effort to do it automatically, instead of care-fully weighing details that don't matter. You can substitute either a dash or a colon for the comma, if you prefer, or use no punctuation here at all.

4. *The ending.* Don't worry about endings being trite; they are unimportant, and usually unnoticed, formalities. If you happen to think of a more original ending, use it cheerfully; but don't strain for it. "Yours very truly" will do for slight acquaintances. "Sincerely yours," "Cordially yours," and "Yours" are successively warmer, but don't try to weigh them exactly. The other man's scales may be different.

5. *No apologies.* About the only other thing worth noticing is that Dick did not apologize either for writing the letter or for ending it. It seldom adds anything to a letter to begin with "I bet you are sur-prised to be hearing from me," and end with "Well, I guess I'd better stop now. This isn't much of a letter but. . . ." Dick assumes that Bob will be pleased to hear from him, begins with what he has to say, and stops when he has finished. It is an admirable practice.

Even if your only purpose in writing a letter is to ask a favor, an apology is seldom necessary. If what you ask is burdensome, you might say you are sorry to put him to so much trouble. But it is better to begin directly with "Could you do me a favor?" than to pre-tend that you would be writing him anyway, and that the favor is merely incidental. He probably will not be deceived.

"Social" Letters

Dick apparently didn't find it much of a strain to write to Bob, but he might feel oppressed at the idea of composing a letter to Bob's mother to express his thanks for a pleasant weekend or a birthday present. Perhaps the best advice we can give him is not to make too much of a production of it, and to be as nearly natural as he thinks she can stand. Something like the following might do:

Tuesday

Dear Mrs. Cartwright,

I want to tell you what a good time I had at your house last weekend. It was nice of you to have me, and everything we did was fun. The only drawback is that now I'll have to start all over again, getting adjusted to the dining hall food.

Please give my best to Mr. Cartwright. I'm still enjoying that story he told about the Model-T Ford. And tell Nancy I haven't either got more freckles than she has. I just counted.

Thanks again—I don't know when I've had a better time.

Sincerely yours,
Dick Burton

This certainly is not a model of grace and charm, and if you can do better nobody would be less surprised than the author. But Mrs. Cartwright will be pleased to get it. Dick *has* taken the trouble to write, and it sounds as if he'd had a good time and liked the whole family. Also, he hasn't tangled himself up with unnecessary superlatives about "your gracious hospitality" and "your lovely home." He seems to think the weekend was natural as well as pleasant. He is a nice boy, and will probably be asked again.

No return address is given, because no reply is expected. "Tuesday" is at least as good as "November 14," because it will probably mean more at the first glance, and Mrs. Cartwright is not likely to file the letter for reference. The tone is still informal, but not quite as free and easy as in the letter to Bob, except for the message to little sister. This letter should be in longhand, and preferably on reasonably good, but not fancy, stationery.

Bob will probably never have any occasion for anything much more complicated than this in the way of social correspondence. His sister may—and she may feel that a few "perfect's" and "lovely's" are necessary. The only advice I feel competent to offer is, keep it as simple as you can.

Routine Business Letters

A business letter may be headed in one of the following ways:

219 E. Maryland Avenue
Seattle 2, Washington
August 3, 1959

Mutual Insurance Company
64 Fifth Avenue
New York 11, N. Y.

Dear Sirs:

Mr. James A. Whiting
Mutual Insurance Company

Dear Mr. Whiting:

Director of Personnel
Mutual Insurance Company
64 Fifth Avenue
New York 11, N. Y.

Dear Sir:

The street address serves no particular purpose, unless you are corresponding with a number of companies with similar names, and want an extra check to make sure the right letter gets into the right envelope. However, many people feel it looks more businesslike.

The chief thing to remember about a routine business letter is that it will presumably be read by busy people who usually have no interest in either your personality or your problems. There is nothing to be gained by trying to impress them, and you waste everybody's time if you go into unnecessary detail about matters that they will handle by strict routine. You may feel that "Please suspend my subscription to your magazine until further notice" sounds a little curt; but if that is all you have to say, don't pad it. The clerk who handles such requests doesn't care why.

Don't try to write in a special "Business English." Just be as clear as possible, as brief as you can be without sacrificing clarity, and sign yourself "Yours very truly."

Important Business Letters

Of course there are some business letters that are far from routine. If you are trying to get a job or a contract, to make a sale, or to ask for special consideration of any kind, you will want to make a definite impression. Possibly you can do it by "pouring on the old personality." It is well to remember, however, that your reader probably won't be much concerned about your personality unless he can think of a way to use it, and that he is much more likely to be interested in his problems than in yours. You may have sold magazine subscriptions by explaining that you are working your way through college, but you won't sell many tractors that way.

If you are starting a business correspondence on an important matter, the most important thing is to consider the whole matter carefully from the other man's probable point of view, and proceed accordingly. To give your point of view and be prepared to deal with his objections is not enough. He may answer simply that he is not interested, and leave you nothing to argue about. You have nothing to gain by starting out as opponents, and the best way to be on the same side is to find out where he is and work from there.

Letters of Application

One very important kind of business letter is an application for a job, but the number of people who have no idea how to write such a letter is amazing. Of course there is no one pattern that will please everybody, but there are a number of common types that will please nobody. It may therefore be worth your while to consider a few general points about how to write to a prospective employer (hereafter called "he" or "him") before developing your individual variations.

1. Start your letter simply and directly by saying what job or what kind of job you are applying for. Don't apologize for bothering him, or tell him you know how busy he must be—you'll just be wasting a little more of his time. And unless you are quite sure either that you are a genius or that he isn't quite bright, don't try to bowl him over with a fancy opening. Here are two beginnings which, with minor variations, have been closing doors on their writers for years:

"Are you looking for a man who . . . ?" In brief, no.
"Currently working in the research department of Western State Electric Co., I am anxious to locate in a community in the congenial
climate of. . . ." You are, are you?

Not nearly so bad, but still clumsy, is "I am interested in applying
for a position as a technician in your department. I should like to
know whether there is an opening. I am etc." Never mind the interest
—say "I am applying" or "I wish to apply." And never mind asking
whether there is an opening. You are writing the letter on the chance
that there is.

2. Even if it means a little extra work for you, give him all the
information you think he might want in the first letter. Some applica-
tions say in effect: "I'm male, twenty-six years old, and would like
a job. If you have any further questions I'll be glad to answer them."
He won't have any further questions—why should he? Unless you tell
him enough to interest him, you won't get more than a form letter in
reply.

3. Don't ask him any questions in the first letter, or put any other
burden on him. If he gets a number of letters that seem about
equally promising, he'll probably answer those that take least effort.
Wait until he shows an interest in you before bothering him.

4. If you enclose a picture, choose one that is appropriate for the
job you are seeking, not merely one that flatters your vanity.

5. Don't enclose a stamped, self-addressed envelope. If he can't
or won't answer without one, you don't want the job anyway.

The Data Sheet

Most important of all, *enclose a data sheet*. This device has at
least three advantages. First, it puts the essential facts together in
convenient form, where they can be scanned almost at a glance—to
see if the rest of the letter is worth reading. Second, it provides some
protection against leaving out essential information. Third, it allows
you to do your boasting impersonally. After all, the main purpose of
a letter of application is to tell how good the applicant is; but since
some of us feel uncomfortable about bragging, and most of us are
easily irritated by other people's bragging, the problem of how to
do this effectively is a delicate one. The best general solution is the
data sheet (also known by various other names ranging from *poop*

sheet to *curriculum vitae*). There is no one form for these, but the following would be reasonable for a college freshman applying for a summer job that he hoped might lead to eventual permanent employment.

DATA SHEET
Ronald F. Sebring

Year of Birth: 1945   *Height:* 5′ 11″   *Weight:* 175   *Health:* Excellent
Marital status: single   *Draft status:* 2 S   *Rel. Pref:* Methodist
Education: Graduated from Chandler, Arizona High School, 1963
            Now freshman at Carradine College.
            Major: Economics
            Grade average, first semester: B+
High School activities:
    Basketball: three letters. Captain senior year.
    Tennis: one letter.
    Organizations: Hi-Y, International Relations Club (vice-president),
                Lettermen's Club (president). Several class offices.
College activities:
    Basketball: freshman numerals.
    Tennis: squad member.
    Organizations: International Relations Club,
                Wesleyan Foundation.
Working experience:
    Have earned all spending money since I was twelve, and am now
        paying over half of my college expenses. Paper route, 2 years.
        Yard work etc., 3 years. Carry-out boy, Bayliss Market, summer
        of 1962. Checker, same store, summer of 1963.

References:
    The following people have offered to write references for me:
James F. Finton, Assistant Manager, Bayliss Market, 746 Morton Avenue,
    Chandler, Arizona.
Homer Mattux, Supervisor of Grounds and Buildings, Carradine College.
Professor J. T. Simmons, Economics Department, Carradine College (my
    adviser).

Ronald could have this duplicated and send a copy with every letter of application. Some employers won't care whether he is a Methodist or a Buddhist, and they might count a point against him if he wrote a sentence about his religion in his letter; but they are used to seeing this entry on data sheets, and can simply skip over it if they are not interested. And for some jobs, such as counseling at a boy's camp, the information may be required. Not every employer will care if he is an athlete, but his record in basketball and tennis support his statement that his health is excellent. His activities and offices indicate that he gets along well with people and has some ability as a leader, and he seems to be both responsible and hard working, though possibly a trifle serious-minded for some tastes. The fact that he worked the second summer for the same store, but at a better job, is especially significant. Altogether, he has given a fairly attractive picture of himself without sounding in the least conceited.

Your own qualifications will of course be different. If you are the same height as Ronald but weigh only a hundred and fifteen pounds and have asthma, you can't put your health down as excellent. But you may be able to put down something like this:

> *Health:* Good, except for uncomfortable but not disabling asthma. Have missed only nine days of work or school in last five years, and quality of work has not suffered.

You are not supposed to lie, but you are entitled to present the facts in a favorable light.

Using the Data Sheet

Important as the data sheet is, it needs a little help from the letter. If the sheet is impressive in itself and the job is purely technical the letter can be brief and colorless. But usually an employer will want to know what you are like as well as what you can do, and most employers have a firm (though often unjustified) belief that they can read character from a letter. In general the best method is to be simple and direct. You may wish to call his attention to one or two items in the data sheet that you think are especially important for his job, and perhaps to explain them a little more fully. It is also reasonable to explain why you want this particular job; but do it in a way that shows your preference is to his advantage as well as yours.

For instance, if you apply for a job in Southern California on the grounds that you "have always wanted to see the West Coast," why should he care? But if you explain that the doctors have told your dependent sister that she needs a warmer climate, there are two small points in your favor. First, you sound like somebody who might stay long enough to be worth hiring. Second, you apparently have some sense of responsibility. It is even possible that he might be moved by a third, or humanitarian, reason. But you shouldn't count on that one, and you certainly shouldn't emphasize it. He wouldn't hold *his* job long if he hired people mainly out of charity or benevolence.

No model letter of application will be given here, mostly because experience shows that students tend to follow such a model far too closely, and your instructor might get tired of correcting minor variations. But remember at·least the following three points: use a data sheet, keep the letter simple and direct, and concentrate on what *he* will want to know.

Exercises—Chapter 23

Mark the following entries *Y* (yes) or *N* (no), indicating whether you think them appropriate for use in business letters. Give a brief reason for every one you reject, and offer a substitute expression if one seems necessary.

1. Yours very truly,
2. Attached please find . . .
3. Please suspend my subscription to your magazine until further notice.
4. A prompt reply will be deeply appreciated.
5. Forgive me for being presumptuous, but . . .
6. Dear Sirs:
7. Are you looking for a man who . . . ?
8. I wish to apply . . .
9. I note that you have failed to specify what the job will pay . . .
10. I hereby acknowledge your letter of April 10, and wish to state . . .
11. (Letter of application) I am enclosing a stamped, self-addressed envelope.
12. Looking forward to hearing from you, I am . . .
13. Currently working in the research department of Western State Electric Co., I am anxious to locate in a community in the congenial climate of . . .
14. I realize this letter has run to some length, but . . .
15. I am applying . . .
16. About item #6, of the enclosed data sheet, I would like to add . . .
17. Your letter of April 8 has been received and the contents of same duly noted.

18. If you want an interview it will have to be next week at the latest . . .

19. There may be others equally qualified, but I really need the job.

20. I am in receipt of your communication dated August 4, and I wish to reply . . .

Suggestions for Discussion or Theme Writing—Chapter 23

1. Draw up a personal data sheet for yourself, as you actually are now, for use in actual application for a definite job you are interested in, perhaps for next summer's work. Be sure to name references.

2. Prepare a letter of application to the actual person, by name or title, who is in charge of this job (#1 above). If you do not want an interview in the near future, indicate when you would be available for it.

3. Prepare a letter to one person listed in your personal data sheet, telling him that you have given him as a reference.

4. Prepare a letter to the friend or member of your family who would be most interested in helping or advising you in getting this job. Tell him, among other things, what you have done, whom you have given as references, and what your hopes are for the future with this job.

THE RESEARCH
PAPER
24

The general aim of research is to answer questions by giving fair consideration to the best available evidence. Research may be conducted in a laboratory, by a field investigation, or in many other ways; but the research for a freshman paper is usually confined to printed material, either collected in a source-book or waiting to be discovered in the college library. The job may be broken down into the following five steps: (a) finding a good question; (b) locating the best printed evidence on this question; (c) considering this evidence until you reach a reasonable conclusion; (d) organizing your findings; (e) presenting these findings in such a way that a reader can easily check their accuracy and completeness.

A good many students concentrate too much and too early on the fifth step. The mechanics of a term paper—physical organization, footnotes, bibliography, and so forth—are certainly important, and will be explained in this chapter at some length. But these things are only means to an end. If you understand how and why they work you should be able to get them straight and use them reasonably and accurately. If you don't you may well blunder along, trying to get two footnotes on a page (whether it needs ten or none), oppressed by a sense of futility and feeling extremely vague about what you are trying to do. We shall therefore examine the general principles of research writing first, and then try to show how sound mechanics fit in with these principles.

Step One: Finding a Good Question
There are at least three requirements for a good question:

1. It should interest you. It will take you a good many hours to

write a respectable term paper, and there is no use being bored when you might be finding out something that you want to know.

2. It should lead to a fairly definite answer. If you ask "Is jazz better than classical music?" you can wander around indefinitely, and you may develop an interesting essay; but you'll never have a satisfactory term paper. You would do much better to ask (a) "What are the technical contributions of jazz?" or (b) "What proportion of music critics now consider jazz a serious and important form of music?"

3. It should be limited enough to be handled adequately within the assigned length.

Limiting the Question

Most students begin by asking a much bigger question than they can answer satisfactorily in a paper of perhaps 2,500 words. This is natural, and nothing to worry about. You are not committed to answering all of the original question. When you learn enough to realize that it is too big, narrow it down; and when you learn still more, narrow it down again. It does not matter how small the eventual question is, as long as you treat it adequately. For instance, if you began by asking "What kind of man was Abraham Lincoln?" you would find thousands of pages on the subject, and you could not compress all the information into a term paper. But if you finally narrowed it down to something like "What kind of a soldier was Lincoln in the Black Hawk war?" you would find comparatively little material scattered through your various sources. By getting all this material together, and comparing it carefully, you might construct an interesting paper.

Here are some other examples of topics narrowed down to a reasonable scope:

1. General topic: Winter Sports
   First reduction: Skiing
   Second reduction: Skiing Techniques
   Final form: Changes in Skiing Techniques Since 1940
2. General topic: Poetry
   First reduction: Ballads
   Second reduction: American Ballads
   Third reduction: Cowboy Ballads
   Final form: The Dying Cowboy Theme in American Ballads

3. General topic: Furniture
  First reduction: Antique Furniture
  Second reduction: American Antique Furniture
  Final form: Duncan Phyfe Chairs

The sooner you narrow down your question, the sooner you will know what sort of material to look for and what you can afford to disregard; but you can expect to lose some time exploring the area before you have selected your particular subject. This lost time is not entirely wasted; you need some general background in order to treat your subject with some sense of proportion.

Step Two: Gathering the Evidence

If you are writing a "controlled" research paper the evidence you are to use has already been collected for you. If you are writing a "library" paper you must try to gather the *best* available evidence that bears on your question. A freshman is not expected to be completely successful, for it takes some experience to find out what the "best available evidence" is and how to locate it. But your instructor will certainly expect you to do more than pick up the first few books and articles that seem to pertain to your subject and leave yourself at their mercy, regardless of their value. So will instructors in other courses; and so should you, if you want a college education to go along with your degree. Some of the things which should be considered are listed below:

1. What are the author's qualifications? Anything that you can find out about his position, training, and experience is worth considering.

2. What evidence does he give that he has done his work carefully? Footnotes indicate that he is willing for a reader to check his sources. A bibliography gives some idea of the extent of his study. A good index shows that he expects readers to look up specific points, and not merely read through once.

3. Who published the work? An article in a scientific journal is more likely to be accurate than one in a popular magazine. A book put out by a university press or by a well established publishing house that does a good deal of business with colleges has something in its favor—so many faces would be red if the critics made fun of it.

4. How is the work regarded by competent critics? You may be able to find book reviews or references to it in other works on the same subject.

5. Does the author impress you as writing carefully and impartially, or does he show a definite bias? Does he seem to be more interested in dramatic effect than in accuracy?

The next few sections contain some suggestions on how to find not only material but good material. There are several ways to begin, and no one of them is always best. You will have to work out one for yourself—and probably modify it next time.

The Card Catalog

Before deciding which books to use, you must find some books to examine. One place to begin looking is in the card catalog of your library. This should have at least three cards for every non-fiction book—one for the author, one for the title, and one for the subject. The listings by author and title are simple and very reliable, but no library has ever devised a completely satisfactory listing by subject. Some books deal with dozens of different subjects, and it would not be practicable to have a separate card for each one. Accordingly, a card is made out for the most obvious subject, and perhaps additional cards are made out for one or two others, but there are a good many gaps. If you don't find enough under what seems to you the obvious heading, try to think of other headings that might be applied to the same subject, or to a broader field including that subject. Thus you might find useful material on skiing in books listed under "Winter Sports," "Outdoor Sports," or "Athletics."

It is therefore not advisable to try to get too much from the card catalog at the first attempt. It is better to draw two or three books pertaining to your subject whose cards indicate that they contain *bibliographies* (lists of books in the same field or in closely related ones). These bibliographies will give you the authors and titles of other books, which you can then look up in the card catalog with much less effort. Moreover, the bibliographies often give information about the contents and value of the books listed, and are therefore useful in helping you to find the "best evidence."

Indexes to Periodical Literature

Some of the material that you need has probably been published in periodicals rather than in book form. Such material may be located through various periodical indexes:

The Reader's Guide to Periodical Literature is the index that freshmen are most likely to find useful (and also the one that almost all college libraries have). It covers popular magazines that contain at least some serious information—roughly, the range from *Look* to *Scientific American*. It is published monthly, but "cumulated quarterly." That is, the February issue covers January articles, and the March issue covers February articles; but the April issue is a combined listing for January, February, and March. Later the quarterly issues will be combined into yearly issues. If your subject is of contemporary interest, be sure that you examine the latest issues available, even if they are not yet bound in permanent form. In some libraries the monthly issues are kept in a different place from the permanent volumes.

The International Index to Periodicals covers more specialized American scholarly and technical journals, and most of the important foreign ones. Small libraries often do not have this, because they do not have enough of the journals indexed to make it worth while. It is generally more useful for advanced research than the *Reader's Guide;* if it is available it should certainly be examined, even for a freshman paper.

The entries in these indexes are highly condensed to save space, and may not always be clear at the first glance. The best way to master them is to examine the explanations at the front of the volume, then check out a couple of magazines covered by the index you are using. Every item in an entry means something. Examine the magazine until you are sure just what it does mean and you should have no further trouble. If there is anything you can't make out after a fair try, ask your instructor to help you; but don't expect him to explain it all before you start.

In addition to the two mentioned above, there are several other indexes which you may find helpful. Most of them are limited to certain fields, and some of them list books, pamphlets, and bulletins as well as magazine articles. You will not need all of them for any one paper; but if you examine the list and then look up the ones that apply to your own field, you may find them very helpful.

Agricultural Index
Book Review Digest
Education Index
Essay and General Literature Index
Index to Short Stories
Industrial Arts Index
International Catalogue of Scientific Literature
Poole's Index to Periodical Literature (Predecessor to the *Reader's Guide*—covers the years before 1907)
Portrait Index
Public Affairs Information Service
Song Index
United States Document Catalog
Writings on American History

These vary considerably in both the quality of the editing and the periods covered; and your library may not have them all. But since any one of them may save you hours of looking for needles in haystacks, it is worth while looking for any that seem appropriate.

The *New York Times Index* will help you locate immediate accounts of news events. Even if the *Times* itself is not available, the dates will probably enable you to find stories in other papers or news magazines.

General Reference Works

The indexes listed in the preceding section merely tell you where to go for information. In this section are listed a few of the more important general works which can be used as direct sources. Some of them (particularly the encyclopedias) also indicate further sources. It will be worth your while to examine each of these, even if you have no immediate need for them. There are other things that you will want to know later, and it is useful to have an idea of the sorts of information that are available.

1. General encyclopedias
   Collier's Encyclopedia
   Columbia Encyclopedia

Encyclopaedia Britannica (for material before the first World War, the 11th edition as well as the latest should be examined)
Encyclopedia Americana
New International Encyclopaedia

2. Special encyclopedias

Catholic Encyclopedia
Hastings's *Encyclopaedia of Religion and Ethics*
Jewish Encyclopedia
New Schaff-Herzog Encyclopedia of Religious Knowledge
Encyclopaedia of the Social Sciences

3. Annual compilations of facts and figures

Annual supplements to the *Britannica,* the *Americana,* and the *New International*
Facts on File
Statesman's Yearbook
Statistical Abstract of the United States
World Almanac

4. Collections of biographical information

American Men of Science
Current Biography: Who's News and Why
Dictionary of American Biography
Dictionary of National Biography (British)
Living Authors
Webster's Biographical Dictionary
Who's Who (British)
Who's Who in America

There are, of course, a great many other important and useful reference works. These are listed merely as a hint. They are not discussed because there is very little value in knowing facts about them. The important thing is to get used to handling a good many of them.

Bibliography Cards

Whenever you find a title that looks really promising, you will do well to make out a bibliography card at once. You may eventually decide not to use the source, but it is less trouble to make out a number of unnecessary cards than to search again for the exact material needed for one. Use a 3 x 5 inch card and follow the basic form indicated in the accompanying illustration.

*Laird, Charlton, The Miracle of
    Language (Cleveland:
    World Publishing Company,
    1953)*

Many interesting examples

400
La.23m
1953

Notice:

1. The last name of the author is given first, followed by his first name (as above) or initials. This makes it easy to arrange the cards in alphabetical order.

2. The title is underlined. It is very unwise to use abbreviations in copying the title. You might expand them incorrectly when you list them in your paper.

3. The city of publication, the publisher, and the date are given in that order, and punctuated as illustrated. If no date is given, put "n.d." in place of date.

4. The call number is noted in the lower left-hand corner so that you won't have to look it up again when you want to draw the book. (You can get this from the card catalog.)

5. The number *4* in the upper right-hand corner is an arbitrary code number. You can save trouble by using this number instead of the title on your note cards (to be discussed later) and in the first draft of your paper.

6. Any comment that you think may be helpful to you may be written in the remaining space.

7. The example shown is for a book by a single author. Minor variations for other types of sources are indicated in the following list:

(a) Basic form:

> Flesch, Rudolph, *How to Test Readability* (New York: Harper, 1951).

(b) Two or three authors:

> Loomis, Roger Sherman, and Donald Lemen Clark, eds., *Modern English Readings,* Sixth ed. (New York: Rinehart, 1950).

(c) More than three authors:

> Grebanier, Bernard D., and others, eds., *English Literature and Its Backgrounds,* Revised ed. (New York: Dryden Press, 1949). 2 vols.

(d) Indication of a particular edition:

> [See (b) and (c), above.]

(e) A work of several volumes:

> [See (c), above.]

(f) Edited or compiled volume:

> Tennyson, Alfred Lord, *Representative Poems,* Selected and ed. by Samuel C. Chew (New York: Odyssey Press, 1941). (Odyssey Series in Literature.)

> [For an anthology see (b) and (c), above.]

(g) Selection from an edited volume:

> Holmes, Roger, "What Every Freshman Should Know," *Readings for Opinion.* Ed. by Earle Davis and William C. Hummel (Englewood Cliffs, N.J.: Prentice-Hall, 1952), pp. 4-9. (Prentice-Hall English Composition and Introduction to Literature Series.)

(h) Chapter from a book:

> Perrin, Porter G., "The Reference Paper," *Writer's Guide and Index to English,* Revised ed. (Chicago: Scott, Foresman, 1950), Chap. 13.

(i) Books in a series:

> [See (f) and (g), above.]

(j) Encyclopedia:

> *Encyclopedia Americana,* 1936 issue.
> *Encyclopaedia Britannica,* 14th ed., 1929.

(k) Selection from an encyclopedia:

"Cosmogony," *Encyclopaedia Britannica* (14th ed., 1929), VI, 488-493.

(l) No author ascertainable:

Manual of Style, Tenth ed. (Chicago: University of Chicago Press, 1937).

(m) Magazines, basic form:

Dykema, Karl, "Progress in Grammar," *College English,* XIV (Nov. 1952), 93-100.

(Notice that the title of the article is in quotation marks, and the name of the publication is in italics. The number of the volume is given because bound periodicals often have the volume number rather than the date on the back. Roman numerals are used to prevent any possible confusion with page numbers.)

(n) Magazines, no author ascertainable:

"What Is Meant by 'Air Conditioning'?" *American Home,* XV (Mar. 1936), 74.

(o) Newspapers:

Arizona Republic, Nov. 4, 1952.

(Headlines and page references are generally included only in the footnotes referring to a newspaper article.)

(p) Pamphlets and Bulletins:

The Short Ballot. Constitutional Convention Bulletin No. 5 (Springfield, Illinois: Legislative Reference Bureau, 1919).

U. S. Department of State, *The Constitution of the United States of America.* Literal Print (Washington: U. S. Govt. Printing Office, 1934).

Step Three: Considering the Evidence

One way to compose a term paper is to read a few books and articles, write from memory, and then put in as many footnotes as seem reasonably impressive, either by desperately trying to find the actual sources again or by making guesses that you think will get by.

This method is not likely to earn you a good grade, and will most certainly cheat you of an opportunity for valuable training. A more systematic approach is therefore desirable.

Making a Tentative Outline

Your first few hours of reading will be largely exploratory. You will want to get a general picture of the subject and some idea about how much of it you can reasonably cover. You began by asking a question, but your paper is to be a statement of what you have found. As soon as you have done enough exploring to have some idea of what you are going to cover, you can save yourself a good deal of time by making a tentative outline. This should be in the form of topics and subtopics rather than sentences, because you should not decide exactly what you are going to say until you have seen the evidence. There should be plenty of space between the lines to permit the insertion of new subtopics as you discover them. The growing outline will serve several purposes:

1. It will help you to look for the material that you need—and to avoid wasting many hours on material that is not pertinent to your purpose.

2. It will help in the narrowing-down process. If you find that the job is bigger than you thought, and you are now most interested in Section III, you can throw out Sections I and II and concentrate on III. This is much better than pretending to cover the larger subject but actually skimping two-thirds of it.

3. It may suggest gaps that you should fill in.

Using Note Cards

Once you have made your tentative outline, do all the rest of your reading with a pencil in hand and a stack of cards available. You are now looking for specific information, and you are responsible both for getting it exactly right and for telling your reader exactly where you got it. You will save yourself time and agony if you make your notes clear enough and full enough so that you can use them without going back to the source, which another student may have borrowed by the time you want it again—leaving you completely helpless. Take your notes on cards or card-sized slips of paper (either 3 x 5 or 4 x 6 inches), and follow three invariable rules:

1. Never put more than one item on a card—this is the main reason for using cards rather than sheets of paper. You will have to rearrange the information you gather in the order demanded by *your* organization of material, which may be quite different from that of your source; and you will have to bring together material on the same point from different sources. The easiest way to do this is to arrange your cards to fit your outline. If you have several items on one card you will have to choose between cutting it into unmanageable scraps and doing extra copying.

2. Be sure that your notes are full and clear enough to be usable a month later. An abbreviation that seems obvious now may be meaningless then. If you use your cards as a piecemeal first draft rather than as an extra step, you can save a great deal of trouble.

3. Be sure that each card contains an exact reference to the source, and an indication of the place in your paper where you expect to use the information.

Below are two examples of cards that follow these principles. The first indicates the place in the paper by a reference to the outline, and the source by a code number. The second indicates the place by a subject heading and the source by the actual title. Either method will do.

II A   6,259

Military planes produced in the U.S. in 1945. 46,819

Plane production, U.S. Information Please Almanac, 1947　p.259

Military planes produced in the U.S. in 1945: 46,819

Why All the Notes?

Most students—and particularly many bright students—do not want to take nearly as many notes as they should. Their unwillingness comes partly from laziness and partly from exaggerated optimism about their memory; but perhaps the chief reason is the fear that too much borrowing will leave no room for originality. This fear is quite unjustified. Originality in research depends mostly on looking at evidence from a fresh point of view, not on digging up entirely new evidence—and certainly not on stealing evidence without acknowledgment. Remember two things:

1. You are expected to emphasize rather than minimize what you have taken from your sources.

2. You are expected to make your mistakes as easy to find as possible.

These may seem like rather stern principles, but a little thought will show that they are absolutely necessary. Research is a cooperative effort, perhaps the most important effort of contemporary society. There is simply no point in doing it, even on an apprentice scale, unless you realize this.

The writer of a legitimate research paper has two principal aims: *first,* to find and evaluate the most useful evidence on a given problem; *second,* to present his findings in such a way that a reader can use them with as little wasted effort and as much confidence as possible.

To repeat, research is cooperative. Even when a man does a particular bit of it "all by himself" he is using techniques and evidence developed by those who went before him, and the whole value of his report lies in its usefulness to those who come after. Since his aim is quite different from those of a journalist, a novelist, or a critic, he must naturally use a different method. The details of that method may at first seem bewildering, even ridiculous, but their purpose is simple efficiency. To put the matter on the lowest possible level, suppose your instructor suspects some statement that you have made. He should be able to find your source with the least possible effort, and check it. He can forgive you for being wrong much more readily than for wasting his time.

Several Kinds of Notes

You cannot take notes successfully unless you have a fairly definite idea of what you are looking for. You should use your tentative outline as a rough guide—remembering that it may be wise to revise it somewhat as you go along. You should also realize that your paper will probably contain at least three kinds of material, and it is wise to take clear and full notes for each of the three kinds. *Get as much of your paper as you can on your cards.* You are going to have to write it some time, and the easiest time is when you have your sources before your eyes. If you want to write something too extensive to put on a card, you can write it on a sheet of paper, then fold the paper and clip it to a card. But don't do this unless you are fairly sure that what you write is a single unit. It is easier to rearrange cards than to cut up paper or recopy.

The three main kinds of material are listed below. Since the first two should be indicated by footnotes when you put them into your paper, make sure your cards show the exact page references. The third kind may not require footnotes, but it is wise to make your notes as soon as they occur to you, and to put them on cards that can be fitted in with the others.

1. Facts found in various sources and organized to suit your own purpose. You do not need a footnote for any statement that is original with you or for any matter of really general knowledge; but you do need one for *every fact* that you have found in your research. Don't

fail to put one in just because you have seen the fact mentioned in several different books and *now* think you can take it for granted. Show your reader where you got it. If you find a dozen facts on the same page you may put them all into one paragraph, with a single footnote for the whole paragraph. The thing to remember is that a reader who wants to check the authority for any one fact should be able to turn directly to the page on which it occurs. Make a note of every fact that you expect to use. Then you will have no trouble putting in a footnote.

2. The opinions of your sources about the significance of these facts. If you say that the Sioux Indians were better fighters than the Blackfeet, your readers are going to wonder how you know. It is much better to say that "Major Langham, who had fought against both, considered the Sioux Indians betters fighters than the Blackfeet." This is not proof, but it is evidence worth considering.

3. Your own conclusions, based on a study of both the facts and the opinions of your sources. Remember that, although you get your raw material from other people, the final paper is your own. You are not supposed to accept evidence unless it convinces you. It is particularly unfortunate to cite contradictory evidence as if you believed both sides, but a good many students do exactly this. Suppose you have not only Langham's statement that the Sioux were better fighters, but Colonel Hamill's statement that the Blackfeet were better. What are you going to do about them?

There are any number of possibilities. Perhaps the statements were made fifty years apart. Then there is no real contradiction, merely evidence of a shift. Perhaps you can find evidence that one man was prejudiced, or that one had much more experience than the other. In any case, it is your job to evaluate both statements and to indicate your own conclusion. If you find that you can reach no conclusion, say so definitely. It is much better to say "The evidence is conflicting and I can't decide" than to write as if you didn't notice the conflict.

Quotations

Sometimes you may want to use the exact words of one of your sources, particularly when they indicate opinions. When you do, be sure that you enclose them in quotation marks on your cards, so that you can identify them as quotations when you use them in your paper. Remember also that you should not make any change whatever without indicating it clearly. Use the following devices:

1. Indicate omissions by three dots.

Original: Smith, who had been ill for weeks, died November 23.
Quotation: "Smith . . . died November 23."

2. Enclose corrections or clarifications in brackets.

Original: He knew that Brown had lived there since 1863.
Quotation: "He knew that [Charles A.] Brown had lived there since 1863 [actually 1861]."

3. If you want to leave a mistake uncorrected, indicate that you are doing so intentionally by putting *sic,* underlined or italicized and in brackets, immediately after the mistake. *Sic* is Latin for "thus." In this use it means "That is the way he wrote it."

Original: He left New Orlins in 1926.
Quotation: "He left New Orlins [*sic*] in 1926."

In the finished paper a quotation of more than four lines should be indicated by single spacing and indenting rather than by quotation marks.

Paraphrases and Summaries

You should use quotations only when the exact words of the source are important for your purpose. Ordinarily you should simply take the material and find words of your own. Two rather common tendencies are particularly unfortunate:

1. Quoting without acknowledgment. Your instructor will be *so* surprised to find that you are suddenly writing like Walter Pater. The fact that you change an occasional word does not justify this kind of copying.

2. Deliberately changing the words while slavishly following the ideas. This is perhaps a little better than (1), but not much. When you copy from a writer, do it exactly and give him credit. When you

merely use his facts and opinions, you should still acknowledge whatever you have taken (and there is nothing shameful in taking a great deal). But remember that your purpose is different from his. Take what you need in as few words as possible. Then write your own paragraphs in your own way.

Sometimes you will want to expand a statement found in a source. More frequently you will have reason to condense it. Everything he says may be important, interesting, and concisely expressed; but if you take only what is useful for your immediate purpose, you can usually save a good many words.

Step Four: Organizing Your Findings

When you have finished taking your notes you are ready to begin putting the paper together; and if you have done a good job so far, you should have practically all the material available except for some fairly obvious expansions. The first step is to rearrange your notes according to the headings of your outline. You will probably find that some of the notes should now be discarded—for instance a card made from one book may have been superseded by a better card taken from a second book. You may also find that there are some obvious gaps. You will then have to consider the notes and outline together, and decide either that you can afford to eliminate part of the outline or that you should take additional notes. When your notes and outline match you will probably find it advisable to rewrite the outline in the full sentence form discussed in Chapter 15 before going any further. Your tentative topic outline shows only what you are going to talk about. A sentence outline will help you to decide and clarify exactly what you are going to say.

The process of transferring material from good notes to sheets of paper is mostly mechanical, but you will probably need an intermediate draft before the final copy. Be extremely careful to copy accurately, and to *document* as you go along—that is, to indicate where you got each piece of information that is not either original with you or a matter of common knowledge. Once again, don't be afraid that too much documentation will give the impression that you have no originality. You will be judged on your ability to collect reliable information and arrange it to suit your purpose. How much of your own you will be able to add is largely a matter of pure luck. At any rate, it is secondary.

Footnotes

You indicate a footnote by placing its number at the end of the information to which it refers, and slightly above the line. At the bottom of the page you indent five spaces and repeat the same number, again slightly above the level of the line you are going to write. Follow this number with an indication of the exact page where you found the information. In your draft you may give simply the code number of your source, thus:

Smith left Springfield on April 2, 1837.[1] He went first to . . .

----
[1] 6, 323.

In your final copy you will replace the code number 6 with the exact information on your bibliography card. Be sure to indicate all your footnotes on your draft. If you wait until the final copy, the task of putting them in correctly will be much more difficult.

Step Five: Putting Your Paper in Final Form

Before typing the final version of your paper it is well to go over your draft with the idea of making it as useful as possible. The primary aim of research writing is neither to impress nor to charm the reader, but to give him reliable information as directly and economically as possible. The cardinal virtues are accuracy, clarity, and brevity, in that order. If you are writing about Lincoln, for instance, it is usually better to call him *Lincoln* eight times on one page than to try to "avoid monotony" by referring to him under eight different disguises which may confuse and will certainly delay a reader. Above all, make sure that you haven't tried to smooth over any weak spots by being vague. If you don't know something, say so.

When you actually type the final version follow the directions in the next two sections unless your instructor directs you otherwise.

Footnote Form

The first footnote reference to a source is taken from the entry on the bibliography card with two slight changes:

1. The author's name is given in normal order instead of with the last name first. Since footnotes are not arranged alphabetically, there is no reason for reversing the normal order.

2. The name of the publisher is usually omitted. A curious reader can refer to your bibliography if he wants this information, but he is not likely to want it at the instant he is reading. He may, however, want to know at once both the date and city of publication (*London,* for instance, might indicate a British viewpoint). Compare the two following entries:

BIBLIOGRAPHY CARD

Black, Max, *Critical Thinking: An Introduction to Logic and Scientific Method* (Englewood Cliffs, N.J.: Prentice-Hall, 1946).

FOOTNOTE

[1] Max Black, *Critical Thinking: An Introduction to Logic and Scientific Method* (Englewood Cliffs, N.J., 1946), p. 231.

(In addition to the differences in content, notice the reverse indentation of the bibliography entry, which makes the author's name stand out.)

Later references to the same source should be abbreviated. For instance:

[16] Black, *Critical Thinking,* p. 267.

When a footnote refers to the same source as the *immediately preceding footnote,* it should be abbreviated still further by using *ibid.* (from Latin *ibidem,* "in the same place").

[17] *Ibid.,* p. 279.

Notice that *ibid.* is capitalized when it begins a footnote, is in italics (in a term paper, underline it), and is followed by both a period and a comma.

Other Latin abbreviations are sometimes used, but most students find they lose more time in learning them than they gain by shortening their footnotes. If you run across one in your research, you can find its meaning in the dictionary.

You should be able to figure out the forms for footnotes referring to articles, books by more than one author, and so forth by applying the principles just explained to the information on your bibliography cards. However, a possible series of footnotes is given here as an additional check:

[1] Bernard D. Grebanier and others, *English Literature and Its Backgrounds* (New York, 1949), II, 393-394.

[2] *Ibid.*, p. 397.

[3] Karl Dykema, "Progress in Grammar," *College English,* XIV (Nov. 1952), 95.

[4] Archibald A. Hill, *Introduction to Linguistic Structures* (New York, 1958), p. 79.

[5] Dykema, "Progress in Grammar," p. 94.

[6] Grebanier and others, *English Literature* . . ., I, 435.

[7] Hill, *Introduction to Linguistic Structures,* p. 85.

[8] *Ibid.*, p. 169.

Number the footnotes consecutively throughout the paper. Single-space the footnotes, and double-space between them.

Mechanics of Final Copy

In its final form, your term paper should have the following parts:

1. Title page

THE MAJOR USES OF DIESEL OIL

Term Paper Prepared for English 102

Stewart A. Jelliffe

2. Outline or Table of Contents
3. The Body of the Paper (complete with footnotes)
4. Bibliography (an alphabetical list of the sources mentioned in your footnotes). Use the exact form on your bibliography cards (assuming that you have followed instructions in making them out). The bibliography for the works to which the footnotes in the previous section refer would then appear as follows:

Dykema, Karl, "Progress in Grammar," *College English,* XIV (Nov. 1952), 93-100.

Grebanier, Bernard D., and others, eds., *English Literature and Its Backgrounds* (New York: Dryden Press, 1949). 2 vols.

Hill, Archibald A., *Introduction to Linguistic Structures* (New York: Harcourt, Brace, 1958).

Listed below are most of the more obvious mechanical rules you should follow in preparing the final copy of your paper:

1. Type your paper double-spaced on 8½ x 11 inch unlined paper. Single-space long quotations (five lines or more) and indent them five spaces. Single-space bibliographical entries and footnotes. Leave a double space between footnotes and between the items in the bibliography.

2. Margins: left, 15 spaces; right, 10 spaces; top, 10 spaces; bottom, 6 spaces.

3. Number your pages (except the first page). Place the number even with the right margin, 8 spaces down.

4. Indent the first line of each paragraph 5 spaces.

5. If you are going to use graphs, tables, or illustrations, consult your instructor about their placement and form of acknowledgment.

6. Do not fold your paper. Fasten it with a paper clip, staple it along the left side, or bind it in a folder.

7. Make at least one carbon copy.

Possible Variations

The rules just given are distinctly arbitrary. The sky will not fall if you follow a slightly different model. You may find some variation, also, in the exact form of the footnotes and bibliographical entries in different sources. If your instructor suggests some departure from the form suggested here, you will do well to follow him. But you had better follow some one definite form throughout. If you waver between several, the result is likely to be ambiguous, and is almost certain to draw criticism.

Exercises—Chapter 24

Answer the following questions briefly and simply:

1. By what device may a writer indicate that he is leaving an author's mistake uncorrected when he is quoting from that author?

2. What are three rules for note takers suggested in the chapter?

3. Quote the following passage properly, omitting the reference to the North Korean:

   The American soldier, unlike the North Korean, was not disadvantaged by the conversion to heavy weapons.

4. Quote the following statement, but indicate your awareness of its errors, although you leave them uncorrected:

   At that time President Rosavelt was in Worm Springs, Georgia.

5. What is the smallest number of catalog cards for one book that should be found in a card catalog? Identify each of them.

6. Briefly summarize the differences between the forms of a *bibliography entry* for a book and a *footnote entry* for the same source. Do the same for a magazine reference.

7. Write three statements, each characteristic of one of the three separate and distinct *kinds* of information which are likely to be found in any research paper.

8. Name the four *kinds* of general reference works discussed in the chapter. What is the nature of the information each is apt to contain?

9. How are long quotes (more than four lines) to be handled in a finished paper?

10. The research paper process can be broken down in five rather logical steps. What are they?

11. A good research question should meet what three requirements?

12. What purposes may be served by a *tentative outline?* Explain briefly.

13. Testing the reliability of a source involves at least five questions one must ask about the writer, the work and the publisher. What are those five questions?

14. The *World Almanac* is typical of what larger category of general reference works?

15. Are you expected to *emphasize* what you have taken from your sources, or *minimize* it—and are you expected to make your mistakes *as easy* or *as hard* as possible to find?

16. .What possible logic might explain why an author's last name comes first in the bibliography, but his first name comes first in a footnote entry?

17. How are footnotes spaced on the typewritten page? Illustrate.

18. *Who's Who* is typical of what category of general reference works?

19. What purpose may be served by code numbers on bibliography cards?

20. Generally speaking, how does *The International Index to Periodi-*

cals differ from the more commonly used *Reader's Guide to Periodical Literature?*

21. Why might one choose Roman numerals to indicate volume numbers in bibliography entries?

22. In handling of quoted material what two common (often fatal) tendencies are to be particularly avoided?

23. The *Jewish Encyclopedia* is typical of what larger category of general reference works?

24. Name three other indexes to periodicals not already mentioned in these questions.

25. How often is the *Reader's Guide to Periodical Literature* published? Explain briefly.

Suggestions for Discussion or Theme Writing—Chapter 24

1. Imagine that you have found the following research questions too cumbersome. Revise each one by narrowing the subject matter area or by making the question more specific, or by doing both:

(a) What has Baseball done for America?

(b) What is Subliminal Perception?

(c) What are the Basic Doctrines of the World's Great Religions?

(d) How much does American Foreign Policy change with the Times?

(e) What do the Experts say about Dating?

2. Discuss the relative merit of the following, as sources for a paper on the subject of *protective tariffs:* (a) the head of the National Association of Manufacturers, (b) the mayor of your town, (c) official reports of the U.S. Bureau of Internal Revenue, (d) the head of a European import firm, (e) a university professor of history whose field is international trade, and (f) a movie star.

3. Which of the following might best provide information on the *life of the common soldier:* (a) a newspaper account of a battle, (b) a private's diary picked up on the battlefield, (c) the memoirs of the general in command? Which source might provide the best information for a paper on *battle tactics?* Explain your reasoning in both instances.

4. Discuss the relative merit of source material by unknown authors (all named Professor William Smith) on the subject of *the international intentions of the United States,* published recently by the following:

(a) Avid Comics, Incorporated, Tempe, Arizona

(b) Encyclopaedia Britannica, Ltd., London, England

(c) Friends of America Press, Moscow, U.S.S.R.

(d) Acme Lithographing Company, Bumblebee, Arizona

(e) Charles Scribner's Sons, New York, N. Y.

(f) Harvard University Press, Cambridge, Massachusetts

part

INDEX
TO USAGE

III

INDEX TO USAGE

a, an

The two forms *a* and *an* are called the *indefinite articles. A* is used before a consonant sound (*a* book, *a* union). *An* is used before a vowel sound (*an* error, *an* honor). Since initial *h* is pronounced more lightly in British usage than in American, you may find *an* printed before some words where you would expect *a* (*an* hotel, *an* historical novel). *A* is the normal American form in such places.

abbreviations

1. *For economy.* Abbreviations may be used freely whenever economy of effort, space, or printing cost is more important than appearance. They are therefore common in footnotes, concise reference books, catalogs, merchandise orders, etc. The writer should avoid any abbreviations that will not be immediately clear to his expected readers unless (a) he provides a list of the abbreviations he uses; and (b) he uses each abbreviation often enough to effect a real economy. For instance, if he refers twenty times to the *Publications of the Modern Language Association,* it is worth while to use the abbreviation *PMLA;* but if he refers only twice to the *Journal of Modern Philology* he would do better to write it out both times instead of using *JMP.*

2. *Titles. Dr., Mr., Mrs.,* and *Messrs.* are regularly abbreviated when used with names. Such other titles as *Captain, Colonel, President, Professor,* and *Reverend* may be abbreviated when used with initials or given names, but not when used with last names only. Thus: *Capt.* (or *Captain*) *Henry Wade,* but always *Captain Wade; Prof. E. H. Walker,* but *Professor Walker.*

3. *Months.* In dates, the months may be abbreviated as follows:

Jan.	Apr.	Oct.
Feb.	Aug.	Nov.
Mar.	Sept.	Dec.

Notice that the three shortest names (*May, June,* and *July*) are not abbreviated, and that *Sept.* is the only abbreviation containing four letters.

Abbreviations are used only for exact dates:

Dec. 17, 1962, but *January,* 1963

4. *The pronunciation test.* In ordinary writing, you should use abbreviations other than titles *only if you would pronounce them as written.* Thus *10 a.m.* and an *FHA loan* are satisfactory, but a *ten ft. pole* and *govt. bonds* are not. When a pronounceable abbreviation is a shorter form of a standard word, its use is definitely informal, but not necessarily objectionable. "I have three *exams* next week" is appropriate in a friendly letter (even from one *prof* to another), though we should probably tell a prospective employer that they were *examinations.*

5. *Periods with abbreviations.* It used to be the general rule to put a period after every abbreviation, and after every letter in an abbreviation consisting of a series of initials. There is now a growing tendency to omit many of these periods. Practice varies so much that it is impossible to give absolute rules, but those that follow are reasonably reliable:

(a) In series of initials, periods are required after small letters, but are optional after capitals. Thus *a.m., f.o.b.,* and *i.e.;* but *FHA* or *F.H.A., RAF* or *R.A.F.* The reason for this is that abbreviations written in small letters without periods might be mistaken for ordinary words (such as *am* and *fob*). There is less danger of this with series of capitals.

(b) Other abbreviations which represent actual pronunciation are not followed by periods. Compare "one *prof* to another" with *Prof.* (pronounced *Professor*) E. H. Walker.

(c) There is now some tendency to omit the period after an abbreviation that ends with the last letter of the word abbreviated, as in *Mr Smith, Dr Jones,* and *vs* (for *versus*). Some publishers insist on this practice, but it has not yet made much headway in general use.

ability (to)

"He has the *ability to learn* languages easily" is in much better standing than "he has the *ability of learning.*" It is usually still better to say "He *can learn*" or even "He *learns* languages easily."

-able, -ible

The following rules are helpful, though not completely reliable:

1. If there is a closely related word with either an *a* or an *i* in the same relative position, it is usually a safe guide:

admiration	admirable	admission	admissible
imagination	imaginable	conversion	convertible
potation	potable	horrid	horrible
separation	inseparable	suggestion	suggestible

2. If the form without either ending is a word in itself, and there is no related word ending in *-ation, -ition,* or *-ion,* the *-able* ending is probably right: bearable, eatable, teachable, unknowable.

(at) about

Theoretically, *at ten o'clock* means one thing, *about ten o'clock* means another, and *at about ten o'clock* is an illogical construction that should never be used. Actually, *at about ten o'clock* is in standard usage; people start out to set a definite time, then decide to leave themselves a margin. However, you might as well cross out the *at* in revisions, since it adds nothing to *about.*

above

"The paragraph *above*" is unquestionably standard, but many people object strongly to "the *above* paragraph." The use of *above* to refer to something several pages back is often confusing; it is better to give the page number.

accent

The noun *accent* always has the stress on the first syllable. The verb may have it on either syllable. The noun may mean (among other things): (1) stress ("The *accent* is on the first syllable"); (2) an accent mark (" 'Negligée' is written with an *accent*"); (3) a characteristic way of speaking ("a Brooklyn *accent*"). The verb usually means to stress.

accept

Accept (to receive willingly) is often confused with *except* (to leave out). The easiest way to keep the words straight is to remember that *ex-* usually means "out."

"I will *accept* all the papers *except* the ones written in pencil."

ad

When *ad* is used informally for *advertisement,* it should be written without a period.

A.D. and B.C.

A.D. (from *anno domini,* "in the year of our Lord") was originally placed before the date (A.D. 236). It is now more often placed after the date, as B.C. (before Christ) regularly is.

B.C. is used regularly for dates before the Christian era. A.D. is used only for dates so early that there might be some doubt about which era was meant, or to give a touch of formality.

Adjectives and Adverbs

There is a clear difference between the uses of the modifiers in the following pairs of sentences:

He is a *happy* man.	He sang *happily.*
She was a *beautiful* girl.	It was *beautifully* clear.
He is *glad* you came in.	He will *gladly* do it.
That is an *extreme* case.	He drove *extremely* carefully.
He has a *bad* foot.	He has a *badly* injured foot.
A *certain* truth is rare.	*Certainly,* it is true.

In the left-hand sentences the adjectives are used to modify only nouns and pronouns. In the right-hand sentences the adverbs are used to modify anything else, such as verbs, participles, adjectives, other adverbs, and even (as in the last example) the whole sentence.

Unfortunately, not all our modifiers come in such convenient pairs, and not all uses are as clear-cut as those shown above. Should we say "He walked slow" or "He walked slowly"? And if (as the evidence indicates) both of these sentences are standard, is there a provable difference between them? And when *slow* modifies *walked* should we call it a "flat adverb" or merely a versatile adjective? These are (to some people) fascinating questions, but we won't go into them here. Instead we will give two general rules, which work about as well as rules can when practice is so divided that nobody can please everybody.

1. When a modifier *clearly* refers to the action of the verb, and not to the subject, use the adverb.

2. When the modifier refers to the subject, *or when it could be taken either way,* use the adjective.

Thus we say "Ann looks beautiful," even though an argument that the modifier tells how she *looks* is at least as logical as one that says *looks* is more nearly parallel to *is* in "Ann is beautiful" than it is to *sings* in "Ann sings beautifully." In borderline cases both adjective and adverb may be in standard use, but there is a better chance that the adjective will be. We can say "They lived *happy*" as well as "They lived *happily*"; but if we say "The roses smelled *sweetly*" we give the impression that we are trying too hard and still missing.

adopt, adapt

To *adopt* is to take as your own. To *adapt* is to change to meet a special purpose.

adviser, advisor

Either spelling will do.

affect, effect

These two words give little trouble as nouns, since *affect* is only used as a technical, psychological term; but they cause much trouble as verbs, since they are pronounced alike and have rather closely related meanings. To *affect* means to influence; to *effect* means to bring about a result. In informal English, *effect* is usually a noun and *affect* a verb.

aggravate

Originally this meant only "to make more serious," as in "The long trip aggravated his injury." Many people still object rather strongly to the meaning "to irritate or annoy," but this usage is probably now more common than the original one.

Agreement

Grammatical *agreement* is a matching of inflections to indicate which words go together.

1. *Agreement of verb with subject.* English verbs have lost so many of their inflections that agreement is often impossible (*had* agrees, or rather fails to disagree, with any subject) and almost never important to the meaning of a sentence. But we have become used to certain *patterns of sound,* and clear-cut violations of these patterns strike most of us as very serious mistakes.

Simple Agreement

Most of us are accustomed to the following combinations:

I	am
he, she, it, the man	is
we, you, they, the men	are
I, he, she, it, the man	was
we, you, they, the men	were
he, she, it, the man	sings
I, we, you, they, the men	sing

Unless all of these sound completely natural, you had better practice them. Some dialects have very different patterns, but the only common mistakes among people whose general usage is standard are *you was* for *you were* and *he don't* for *he doesn't.*

Singular Subjects with Plural Meanings and Plural Subjects with Singular Meanings

When a singular subject has a plural meaning or vice versa, the general tendency is to make the verb agree with the idea instead of the form, unless a strong sound-pattern is involved.

The *jury is* making its decision. (Jury considered as unit)
The *jury are* eating their dinners. (Jury considered as individuals)

My *family like* (or *likes*) you. (Either will do)
Everybody is coming. (*-body are* would sound wrong)
None of them *are* (or *is*) coming. (Although *none* is actually a negative
  compound ending in *one,* most people do not think of it in this way.
  Also, *none* does not usually come immediately before the verb)
Neither of his parents *is* (or *are*) still living. (Both are dead)

Ten thousand *dollars is* a lot of money. (*Are* would be possible, but we
  generally consider the money as one sum rather than as many dollars)
Her *patience and understanding is* (or *are*) amazing. Depending on
  whether we consider that she has two separate virtues or one compound one)

Verb Separated from Subject by Intervening Noun of Different Number

The *collector* of all these objects *was* a Frenchman.
This *kind* of mushrooms *is* (or *are*) good to eat.

In the first of these, the verb refers not only to a singular subject
but to a single person, and there can be no reason except carelessness
for using a plural form. But in the second, while the formal subject
(*kind*) is singular, it is actually the plural *mushrooms* that are good
to eat; and the verb may agree with either. The tendency is to use the
form appropriate to the *idea in mind at the time,* rather than to the
particular word by which that idea has been previously indicated.

Since a faulty agreement seldom interferes with meaning, it doesn't
always pay to be too particular.

I hope the *box gets* here in good condition.
I hope the *box* of *apples* gets here in good condition.
I hope the *box* of those delicious Hood River apples *gets* here in good
  condition.

We could not say *box get,* but *box of apples get* would be likely to
pass unnoticed; and *box of those delicious Hood River apples get*
would probably sound to most people more normal than *box . . .
gets.* Since the only importance of the form is the impression it makes
on the audience, there is not much advantage in being too correct to
be appreciated.

Agreement after Who

Another type of agreement that causes more trouble than it is worth occurs when the form of the verb is supposed to be determined by whether *who* refers to a singular or plural noun—a matter to which the speaker has often given no thought.

a. He is one of those *men who* always *know* what to do. It is often said that *knows* would be wrong here, because there are a number of men who know. However, the meaning of the statement is that he, among others, *knows* what to do; and the temptation to use the singular form is hardly worth resisting.

b. He is the only *one* of those men *who* always *knows* what to do. Here theory and natural practice agree on the singular form. Only one man *knows*.

c. He is the only one of those *men who* always *know* what to do that I like. This is the kind of sentence that is devised by writers of textbooks to prove that theoretical agreement is important. It is not recommended for any other purpose.

Agreement after It and There

a. *It* is always followed by a singular verb: "It *is* the Browns."

b. After *there* the verb normally agrees with the following subject: "There *is* a man," "There *are* three men."

c. When *there* is followed by a compound subject of which the first member is singular, the verb may be either singular or plural: "There *is* (or *are*) a man and a couple of boys over there."

2. *Agreement of pronoun with antecedent or referent.* See pages, 407-408.

ain't

Originally a contraction of *am not,* then used as a substitute for *aren't* and *isn't,* and finally for *hasn't* and *haven't*. Most people (including many who are sure they don't) use it in some or all of these meanings in informal speech, though often only in a supposedly humorous way. However, since it is quite generally regarded as the very battle flag of "bad grammar," it is well to avoid it if you are concerned about the impression you are making. It should not be used in writing except in dialog or as a mild attempt at humor.

Many linguists now say that *ain't* has a much better standing as a contraction for *am not* than in any of its other uses, partly because of its origin, and partly because there is no satisfactory standard equivalent, especially in questions. The Irish *amn't I?* and the British *aren't I?* have never been generally accepted in this country, and *am I not?* sounds inhumanly formal.

This sounds very logical, but the fact is that most people either accept *ain't* freely or don't accept it at all.

alibi

In Latin, *alibi* means "elsewhere." In legal English an alibi is a defense that the accused was somewhere else at the time of the crime, and therefore could not have committed it. The word is now often used for any kind of excuse, frequently with the implication that the excuse is not a very sound one: "What's your *alibi* this time?"

all (of)

We say *some of it, some of them, all of it, all of them.* If we replace the pronouns with nouns, we still say *some of the money, some of the boys;* but in such expressions as *all (of) the money, all (of) the boys,* the *of* somehow seems unnecessary. It is therefore better to leave it out, at least in writing.

all ready, already

The two separate words preserve their original meaning. The compound word has the entirely different meaning, "by now" or "by that time." "They are *all ready* there" means "All of them are ready there." "They are already there" means "They are there by now."

all right, alright

The form *alright* is patterned after *already* but developed much later. It will probably be accepted without question in a few years; but today many people regard it as a serious mistake and nobody seems to praise it particularly, so you might as well avoid it.

all the farther, all the harder, etc.

Phrases of this type are standard in such sentences as "He worked *all the harder* because he had been advised to take it easy." As substitutes for such expressions as *as far as,* they are not generally accepted as standard, though they are used by educated people in some areas ("Is that *all the farther* you can go?").

all together, altogether

The two separate words preserve their original meanings. The compound means "completely," "in all," or "on the whole."

They are *all together.* (all of them are together)
They are *altogether* trustworthy. (completely)
He has five cars *altogether.* (in all, but not necessarily in one place)
Altogether, I don't think much of him. (on the whole)

almost

Almost is often shortened to *most* in conversation. If you use the shorter form in informal writing, use it firmly, and don't write *'most,* which looks cute.

although

Interchangeable with *though.* Use whichever you think sounds better in a given sentence. The spelling *altho* is growing in favor, but still meets a good deal of objection.

alumna—alumni

A woman graduate is an *alumna,* plural *alumnae* (pronounced *alumnee* or *alumnay*). A male graduate is an *alumnus,* plural *alumni* (pronounced *alumneye*).

A.M. and P.M.

Abbreviations for *ante meridiem* and *post meridiem,* meaning "before noon" and "afternoon." Midnight is 12 P.M., noon 12 M. Either small or capital letters may be used. These abbreviations are not in good standing except for specific times. "From 3 to 5 p.m." is standard, but "This a.m." is not. Such redundant expressions as "10 A.M. in the morning" are never justified.

Ambiguity

A statement that can reasonably be understood in two ways is said to be *ambiguous*. Intentional *ambiguity* is sometimes convenient (so is lying). Unintentional ambiguity is one of the most serious errors in communication. It doesn't do much good to prove that a sentence *could* be read the way you intended it. If it is not completely clear at first reading, don't try to justify it—rearrange it so that a reader will automatically get the meaning that you intend. Two of the commonest causes of ambiguity are carelessly placed modifiers (see pages 83-85) and pronouns that might refer to more than one thing (see pages 407-408).

among, between

Among always implies more than two. *Between* originally implied only two, but is now generally recognized as acceptable with larger numbers.

amount, number

Amount is used of things considered in bulk; *number,* of things that can be counted.

> A large *amount* of money.
> A large *number* of nickels.

analytic and synthetic

An *analytic* language (such as English) indicates the relation of ideas principally by word-order, connectives, and auxiliary verbs. A *synthetic* language (such as Latin) indicates the relation of ideas primarily by changes in the forms of the words.

and etc.

Since the *et* in *etc.* is the Latin word for *and,* an extra *and* before it is quite useless, and to many readers distinctly annoying.

and/or

And/or is a recent and useful invention, and is already widely used in business and legal language (though there are many people who object to it even in these fields). It is not firmly established as standard in general writing, and the small economy achieved by writing "pie and/or ice cream" instead of "pie or ice cream or both" is hardly worth the criticism it is likely to arouse.

and which

And which should be used only after an earlier *which*.

This plan, *which* was proposed by Mr. Moore, *and which* certainly seems promising . . .

but

The plan proposed by Mr. Moore, *which* (no *and*) certainly seems promising . . .

ante-, anti-

Ante- means before, as in *antecedent* (going before). *Anti-* means against.

Anti- (pronounced *antee* or *anteye*) is much the more common of the two. It is followed by a hyphen only when the word to which it is prefixed begins with *i* or with a capital letter (anti-intellectual, anti-American, but antiaircraft).

Antecedent

An antecedent is the word to which a pronoun refers. In the sentence "Bathgate did his best, but he couldn't manage it," *Bathgate* is the antecedent of both *his* and *he*. *It* has no antecedent in this sentence. Consequently, we cannot tell from this sentence alone what *it* stands for. Unless the reference is perfectly clear from an earlier sentence, some change should be made. See also pages 407-409.

Antonym

When two words have opposite meanings, each is called the *antonym* of the other. Thus *good* and *bad, long* and *short, wet* and *dry* are pairs of antonyms.

any and its compounds

1. Such expressions as "This is the best of any hotel in town" are not standard. Say "This is better than any other hotel in town" or simply "This is the best hotel in town."

2. The following compounds should be written as single words whenever the stress is on the first syllable: *anybody, anyhow, anyone,*

anything, anyway, anywhere. Some of them may be written as two separate words when the stress is divided (*any body* of water, *any one* thing).

Anyways is sometimes used as a variant form of both *anyway* and *anywise,* but is often criticized. *Anywheres* is definitely not standard. No other compounds of *any* are recognized.

The use of *any place* for *anywhere* is not exactly wrong, but it won't get you any extra points.

Apologies

One of the best ways to get a paper marked down is to begin it with an apology. The instructor ought to be able to find something wrong with it without your telling him—but if you insist on helping him you should be prepared to take the consequences. Moreover, if he has demanded five hundred words, he means five hundred words on the subject, and probably won't count those used to excuse it— though of course he will notice any errors in this part.

Apostrophe (')

The principal uses of the apostrophe are:

1. To indicate the possessive forms of nouns (the *boy's* hat, the *girls'* faces), but not of pronouns (*its* head; that is *yours*).
2. To show the omission of one or more letters in a contraction (*it's* true; they *can't* do it).
3. To indicate the plural of figures, letters, and words considered as words (three *2's;* two *t's;* too many *and's*). It is permissible to omit this apostrophe unless the result would be confusing. We could write *2s, ts,* and *ands;* but if we wrote *is* instead of *i's* it would probably be mistaken for the verb.
4. In representing conversation, apostrophes may be used to indicate the omission of certain sounds: "He an' John were drivin' on one o' the back roads." It is advisable to use apostrophes rather lightly for this purpose. Too many of them interfere with comfort in reading. Moreover, they may be quite unfair. Are you sure that *you* always pronounce *and* and *of* in a sentence exactly as you would if you were reading them from a list? And would it really be an improvement if you did?

Apposition, Appositive

When a noun is placed immediately after another noun or pronoun to explain it, it may be called an *appositive,* and the construction is called *apposition.* The second term may or may not be set off by commas or parentheses, and it may be either a single word or a phrase.

> My brother *Everett* is in California.
> Everett, *my oldest brother,* is in California.
> His sister (*the youngest one*) will be here tomorrow.
> That is Ernest Hemingway, *the famous novelist.*

This construction usually gives little trouble, although over-elaborate theories of punctuation sometimes cause confusion. It is sometimes said, for instance, that the sentence "My brother John is here" implies that I have several brothers, while the sentence "My brother, John, is here" implies that I have only one. This is putting more strain on the commas than they can be depended on to bear. If we wish to indicate that we have only one brother, or more than one, we had better say so in definite words, and depend on our ears rather than rules for the decision whether or not to use commas. "My brother John is here" and "My brother, John, is here" are both acceptable sentences, regardless of the size of our families.

apt to, liable to, likely to

The traditional distinction between these phrases is that *apt to* indicates a natural tendency (he is *apt to* work too fast); *liable to* indicates exposure to consequences, particularly legal ones (he is *liable to* be sued); and *likely to* indicates simple probability (it is *likely to* rain tomorrow).

However, anybody who attempts to follow these distinctions exactly runs into a good many hairsplitting decisions, and most people have given up the attempt. Both *apt to* and *likely to* are now in standard use for all three purposes. *Liable to* is more likely to be criticized except in its original meaning.

archaic, current, obsolete

Current means still in normal use.
Archaic means still in use, but having a distinctly antique flavor.

Smitten is current, especially when it refers to being hit by Cupid's arrows, but *smote* is archaic.

Obsolete means no longer in use. *Obsolescent* means disappearing from use. *Eke* in the sense of "also" is completely obsolete. *Vaudeville* now seems to be obsolescent because there is practically none left to talk about.

around, round

Only *round* can be used as an adjective (a *round* table). In most other uses the two are interchangeable. Those people who make distinctions between the two do not agree on what the distinctions are. However, only *around* is generally used as a synonym for *about*. In the sense of "approximately" (they have *around* fifty cows) this is definitely informal. In the sense of "in the neighborhood" *around* has pretty well replaced *about* in American, though not in British, usage.

athlete

This word has only two syllables, but is often both written and pronounced with an unjustified extra syllable ("ath*e*lete"). The same mistake is often made with *athletic* and *athletics*.

Auxiliary Verbs

The last form in a verb-phrase normally indicates the principal idea involved and is called the *main verb*. The other forms indicate such shadings as time, definiteness, obligation, and direction of action, and are called *auxiliary verbs* or *helping verbs*.

Occasional Auxiliaries

A number of verbs may be used in either main or auxiliary functions:

MAIN	AUXILIARY
He *is* a man.	He *is* working.
He *has* a boat.	He *has* built a boat.
He *got* the money.	He has *got* to be there.
He is *going* there.	He is *going* to be there.
Let us alone.	*Let* us consider the facts.
He *used* the books.	He *used* to read in bed.

There is often a difference of opinion on whether a combination of verb-forms should be considered as one verb-phrase or as two or more successive verbs. It makes little difference—the combinations exist, whatever we call them.

The "Pure" or "Modal" Auxiliaries

The verbs *can, may, must, ought, will,* and *shall,* sometimes called "pure" or "modal" auxiliaries, form a curious group. The historical reasons for their peculiarities are too complicated to go into here, but the net result is that all of them have lost both some of their forms and some of their uses.

1. None of them has an *-s* form, a participle, or an infinitive.

2. When used in verb-phrases, they can only stand first. Such combinations as *may can, used to could,* and *hadn't ought* are not in standard use. The first two have some standing in parts of the South, and would be useful everywhere to avoid the "be able to" construction, but they have not been generally accepted.

3. They have nearly lost their independent functions. Even when they are used alone, they almost always invite attention to verbs previously used.

Who can finish this?	I *can (finish).*
Are you going to work?	I *ought to (work).*

awful, awfully

A generation ago schoolteachers were making a determined effort to stop the use of *awful* and *awfully* in any sense not connected with "awe-inspiring." Now most of them are willing to settle for a careful distinction between the adjective (it was simply *awful*) and the adverb (I had an *awfully* nice time). However, you might as well avoid both forms in formal writing.

Back Formation

Sometimes a noun like *beggar* is mistakenly thought to have come from a shorter verb plus a suffix; then the verb *beg* is accidentally invented in the belief that it already exists. (*Beggar* actually came from *Beghard,* not from *beg + -er.*) This process is called *back formation. Opine* from *opinion* and *enthuse* from *enthusiasm* are other examples—not universally admired.

bad, badly

"I felt bad" was standard English long before "I felt badly" developed in a mistaken attempt to be "correct." However, the mistake became so common that both expressions must now be accepted, on the evidence, as standard.

With other verbs indicating sensation (*taste, smell,* etc.) only *bad* is standard.

balance

Balance is a standard bookkeeping term, but is not generally considered an improvement over *rest* in such sentences as "They kept the rest of them for themselves."

because

The first syllable is often dropped in conversation, but it isn't wise to indicate this in writing. It looks too cute for anything.

being as

Being as and *being as how* are not standard. Use *since* or *because.*

beside, besides

Beside means "by the side of" or "not included in" (*beside* the question).

Besides means "in addition to."

between

Between originally implied only two, but the numeral sense has been largely lost, and *among* is not always a satisfactory substitute. We could hardly say "She was torn *among* three possible decisions." Let nature take its course.

blame

"He *blamed* John *for* it" is often said to be better usage than "He *blamed* it *on* John." Both expressions are standard.

blond, blonde

In French, *blond* is masculine and *blonde* is feminine. Some people preserve the distinction in English, speaking of a man as a *blond* and of a woman as a *blonde;* but the general tendency now is to use *blond* for all purposes.

born, borne

We say that a child was *born* except in a phrase that explains who bore it.

> He had two children *borne* by his first wife.
> He had two children *born* of a former marriage.
> She had *borne* him a son.

In any sense not involving birth, the form is always *borne.*

boy friend, girl friend

A few years ago these expressions were generally considered, by people who did not themselves use them, to be somewhere between comic and pathetic. They continue to be widely used, probably because there are no entirely satisfactory standard equivalents. However, when *boy, girl,* or *friend* is sufficiently clear, it is just as well to avoid the combination. For *girl* friend, a man can always substitute *girl,* and a woman can use either *friend* or *another girl.* A man is not supposed to have a *boy friend,* but a woman is, and I suppose she can call him that if she wants to.

Brackets [ ]

The principal use of *brackets* is to insert in quoted material something that was not in the original. Since it is a scholarly principle that quoted material may never be changed, even when it is unclear or actually wrong, brackets are a very useful device, and may often be used to avoid cumbersome footnotes. For instance: "He was born in 1853 [actually 1855] in Springfield, Illinois."

Brackets may be made on a typewriter by combining underlining and slant marks.

broadcast

Past tense either *broadcast* or *broadcasted.* The latter is gaining.

broke

Broke may be slang, but it's better than "financially embarrassed" or—well, what else would you say?

bunch

Bunch is unquestionable in such expressions as *bunch* of grapes, *bunch* of keys. To designate a group of animals, *bunch* is rather informal, but apparently growing more popular. Such expressions as *bunch of people* and *bunch of money* are decidedly free-and-easy.

burst, bust

Burst (past tense also *burst*) is an old verb meaning to break because of an expanding force from within. Pipes, fruits, and blood vessels can *burst,* and orators can *burst out* or *forth,* and so can prisoners.

Bust was originally a corrupted form of *burst,* but is rapidly becoming recognized as a legitimate and different word meaning *break* in any sense, especially figurative ones.

To *bust* a bronco or a trust is now standard.

To *bust* a leg is decidedly informal.

To go *busted* is slang.

Bust has the regular past form, *busted.*

bus

Plural usually *buses,* sometimes *busses.* Formerly often written *'bus* to indicate that it was originally a shortened form of *omnibus.*

but

A number of very peculiar rules about *but* have been invented. Actually, it is very hard to misuse. Both "Nobody came *but* I" and "Nobody came *but* me" are standard. So is "There aren't *but* two of them," even though some writers criticize this as a double negative. It is also permissible to begin a sentence with *but.* But it gets monotonous if you do it often.

but that, but what

Such sentences as "I don't doubt *but that* it will rain tomorrow" would be at least as good without the *but.* The use of *but what* for *but that* in such sentences is not standard.

calculate, guess, reckon

A generation ago *calculate, guess,* and *reckon* were quite generally condemned in schoolrooms as inferior regional expressions for *think* or *suppose*. Now *guess* is firmly established throughout most of the country, though it is still sometimes considered a "Yankee word" in the South. The Southern *reckon* now seems to be generally accepted but seldom used by Northerners. *Calculate* was always confined to a much smaller area than either of the others, and seems to be losing ground.

can, may, could, might

Schoolteachers have been battling against the use of *can* to indicate permission for generations, and have achieved some success. A good many people are careful to use *may* in this sense, and some of them are quite critical about those who say "*Can* I go now?" But the general tendency is now to reserve *may* for possibility (He *may* go tomorrow), and to use *can* to indicate either permission or ability.

Could and *might* are sometimes used simply as the past tenses of *can* and *may*. They are also sometimes used to indicate a small probability. "I could do it tomorrow" is much less promising than "I *can* do it tomorrow." "I *might* go next week" often implies doubt, while "I *may* go next week" leaves the question completely open.

cannot, can not

Usage is about evenly divided between these two forms. Any statement about comparative emphasis or general preference would be very hard to prove.

can't

Like all contractions, this is somewhat less formal than the uncontracted form. Otherwise there is nothing wrong with it.

can't help (but)

Notice the difference between the following sentences:

> I can't help *liking* him.
> I can't help but *like* him.

The construction with *but* is often condemned, probably because it is hard to explain "logically" or to diagram. But it is certainly widely used by standard speakers.

Capitalization

Capital letters are used for:

1. *Proper nouns.* See pages 335-336.
2. *Proper adjectives.* See page 401.
3. The pronoun *I*, both alone and in such contractions as *I'll, I'm,* and *I've.*
4. *Sentence capitals.* The first word of a sentence is normally capitalized, though advertisers and experimental writers sometimes use lower case to get a special effect. The first word of a quotation is capitalized only if it is also the first word of a sentence.

> A cynic once remarked, "Virtue is its only reward."
> "Virtue," a cynic once remarked, "is its only reward."
> He called the new law "a fantastically silly piece of legislation."

5. *Lines of verse.* The first word in each line of verse is usually capitalized. If you are writing original verse you can suit yourself. If you are copying somebody else's verse, follow his practice.
6. *Titles of books, poems, articles, etc.* The most usual practice is to capitalize all words in a title except unimportant words of three letters or less that stand neither first nor last.

> *For Whom the Bell Tolls*   *A Bell for Adano*
> "The Man With the Hoe"

Cardinal Numerals

The numerals *one, two, three,* etc. are called *cardinal,* as opposed to the *ordinal* numerals, *first, second, third,* etc.

Caret

An inverted v used to indicate an omission.

>   daughter
> She was the youngest of John Davies.
>   ∧

Case

A *case* is a form of a noun or pronoun which originally indicated its grammatical relation to the rest of the sentence. Modern English nouns may have two cases, plain (or *common*) and possessive (or *genitive*). Pronouns may have three, nominative (*he*), possessive (*his*), and objective (*him*). In this book these are called the subject, possessive, and object forms.

1. *Uses of the subject forms.* The forms *I, he, she, we,* and *they* are always required as the subjects of verbs. This causes little trouble with single subjects, but double subjects and subjects followed by explanatory nouns need special attention:

STANDARD	POPULAR
He and *I* did it.	*Me* and *him* did it.
We girls had a picnic.	*Us* girls had a picnic.

The rule is simply to use the same form of the pronoun that you would use if it stood alone.

In distinctly formal English the subject form is also required when the pronoun is joined to the subject by any form of the verb *to be*.

It is *I*.   That must be *they*.

In good informal English, however, practice on this point is divided. The general feeling seems to be that the subject form is more correct, but that the object form is more natural and human. In spite of the general schoolroom insistence on the "correct" forms, a great many cultured people definitely prefer "It is *me*" and "That must be *them*." This is a point on which we can't please everybody, so we might as well please ourselves. The only variations really to be avoided are, "It is *me*—I mean *I*," and "It was *her*—ain't my grammar awful?"

About the same sort of divided practice is found in such sentences as:

He is as tall as *I* (or *me*).
She is better than *he* (or *him*).

If you want to avoid argument, you can say "as tall as *I am*" and "better than *he is*." Otherwise, take your choice.

2. *Uses of the object forms.* The object forms, like the subject forms, give little trouble when used alone. Very few people would say "I saw *he*," "Give *she* the book," or "That belongs to *they*." But a good many people do use the subject forms erroneously when the pronouns occur in pairs or are coupled with nouns.

STANDARD	POPULAR
Between you and *me*.	Between you and *I*.
I saw John and *her*.	I saw John and *she*.

The popular use seems to grow out of a feeling that the subject forms are somehow more elegant. It is the natural, though unfortunate, result of being corrected for saying "John and *me* were there." Mistakes in both directions may be corrected by the simple rule that *the form of a pronoun that would be used if it stood alone should also be used if it is coupled with another pronoun or a noun.*

If this sounds too complicated, try the following rules:

(a) *Always* use the forms *I, he, she, we,* and *they,* as subjects, whether they are used alone or joined with other words.

(b) *Never* use these forms as anything but subjects, unless you are perfectly sure you know all about grammar.

3. *Uses of the possessive forms.* For the form used before a participle see under **Gerund,** page 359. For other uses of the possessive forms see pages 396-397.

cast, caste

Caste was originally a technical name for any of the strictly observed levels in Hindu society (*Brahmin caste,* etc.). It came to be used loosely for social position in any society. Thus a man who has lost the respect of his social group may be said to have *lost caste.* A Eurasian is often called, with rather muddy logic, a *half-caste.* In all other uses, including the list of actors in a play, the spelling *cast* is used.

A man who has been rejected by society may be called either an *outcast* because he has been thrown out or an *outcaste* because caste is what he has been thrown out of.

censor, censure, censer

A *censor* (if he isn't taking a census) prohibits a book or deletes a passage. To *censure* is simply to blame without taking restrictive action; *censure* may also be used as a noun meaning adverse criticism. A *censer* contains incense.

center around

To *center around* is less logical than to *center on* or *upon,* but it certainly occurs more frequently, even in highly respectable writing.

central

This word is often used in a rather gasping attempt to sound important. "Occupies a *central* position in relation to" means "is in the middle of." The expression "is central to" presumably means "is important to" when it means anything.

centuries

If you recall that this is the twentieth century you should be able to figure out that 1345 was in the fourteenth century. If this confuses you, or you are afraid it will confuse your audience, you can say that something took place in "the thirteen hundreds."

Chinaman, Chinese

Most Americans think of *Chinaman* as the normal noun for a Chinese national. But the Chinese people prefer *Chinese* as both noun and adjective, and consider *Chinaman* to be a rather insulting term, like *Wop* or *Hunky.*

cite, site, sight

To *cite* means to call attention to, to refer to, or to summon before a court. A *site* is a place where something is, or is to be, situated. *Sight,* aside from the meanings connected with vision, is often used colloquially to mean "a great deal":

> that will take a *sight* of doing; not by a long *sight.*

Cities

When the name of a city is followed by the name of a state or country, it is set off by a comma. Ordinarily the name of the state or country is not mentioned unless it is actually needed for identification. Thus we would normally write *Paris, Texas;* but our readers might consider *Paris, France* rather countrified.

Coining Words

To make up a new word is to *coin* it. Obviously, all of our words must have been coined by somebody, and you have as much right to coin as anybody else, but it isn't wise to overdo it.

If you feel like coining a word for a special occasion, and do it in a way that is clear to your audience (for instance, "She is very *Aunt Lucified*"), suit yourself and take your chances. But if you coin by depending on an inaccurate memory, or by making a bad guess at words that are already in existence (for instance, if you write *sensitivify* instead of *sensitize*), you might as well expect unfavorable criticism.

Collective Nouns

Such words as *group, family,* and *set* are singular in form, but refer to a number of people or things. They are called *collective nouns,* and there is often a question whether they should be used with singular or plural verbs and pronouns.

As a general rule, if you think of the group referred to as a unit, use singular forms:

> My family *owns its* own home.

If you think of the members of the group as individuals, use plural forms:

> The majority *are* driving *their* own cars.

Don't worry about borderline cases—practice varies, and some people will think you are wrong whatever you do. It is better to write in a way that is clear, even if it is open to criticism, than to twist a sentence until it is "correct" but awkward or wordy. Even a mixture like "The committee *has* decided to make up *their* own minds" is at least as good as "The committee has decided that each of its members will make up his or her own mind."

Colloquial

The term *colloquial* originally meant simply "conversational." Most modern books on usage agree that *colloquial* now means something like "appropriate to the conversation and informal writing of educated people." Unfortunately, the word seems to be used in many schoolrooms as a term of reproach, almost equivalent to "illiterate." There seems to be no reasonable excuse for this attitude. Much of our best writing is decidedly colloquial.

Colon (:)

The principal uses of the *colon* today are:

1. After the salutation of a business or formal letter: Dear Sir: (Many writers use the *colon* after the salutation in any letter. Others use a comma or dash in informal letters. *Please* don't use a semicolon.)
2. To introduce an explanation (as in the first line of this entry) or list:

   The following men will report for shots tomorrow: Baker, Colwell, Cummings, Novak, and Serna.

3. To introduce a quotation of more than one sentence, especially in rather formal writing.
4. To separate figures for hours from figures for minutes (10:45).
5. Some publishers use *colons* to separate certain items in references to books, but their uses vary so much that it is hopeless to learn a general principle. Follow whatever form is prescribed for a given publication.
6. The use of *colons* to separate certain types of clauses is much less common than it used to be, which is probably just as well.

combine

The verb *combine* takes the stress on the second syllable, with the first slurred. In the noun *combine,* both syllables are pronounced distinctly, with a slightly greater stress on the first. *Combine* is the correct technical name for a reaping-and-threshing machine, and is in fairly good informal use to indicate a political or business alliance, especially if you disapprove of its purpose.

We can expect trouble from the Schmidt-Davis *combine.*

It is not in good use as a substitute for *combination* in other senses.

Comma (,)

A comma indicates a minor pause, and anybody who can read aloud with reasonable skill can put in most of the necessary commas by ear. This is especially true if he realizes that the purpose of a comma is to help the reader understand the sentence with as little effort as possible, rather than to conform to rules. The principal uses of the comma are as follows:

1. *To prevent a false connection of ideas.*

   Dick took Mary, and Betty took Jane.

Without the comma a reader would first get the impression that "Dick took Mary and Betty." Of course he could straighten it out, but he would have to back-track.

> While we were out shooting, Dick found a purse.

We don't want to give the impression that we were shooting Dick, or even out-shooting him. If the second clause read "*we* found a purse," there would be no reasonable chance of a misunderstanding, and the comma would be optional.

> We had to work fast, for John wanted to get home.
> Jim, put up the car.
> When we went out to milk, the sun was just setting

2. *In pairs, to set apart something not in the main line of thought.*

> He is, I realize, trying as hard as he can.
> Mr. Davis, who has a lot of experience, thinks it won't work.
> His decision was, in the opinion of most of his friends, a serious mistake.
> He had, to some extent, failed in his efforts.

In the last sentence above, as in many others, the pair of commas is optional. Since the interruption *to some extent* is too short to be confusing, we could write the whole sentence with no punctuation but the period. But *two commas or none* should be used. Either comma alone is worse than useless, since it breaks the main statement instead of setting off the interruption.

3. *To indicate the place for a necessary pause.* When a sentence is long enough to require a pause somewhere, a comma is useful to show where the pause should be. Compare the following sentences:

> If John were here we could do it.
> If only the president of the Board of Athletic Control were here, we could probably do it without too much trouble.

It would break no absolute rules to take the comma out of the second sentence and put it in the first. But a comma would not make the first sentence any clearer, and it is a sound principle not to use a punctuation mark unless it accomplishes something. On the other hand, it is rather hard to read the second sentence without a pause, and a comma shows the best place for the pause—between the two clauses. If you prefer, you may learn the rule that "An introductory adverbial clause should be set off by a comma unless it is short and intimately connected with the movement of the sentence."

4. *To separate members of a series.*

> He ordered orange juice, cereal, eggs, toast (,) and coffee.

The question whether the comma is necessary before the *and* has been bitterly debated, but the plain fact is that usage is fairly evenly divided. Most English instructors (including this one) use the comma in such positions, and miss it when it does not appear. But except for trick sentences, the omission of the comma would probably not cause any real ambiguity once in a year's reading.

5. *Between successive adjectives.* Compare the two following sentences:

> He was a young, healthy man.
> He was a healthy young man.

In the first, both *young* and *healthy* modify *man*. They therefore form a series and should be separated by a comma. In the second, *young* modifies *man,* and *healthy* modifies the combination *young man.* There is no series, and no comma is required, as you can probably tell by reading the sentence aloud. In borderline cases it is usually better to leave the comma out.

6. *Conventional uses.* There are a few special situations in which commas are expected regardless of whether a pause is indicated.

(a) To separate two geographical units, one of which is included in the other:

> Lima, Peru   Seattle, Washington
> Essex County, New York

(b) To separate the day of the month from the year:

> June 18, 1947

When no day is indicated, a comma after the month is optional:

> June (,) 1947

(c) In figures containing more than four digits, commas are used to set off thousands, millions, etc.:

> 10,000   3,487,291

In four-figure groups a comma is optional except in dates, where it is not used.

(d) To set off a name from a following degree or title:

J. F. Smith, Ph.D.   Robert Clark, Jr.
John Aley, M.A., LL.D.   Matthew K. Reis, Colonel (,) USAR

7. *Commas with other marks.* A comma is usually placed within final quotes, but after parentheses. It is not generally used after an exclamation point or question mark; but it should be used after a period indicating an abbreviation exactly as if the abbreviated word were written in full.

Comma Fault; Comma Splice

See *Run-on sentence,* pages 205-208.

common

Originally *common* meant "belonging to the community," hence "shared" (common property), or "frequent" (a common idea). Later it came to mean characteristic of the lower classes. ("His manners are rather *common.*") This led to some ambiguity: a *common taste* might indicate either a shared one or a low one. Probably for this reason the phrase "a common friend" seemed to some speakers insulting, and "a mutual friend" was substituted. Since *mutual* originally meant "having the same relation to each other," this was illogical, and it is still regarded as highly objectionable by many speakers. However, the phrase is now very *common* (in any sense you like) in standard use.

Common and Proper Nouns

Theoretically, a noun which designates a particular thing is *proper* and should be begun with a capital; and a noun which can designate any member of a class is *common,* requiring no capital unless it begins a sentence. Actually our habits of capitalization are too complicated to be covered in any definition of reasonable length. The following kinds of nouns are usually considered *proper* and written with capitals:

1. Names and nicknames of people and animals: *Robin Hood, Billy the Kid, the Brown Bomber, Man o' War.*

2. Names of specific institutions, events, ships, classes, etc.: *Phoenix Union High School,* the *First National Bank,* the *Western*

Open, the *Civil War,* the *Normandie,* the *Twentieth Century Limited, Geography* 100.

3. Names of specific geographic features: *Lake Superior,* the *Rocky Mountains,* the *Mojave Desert, Tonto Creek.*

.4. Names of cities, states, countries, regions, etc.: *Springfield, Idaho, France,* the *Near East.*

5. Names of the inhabitants of such places: a *New Yorker,* the *Texans,* an *Irishman.*

6. Titles when used to designate individuals: *Major Brown* asked the *Colonel* to assign him another captain.

7. Names of the months, days of the week, and holidays: The first *Tuesday* after the first *Monday* in *November* is *Election Day.*

8. Brand names: *Frigidaire, Eversharp, Camels.*

9. Nouns designating the Deity: *God, Jehovah,* the *Almighty.*

All other nouns are usually considered *common,* and written without capitals.

There has never been a perfect agreement about which nouns are to be capitalized, and there isn't now. The style sheets of newspapers and publishing houses show some differences. Borderline cases are not worth worrying about, since there is no final authority.

compare (to or with), contrast

To *compare* one thing *to* another is to point out similarities. To *compare* a thing *with* another is to examine or point out both similarities and differences. To *contrast* a thing *with* another is to point out differences.

complected, complexioned

Originally, the only correct phrase was *dark-complexioned.* The substitute *complected* is a back formation, coined (probably independently by a number of different people) in error. It is now widely used, but is certainly not fully accepted as standard, and is often ridiculed.

complement, compliment

Complement always refers in some way to completeness.

The ship had her full *complement* of men.
Boyd's practical experience *complemented* his partner's theoretical training.

The normal order of a sentence is subject, verb, *complement.*
Compliment refers only to praise or respect.

> He paid her a *compliment.*
> He *complimented* Suzanne on her dancing.

Complex Sentence

A sentence containing at least one subordinate clause. See pages 79-80.

Compound Predicate

Two or more verbs having the same subject are sometimes called a *compound predicate.*

> He *lives* and *works* in New York.
> She *has been* here for a long time and *ought to know* better.

Compound Sentence

A sentence containing two or more independent clauses and no subordinate clause is called a *compound sentence.* See pages 78-79.

Compound Subject

When two or more subjects take the same verb, they are called collectively the *compound subject.*

> *He and Leroy* were there.
> *Dorfmann or Adams* will pitch today.

Compound Words

A simple word such as *take* may be combined with another word or with a prefix or suffix to make a compound word—*overtake, retake, take-off, unmistakable,* etc. It is sometimes difficult (and it is for most people unimportant) to determine whether a given word is simple or compound. The chief questions that come up concern whether a compound word should be hyphenated (see *hyphen*) and how the plural forms of compound nouns should be written (see page 52).

concerning

Concerning should not be used as a substitute for either *of* or *about,* but only when neither of those words will quite do.

(in) connection with

One of the single words *about, in,* and *with* will usually do at least as well as this phrase.

I want to see you *in connection with* (*about*) your request.
His experience *in connection with* the college was unfortunate.

(Either *in* or *with* would be clearer, depending on the meaning intended.)

Connotation and Denotation

As a technical term in logic the *denotation* of a term is the class of things to which it refers, and the *connotation* is the sum of what the term tells about those things. Thus the denotation of *planets* is simply Mars, Venus, Mercury, and so forth; the connotation is the sum of qualities that distinguish them from stars and other objects.

In ordinary use denotation is the simple and direct meaning of a word and connotation is what is implied in addition. It is difficult to draw an exact line between connotation and denotation in this use, and ridiculous to be dogmatic about "exact connotation," since people react very differently to the same words. However, the terms are useful if not overstrained. If a girl is five feet seven and weighs a hundred and eleven pounds, she'd probably rather have you call her *slender* than *skinny*.

conscience, conscious

Your *conscience* is supposed to guide your moral decisions. *Conscious* means "aware."

consensus

Consensus by itself means "the general opinion" or "an agreement in opinion," so that "*consensus* of opinion" is theoretically repetitious, and is avoided by many careful writers.

considerable

Considerable is a perfectly good adjective, but is often misused in two ways:

1. To modify a verb, usually *help:* "That helped considerable" (should be *considerably*).

2. As a condensation for *a considerable* amount: "He wants *considerable* for his car."

Consonants

See ***Vowels and Consonants.***

Construction

A grammatical pattern is often called a *construction.* For instance, "Eustace caught the fish" is in the *active construction,* while "The fish was caught by Eustace" is in the *passive construction.*

contact

Many English teachers are almost fanatically opposed to *contact* as a verb, presumably because it is much used by salesmen, and English teachers usually don't like salesmen (possibly because they usually can't afford to buy whatever is being sold). I don't use it myself, but it is obviously here to stay, even in standard usage.

content, contented, contents

We can say that a man is either *content* or *contented* (both stressed on the second syllable), but only "a *contented* man." When there is a choice, *content* is rather more formal.

The nouns *content* and *contents* take the stress on the first syllable. *Content* is used for the intellectual make-up, as "the *content* of a course," and for the proportion contained, as "the sugar *content* of the blood." *Contents* is used in a more physical sense, as "the *contents* of a box" or "the *contents* of a book" (you can get an idea of the general *content* of a book by examining the table of its specific *contents*). *Contents* may be used with either a singular or plural verb.

Context

The *context* is the language that accompanies the particular word or passage that is being considered. It is often necessary to examine the context in order to determine even approximately what is meant by a given word or statement. Thus to quote out of context often gives a very false impression. If a man says "According to the John Birchers I am not a loyal citizen," it is decidedly dishonest to quote him as saying "I am not a loyal citizen."

The word *context* is sometimes used to mean the situation as well as the surrounding language, but this extended use is likely to be confusing.

continual(ly), continuous(ly)

Careful speakers use *continual* to mean "frequently repeated," and *continuous* to mean "without interruption."

He was in Paris *continually* for ten years. (He made many visits during this period.)
He was in Paris *continuously* for ten years. (He was there the whole time.)

Contractions

Such contractions as *can't, doesn't, he'll, I'd,* and *won't* are completely standard but rather informal. Since they look more informal than they sound, many people feel that they detract from the dignity of serious writing. It's a matter of taste.

could

See **can, may.**

council, counsel, consul

A *council* is always a group (the city *council*). *Counsel* means advice or the lawyer who gives it. A *consul* is a government representative in a foreign city. A *councilor* is a member of a council. A *counselor* is a person who gives *counsel*. A lawyer is a *counselor*, but may act as *counsel* for the defense.

couple

Originally *couple* meant a set of two joined in some distinctive way, as a married *couple*. Now it is often used to mean either simply two or a vague small number which there is some reason to minimize.

> We had a *couple* of drinks.
> Could you let me have a *couple* of eggs?

In such uses as the last two, the *of* is often omitted.

> A couple fellows were over last night.

This usage is not standard.

Course Names

The names of specific courses, such as *Zoology 100,* are regularly capitalized.

It is not necessary to capitalize such words as *history* and *zoology* when they refer simply to subjects, but it is natural and permissible to do so when they are listed along with such subjects as *English* and *French,* which must be capitalized.

The names of all college departments are capitalized.

credible, credulous

Credible means *believable; credulous* means *too ready to believe* (all suckers are *credulous*). While we're in the neighborhood, *creditable* means *deserving praise.*

cunning, cute

Cunning used to mean "craft" or "crafty," and sometimes still does. *Cute* is an abbreviation of *acute,* and formerly meant *sharp.* We can't stop the ladies from using them the way they do, but men should find other adjectives.

current

See *archaic.*

curriculum

The new plural *curriculums* now seems to appear at least as often as the Latin plural *curricula.*

Dangling Modifiers

The phrase at the beginning of the following sentence is called a *dangling modifier:*

> Raising the foaming glass to his lips, the minister suddenly appeared at the door.

A careful consideration of customs and probabilities suggests that somebody other than the minister was raising the foaming glass— after all, the minister wasn't even in the room yet; but the author of the sentence is certainly leaving himself open to either misunderstanding or ridicule. He should have written, "Raising the foaming glass to his lips, Eric suddenly saw the minister at the door." The word which a phrase is intended to modify should never be taken for granted, but should be put in as close to the phrase as possible so that a reader will automatically make the intended association. Dangling modifiers usually, though not always, contain participles. A few other examples follow:

> *After doing the dishes,* the floor was scrubbed.
> Revised: *After doing the dishes, they* scrubbed the floor.
> *To be a good pitcher,* the batters must be studied.
> Revised: *To be a good pitcher, you* must study the batters.
> *While driving to Prescott,* a tire went flat.
> Revised: *While driving to Prescott, we* had a flat tire.

Notice that the dangling effect is often caused by an unnecessary shift to the passive construction.

Dash (—)

The main purpose of a *dash* is to indicate some kind of a break in thought. Its meaning is less specialized than that of most of the other punctuation marks. It is therefore very popular with those who don't want to bother to decide between more precise marks—and equally unpopular with many instructors, who regard it as a lazy way of avoiding difficulties. It is now used far more, even in quite formal writing, than it used to be. One reason is that it is visually effective—it shows up well and indicates a break in thought even to a reader who knows nothing about theories of punctuation.

Some writers, principally women, use nothing but *dashes* in letters. They seem to feel that, aside from the trouble this habit saves, it gives an impression of agreeable informality. (A girl I used to know broke off her engagement because her fiancé used semicolons in his love letters. She felt that true passion could not be accompanied by such precise punctuation.) This is, of course, a matter of taste. In general, a short passage containing nothing but dashes may be quite effective if the impression desired is either intimate chattiness or the sort of headlong rush of events that some radio announcers aim at.

The use of too many dashes in long passages is likely to be boring. They give the effect of unconnected bits of information, rather than ideas accurately fitted together. The four best recognized uses of the dash are:

1. To indicate a sharp break in the line of the sentence:

> He was very—but why go into that?

2. To serve as informal parentheses:

His war experiences—he had served in the Pacific—had taught him a good deal.

3. To introduce a rephrasing or summary:

His family, his education, his business experience—all his background had prepared him for this.

4. To indicate that a sentence is unfinished:

> "I don't really think—"

data

This is a Latin plural form meaning "the given facts." There is not much occasion to use the singular form *datum* except in the technical sense of "point of departure." In other senses we are more likely to say "one of the *data*" than "one *datum*." Since *data* is collective, it may be followed by either a singular or plural verb. The singular is more usual.

date

As a synonym for "engagement" this is now standard and only slightly informal.

> He has three speaking *dates* in March.

As a term for the person who shares the engagement it might be called a technical term in college, and slang thereafter.

Dates

The traditional form for *dates* in the United States is

> April 2, 1957

The months are not usually abbreviated in the body of a paper. In references and other places where saving space is important, *May, June,* and *July* are written in full, *September* is shortened to *Sept.,* and all the others are reduced to their first three letters. When figures only are used, the order is the same as when the date is written out. Thus April 2, 1957 would be shown as 4/2/57.

There is now a growing tendency to put the day before the month, a practice which has advantages. If you write

23 April 1957

you keep the two sets of figures distinct. But if you use this order and abbreviate it, you should use either letters or Roman numerals for the month to avoid misunderstanding. During World War II the Army adopted the form 23 Apr 57 (using the first three letters of each month, with no period). Many people now use the form 2/IV/57. Since most of us are too lazy to write a big number like 29 as XXIX, it is quite easy to remember that 2/IV must mean the second of April, not the fourth of February.

Any of these forms is acceptable, but 4/2/57 is more likely to be misinterpreted than any of the others.

Dative Case

In Latin the *dative case* was a separate form, used primarily to indicate the indirect object of a verb. No useful purpose is served by talking about *dative cases* in English.

Defining Terms

If you use terms that might be confusing or ambiguous, explain what *you mean* by them. But don't assume that your meaning is the only legitimate one, or that your readers will throw aside the habits of years just to conform to your practice. See also pages 185-190.

Denotation

See **Connotation and Denotation.**

Dialect

Some writers on the language still believe that there is one standard of "pure English" and that all other varieties are dialects, usually regional or characteristic of national groups, as *Scottish dialect.* Modern linguists take the view that there is no one uniform standard, and that anyone who speaks English at all must speak either some one dialect or a mixture of several. The three generally recognized major dialects in the United States are *New England, Southern,* and *Western* or *General American* (though some linguists use a different division and terminology). All of these can be subdivided almost indefinitely. Some regions with particularly strong foreign backgrounds have special dialects almost unrelated to the major dialects which surround them, e.g., Pennsylvania Dutch.

different from (than, to)

The traditionally standard American usage is *different from. Different than* is frequently condemned, but has actually been in good usage for centuries, and shows no signs of disappearing. In simple comparisons, *from* is generally preferable:

<blockquote>This is different from that.</blockquote>

In such expressions as "This is *different than* I expected" or "He does it *differently than* John used to," *than* has its advantages. We could not substitute *from* alone, but would have to use *from what* and *from the way.*

Different to is standard British usage, but very rare in America.

Diphthong, Digraph, and Ligature

A *diphthong* (pronounced *dif'thong* or *dip'thong*) is a combination of two vowel *sounds* running together in the same syllable; for instance, the sound of *oi* in *coin* or of *i* in *bite* (pronounced *bah-eet,* with the *ah* and the *ee* running rapidly together). The so-called "long vowels" which serve as the names of the letters *a, e, i, o,* and *u* and which appear in such words as d*a*te, m*e*ter, r*i*ce, p*o*se, and c*u*te are all actually diphthongs, as you will see if you pronounce them slowly and carefully (for a few people long *e* is a pure vowel, but most of us begin it with a sound like the *i* in bit).

A *digraph* is a combination of two letters used to represent a single sound; for instance the *ea* in *breath* or the *th* in *that* (the sound represented by *th* is just as simple as the sound represented by *f* in *fat*).

A *ligature* is a special character consisting of two letters joined; for instance, *æ.*

Unfortunately the three terms are often confused. It is not uncommon to hear digraphs called diphthongs or ligatures called digraphs. It is therefore important to make sure that you understand how a given writer or speaker is using each term.

If changes in English spelling had kept up with changes in pronunciation most of this confusion could be avoided; but we have to get along with what we have.

disinterested, interested, uninterested

An *interest* may be either a matter of curiosity (an *interest* in botany) or a definite share (an *interest* in a mine). *Interested* may mean having either kind of interest. The word for "not curious" is *uninterested. Disinterested* means "having no share in the matter and therefore unbiased."

A judge or referee should be *disinterested* but not *uninterested.* A student should be *interested;* but when he is bored he should call himself *un-,* not *dis-.*

Division of Words

The best general rule for dividing words at the end of a line is, "When in doubt, don't do it." It is easier to read a paper with a fairly irregular right-hand margin than one with many divided words. When a word is obviously composed of several parts, the division should come between the parts (*re-store,* but *rest-ing*). Otherwise, the division should reflect pronunciation (*cam-el* but *cha-meleon*). Double consonants are usually split, unless they come at the end of a word to which an inflectional ending as distinguished from a suffix is added (*pas-sage* but *pass-ing*).

There are so many borderline cases that even the most elaborate set of rules is not completely reliable. Never divide a word in the middle of a syllable, and go by pronunciation, not appearance. *Walk-ed* is as bad as *thro-ugh,* though *add-ed* is permissible because the *-ed* is pronounced separately. Also, never leave a single letter on either line: both *a-bout* and *man-y* are considered wrong.

don't

As a contraction for *do not, don't* is appropriate except in very formal writing. As a substitute for *doesn't* it is widely used and sometimes defended, but a great many people who are broadminded about speech in general find this use particularly irritating.

Double Comparisons

Double comparatives and superlatives, such as *more dearer* and *most unkindest* were once in good use, but are now generally considered illiterate.

Double Negative

In older English double (not to mention triple and quadruple) negatives were common even in literature; and the statement that "two negatives make an affirmative" is not accurate, no matter how often it has been repeated. It is true, however, that some types of double negative are no longer standard.

1. A speaker who applies two negatives to *different* words usually means to strengthen the negative idea rather than to reverse it; and his intention is usually perfectly clear to the audience:

> I have money.
> I have *no* money.
> I have*n't no* money.

It is silly to say that the third sentence "really means" the same thing as the first. But it is quite accurate to say that it is not standard English. Most educated people carefully avoid clear-cut double negatives of this type.

2. There are some words in English that have a negative implication without an obviously negative form, such as *but, hardly,* and *only*. Look at these three sentences:

> There are*n't but* two of them.
> He has*n't* made *hardly* any effort.
> There are*n't only* two days left.

The first of these is standard, in spite of theoretical objections. The second is a careless slip, which should be corrected in revision. The third is practically illiterate.

Two negatives applied to the same word are unquestionably standard. They more or less cancel each other, though the meaning is never quite the same as that of the positive word: *happy, unhappy, not unhappy.*

doubt

Doubt that means quite as much as *doubt but that* or *doubt but what*. When the more formal usage is also shorter and simpler it might as well be used.

dove, dived

Both forms are common in standard use; but *dived* is seldom questioned, and *dove* is often criticized.

draft, draught

Both forms are pronounced *draft,* and are interchangeable in most uses. *Draft* is gaining rapidly.

drought, drouth

Interchangeable. *Drouth* seems to be gaining.

due to

Many English instructors object strongly to *due to* as a connective ("*Due to* the lack of rain, the crops were in poor condition"). Nevertheless, such uses appear frequently in standard writing. They are a rather natural development of the undoubtedly correct use: "The poor condition of the crops was *due to* the lack of rain." In other words, *due to* has developed exactly like *owing to,* but rather later.

As a matter of effective style, *due to* is as good (aside from prejudice) as *owing to* or *because of;* but a simple *because* is often preferable to any of the three, since it leads naturally to a more direct statement:

We could not get anything done, *due to* (or *owing to,* or *because of*) the absence of the president.
We couldn't get anything done *because* the president was absent.

Because is always better than *due to the fact that.*

each

When *each* is the subject, it takes a single verb.

Each of the houses *has* its own candidate.

When *each* merely modifies the subject, it does not affect the form of the verb.

The four *boys each make* their own decisions.

effect

See *affect.*

e.g.

E.g. means "for example" (from Latin *exempli gratia*). There is not much point in using it except when space is precious.

either

The usual American pronunciation is *eether*. The pronunciation *eyether* is legitimate if it comes naturally; but if you deliberately change to it you will probably lose more admirers than you will gain.

Either usually refers to choice between two. When the reference is to more than two, *any* or *anyone* is preferable.

Either normally takes a singular verb, and is referred to by a singular pronoun.

elder, eldest

These old forms of *older* and *oldest* have practically passed out of use except in such set phrases as *elder statesmen* and (very formally) *eldest son.*

Ellipsis (. . .)

The principal use of the *ellipsis* is to indicate that something has been omitted from quoted material. This makes it possible to leave out parts that are not important to your purpose. It is never permissible to shorten a quotation without indicating that something has been left out.

Original: The bill, which had been hotly debated for several days, was finally passed by a vote of forty-two to thirty-nine.
Quotation: According to Hofstetter, "The bill . . . was finally passed by a vote of forty-two to thirty-nine."

Some careful writers use a fourth period when the material omitted comes at the end of a sentence in the original.

Original: He died twenty minutes later, in spite of all our efforts to save him. We buried him the next day.
Quotation: J. F. Buchsbaum says: "He died twenty minutes later. . . . We buried him the next day."

Some writers use the ellipsis for other purposes, such as to indicate a decided break in thought, or to show that sentences of their own are unfinished. There is nothing wrong with doing this if you like the effect, but there is no reason for learning rules about it.

Elliptical Constructions

An elliptical expression is one in which one or more words are implied rather than directly stated. There are two common and legitimate types:

1. Omission of one or more words to avoid repetition.

> John went one way, Dick (went) the other (way).
> She sings better than Mary (sings).

The word omitted need not be in exactly the same form as the word expressed. "She sings better than you (sing)" is as correct as "She sings better than Mary."

The rule that all comparisons must be completely expressed need not be taken seriously. "I feel better today" is just as good as "I feel better today than I did yesterday," unless the speaker wishes to emphasize a contrast between the two times. The *as . . . than* construction has also been given more attention than it is worth.

He is *as tall or taller than* John. (In standard use, in spite of theoretical objections)
He is *as tall as or taller than* John. (Theoretically correct, but hardly attractive)

He is *as tall as* John, *or taller*. (Correct *and* natural)

2. Omission of elements which are obvious because of either the situation or the neighboring words.

> (I) am leaving tomorrow.
> (You had) better not drive so fast.
> While (he was) in the Army Jake learned a good deal about radios.
> Two, please.

Obviously, an element should not be omitted unless the meaning is clear without it. In "Two, please" the situation should tell us whether the request is for tickets or doughnuts. But it is rather silly to theorize that this is a sentence with both subject and verb "understood." We need be concerned only with whether it is clear and appropriate.

else

There are still a few people who write *somebody's else* as a matter of flaming principle; but *somebody else's* is now almost universal in standard English.

emigrant, immigrant

Both words refer to the same person, but from different viewpoints. An *emigrant* from Austria is an *immigrant* when he gets to America. The *e-* comes from the same word as *ex-*, meaning out, and the *im-* is a modification of *in*. Since most migration is in this direction, we have many more occasions to use *immigrant*.

en-, in-

The prefix *in-* sometimes has the general meaning of *in* or *on,* sometimes a negative meaning (*inanimate, inedible*). *En-* is a variant for the first of these only.

Some words are spelled only with one or the other of these forms—*encourage, enforce, infect, insist*. Others may be spelled either way, with usage quite evenly divided.

If you are quite sure that one form is correct, use it and don't worry about whether it is "preferred." If you are not, look it up.

Endorsing Papers

Your instructor will probably tell you where on your paper he wants you to put your name, and what other information he wants—perhaps course titles, date, and section number. Many students forget these instructions, and some free souls disregard them as a matter of principle. This is not bright. Your instructor handles each paper several times, and he often has to deal with several batches at once. If they are not marked uniformly he loses a good deal of time, and he may lose his sunny disposition. Of course he is an honorable man —but why prejudice him against you?

en route

The French pronunciation is beyond most Americans. The modified pronunciation *on root* (riming with *toot,* not *foot*) is satisfactory. "On the way" is usually even better.

enthuse

Enthuse is what is called a "back formation." People familiar with the noun *enthusiasm* assumed that it must have developed from a verb *enthuse,* so they used the verb—coining it without knowing that they were doing so.

A great many people, including this writer, do not like the word, but it is obviously more economical than "be enthusiastic" and often appears in standard English.

envelop, envelope

The verb has no final *e* and is pronounced *en-vel'-up.* The noun has a final *e* and takes the stress on the first syllable, which is usually pronounced *en,* but sometimes *on.*

equally as

If one thing is *as good as* another, the two are *equally* good. The combination *equally as* is seldom necessary.

etc.

An abbreviation for *et cetera,* which is equivalent to *and so forth.*

1. Notice that the *t* comes before the *c.*

2. This form should be used only when there is a real need for saving space. Most instructors dislike it in the body of the paper.

3. If you do not abbreviate, *and so forth* is usually preferred to *et cetera* written in full.

4. There is no justification for the form *and etc.,* which invites, and usually receives, ridicule.

euphemism, euphuism, euphony

A *euphemism* is a pleasant or colorless term substituted for one regarded as unpleasant. *Pass away* for *die* and *social disease* for *syphilis* are examples. One trouble with the process is that the substitute often becomes the normal direct term, and a further euphemism is developed. During the nineteenth century this verbal delicacy was carried to lengths now generally regarded as ridiculous.

The current standard tendency is to use the direct and simple word unless there is a real social taboo, as there is about some of our four-letter words.

The best advice is probably to call a spade a spade whenever you can do it simply and naturally. If you do it with a sense of great daring you will probably be considered young rather than sophisticated.

Euphuism is the name given to a very elaborate and artificial style that characterized some writing in the Elizabethan period.

Euphony means simply the quality of "sounding well." Since we don't all have the same tastes, it is hard to be successfully dogmatic about this subject; but if you write a sentence that is difficult to read aloud, or has too strong an unintentional rhythm, or has a sound effect inappropriate to the subject, you may be told that it is not euphonious.

everybody, everyone

Everybody and *everyone* are interchangeable. In their usual meanings they are written as single words, but when the second element is stressed they are divided.

> Almost *everybody* was there.
> Almost *everyone* was there.
> Almost *every body* of water in the state is low.
> Almost *every one* of the pieces was broken.

Everybody and *everyone* should be used with singular verbs, but may be referred to by plural pronouns.

> *Everybody is* expected to bring *his* (or *their*) own tools.
> Practically *everybody is* coming, but *they aren't* all staying.

ex-

Ex-, meaning "former," may be used as a hyphenated prefix with anything reasonable:

> *ex-husband*   *ex-schoolteacher*   *ex-senator*

except, accept

Except means "leave out"; *accept* means "receive" or "agree to."

Exclamation Point (!)

The *exclamation point* may be used to give emphasis to a whole sentence or to a particular word.

Ouch, that hurts!
Ouch! That hurts.
Ouch! That hurts!
I should say not!

It is usually considered as ending a sentence, and is thus followed by a capital letter. It may be enclosed in parentheses to call special attention to a word within a sentence.

He had seventeen (!) hats and half a dozen overcoats.

If there is the slightest doubt about using an exclamation point, leave it out. Too many of these marks are likely to give an effect of gushing.

excuse, pardon

The choice between these words is, of course, a matter of taste and habit. On the whole, "excuse me" has the better standing as a social term. "Pardon me" seems to be considered more elegant by some speakers, but for this very reason is regarded as rather ridiculous by many others, who use it only when they want to be slightly sarcastic. "I beg your pardon" is often used to mean "I disagree." "Pardon" alone sounds very small-townish to many ears.

expect

Expect, in the sense of "suppose," is a normal British idiom, but has hardly been naturalized in America.

falls

We usually say "The *falls* are thirty feet high," but we may speak of "a *falls.*" There is no logic whatever in this combination of practices, but it is convenient.

famed

Famed is often used in newspapers as a substitute for *famous,* presumably because it is shorter. In other types of writing there is usually room for the extra letter.

farther, further

As a verb, only *further* is used. In other uses the two forms are interchangeable. The "rule" that *farther* should be used for physical distance and *further* for all other senses was a pure invention and has never been generally followed, though there are some people who take it seriously.

faze

Faze is a respectable, though slightly informal, word meaning to embarrass or disconcert. It may also be spelled *feaze* or *feeze*, but not *phase*, which is an entirely different word.

feel (bad or badly, good or well)

"He *feels bad*" is generally preferred to "he *feels badly*." "He *feels good*" generally refers to a mental attitude.

"He *feels well*" refers to the state of his health.

fewer

See *less*.

fiancé, fiancée

One *e* for a man and two for a woman. The accent mark is beginning to disappear. Usually pronounced something like *fee-on-say*.

Figures of Speech

The two most important *figures of speech* are *metaphors* and *similes* (which see). The passion for classifying which resulted in the development of special terms for sub-varieties of metaphors (*hendiadys, metonymy, synecdoche,* etc.) and for almost every other use of language that was not completely straightforward (from *anacoluthon* to *zeugma*) has now abated considerably.

fine

In spite of objections, *fine* is in widespread standard use to modify verbs:

That works *fine*.

first rate, first-rate

With or without a hyphen, *first rate* is in standard use to modify a noun (a *first rate* play), but not to modify a verb (he did *first rate*).

fish

The usual plural is *fish,* though *fishes* may be used either to individualize as in the song title "The Three Little Fishes" or to indicate separate species, as in "Bass and trout are the two *fishes* that I most like to catch." In the latter use, *kinds of fish* is more usual than *fishes.*

fix

Fix is now standard in the sense of "repair" or "arrange satisfactorily" as well as in earlier meanings. As a noun meaning "predicament" it is still considered very informal; but since comparatively few people ever use *predicament, fix* will probably soon be fully accepted in this use also.

folk, folks

In the sense of "family," British usage calls for *folk.* American usage calls for either *folks* or some entirely different word.

Foreign Plurals

The tendency now is to use English plurals for words of foreign origin whenever both English and foreign forms are current. For the formation of the most common plurals, see pages 51-52.

Foreign Words in English

There was a time when it was rather generally felt that foreign terms added a touch of grace to English. Now the tendency is to feel that a foreign word should be used only when there is no satisfactory English substitute (*geisha, samovar*). Exceptions may reasonably be made in fiction when a foreign flavor is desired, or when addressing a selected audience who may be expected to know the foreign words.

Formal English

A generation ago "Formal English" was often regarded as the only really "correct" English. Now the tendency is to use the word *formal* literally, to indicate an attitude rather than a "level."

former, latter

These two words are not exactly obsolescent, but they are certainly used much less than they used to be. The current tendency is to use either *first* and *second* or *first* and *last* when comparing two units. A football game never seems to have a *latter* half, though a book still may. Neither now has a *former* half. Moreover, if you refer to Smith and Jones in one sentence, it is usually better to repeat the names in the next sentence than to call one of them the *former* and the other the *latter*.

Fragments

A group of words punctuated as a sentence, but lacking either the subject or the main verb, is called a *fragment*—unless the instructor thinks that the lack is both intentional and satisfactory. See pages 109-110.

freshman

Only the singular form is used as a modifier (the *freshman* class). As nouns we use one *freshman,* several *freshmen.* A capital is not required, but may be used when the *Freshman Class* is mentioned as a specific organization.

full, -ful

When *full* is used as the last half of a word it is shortened to *-ful* (*careful, spoonful*).

Function Words

Words which have no definite meaning of their own, but are used merely to fill out a grammatical pattern, or to indicate the particular way in which other words are used, are called *function words.* Auxiliary verbs and connectives are most often used in this way. In the sentence "He has money," *has* is equivalent to *possesses,* and is a "full" word. But in the sentence "He has gone," *has* merely indicates the time of the main verb, and is a function word. The words italicized in the following sentence are all function words:

The wife *of the* gardener works *more* rapidly.

Compare this with:

Johnson's wife works faster.

It is impossible to draw a clear line between function words and "full" words, and useless to split hairs about them. It does little good to attempt to analyze function words logically. We simply have to develop the accepted habits, and the less we think about them the better. They are hard on foreigners simply because a logical approach to them will not work. We could just as well say "attorney *of* law" and "doctor *at* medicine," but we don't.

funny

Except in very formal English, *funny* is a perfectly good word for "odd."

further

See **farther.**

Fused Sentence

See *Run-on sentence,* pages 205-207.

Gender

It is often said that English has "natural gender," while many other languages have "grammatical gender." For instance, in French the word for *pencil* is masculine and the word for *pen* is feminine. Actually, *gender* is a purely grammatical phenomenon, and English has none. We use some words only to refer to female beings, or as things personified as female, but we do not have special forms of adjectives to modify them. If we refer to an actress as *she,* it is because the actress is a woman, and not because the word *actress* is feminine. If the term *gender* were dropped entirely in discussing English grammar, nothing would be lost.

Genitive Case

Another term for the possessive case, always used in referring to Latin and German, and preferred by some grammarians in referring to English. If you use it, notice that the middle vowel is *i,* not *e.*

genteel

This word formerly meant "well bred." Now it usually means something like "trying to act well bred and not making it."

gentleman

There was a time when a man of assured social position was regularly referred to as a *gentleman;* to call him a *man* was almost insulting. The general feeling now is that *man* is good enough for anybody, and should be used unless you are specifically calling attention to certain (or perhaps uncertain) desirable qualities, as in "That *man* is a real *gentleman.*"

Gerunds

Some grammarians call present participles *gerunds* whenever they are used as nouns. By so doing they can distinguish between the two following sentences:

> I don't like Betty's working. (I disapprove of Betty's activity)
> I don't like Betty working. (I don't like Betty when she works)

In the first they call *working* a gerund modified by *Betty's;* in the second they call it a participle modifying *Betty.*

This theory is ingenious rather than sound. In Latin the gerund *operandum* is obviously different from the participle *operantem,* but in English the one form *working* serves both purposes and might as well be called a participle all the time. The fact is that both expressions are in good use in the first meaning, with the plain form gaining ground. Moreover, since the supposed distinction between the two will not be caught by one reader in a hundred, it is clearly not a very dependable basis for communication. We can therefore forget about the "gerund" and notice only the following points:

We automatically use the possessive form:

1. When the participle indicates an accomplishment rather than a temporary activity:

> He likes *Betty's* cooking.

2. When the participle is used as the subject:

> *Schlegelmeyer's* pitching won the game.

Otherwise we may take our choice.

get

The verb *get* has a very wide range of meanings. The simple sentence "I *got* him," for instance, might mean "I engaged him," "I killed him," "I understood him," or several other things. *Get* also enters into a bewildering variety of combinations. We may *get up* or *down, hot* or *cold, sick* or *left, away* or *away with something.* We may *get going.* We don't *get coming,* but we may *have got it coming.* Possibly one reason so many teachers have a strong prejudice against *get* is that it is very hard to explain.

Some of the uses of *get* are definitely informal, some are not standard, and some are slang. But it would be hopeless to attempt a complete analysis—there is too much disagreement about which is which. Only a few of the most debated uses will be discussed here.

1. It is often said that *got* is redundant when used with *have* whether to indicate possession or necessity.

> Have you *got* any apples? (Have you any apples?)
> He has *got* to do it. (He has to do it.)

It is true that *got* does not add anything to the theoretical meaning of these sentences; but it is also true that *have* is used so often as an auxiliary that it is likely to seem a little bare when used alone. Since we regularly say "Have you found any apples?" "Have you sold any apples?" and so forth, it seems natural to say "Have you got any apples?" rather than to vary the pattern by using *have* alone.

To indicate necessity, *has got to* strikes many people as more satisfactorily emphatic than *has to.* Both idioms are certainly standard, no matter how often they are criticized.

The practice of leaving out the *have* and using *got* alone in these meanings is not recognized as standard, though many standard speakers who think they are saying "I've got" often sound as if they were saying "I got to go" or "I got enough now."

2. The past participle *gotten* has disappeared in British usage, but is a permissible form in American usage in the sense of "become" or "procured." Thus we can say either "He had *got* tired of it" or "He had *gotten* tired of it," "He has *got* the tickets" or "He has *gotten* the tickets." It is also permissible in many verb-connective combinations, as "It had *got* (or *gotten*) away from him." But *gotten*

is never used to indicate either necessity (He has *got* to do it) or simple possession (He has *got* a farm in Pennsylvania). It is not necessary to memorize rules about this. If you can't trust your ears, remember that *got* can be used in any sense, and avoid *gotten*. But *forgotten* is the only standard past participle of *forget*.

good, well

In standard usage *good* is used only to modify nouns and pronouns. There is no logical reason why "He pitched *good*" should be any worse than "He pitched *fast*," but so much classroom time has been spent objecting to the extended use of *good* to modify verbs and other modifiers that it has become an important shibboleth.

Well is used as an adjective when it refers to health. It is also used as the adverbial equivalent of *good*.

> He pitched *well* today.

good-bye, good-by

The form with the final *e* is older, but both are now standard. With either spelling the hyphen is optional.

graduate

The passive construction ("He *was graduated* from Cornell") has been almost completely replaced by the active ("He *graduated* from Cornell"). However, if you like the academic flavor of the former, it is still permissible and will impress some people favorably.

guess

Guess, in the sense of "suppose" is now standard throughout most of this country. Some Southerners (who say "reckon") and some Britons (who say "fancy") object to it; but the schoolroom opposition throughout most of the country has about died out.

had better, had rather; would better, would rather

Had better, had rather, and *would rather* are all standard. *Would better* is decidedly questionable, though often used with conscious pride.

half

A half is more specific than *half a.*

> He ran *a half* mile. (880 yards)
> He ran *half a* mile. (Approximately)

Similarly, *a half dollar* is a coin, while *half a dollar* is a sum.

The double construction *a half a* is common speech, but is generally considered careless or ignorant in writing.

hanged, hung

In legal language, murderers are *hanged* when they are executed, and many careful users of standard insist on *hanged* in this sense even in ordinary English. But the tendency to use *hung* in all senses is so strong and general (not to mention sensible) that "He was *hung* for murder" is now, on the evidence, in standard usage, though it is very likely to be criticized.

happen to be

Happen to be is a perfectly good idiom when there is a reason to bring out the element of chance:

> I just *happened to be* working late when he called.

When there is no reason to emphasize chance, some form of *be* is usually better.

In other words, don't substitute "He *happened to be* hungry" for "He *was* hungry" unless you want to bring out an idea of rarity or coincidence. *Happened to be* for *was* is not only wordy, but often sounds apologetic or uncertain.

hardly

"I *have hardly* any left" means just as much as "I *haven't hardly* any left," and is more generally admired.

he or she (his or her)

The use of the double pronoun is overfussy. Ordinary *he* or *his* will do for a reference to mixed as well as purely male company. In a sentence like "Neither John nor Mary liked——assignment," the best way to fill the blank is with *their.*

height (*not* heighth)

Maybe the form with the extra *h* ought to exist in standard English, to go along with *width, breadth,* and *length;* but it doesn't.

help but

Such expressions as "I can't *help but* admire him," are criticized on theoretical grounds; but they have been in standard use for a long time and still are.

high school

High school may always be written as two separate words. Some writers hyphenate the combination, or even write it as a single word, when they use it to modify another word.

> He went to *high school.*
> A *high school* (or *high-school* or *highschool*) text.

It is usually capitalized when it refers to a specific school:

He went to *Richfield High School* for two years. (Some newspapers would say *Richfield high school*)

Historical Present

We are likely to be more interested in something that is still going on than in something that has already happened. Consequently there is a fairly general tendency to make past events seem more vivid by talking about them in the present tense. When a respected authority does this, we call it the *historical present:*

There *is* a silence in the great hall. The audience *is* tense, expectant. Then Washington *rises* to speak. . . .

If a less respected person does the same sort of thing, we call it vulgar:

I *play* an interesting hand last week. The bid *is* four spades and I *hold.* . . .

There is no justice.

A special (and paradoxical) use of the historical present is to refer to fiction and drama. We usually say that the historical Richard II *died* in 1400, but Shakespeare's Richard II *dies* in Act V.

There is no justice at all.

home

In spite of theoretical objections, "He is *home*" is established in both literary and conversational standard usage, along with "He is *at home*." On the other hand, "He is *to home*" is good colloquial English only in limited areas.

homey, homely

The British call a girl *homely* as a compliment, implying that she would be a nice, comfortable person to have around the house. We don't. Both we and the British may speak of a club as having a nice, *homely* atmosphere, but Americans are more likely to substitute *homey* or (better) *homelike*.

Homonyms

Words with the same sound but different meanings are called *homonyms* (*sun, son; sight, cite, site*). Sometimes *homonyms* have the same spelling, in spite of different origins. Thus the verb *rock* (sway) comes from an Old English word. The noun *rock* (stone) comes from an unrelated French word. On the other hand, the same original word may have developed different spellings in different meanings. Thus we call the *flower* (best part) of the grain simply *flour*, though we have not found it necessary to develop a special spelling of *cream* in similar senses (*cream* of the crop, *cream* of wheat).

hope, hopes

We often use the plural where the singular would be at least as reasonable, especially with *high*.

> His *hopes* were high.
> He had high *hopes* of accomplishing something.

But the phrase *in hopes of* is not a standard variation of *in (the) hope of*.

however

The chief difficulty with *however* is in the question of what punctuation to use with it when it joins two clauses. Standard practice usually follows the following rule: separate *however* from the rest of the clause to which it belongs by a comma, and from the other clause by a semicolon.

They will make every possible effort; *however,* we should not expect too much.
Most people think of oranges as sweet and lemons as sour. This is not always true, *however;* there are sour oranges and sweet lemons.

When *however* in the sense of "nevertheless" occurs within a clause instead of between two clauses, it is set off by a pair of commas:

The president, *however,* decided on a different policy.

When *however* means "no matter how," it is not separated from the word it modifies:

However little he knows about a subject, he always expresses an opinion.

Hyphen (-)

1. *At the end of a line.* The *hyphen* is used to mark the division in a word carried over from the end of one line to the beginning of another.

(a) The division must be between pronounced syllables:

thought-less, but never *thou-ght* or *walk-ed*

(b) There must be at least two letters before and after the *hyphen:*

Scar-ing and *ac-cuse,* but not *scar-y* or *a-cross*

(c) Double consonants are usually divided unless they come at the end of a simple word to which an ending is added:

com-mittee or *commit-tee* and *let-ting,* but *bless-ing*

(d) In doubtful cases, the tendency is to put as many letters as possible without distorting the pronunciation after the *hyphen:*

hy-phen   *re-store*   *res-piration*

2. *With prefixes.* Prefixes are usually hyphenated when:
(a) The root word begins with the vowel with which the prefix ends:

pre-eminent   *anti-intellectual*

(b) The root word begins with a capital letter:

pre-Christmas   *un-American*

(c) Confusion with another word might result:

re-mark (mark again), *remark*
super-vision (Superman has it), *supervision*

(d) *Ex-* is used in the sense of *former:*

ex-professional   *ex-wife*

3. *To make compound words.*
   (a) Two-word numbers from *twenty-one* to *ninety-nine,* fractions (*five-eighths*), and words indicating relation by marriage (*brother-in-law,* etc.) are treated as permanent compounds.
   (b) Groups of words used as a unit to modify a following noun may be hyphenated in such uses.

He lived in the *eighteenth century.*   An *eighteenth-century* poet
He kept to the *middle of the road.*   A *middle-of-the-road* policy

Such hyphens may be omitted when there is no possible ambiguity (we could say "An eighteenth century poet"), but are very useful in indicating just which connections are closest. Compare:

The middle-of-the-road policy satisfied nobody.
Johnson had to leave in the middle of the road-policy debate.

   (c) In many words there is a variety in practice. *Tax payers, tax-payers,* and *taxpayers* are all in use. If you have to guess, the form with two separate words is probably the safest.

ibid.

Ibid. is an abbreviation of *ibidem,* a Latin word meaning "in the same place." It is used principally in footnotes, and refers to the work mentioned in the *immediately preceding* footnote. It should be underlined or printed in italics.

[1] Archibald A. Hill, *Introduction to Linguistic Structures* (New York, 1958), p. 126.
[2] *Ibid.,* p. 173.

Notice that *ibid.* is separated from the page number by both a period and a comma.

-ics

Nouns ending in *-ics* are usually treated as singular when they refer to a subject of study, but as plural when they refer to activities or qualities:

>*Tactics* is a difficult subject. *His tactics* are sound.
>*Acoustics* is the science of sounds. *The acoustics* are bad.

Idiom

The most frequent meaning of *idiom* is an expression which departs from the normal pattern of a language, or has a meaning that is not quite what you would expect, considering the meanings of the individual words.

>He *had better* be there.   They will be *on hand*.

We learn these *idioms* by simple exposure, not by grammatical theory, and they are *hard on* foreigners.

The term *idiom* is also used in a quite different sense, to mean the characteristic expression of a language or dialect. Thus we might say that the English *idiom* is more direct than the German, or that a certain character speaks in the *idiom* of Brooklyn.

i.e.

I.e. is an abbreviation of *id est,* a Latin phrase meaning "that is." It is used chiefly when space is important, as in compact reference works.

immigrate, emigrate

Immigrate means "migrate to." *Emigrate* means "migrate from."

Imperative Mood

In commands and requests with no expressed subject ("Be quiet," "Please come here"), the verbs are often said to be in the *imperative mood*. There seems to be no reasonable way of making mistakes in such constructions.

Impersonal Style

In many types of writing it is inappropriate for the writer to call attention to himself when he can reasonably avoid it; yet there are times when he must make a clear distinction between his personal opinions and established fact. About the best general principle to follow is to *be* as impersonal as is reasonable, but not to *pretend to be* more impersonal than you are. "It is the opinion of the writer of the present paper" is a very roundabout way of saying "I think."

imply, infer

Imply and *infer* are complementary terms. To *imply* is to indicate something without saying it directly. To *infer* is to gather more than has been directly stated.

> His words *implied* that he did not trust me.
> I *inferred* that he did not trust me.

in, into

> The piano is *in* the next room.
> They went *into* the next room.

These two sentences show the general difference between *in* and *into*. *In* primarily indicates mere location (in time, in space, or figuratively); *into* indicates a change of position or condition. When in doubt it is usually better to use *in*. "They went *in* the next room" is in good general usage, while "The piano is *into* the next room" is typical only of a few regional dialects.

The choice between *into* and *in to* can be determined by the natural pronunciation.

> He came *into* (*into*) some money.
> He came *in to* play.

in back of

Many school texts describe the phrase *in back of* as objectionable for one reason or another. Some of these prefer *back of,* and some insist on *behind.* But *in back of* goes naturally with *in front of,* and is definitely established in standard usage.

in-, un-

Both *in-* and *un-* may be used as prefixes meaning *not.* There is no satisfactory general rule on which prefix should be used. Only *un-* is used with English roots (*unsung, unworkable*), but either may be used with Latin roots.

incidentally

This adverb is formed from the adjective *incidental,* not directly from the noun *incident.* The very common misspelling *incidently* has no standing whatever.

incredible, incredulous

Incredible means *unbelievable; incredulous* means *unbelieving.*

Indicative

An unnecessary term in English. See *Mood* if you are really curious.

Indirect Discourse

See page 99.

Indirect Questions

A question reported in a statement, but not quoted exactly, is called an *indirect question,* and does not require a question mark.

> *Original question:* When are they coming?
> *Quoted question:* He asked, "When are they coming?"
> *Indirect question:* He asked when they were coming.

individual

For *each individual* read *everybody;* for *the majority of individuals* read *most people.* In fact, whenever you come across a writer who uses *individual* when he could just as well say *man* or *person,* it might be a good idea to change authors and read another book. *Individual* is occasionally useful as an adjective (*individual* portions) or even as a definitely technical noun (for instance, when the *individual* is contrasted with *society*); but it is far more often the first symptom of a creeping inflation of the vocabulary. A precautionary attitude is indicated, in order that exposure to this practice may not ultimately be reflected, with adverse results, in the stylistic characteristics of the individual. (This means "Look out or you'll be doing it yourself.")

Infinitive

In some languages the *infinitive* is a special form of the verb, not used alone to make a definite statement, and not limited as to person or number (hence the name). English has no exact equivalent of this form, but the term *infinitive* is often used to designate:

1. The plain form of the verb when it comes directly after another verb:

He will *go.*   They must *try.*

2. The phrase consisting of *to* plus the plain form:

> *To drive* so fast is dangerous.
> That is a silly thing *to do.*
> He is going *to be* there.

Only the *to go* construction is called an *infinitive* in this book. As the examples above indicate, an *infinitive* may be used as a noun (*to drive* . . . is), as a modifier (thing *to do*), or as part of a verb phrase (is going *to be*). It may also be used in such sentences as:

> He asked his friend *to do* that.

However, it is never used alone as the main verb of a sentence ("The Johnsons *to be* here today"). See also **Split Infinitive.**

inside (of)

      Inside the house   The *inside of* the house

In expressions of time rather than space, *inside of* is used without the preceding *the* (*inside of* two months). More formal equivalents are *within* and *in less than.*

Intensive Pronouns

The compound personal pronouns (*myself,* etc.) are often called *intensive* when they are used to emphasize ("He did it *himself*") rather than to show "reflexive" action ("He cut *himself*").

Intensives

Words intended to increase the force of following words (such as *extremely, terribly,* and *very*) are called *intensives.* Our general tendency to exaggerate tempts us to overuse intensives, and thus to weaken them. Such words as *awfully* and *terribly* have pretty well lost their original meaning and are now practically synonymous, with considerably weakened force. *Quite,* which originally meant *completely,* now often weakens rather than strengthens the word it modifies. Other intensives tend to have the same effect unless they are pronounced with a strong stress.

inter-, intra-

Inter- means *between; intra-* means *within.* Thus *intercollegiate* sports are between different colleges, while *intramural* sports take place "within the walls" (*murōs* is Latin for *walls*) of a single college.

invite

Not standard as a noun.

Irony

Irony might be defined as a method of implying the opposite of what is actually said with a little more restraint than is characteristic of *sarcasm.* Suppose your roommate has borrowed your last clean shirt on the night of the junior prom. If you say "You're a real pal!" you are being sarcastic. If you remark with apparent calmness "There's nothing like having a bosom friend" you are being ironical. Never use *irony* unless you are either sure he'll get it or sure he won't.

We also speak of the *irony of fate* or *of events* when something happens that seems to make light of all human efforts or experience. When a star tackle breaks his leg playing ping pong or a man dies of thirst just an hour before a heavy rain, it is kinder to say "ironical" than "funny."

-ise, -ize

If you have to guess between an *-ise* and an *-ize* ending, the best rule of thumb is the following:

1. When the part of the word before the ending is complete or nearly so, add *-ize.*

apologize   characterize   memorize   standardize

2. When the part before the ending doesn't look much like a word all by itself, add *-ise.*

advise   despise   disguise   franchise   surprise

Many words are spelled with either ending.

Italics

See *Underlining.*

its, it's

Like all pronouns, *it* forms *its* possessive with no apostrophe. *It's* is legitimate only as a contraction of *it is.* If you remember that the apostrophe must be used to show the omission of the second *i* in *it is,* you may figure out that the possessive form does not need one.

it's me, it's I

In spite of almost frantic opposition, *it's me* has become the normal form in standard English. *It's I* is also permissible if you can say it without feeling self-conscious or overvirtuous, but it isn't worth a special effort, since it will probably lose you more admirers than it will gain. The same is true of *it's we.*

The expressions *it's her, it's him,* and *it's them* are not quite so well established, probably because we can usually substitute *it's Helen,* or *Jack,* or *the Smiths.*

Insistence on using the subject forms of any of these pronouns is now an indication rather of petty snobbery than of "good English."

-ize

See *-ise.*

Jargon

Jargon means a form of language that is for some reason unintelligible. It is now most frequently used to indicate a kind of shoptalk which not only mystifies outsiders but often fools the speakers into believing that they are saying something much more important than they actually are. We can forgive a young doctor for saying "lacerations and contusions" for "scratches and bruises"—after all, he may have enough trouble collecting his fees, even with the aid of big words. It is not so easy to forgive people who say things like "His failure to provide optimum motivation for his classes was traceable to the deficiencies of his preparation in subject matter areas, which resulted in an incapacity to provide adequate stimulation through the broadening of their intellectual horizons." This really is not a very good way to say "He bored his classes because he didn't know enough to teach them anything."

job

There are still people who think that *job* is less dignified than *position*. On the other hand, many employers feel that an applicant for a *job* might be willing to work, whereas a seeker after a *position* might be looking merely for a comfortable place.

It is still definitely slang to call a car or a girl "a nice *job*."

judgment, judgement

The spelling without *e* in the middle is "preferred"—largely because it is so unnatural that people who know it are proud of their knowledge. The other spelling is now definitely established also. The same statements apply to *acknowledgment, acknowledgement.*

kind, sort

1. *Kind of* and *sort of* are both often used informally for *rather* or *somewhat:*

> I feel *kind of* sorry about that.

Like many colloquial expressions, they look more informal than they sound, and sometimes seem rather undignified in writing.

2. *Kind of a, sort of a.* In such expressions as *a sort of a* handyman and *some kind of a* story, the *a* after *of* could certainly be dropped without affecting the meaning, and is often criticized as incorrect; but it is clearly established in standard usage.

3. Such expressions as *these kind of apples* and *those sort of people* have been in standard use for some seven centuries, and will probably continue in spite of frequent protests that *this kind* and *that sort* are required by the rules of agreement. It is just as well to "correct" these phrases in revision if you notice them.

lady

A generation ago it was rather generally considered almost insulting to call a woman a *woman,* unless she definitely belonged to what used to be called "the working class." It is now generally felt that *woman* is good enough to designate anybody, and that *lady* should only be used to indicate certain admirable qualities. Thus a speaker might reasonably make the following remarks about the same friend:

> Helen is the tallest *woman* in the club.
> You can always depend on Helen—she's a *lady*.

last, latest

Last may mean either *final* or *most recent*. *Latest* means *most recent*.

last, latter

Latter is used only in referring to a group of two units or two parts. *Last* must be used when there are more than two, and may be used when there are only two. We can say either the *latter half* or the *last half* of the month, but always the *last day*.

lay, lie

The following expressions are standard.

> I *lie*　　　　in bed.
> 　*lay*
> 　have *lain*
> I *lay*　　　　the book down.
> 　*laid*
> 　have *laid*

"I lay down" may sound like "I laid down," and the fact that the past form of one verb is the present form of the other may seem unfair; but it really does not take a superhuman effort to master the standard uses, and enough people think the difference is important to make the effort it does take worth while.

l.c.

L.c. is an abbreviation for *lower case,* and means "use small letters instead of capitals."

lead, led

The noun *lead* is pronounced *led* when it refers to a metal, otherwise *leed*.

The present tense of the verb is spelled *lead* and pronounced *leed*. The past tense is spelled and pronounced *led*.

learn, teach

Such expressions as "That will *learn* him" and "The teacher *learned* them to spell" are not standard. Use *teach* and *taught*.

leave

As a synonym for *let*, *leave* is standard in the expression "*Leave* (or *let*) him alone," but not in such expressions as "Let him go."

However, Damon Runyon's very popular stories of Broadway characters started a widespread fad for a sort of slumming use of such expressions as "*Leave* us not be hasty." If you say things like this you are supposed to indicate by your tone that you really know better.

less, lesser

Less may be used in place of *fewer* in referring to numbers, as well as in comparing size or quantity.

> There were *less* (or *fewer*) than ten members present.

Lesser is a rather formal equivalent of *smaller*, now little used.

let's

Let's is an abbreviation of *let us*, and should be treated accordingly.

> *Let's* do it. (Not "*Let's us* do it")
> *Let's not* go. (Not "*Let's don't* go")

liable

See **apt to.**

lie

See **lay, lie.**

like, as

The idea that *like* should never be used to introduce a clause has no sound basis in either theory or actual usage; but a good many people believe it firmly, and are much disturbed by such sentences as:

> He did it *like* I told him.
> He acts *like* he is tired.

If you want to avoid their criticism, substitute *as* in the first sentence and *as if* in the second.

likely

See *apt to.*

loan

Loan is now completely established as a verb in business transactions, but not otherwise:

The bank *loaned* (or *lent*) him four hundred dollars. Many people whose general usage is standard would also say:

> She *loaned* him a book.

Many others would insist that only *lent* is permissible in this sentence. If you don't mind criticism, suit yourself. If you do, use *lent.*

Localism

A word, expression, or pronunciation which is current in only a limited region is called a *localism.*

locate

Locate is a convenient word for "Find (or explain) the position of." It is seldom advisable in any other use. *Is located* seldom means any more than simple *is.*

loose, lose

Perhaps the best way to keep these straight is to remember that the verb *lose-lost* has only one *o* in both tenses; and that the expression *"loose* as a *goose"* rimes to the eye as well as the ear.

lot, lots

Such expressions as "a *lot* of money" and *"lots* of friends" are standard, though a bit informal. Notice that the first of these contains two words (not *alot*).

mad

In America, *mad* normally means *angry,* not *insane.* When insanity is suggested, it is usually of a mild and often pleasant kind:

> Such delightful people—quite *mad,* of course.
> We were in a *mad* rush to get off.

madam

"Dear *Madam*" is the feminine equivalent of "Dear Sir," and may be used in a letter to any woman, married or unmarried. In speech, the contraction *ma'am* is generally preferred among friends, though *madam* is generally used by store clerks and waiters.

madame, mademoiselle, mesdames, mesdemoiselles

These are French words, and may be reasonably used to refer to French women. Otherwise, they are appropriate to advertisements in women's magazines, and common in small-town newspaper reporting.

Malapropism

Mrs. Malaprop (from *mal à propos*—inappropriate) is a character in Sheridan's *The Rivals,* who knew a good many big words but had very vague ideas about what they meant. If you use a word which sounds something like the one you are reaching for but has a very different meaning, you commit a *malapropism*. Example:

He proved it by *seductive* (for *deductive*) reasoning.

man, woman

In a more genteel age it seems to have been felt that to call men and women *men* and *women* implied that they were not ladies and gentlemen. This feeling has now largely disappeared. It is still conventional to *address* a group as "ladies," "gentlemen," or both; but we now usually *refer* to them as *men* and *women*.

may

See *can*.

maybe, may be

Maybe is written as a single word only when it means *perhaps*.

Messrs.

This is an abbreviation for the French *messieurs,* and can be used as the plural of Mr. (*Messrs.* Smith and Brown). It is now dropping out of general use, and there seems to be no reason to mourn its passing. See also *Miss, Mr.,* and *Mrs.*

Metaphors and Similes

A *simile* is a fully expressed comparison:

> He is *as big as a moose.*

A *metaphor* is an expression which is not literally accurate, but which suggests a quality, perhaps more vividly than a simile:

> He is *a moose.*

Mixed metaphors, in which the implied comparison changes without warning, are often ridiculous ("the hand that rocked the cradle has kicked the bucket"). It seems a little hasty, however, to condemn all mixed metaphors on principle. Hamlet's "to take arms against a sea of troubles" has worn very well.

Metaphorical uses of words are often so satisfactory that they become standard, and what was originally an imaginative suggestion becomes a new literal meaning—for example, "The *head* of any *body* needs a good *staff* to *carry out* his *plans.*"

Meter

The *er* spelling is now more common than the *re* in all senses.

In referring to verse, *meter* designates the rhythmical pattern.

Specific *meters* are usually indicated by a pair of words, the first showing the stress-pattern (or in Greek or Latin the time-pattern) of the foot, the second showing the number of feet in the line.

The most common types of feet in English are:

iambic—*along*	dactylic—*easily*
trochaic—*many*	anapestic—*in a rush*

A *spondee* (*manlike*) may be substituted for a dactyl, but is seldom the basic foot of a meter.

The number of feet is shown by compound words consisting of Greek numerals followed by -*meter.*

Dimeter—two feet	Pentameter—five feet
Trimeter—three feet	Hexameter—six feet
Tetrameter—four feet	Heptameter—seven feet

Thus a poem in iambic pentameter has a basic pattern of five iambic feet:

> A bóok of vérses úndernéath the boúgh

might

See **can, may.**

Miss, Mr., and Mrs.

In standard English these three words are fully satisfactory only when followed by proper names. The last two are used only in their abbreviated forms. Only *Miss* has a plural, and that is dropping out of ordinary use (most of us would say *The Miss Smiths* rather than *The Misses Smith*). The whole situation is very curious, and quite different from what we find in most other languages. We simply do not have any fully acceptable way of addressing strangers.

In French, for instance, you can call a stranger *Madame, Mademoiselle,* or *Monsieur,* whichever happens to be appropriate, without being either rude or overpolite. Even if you know (or are supposed to know) the person's name, the forms are perfectly acceptable. This is very handy if you are not quite sure of the name, or if it is too long to be convenient. But in English we almost have to choose between saying "Mr. Titherington" or "Hey, you!" Of course we can put in a *sir* or *ma'am,* but we don't often begin sentences with these words except in situations prescribed by discipline. The following suggestions for addressing people whose names you do not know are offered:

1. If it doesn't seem reasonable to call a man "Mac" or "Pardner," say *Sir* rather than *Mister.*
2. *Ma(d)am* stands higher than *Miss,* and should be used in all borderline cases.

The French plurals *mesdames* and *messrs.* (for *messieurs*) seem to be established in the society pages of newspapers, where they save a good deal of space; but most of us can get along without them elsewhere.

Mixed Construction

We often forget how we have started a sentence, and finish it on a different pattern. The first two of the sentences below are satisfactory; but the third, which changes from one pattern to the other, is an example of a *mixed construction.*

> My father practices law, and I want to too.
> My father is a lawyer, and I want to be one too.
> My father practices law, and I want to be one too.

There are many varieties of mixed construction, and anybody is apt to slip into one in a hurried first draft. The way to catch them in revision is to be sure that you consider each sentence as a whole, and notice how the parts fit together.

Mode

A variant of the grammatical term *mood*.

Money

Sums of *money* should be expressed in figures when you want them to be easy to pick out (as in a business letter) or when it would be quite cumbersome to write them in words ($183.67). Otherwise, they should usually be written out, especially if they are round sums. There are no reliable rules.

The practice of writing out sums in words and then repeating them parenthetically in figures has now been generally abandoned except in certain legal forms.

Mood

Latin has three sets of verb forms, called respectively the *indicative,* the *subjunctive,* and the *imperative mood.* Some grammarians call the *infinitive* a fourth mood. Since English has only one set for all purposes, the term *mood* is unnecessary. However, there are a few idiomatic expressions which may be traced back to the time when English did have separate moods. These are discussed under *Subjunctive.*

moral, morale

Moral is connected with morals. *Morale* (rimes with *pal*) means "spirit."

The student body may not be particularly *moral,* but its *morale* is high.

most

Almost is often shortened to *most* in conversation. This is not advisable in writing, but if you do it, do it firmly and don't write *'most.*

muchly

Much can do anything that *muchly* can, and do it better.

must

The use of *must* as a noun ("This book is a *must"*) and a modifier (*must* legislation) is quite recent; but on the evidence it *must* now be called standard.

mutual

See **common.**

myself

This is normal for emphasis ("I saw it *myself"*) or for reflexive action ("I cut *myself"*), but should not ordinarily be used simply as a substitute for either *I* or *me*.

naive

Pronounced *nah-éev,* and now usually spelled with only one dot over the *i*. *Naive* is both French and English. *Naif* is purely French, and quite unnecessary in English. The word means "unsophisticated" or "unworldly," often with a suggestion that the unworldliness is not quite bright.

need

In most uses *need* is a perfectly regular verb. However, in questions and negative statements, when *need* is followed by the plain form of another verb, we may use *need* instead of *needs* even with a singular subject:

> *Need* he ask that?
> He *need* not try that again.

It is now more usual to say:

> *Does* he *need to* ask that?
> He *doesn't need to* try that again.

neither

The usual pronunciation is *nee'ther*. *Neye'ther* is all right if it comes naturally, but is not worth practicing.

Neither should be followed by *nor* rather than *or:*

> *Neither* John *nor* his brother has been here.

Notice that *has* is singular.

nice

Nice is a word with a curious history. It meant first *ignorant,* then *silly,* then *precise,* and finally became a general expression of approval. It is a useful word when you want to be a little vague, or when you are too lazy to figure out exactly what you do mean, and it is often quite satisfactory in conversation. In writing, a more definite word is usually preferable.

Nominative Case

In English the only discoverable traces of the *nominative case* are the six pronoun forms, *I, he, she, we, they,* and *who,* which can just as easily be called the *subject forms.* The statement that "nouns used as subjects must be in the nominative case" is a meaningless carry-over from Latin grammar.

none, no one

None was originally the negative form of *one,* and always took a singular verb. Now it seems natural to think of it as the opposite of *some,* and to use it with a plural verb. Take your choice.

> *None* of them *has* (or *have*) any real interest in it.

No one is rather more emphatic than *none.* It always takes a singular verb.

> *No one* of these books *is* very useful by itself.

Nonrestrictive Clauses

Another term for amplifying clauses.

not as or not so

In negative comparisons, either *as* or *so* may be used. *As* is now more usual:

> This is not *as* (or *so*) good as the other.
> He is not *as* (or *so*) old as I thought.

notoriety, notorious

Notoriety normally means a sort of cheap substitute for fame, and *notorious* means "well known for unworthy reasons." Neither word is complimentary unless used by somebody who thinks that any advertising is good advertising.

Noun and Verb Stress

There are a good many pairs of nouns and verbs which are identical in their written forms, but are pronounced with a different stress.

NOUNS	VERBS
con'trast	con-trast'
in'sult	in-sult'
rec'ord	re-cord'

The unstressed syllable is often slurred. When there is a difference in stress, nouns take the stress on the first syllable, verbs on the second. There are many other pairs which are pronounced as well as spelled alike.

number

When *number* is preceded by *the* it usually indicates a definite (though perhaps unspecified) number, and takes a singular verb:

The *number* of people who still believe in magic *is* amazing.

A number of is usually equivalent to *many* and takes a plural verb:

A *number* of the trees *were* damaged by the storm.

Number

There are two grammatical numbers in English, *singular* and *plural*. Most nouns have separate forms for the two numbers, and all the pronouns except *you* and *who* are limited to one number or the other. *Number* has disappeared from adjectives except in the pairs *this-these* and *that-those*. The only traces left in verbs are *am, was,* and the *-s* form of the present tense. See *Agreement*.

Number Forms of Nouns

Ordinarily there is no problem in choosing between the singular and plural forms of nouns. However, there are a few peculiarities in the uses of nouns indicating number, quantity, and measurement.

1. Such hyphenated compounds as the following are always used as modifiers, and therefore never take the plural form:

a *six-foot* tackle	a *forty-acre* pasture
three *two-quart* jars	ten *five-dollar* bills

2. When nouns indicating *number* are preceded by a word indicating plurality, they are usually put in the singular form. When they are not so preceded, the plurality-of-their-plurality can only be shown by their endings:

Three *hundred* came.   *Hundreds* came.
She has two *dozen* eggs.   She has *dozens* of eggs.

3. Traces of this same distinction can still be found in nouns indicating *quantity* and *measurement,* but in standard usage these are now usually put in the plural even when preceded by a plural number, except in hyphenated compounds.

ten *tons* of coal (sometimes ten *ton*)
He was six *feet* tall. (sometimes six *foot*)

Numbers

Types of numbers. The numbers *one, two, three,* and so forth are called *cardinal numbers.* The numbers *first, second, third,* and so forth are called *ordinal numbers.* The population of America is divided into three main classes: those who have never heard of these terms; those who have forgotten them; and those who get them mixed up. If you want to join the select group that knows them, perhaps you can remember that *cardinal* is a more common word than *ordinal,* and is used for the more common type of numbers.

Types of numerals. The ordinary figures 1, 2, 3, and so forth are called *Arabic.* When the letters I, V, X, L, C, D, and M are used to indicate numbers, they are called *Roman numerals.* Roman numerals are not used with perfect consistency (for instance, 9 may be indicated by IX, VIIII, or VIIIJ) but the most usual system is indicated below.

1—I	13—XIII	40—XL
2—II	14—XIV	. . .
3—III	15—XV	50—L
4—IV	16—XVI	. . .
5—V	17—XVII	60—LX
6—VI	18—XVIII	. . .
7—VII	19—XIX	90—XC
8—VIII	20—XX	. . .
9—IX	21—XXI	100—C
10—X	. . .	. . .
11—XI	30—XXX	110—CX
12—XII	. . .	. . .

140—CXL		1,000—M
. . .	600—DC	. . .
400—CD	. . .	1955—MCMLV
. . .	900—CM	
500—D	. . .	

You will notice certain principles in this system:

1. The basic letters stand for 1, 5, 10, 50, 100, 500, and 1,000.

2. No letter occurs more than three times in a row.

3. The normal procedure is to put the letters in descending order of size. Thus 1873 is represented by MDCCCLXXIII.

4. To prevent a letter from coming four times in a row, the numbers 4 and 9, 40 and 90, 400 and 900 are indicated by a kind of subtraction. Thus IV means 1 from 5, or 4; XC means 10 from 100, or 90.

5. Although small letters may be used for Roman numerals, capital letters are now more common.

6. Except for carving dates on banks built to look more or less like Roman temples, Roman numerals should seldom be used alone. However, they are useful when different kinds of numbers to indicate different levels are needed, as in outlines (II, A, 3), to distinguish volume numbers from page numbers of books, and so forth.

When to use words. Apparently there used to be a feeling that figures were a rather undignified substitute for words, and perhaps not quite legal. Formal documents gave even dates as "One thousand seven hundred and fifty-three," and businessmen played safe by writing out the words and then putting the figures in parentheses. This attitude has nearly disappeared, but words are generally used in the following situations:

1. At the very beginning of sentences:

Fifteen men, 26 women, and 13 children were on the boat.

2. When round numbers are used approximately:

It will cost you a thousand dollars for the round trip, and fifty dollars a day while you are there.

3. When small numbers are used in such a way that there is no reason to think a reader will want to find them rapidly (some people define "small" as under 100, others as ten or less):

It is only nine miles to Phoenix, but it is sixty-three (or 63) to Wickenburg and 196 to Flagstaff.

4. To indicate hours, when not followed by A.M. or P.M., or by the exact minute:

> He came at seven o'clock and stayed until half past ten.
> He came at 7 A.M. and stayed until 10:32.

When to use figures. In the following situations figures rather than words should be used:

1. For large numbers—see (3) above.

2. For small numbers when you wish to indicate that they are precise and not approximate. If you write "$5.00" your reader knows you have given him the exact figure. "Five dollars" might mean $4.98 or $5.15.

3. Whenever you have reason to think that a reader might want to find the numbers rapidly. Thus you might normally write *five* and *seven,* or even *nineteen* and *sixty-two.* But if you are dealing with percentages or temperatures, in such a way that your reader might reasonably be more interested in your numbers than your words, make it easy for him to find the numbers. Figures are easy to pick out.

Punctuating figures. Decimal fractions (including cents) are set off from whole numbers by a period (6.73%; $18.75).

Minutes are usually set off from hours by a colon, though a period is sometimes used (6:32 A.M. or 6.32 A.M.).

Ordinarily, figures larger than 999 are separated by commas into groups of three, beginning from the right (17,388; $13,466,791.46). But dates are punctuated only by separating the day of the month from the year (June 29, 1954), and street numbers are not punctuated at all (12473 Seventh Avenue). Some stylebooks require the use of commas only when the number contains more than four figures ($1750 but $17,500). This is not yet usual except in advertising.

Plurals of figures. The plural of a figure may be indicated by either *'s* or simple *s* (Three 9's or three 9s).

O, oh

In very formal writing, *O* is a sign of direct address ("*O* king, I hear and obey"), and *oh* is an exclamation, though often a very mild one. Most people now use *oh* for both purposes:

> *Oh* John, will you come over here?
> *Oh,* I don't think so.
> *Oh!* I never thought of that.

obsolete

See *archaic.*

of

Of is often added unnecessarily to other connectives:

> He looked *out* (*of*) the window.
> He stepped *off* (*of*) the porch.
> His place is *outside* (*of*) the city limits.

Of these, *off of* is rather generally regarded as substandard. The others are now generally accepted.

The mistaken writing of *of* for *'ve* is a very common error:

> He might *of* done it. (Should be *might 've* or *might have*)

Omissions

If a subject or verb is omitted a potential sentence becomes a fragment. If something else is omitted the result may be:

1. A logical contradiction:

> [other]
> Jim was older than any boy in the block.
>   ∧

Without the *other* this says that Jim was older than Jim.

2. An unacceptable grammatical construction:

> [had]
> Allen had heard and Pete seen the bear.
>   ∧

3. An obvious blank:

> She had three children, a son in the Army and a married daughter in San Francisco. [Who and where is the third?]

4. Complete ambiguity when something is clearly missing but the reader can't tell what:

> He looked for the knife was no longer there.

Everybody sometimes leaves out words. If you leave out many, make a practice of reading your papers aloud before handing them in —and be careful to read *only* the words that you actually see.

one

The use of *one* as an "indefinite pronoun" is becoming distinctly rare in American English. In spite of the efforts of generations of teachers, we normally say *"We* normally say" or *"You* normally say," rather than *"One* normally says."

The repetition of *one* (*"One* should do *one's* best, shouldn't *one?"*) and its use as a substitute for *I* ("After all, *one* has had some experience in these matters") sound intolerably affected to most Americans.

only

It is often preached in schoolrooms that *only* inevitably modifies the word that immediately follows it, so that "He *only* wants ten cents" means something quite different from "He wants *only* ten cents." This simply is not true. Put *only* where it sounds natural, and only change its position if it is ambiguous.

onto, on to

When *on* and *to* are separate words that just happen to come together, they are written separately.

He went on to say.

The single word *onto* may be used in a way that parallels *into;* that is, it indicates motion with the result of being *on* something. Theoretically, "He jumped *on* the porch" implies that he was already there when he jumped; while "He jumped *onto* the porch" would show that he got there by jumping. When in doubt, use *on* rather than *onto.* Such expressions as "He stood *onto* the porch" are not standard.

-or

In American usage *-or* is always acceptable in place of the British *-our,* though in a few words (*glamour,* the *Saviour*) the *-our* ending is still often used.

Ordinal Numerals

The words *first, second, third,* and so forth are called *ordinal* numerals, while *one, two, three,* and so forth are called *cardinal* numerals.

Such forms as *firstly* and *secondly* are never necessary.

Such abbreviations as *1st* and *2nd* should be used only where there is a real need for economy of space.

ought

In standard English, *ought* is never preceded by *had*. The negative form is *oughtn't to,* not *hadn't ought to.*

out loud

Out loud is considered more informal than *aloud,* as well as more emphatic. Both are in standard use.

over

When *over* is used as a prefix, the compound word is regularly written without a hyphen; *overactive, overcareful,* etc.

Overloaded Sentences

It is all right to put several ideas in a single sentence if:

1. They are closely related
2. The relation is clearly shown
3. The whole sentence is not so complicated as to put an unreasonable strain on a reader's attention

A sentence that fails to meet any one of these conditions is overloaded. It should be either strengthened so that it will carry the load better or split into parts.

pair

After a number the plural may be either *pair* or *pairs;* otherwise it is usually *pairs:*

> He bought three *pair* (or *pairs*) of shoes.
> All the *pairs* were well matched.

pants, trousers, slacks, breeches, levis, denims, shorts, etc.

We consider a garment with two sleeves definitely singular, but we seem to be permanently confused about garments with two legs, or even leg-holes. All of the words in this list normally take plural verbs unless preceded by "pair of," though the people who sell them sometimes speak of *one pant* and *two pants.* For some reason the word *pants* seems to be regarded as rather undignified in serious writings. All the others are completely standard.

Paradox

A *paradox* is either an apparent contradiction or something which has the opposite effect from what might be expected.

> He is so efficient that he never gets anything done.
> The better I know him the less I know about him.
> The more he eats, the thinner he gets.
> She was so good she made him worse.

Parentheses ( )

1. *For insertions. Parentheses* are used to insert illustrations, definitions, or other information not a part of the main structure of the sentence, but useful for a clear understanding.

> In two states (Idaho and Nevada) such laws have already been passed.
> His collection of incunabula (books printed before 1500) is one of the largest in the country.
> Her long theatrical career (she first appeared on the stage in 1902) was now drawing to a close.

In informal writing, commas or dashes may often be used satisfactorily in place of parentheses.

2. *With other punctuation.* A parenthetical expression does not affect the other punctuation of a sentence in which it is inserted. Any mark required at the point of insertion should be placed *after* the second curve:

> The room contained a table (borrowed from the neighbors), three chairs, and a phonograph (probably Edison's first model).

3. *Parentheses and brackets.* In academic writing, parentheses are used only for insertions in a writer's own sentence. Insertions in quoted material should be put in brackets. ([ ]).

Participles

A *participle* is a word derived from a verb but functioning on the borderline between verb and adjective. *Present participles* are always formed by adding *-ing* to the plain form. *Past participles* are formed in various ways, of which the following are examples:

He has *broken* it.
begun
made
finished

You will notice that *broken* and *begun* are special forms, used only as *participles,* while *made* and *finished* are identical with the forms for the past tense.

Any participle may be used as a part of a verb phrase or as an adjective.

The horse *was running.*	He *had broken* the dish.
The *running* horse suddenly swerved.	He had a *broken* arm.

Sometimes a participle is so close to the borderline between verb and adjective that it might be called either:

She had been *smiling* and happy all morning.

Had been smiling looks like a verb phrase. *Smiling and happy* looks like a pair of adjectives. Argument is useless—take your choice.

Any *present participle* may also be used as a noun ("*Running* is a strenuous sport"), although some people call it a *gerund* when it is so used. Comparatively few *past participles* are used as nouns (the *slain,* the *wounded*), and they are not called anything fancy.

Participles are not supposed to be used alone as verbs. Few of us make the mistake of using present participles in this way. Such expressions as "Annie *doing* me a favor" strike us as incomplete. But the substitution of the past participle for the past tense is a very common error:

Annie *done* (should be *did*) me a favor.
We *seen* (should be *saw*) him yesterday.

Such expressions are very common in some dialects, and they are certainly used by millions of intelligent and admirable people. But the prejudice against them is so strong that it is worth whatever time it takes to learn and practice the standard usage.

party

Party is established in legal usage (the *party* of the first part, one *party* to the dispute, etc.). As a substitute for *person* it is not now generally admired.

passé

Out of date, out of style. *Passé* is passé, or ought to be.

passed, past

Passed is a form of the verb *pass:*

> He *passed* the test.
> He had *passed* a good deal of time there.
> The bill was *passed* by the Legislature.

Past indicates former time rather than the action of passing.

> In the *past* this was often done.
> All his *past* efforts were failures.

Passive Constructions

A *passive construction* represents the subject as the receiver rather than the performer of an action. It is therefore appropriate when the performer is unknown, vague, or comparatively unimportant. Otherwise an active construction is usually preferable.

1. *The impersonal passive.* We often want a sentence to tell what happened rather than who did it. Sometimes we can choose between an *active construction* with a pronoun subject and a *passive construction:*

ACTIVE	PASSIVE
They *make* several good cars in England.	Several good cars *are made* in England.
You *can open* it with a screwdriver.	It *can be opened* with a screwdriver.
We *use* the passive construction.	The passive construction *is used*.

In each of these pairs the passive is rather more formal. In the following examples it would be hard to find a natural active construction:

> The crops *are ruined*.   The meadow *was flooded*.

2. *Passive with unknown agent.* When the performer of an action is actually unknown, the passive is the normal construction:

> Smith's grocery store *was robbed* last night.

3. *Passive with unimportant agent.* When the speaker is more

interested in the receiver of the action than in the performer, the passive is appropriate:

> My brother *was bitten* by a dog.

4. *The weak passive*. Unless there is a definite reason for using the passive, an active construction is usually preferable. "John saw Tom" is two words shorter than "Tom was seen by John," and is also more direct and forceful. It is especially unfortunate to begin a sentence containing several clauses with a passive construction, since one passive often leads to another, and a discouraging tangle is likely to result. Compare the following sentences:

ACTIVE	PASSIVE
Ponsonby suggested that Sanders ask the contractor to submit a new bid.	It was suggested by Ponsonby that the submission of a new bid by the contractor be requested by Sanders.

There are people who write whole books in this style.

5. *The cautious passive*. The frequency of the passive construction in military and bureaucratic correspondence is caused partly by official policies of impersonality, but owes something also to the fact that passive statements can be made without indicating exactly who is responsible. The passing of the buck is thereby greatly facilitated— not to mention that the recipient of such communications is often reduced to gibbering frustration, and effectively prevented from making a further nuisance of himself.

peeve, peevish

Peevish is an old and standard word. *Peeve* is a back formation. As a verb it is decidedly informal; as a noun it is slang.

people

A generation ago the use of *people* as a plural of *person* was still frequently condemned. It is now unquestionably standard.

per cent, percent

Per cent may be written as one word or two. The literal meaning is "to the hundred." Thus *ten per cent* equals one tenth. The noun *percentage* originally meant a fixed proportion:

> He gets a *percentage* of the profits.

Percentage is often shortened to *percent,* and is sometimes used to indicate merely a part, with no exact proportion to the whole:

A small *percentage* (or *percent*) of them will always have trouble.

Since this is a mere pretense at exactness, it offers no real advantage over "a small fraction," or even "a few."

"Perfect" Constructions

Verb phrases consisting of some form of *have* followed by the past participle of the main verb are called *perfect* constructions. Here *perfect* has its original meaning of "completed," and does not imply unusual virtue or quality.

He *has finished* the job.	Present perfect.
He *had finished* the job when I got there.	Past perfect.
He *will have finished* the job by Tuesday.	Future perfect.

It is often said that these three constructions are used to show action completed in the present, past, or future. Actually, the future perfect is very little used, since *he will finish* conveys just about the same information as *he will have finished*. The past perfect gives little trouble, though it is often replaced by another construction: *He finished before I came* is equivalent to *He had finished when I came.* But the present perfect is almost impossible to explain—we simply have to get used to it. It does not always indicate completed action. *He has worked there for twenty years* implies that he is still working there, while *he worked there for twenty years* implies that he has left. Moreover, we say *He has already done it* but *He did it yesterday.* A foreigner should simply believe us if we tell him this. We couldn't possibly explain why.

Period (.)

1. *At the end of a sentence.* The principal use of a period is to mark the end of a statement. When there is any doubt about whether the final mark should be a period or one of the other end marks (exclamation point or question mark), the period is usually the better choice.

2. *With abbreviations.* Periods are also used to indicate abbreviations (Sept.; Mr.; Prof. J. D. Hasting; P.S.).

(a) When an abbreviated form is pronounced as spelled, it is considered an informal word, and is not followed by a *period:*

The *Doc* gave me a health *exam* this morning.

(b) Periods are not usually used with abbreviations consisting entirely of capital letters: *FHA, CIO.*

(c) A few publishers follow the theory that a period indicates that something has been omitted after it occurs, and therefore should not be used when the abbreviation ends with the final letter of the original word. They therefore use *Dr, Mr,* and so forth. This practice is not usual in this country.

3. *As a decimal point.* The period (or something that looks very much like it) is used to indicate decimal fractions and to set off cents from dollars (17.89 *miles;* 3.5%; $16.95). This period is not used when cents are indicated without the dollar sign ($0.38 or $.38; 38¢).

4. *To indicate omission.* Three periods (. . .) are called an *ellipsis,* and are used to show an omission of one or more words.

5. *With quotation marks.* The period is usually put within final quotes, even if it does not logically belong there:

I heard him mumble something about "not my fault."

Person

There are three grammatical *persons.* The first represents the speaker; the second, the person spoken to; and the third, the person (or thing) spoken of.

The pronouns *I* and *we* are in the first person. *You* is in the second. The others, and all nouns, are usually considered to be in the third.

Verbs may be said to be in the same person as their subjects, although *am* and the *-s* form are the only ones in which the physical indication of person has remained.

phone

This shortened form of *telephone* is now in general use except in decidedly formal writing. No apostrophe is needed.

photo

Photo is not as thoroughly established as *phone,* probably because a short form is less needed. It is not much shorter than *picture,* and not as short as *snap* or *shot.*

Phrase

In this book any closely related group of words which does not contain both a subject and a predicate (and is therefore not a clause) is called a *phrase*.

In the morning   Driving down the street   Must have been

place

Place is a good word, but the combinations *any place, every place, no place,* and *some place* are not generally considered improvements over *anywhere, everywhere, nowhere,* and *somewhere.*

plan to *and* plan on

Plan to do it is unquestionably standard. *Plan on doing it* is also widely used, but is often criticized.

plenty

Standard usage requires an *of* after *plenty* before a noun:

I have *plenty of* potatoes.

The use of *plenty* as an intensifier ("He was *plenty tired,*" "He worked *plenty hard*") seems to be spreading, but is still generally considered substandard.

Possessive Forms and Of Phrases

1. The *possessive form* is used to show not only ownership but a number of other relations.

> He bought *Walter's* house.
> The ball hit the *pitcher's* foot.
> *Elmo's* brother is here.
> *Sheila's* picture does not do her justice.
> They worked hard for the *Senator's* election.
> *Hemingway's* novels have been very popular.
> Give me a *dollar's* worth.
> He can do it in a *week's* time.
> I don't like *Betty's* (or *Betty*) working so hard.

See also **Gerunds,** page 359.

2. Theoretically, any relation that can be shown by the possessive

form of a noun can also be shown by a phrase consisting of *of* and the plain form. Thus we can choose between:

Ed Ryan's home	The home of Ed Ryan
Aristotle's father	The father of Aristotle
The ship's crew	The crew of the ship

Frequently the choice is completely a matter of personal taste, but two general tendencies are noticeable:

(a) Restriction of possessive forms to living things, or at least things (like ships) that can be personified. This is by no means absolute. There are a number of set phrases like *a day's work, a stone's throw,* and *an hour's time* that are in very common use; and it certainly cannot be proved that "The *house's roof* leaks" is incorrect. But most of us would probably say "The *roof of the house* leaks."

(b) Single personal names are more likely to be used in the possessive form than with an *of* phrase. Although we may say "The home of *Ed Ryan,*" we generally say *"Ed's* home" or *"Ryan's* home," rather than "The home *of Ed,*" or "The home *of Ryan."* Also, we do not usually say "The father *of John,*" though we might say "The father *of John Fink,*" or "The father *of John and Edna."*

3. *The double possessive.* With nouns referring to persons, we sometimes combine the possessive form and the *of* phrase.

> A friend *of my father's*
> That speech *of Lincoln's*
> What business is that *of John's?*

This seems to have originated as a combination of the ideas of "possession" (in its broadest sense) and of selection from a group. Thus "a friend *of my father's"* indicates one of a number of people who are my father's friends.

practicable, practical

A plan or theory that can be put into practice may be called either *practicable* or *practical.* A thing that can be used is almost always called *practical.* A person is always called *practical.*

pre-

Pre- is followed by a hyphen when the word to which it is joined begins with an *e* or a capital letter (pre-eminent, pre-Romantic). Otherwise there is no hyphen (prearrange, prefabricate).

Predicate

The *predicate* of a sentence consists of everything in the sentence except the subject and its modifiers. The verb alone is sometimes called the *simple predicate*.

predominant (-ly), predominate

The adjective is *predominant,* the adverb *predominantly,* and the verb *predominate.* The erroneous form *predominately* results from confusing the verb and adjective.

prefer

In comparing two things, you *prefer* one *to* the other.

Prefix

A *prefix* is a word or word-element that can be placed before another word to make a new word with a changed meaning:

*de*moralize　　　*inter*collegiate　　　*over*take　　　*re*-examine

prejudice, prejudiced

The noun is *prejudice,* the modifier *prejudiced.*

> He has a *prejudice* against women.
> He is *prejudiced* against women.

preventive, preventative

Preventive was the original form. *Preventative* began as a mistake (probably under the influence of *representative*); but it has been used so often that it should now be considered a variant form rather than an error.

principal, principle

Principle is always a noun, and usually means something like an underlying truth, a rule of conduct, or an inherent quality:

> The *principles* of science should be followed.
> He is a man of high *principles.*
> The *principles* on which it works.
> In *principle,* I abhor it.

Principal is used as a noun when it refers to a sum of money or to a person (the *principal* of a school, the *principals* in a law suit).

As an adjective, the form is always *principal.*

Principal Parts of Verbs

The plain form (*take*), the past tense (*took*), and the past participle (*taken*) are called the *principal parts of a verb,* because in irregular verbs they have to be learned individually, while the other two forms (*takes* and *taking*) can be derived regularly from the plain form.

prior to

There is no law against using this phrase (or *previous to*) instead of *before,* but it is hard to think of a good reason for doing so.

privilege

Notice that this ends in *-ege* (pronounced *-ij*).

professor

Professor is spelled with a single *f* and a double *s.* The formal written abbreviation is not used with a last name alone.

Prof. Richard Jones   *Prof.* C. E. Jones   *Professor* Jones

The informal abbreviation *prof* is not followed by a period and should be used with reasonable discretion.

Progressive Constructions

Very roughly, we may say that the simple forms (*calls, called,* and *will call*) indicate the time of an activity only in a general way, and that the progressive forms (*is calling, was calling,* and *will be calling*) place it more specifically. Thus *he calls* usually indicates a habit extending through the present, while *he is calling* usually indicates a specific action taking place right now. For this reason the simple forms are sometimes called "indefinite" and the progressive forms "definite." However, the distinction is by no means uniform. It varies with different verbs, with different tenses, and with different contexts.

Verbs indicating *perceptions* are used more often in the simple tenses than are most other verbs. Thus we say, "I *hear* it now," or "I *see* it now" (perception), but "I *am* listening now" or "I *am looking* now" (effort).

Verbs indicating states of mind or attitude are also likely to be in the simple tenses, probably because the speaker usually thinks of his attitude as continuing. We rarely say "I *am liking,*" "I *am loving,*" "He *is hating,*" or "They *are knowing*" unless we wish to emphasize that we are feeling strongly right now ("I *am* simply *loving* this dance"). Similarly, "I *admire* him" indicates a general attitude; "I *am admiring* him" indicates a temporary, active appraisal.

In the past and future, the progressive forms often indicate action already going on at the time of another event, while the simple forms indicate action starting at or after the other event.

> He *was doing* it when they came.
> He *did* it when they came.
>
> He *will be resting* when you get there.
> He *will rest* when you get there.

When no second event is mentioned, the simple and progressive forms are more nearly interchangeable in the past and future than in the present.

What is he doing now?	He is working (not "He *works*").
What will he do tomorrow?	He *will work* (or *will be working*).
What did he do yesterday?	He *worked* (or *was working*).

In some situations the progressive forms somehow imply inevitability rather than a personal decision, and are therefore more polite than the simple forms.

Want to go fishing tomorrow? Sorry, I'll *play* tennis. (This sounds like a direct refusal)

Sorry, I'll *be playing* tennis. (This implies that I can't help it, and really am sorry)

Why weren't you here last night? I *bowled.* (Presumably by choice)

I *was bowling.* (Caught in the fell clutch of circumstance)

A number of other differences could be added, but these are enough to show that our uses of these forms depend on an erratic set of habits rather than any fixed principles. Actually, most native speakers have little trouble in making appropriate choices, though intelligent foreigners who try to follow rules are often hopelessly confused. It is easy to forgive them.

pronunciation

Notice that the second syllable is *-nun-*, not *-noun-*.

Proper Adjectives

Adjectives formed from proper nouns are called *proper adjectives* and are begun with capital letters: *French* cooking, *Shakespearian* sonnets, etc. However, when they come into common use in a meaning which has little to do with their origin, they may be begun with small letters. Thus we regularly write *French* cooking, because we definitely associate it with France; but we may write either *French* or *french* windows, because here the emphasis is on the shape rather than the origin. When in doubt, it is safer to use the capital letter.

Proper Nouns

See **Common and Proper Nouns.**

proposition

Proposition is a standard word in mathematics, philosophy, and business, and at least a useful word in social relations when it means the opposite of *proposal*. It is not recommended as a general substitute for *plan* or *affair*.

Used as a verb, *proposition* is definitely substandard linguistically, and usually implies a request that is substandard morally.

proved, proven

The verb to *prove* began as a perfectly regular one, and *proved* is always correct. *Proven* got into the language by mistake. However, it has been in for a long time and is now established, though it is not used nearly as often as *proved*.

psychology,psychiatry, *etc.*

There is probably no very good reason for putting these words here, since people who spell them "physcology" etc. would hardly be able to find them here. However, if you happen to find this entry by accident, you might notice how they are spelled.

public

Public may take either a singular or a plural verb.

Punctuation

Punctuation was developed as a method of helping readers to understand the relations of written words. If used in this way, it can obviously be helpful. Unfortunately, we sometimes forget the original purpose of punctuation, and treat it as if it were an end in itself; the "rules of punctuation" often appear to be just as arbitrary as the "rules of grammar," and even more mysterious. Quite naturally, many readers cheerfully disregard much of the punctuation they encounter, and have very vague ideas about what marks to use when it is their turn to write.

There is something rather peculiar about trying to teach punctuation by giving students passages incorrectly punctuated, or not punctuated at all, and telling them to "punctuate this correctly." In the first place, if a passage can be clearly understood without the "correct marks," a student may reasonably decide that it does not really need them; and his idea that punctuation is a system of arbitrary obstacles rather than of helpful hints is likely to be strengthened. In the second place, there are usually a number of equally "correct" ways to punctuate any but the very simplest passages. It might be reasonable to say, "Punctuate this so it will make some kind of sense." But there is usually not enough time available for a fair consideration of all reasonable variants; and at any rate such exercises are appropriate only for students who have already learned a good deal about the subject.

In order to punctuate intelligently we must find out what sort of effect each of the marks may be expected to have in guiding a reader's association of ideas. Then we can use the marks, like the words themselves, as a means to an end. We may miss our aim at times, as we sometimes do in the choice and arranging of our words; but this approach is more promising than trying to remember whether a given comma is used in accordance with Rule 19a.

It is true that a few perfectly arbitrary habits are widely and rather uniformly practiced. For instance, we are expected to separate a city from a state by a comma (*Atlanta, Georgia*) although the meaning would be as clear without the mark, and most of us would not pause between the two words if we read them aloud. But such rigid rules are not as numerous as students are often led to believe, and they are certainly not as important as an understanding of how the marks can be used as actual aids to communication.

Uses of the following marks are discussed under separate entries in this section:

Apostrophe (')	Hyphen (-)
Brackets ([ ])	Parentheses ( )
Caret (∧)	Period (.)
Colon (:)	Question Mark (?)
Comma (,)	Quotation Marks (" ")
Dash (—)	Semicolon (;)
Ellipsis (. . .)	Underlining (_____)
Exclamation point (!)	

A study of these entries should be reinforced by some practice in reading good contemporary prose with careful attention to how each mark is used and whether or not it seems to be effective. Only when you have learned what the marks do *to* you as you read can you expect them to do similar things *for* you when you write.

purist

A *purist* is a man who takes pride in using words exactly as they are defined in an out-of-date dictionary.

Question Mark (?)

1. *In direct questions.* The question mark is required after a direct question:

What is the approximate population of each of the three largest cities in New England?

It is *not* used after an indirect question:

He asked what she was going to do.

2. *In requests.* The question mark is optional after a request phrased as a question:

Will you please fill out the enclosed form?
Will you please check the information in your files, fill out the enclosed form, and return the information to me tomorrow.

There is no fixed rule, and the question mark and period in the two sentences above could be reversed. But a period after a very short question may seem rude unless the situation calls for a direct order. The longer the question, the more appropriate the period.

3. *With other marks.* When a question mark is used with quotation marks, its position depends on whether the sentence as a whole or only the quoted part is a question:

> Are you sure he said "The test will cover only the second chapter"?
> She heard him ask, "Where are our seats?"
> "Who cares?" he remarked, and went on with his work.
> Did he say "What time is it?"
> His first question was "What are the dates of the French Revolution?"; I didn't hear the other one.

Notice that a question mark within quotation marks is not followed by a comma, a period, or a second question mark, but is followed by a semicolon if the structure of the sentence requires it.

questionnaire

Notice the double *n*.

Quotation Marks (" ")

1. *To indicate quotations.* Quotation marks (also called *quotes*) are used to indicate the exact words used by a speaker or previous writer. Double quotes are the usual form, although the practice of using single quotes is gaining ground. For quotations within quotations the forms should alternate:

> John answered, "I distinctly heard Peggy say 'That is mine.' "
> John answered, 'I distinctly heard Peggy say "that is mine." '

Notice that closing marks should not be omitted even when two sets come together.

In academic writing, quotations of more than four lines are usually indicated by indenting and single spacing in typed papers, and by simply indenting in longhand papers, rather than by the use of quotes. This keeps the reader from forgetting where the quotation began, and reduces the necessity for quotes within quotes.

2. *In titles.* In informal writing, titles of books, magazines, and so forth are often put in quotes. In academic writing such titles are put in italics (or underlined to indicate italics), but quotes are used for titles of poems, stories, or articles of less than book length.

> Mrs. Frank's "Heartache on the Campus" first appeared in *The Woman's Home Companion.*

3. *For words used as words.* In informal writing words discussed as words rather than used to express meaning may be put in quotes:

> He was confused by such terms as "protocol" and "implemented."

In academic writing such words would usually be italicized.

4. *The apologetic use.* It is not advisable to use quotes apologetically:

> He was "bawled out" by the first sergeant.

Either say *bawled out* without the quotes or find some such substitute as *severely reprimanded.*

5. *Quotation marks used with other marks.* When a comma or period follows a quoted passage, it is put within the final quotes, regardless of its relation to the sentence as a whole. Other marks are put within or without, depending on the construction of the whole sentence.

> She heard him say "This way," and a moment later, "Here it is."
> He may have said "I dislike her"; but can you really believe that he said "I despise her"?

It used to be generally taught that quoted material should be set off from the rest of the sentence by commas as well as quotation marks. Such commas are now often omitted:

> "The main thing," said Larry, "is to find a place that is still open."
> "The main thing" said Larry "is to find a place that is still open."

A comma should not be used with quotes when a pause would be distinctly unnatural:

> "Very truly yours" sounds better to me than "yours very truly."

raise, rear

We used to be taught that only animals were *raised*—children were *reared.* Perhaps it is a result of progressive education, but now children are generally *raised,* too.

raise, rise

When the subject shifts its whole position, it *rises.* When it moves anything else, including part of itself, it *raises.*

He *rises*   from his seat.   He *raises*   his hand.
   rose   *raised*
   has risen   *has raised*

re-

In long-established words the prefix *re-* has a number of meanings difficult to analyze (*rely, remove, repeat, reverse,* etc.). Its most frequent meaning, and the only one used in new formations, is *again.* It is separated by a hyphen whenever this meaning has to be distinguished from another:

> We must *re-mark* the boundaries. (Not *remark*)

A hyphen is also used between *re-* and a word beginning with *e: re-emphasize.*

real, really

Real is often used in standard English to modify other modifiers: "a *real* nice time"; "He did that *real* well." On the other hand, such expressions are often severely condemned. *Really* is an unquestionably standard substitute.

reason is because, reason why

Such sentences as the following are often criticized as containing unnecessary repetition of an idea:

> The *reason* I failed was *because* I misunderstood the first question.
> That is the *reason why* he did it.

You can avoid criticism by rewriting the sentences as follows:

> The *reason* I failed was *that* I misunderstood the first question.
> That is the *reason* he did it.

or

> That is *why* he did it.

However, if you think *reason . . . because* and *reason why* are satisfactorily emphatic, you will have plenty of good company.

receipt, recipe

You always get a *receipt* (*re-seat'*) for a payment; but the directions for making cookies may be called either a *receipt* or a *recipe* (*ress'-i-pee*).

reckon

See *calculate.*

Redundancy

A word or phrase which repeats an idea already expressed, without adding anything useful, is called *redundant.* The words italicized in the following sentences are all worse than useless.

> Where is he *at?*
> The consensus *of opinion* is that Richards hasn't a chance.
> The trial is set for 3 P.M. tomorrow *afternoon.*
> He said that if he was elected *that* he would clean out the corrupt crowd *of dishonest people* at City Hall.

Reference of Pronouns

1. *Pronouns and antecedents.* One of the main uses of pronouns is to avoid repeating nouns. Thus we can say, "I asked John how *his* sister was getting along, and *he* said *she* was feeling much better." This is obviously neater than saying, "I asked John how John's sister was getting along, and John said John's sister was feeling much better." The noun to which a pronoun refers is called its *antecedent* (literally, "going before"). In the sentence above, *John* is the antecedent of both *his* and *he,* and *sister* is the antecedent of *she.* But the pronoun *I* has no antecedent, any more than the noun *John* has. Both words stand directly for persons, instead of referring to other words previously used. The pronouns *I, we,* and *you* are regularly used without antecedents, and all other pronouns may be.

Whenever we use a pronoun to stand for a noun, we must be careful to do it in such a way that our audience knows just what noun it is supposed to stand for:

> I saw Fred and Annette yesterday, and *he* looked tired. (Clear)
> I saw Fred and Dave yesterday, and *he* looked tired. (Ambiguous)

It is better to repeat a noun than to leave your audience guessing.

The pronoun *it* is often used to refer to the idea contained in a group of words, rather than to any one word:

> They argued about whether they would go fishing, but finally decided that *it* was too much trouble.

This, that, and *which* (sometimes called pronouns) are used in similar ways:

Dick suggested that we try to find one second hand. We decided that *that* was a good idea.
He was driving at fifty miles an hour, *which* is dangerous on that road.

This sort of reference is satisfactory unless the group contains a single word that might be mistaken for an antecedent.

Ambiguous: He was doing fifty on the Apache Trail, *which* is never safe.

The reader can only guess whether the speed or the road itself was dangerous.

Since it is almost impossible to avoid some vague or ambiguous references in a first draft, you should watch for them when you are revising. It isn't enough for *you* to know what every *it, this, that,* and *which* stands for. Unless your reader knows too—automatically and at the first glance—your sentences need tightening up.

2. *Agreement of pronouns.* In some languages pronouns have to "agree" with their antecedents: that is, they have to match *words* that have previously been used. But in English we have a choice between the pronoun that matches the word and the one that best expresses the idea. For instance, we can say either:

Everybody in favor should raise *his* hand. (because the word *everybody* is singular)

or

Everybody in favor should raise *their* hands. (because the idea expressed by *everybody* is plural)

Some people have a theory that a plural pronoun should never be used with *everybody,* but there are sentences in which it can hardly be helped, such as *"Everybody* went to the dance, and I think *they* all had a good time."

When we want to refer to a group noun as a unit, we usually use a singular pronoun:

The jury gave *its* verdict.

But when we want to refer to a group noun with an emphasis on the individuals of which the group is composed, we usually use a plural pronoun:

The jury left *their seats.*

There are a great many sentences in which either a singular or a plural pronoun may be used, and arguments about which is better simply cannot be settled, unless one is definitely clearer than the other. In older English it was customary to make the pronoun match the preceding *noun;* now it is becoming more usual to make it fit the *idea.* About all we can say is that both methods are in good standing, although some people are prejudiced one way or the other.

The same principle applies to such sentences as "I want each of you to do (*his* or *your*) best." Take your choice. You will find authorities on both sides.

Reflexive Pronouns

In such sentences as "He hurt *himself,*" the compound pronoun may be called *reflexive.*

regard, regards

The two expressions *as regards* and *in regard to* are often jumbled into *in regards to.* None of the three adds anything to a good prose style.

regardless

The *-less* makes this word sufficiently negative:

> He will do it, *regardless of what you say.*

The form *irregardless* (probably influenced by *irrespective*) is a double negative that is only used humorously. Even if the user is serious about it his audience is likely not to be. The triple negative *disirregardless* has now begun to appear, and we may hope for *undisirregardless* in the near future.

Relative Clauses

See pages 94-97.

remember

Memory is often followed by *of.* In standard usage, *remember* is not.

> I have a faint *memory of* reading that book.
> I faintly *remember* (no *of*) reading that book.

respectfully, respectively

Respectively means "in the order listed," and has nothing whatever to do with *respectfully*.

Restrictive *and* Nonrestrictive Clauses

In this book the terms "identifying" and "amplifying" clauses are used. See pages 94-96.

reverend

The rules for the "correct" usage of *reverend* are highly formalized:

1. It is properly used only as a title, not as a substitute for *minister* ("The *reverend* told me" may be common, but it is not standard).

2. It is not used with a bare last name—*Reverend John Smith* or *Reverend J. E. Smith,* but not *Reverend Smith.*

3. It is even better with a *the* before it: *the Reverend J. E. Smith.*

4. Best of all is a *the* before it and a *Mr.* after it. This combination makes the first name or initials unnecessary: the Reverend Mr. Smith. However, local ground rules vary a good deal.

The original meaning of *reverend* was "to be revered." *Reverent* is a different word meaning simply "revering," and may be used of laymen as well as ministers.

Rhetorical Question

A *rhetorical question* is one to which the speaker expects no answer, unless he is planning to supply it himself.

rhyme, rime

Rime is the earlier spelling, and seems to be returning to favor after a long period in which *rhyme* (resulting from a mistaken belief that the word was related to *rhythm*) was the usual one.

right

Right in the sense of *very* is used in conversation by many standard speakers throughout the country, but many people consider it too informal for writing.

role

Role (a part in a play) is now usually spelled without the circum-flex accent (*rôle*).

Roman Numerals

See *Numbers.*

round, around

See *around.*

said

As a modifier, *said* is appropriate only in legal phraseology (*said* property, the *said* defendant).

saint

For a particular *saint,* the abbreviation is usually *St.* (*St.* John); for several saints, SS. (SS. Matthew and Mark).

Sarcasm

See *Irony.*

Seasons

The *seasons* (*spring, summer, fall* or *autumn,* and *winter*) need not be capitalized.

seldom

Seldom, by itself, means "hardly ever." There is therefore no need for *seldom ever.*

semi-

A prefix meaning *half.* No hyphen is needed unless the main word begins with an *i* or a capital letter.

Semicolon (;)

A *semicolon* is read like a period, rather than like a comma; but where a period indicates a complete break in thought, a semicolon suggests that the groups of words it separates are parts of a larger whole. Semicolons are rather formal marks, and are seldom absolutely necessary; however, they are convenient for several purposes:

1. *To separate members of a series that contain internal commas.* Compare the two following sentences:

Dinner included meat, bread, vegetables, and fruit.
Dinner included meat, flown in from the continent; bread, freshly baked that afternoon; fresh vegetables; and several kinds of fruit, including some quite strange to me.

With nothing but commas, the second sentence would be rather bumpy; the semicolons show where the main pauses come, and so make it easier to read.

2. *To separate independent clauses when they are rather long and contain internal commas:*

A good many people have tried, but nobody has succeeded.
A good many people, some of them very well prepared, have tried; but nobody, according to the best records available, has succeeded.

3. *To separate independent clauses when no connective is used:*

Some traffic officers think the new code will help; others doubt this.

This sentence could be broken in two, or a comma and *but* could be substituted for the semicolon. A comma alone would not be sufficient.

4. To indicate to which clause such heavy connectives as *consequently, moreover, nevertheless,* and especially *however* belong:

He has failed six times; however, he may finally succeed.
He has failed six times, however; the odds against him are long.

Usually these words belong to the second clause, and are therefore preceded by a semicolon and followed by a comma.

set, sit

Such expressions as "Let's *set* (should be *sit*) awhile" and "We *set* (should be *sat*) there for hours" are widely used, especially in the country, but are not generally accepted as standard.

Sit is seldom misused, though people who have been warned against *set* sometimes go too far and say "*Sit* (should be *set*) this on the table."

shall

See *will* and *shall.*

Shifting Viewpoint

It is all right to shift from one person or tense to another if you do it on purpose in order to accomplish something. But if the shift was made simply because we forget how you started, then one is likely to have a sentence as confused as this one. And unless you are sure you are writing for thousands, you had better keep the same audience in mind throughout. Otherwise you are likely to be explaining the obvious in one paragraph and leaving out essential points in the next.

should

See *will* and *shall.*

sic

Sic is Latin for *thus.* It is used, in brackets, to indicate that a mistake in quoted material was made by the original author and not in copying:

> "He was born in Brooklin [*sic*] in 1873."

sick at, sick to

The usual standard expression is *sick at my stomach,* though *sick to* is current in some regions. The English have solved this problem by deciding that *sick* all by itself means nauseated, and using *ill* as the general term.

similar to

Similar to is longer than *like* and means no more. Besides, *like* is seldom misspelled, while *similar* often is.

similes

See *Metaphors* and *Similes.*

slow, slowly

Slow may be used to modify verbs as well as nouns, though it sounds awkward in some positions. We could say "He walked *slow*" or "He walked *slowly,*" but only "He *slowly* walked to the corner." It is hard to explain why "He *slow* walked to the corner" is wrong, but it is.

so

Though often criticized in classrooms, *so* is standard:

In purpose clauses: He came home early *so* he could work in the garden.
In result clauses: He has lived here a long time, *so* he knows almost everybody.
As an intensive: There are *so* many new people here.

The following expressions are not universally admired:

So you're tired. *So* I should do your work for you? *So* what?

so-called

So-called is likely to sound peevish at best, and ridiculous when the calling is accurate. Describe a man as a *so-called mastermind* if you must, but don't call him a *so-called lawyer* if he *is* a lawyer, even if you don't think he should be.

some, somewhat

A heavily stressed *some* is slang ("That was *some* examination," "They were going *some* when they hit the curve"). Practically all other uses are standard, though in distinctly formal English *somewhat* is generally used to modify participles and comparative forms of adjectives ("He felt *somewhat* rested," "This is *somewhat* larger than the other").

sometime, some time, sometimes

When the idea is "at a certain (or uncertain) time," write *sometime*. When the idea of duration is present, write *some time:*

He went there *sometime* in 1952 and stayed *some time.*

Sometimes means occasionally.

sooner . . . than

If you remember "no *sooner* said *than* done" you won't be tempted to write "He had no *sooner* gone to bed *when* he remembered he had not put the car in the garage."

sort

See **kind.**

specie, species

These words are not the singular and plural of the same word. *Specie* (*spee'she*) means coin as distinguished from paper money.

Species means kind, especially as a biological term. It has the same written form in the singular and plural, and most people pronounce it *spee'sheez* in both numbers, though some pronounce the singular *spee'shiz.*

Split Infinitive

A Latin infinitive cannot be split because it is a single word. An English infinitive can be split and sometimes should. In such a sentence as "I want *to* actually *see* him do it" it would be impossible to move *actually* without either changing the meaning or weakening the force. However, most split infinitives are awkward and weaken rather than strengthen the sentences in which they occur. Such a sentence as "I want *to* eventually *get* to Philadelphia" would be improved by putting *eventually* almost anywhere but where it is. In revising papers, suspect every split infinitive, and leave only those that you are sure you can defend.

Squinting Modifiers

A *squinting modifier* is one that "looks both ways"—that is, it could reasonably be understood as applying either to the preceding or the following element.

He asked me *while I was in New York* to visit his sister.
Revised: He asked me to visit his sister *while I was in New York.*
While I was in New York he asked me to visit his sister.

He advised me *secretly* to go to the police.
Revised: He *secretly* advised me to go to the police.
He advised me to go *secretly* to the police.

She told Algernon *after a few minutes* to get a taxi.
Revised: *After a few minutes* she told Algernon to get a taxi.
She told Algernon to get a taxi *after a few minutes.*

stationary, stationery

Paper, envelopes, and so forth are called *stationery*. In all other uses the form is *stationary*.

statue, stature, statute

Statue means a carved figure. *Stature* can mean either the physical height of a person (He was a man of medium *stature*) or *standing* in the figurative sense (His professional *stature* made him an obvious choice for chairman). *Statute* means a law or rule formally enacted. *Statute law* is often contrasted with *case law*, which is based on judicial decisions rather than legislative enactment.

Strong Verbs

Such verbs as *sing* and *break*, which form their past tenses by a change in the vowel, and *without* adding a *d* or *t*, or changing a *d* to a *t*, are called *strong*. All regular verbs, which add a *d* or *ed*, are *weak*, and so are such verbs as *make* and *think*.

The terms *strong* and *weak* are useful in discussing Old English, but much less satisfactory than *regular* and *irregular* in Modern English.

Stylebooks

A *stylebook* gives the rules on capitalization, punctuation, and other mechanical details to be used by a particular newspaper, publishing house, or other organization. It may include rules (usually antiquated) on grammar and even style. Probably no two stylebooks have ever been in complete agreement, and certainly no stylebook has ever covered all possible cases.

A stylebook may be very useful in getting a number of people to write with comparative uniformity; but if it is taken too solemnly it can lead to wasting endless time on trivial decisions.

Subjunctive

Three kinds of expressions are often said to be in the "subjunctive mood":

1. Wishes, such as "God bless us." This causes no trouble except when we try to explain it, and the simplest way to do that is to say

that it is short for "*May* God *bless* us." It is quite true that our ancestors could have used a subjunctive form of *bless* without the *may,* but that was when there was a subjunctive form to use.

2. Expressions of willed action, such as "They insisted that he *try* again" and "They requested that he *be* given another chance." There is no trouble in understanding these, and no good reason for insisting on their use. They can be explained as short for *should try* and *should be,* which are now more common and quite as respectable.

3. Conditional expressions such as "If he *were* here," and "If it *be* true." With verbs other than *to be* there is no longer a question of form in the past tense. In the present tense, "If he *call*" is now obsolete, since it seems to most people like a simple mistake in agreement, and "If it *be*" is on its last legs. This leaves "If I *were*" and "If he *were*" as the only real excuse for preserving the theory of a subjunctive mood. Even these are visibly losing ground, but they are still considered by many educated people to be of great importance. They are therefore discussed on page 101.

Suffix

An ending, other than an inflection, that can be added to a word to give it a new meaning or function.

> *-able, -ation, -ish, -ly, -ment, -ous,* and so forth.

suite

Suite (pronounced *sweet*) is now most frequently used to indicate a set of connecting rooms. The original meaning is "following," which is retained in the sense of "staff of assistants" and in the musical term for a series of dances.

suspect, suspicion

In standard English, *suspicion* is used only as a noun. *Suspect* is used both as a noun (pronounced *sus'pect*), meaning "a person under suspicion," and as a verb (pronounced *sus-pect'*): "We *suspected* (not *suspicioned*) he was there."

swell

As a general expression of approval, *swell* has resisted the attack of generations of teachers, and is now often heard in standard speech. We must be honest, but we don't have to be enthusiastic.

Synonyms

Words that have approximately the same meaning are called *synonyms* (*couch, davenport, sofa; begin, commence, start*). It is obviously important to choose the *synonym* which will come closest to conveying your exact meaning.

It is often said that no two words are exact synonyms. Whether or not this can be proved, it is much closer to the truth than the rather widespread idea that any synonym of a word can be substituted for it at any time—and probably should be, just for the sake of variety. It is better to repeat an accurate term than to vary it with a less accurate one.

Tense

The word *tense* comes from the Latin word *tempus,* meaning "time," but the relation between time and tense has become very irregular. English has only two clear-cut tenses—the present and the past—and each of these may be used to indicate any of the three natural divisions of time—the present, the past, and the future.

TENSE	TIME	
present	*present*	I *see* it now.
	past	It *is* cold at Valley Forge. (Historical present)
	future	We *play* in Denver next week.
past	*present*	I didn't know he *was* there right now.
	past	We *found* them yesterday.
	future	If you *tried* tomorrow, you might catch him.

If you think this is illogical, you are perfectly right; but we are used to such expressions, and they don't usually cause much trouble unless we think about them too much and try to pretend that they are all perfectly reasonable. The fact is that tense is only one of our ways of indicating time. We also indicate definite time by such words as *yesterday* and *tomorrow* and comparative time by words like *before* and *after*.

Still another way of showing time is by verb phrases like *will go* and *have gone*. Many (but not all) grammarians say that some of these phrases are also tenses. The ones that do usually say that English has six tenses, about as follows:

	SIMPLE	PROGRESSIVE	EMPHATIC
Present	he calls	he is calling	he does call
Past	he called	he was calling	he did call
Future	he will call	he will be call-ing	
Present perfect	he has called	he has been calling	
Past perfect	he had called	he had been calling	
Future perfect	he will have called	he will have been calling	

The first three are said to represent the absolute divisions of time, and the three "perfect" tenses to show relative time: before the present, before the past, and before the future. ("Perfect" in this connection means "completely finished," and has nothing to do with virtue.)

At first glance this arrangement seems logical and reasonably complete, but the more we study it, the more suspicious we become. It would be hard to prove, for instance, that the difference between *called* and *has called* is any greater than that between *called* and *was calling;* yet *has called* is listed as a different tense from *called,* and *was calling* merely as a different form of the same one. Moreover, a number of combinations indicating various aspects of time are left out entirely: *used to call, is going to call,* etc.

On the whole, the evidence seems to show that the main reason we talk about six tenses in English is that there really were six in Latin (you can count them: *vocat, vocabat, vocabit, vocavit, voca-verat,* and *vocaverit*). It is perfectly certain that there were only two tenses in Old English, the present and the past. Since then we have developed a number of verb phrases, some of which are used as substitutes for the missing tenses. You can call them tenses if you want to, but they are not called that in this book.

that

That is used in so many different ways that some grammarians have made arbitrary rules to keep it under control. However, practically all the habitual uses remain standard. The misuses that occur most often are:

1. Unnecessary repetition to introduce a clause ("He said *that* if we could get there by sunrise (*that*) we ought to get some good fishing").

2. Reference to an idea implied but not expressed ("My father practices law, and *that* is what I want to be"). In this sentence, *that* apparently refers to *lawyer*, which isn't there to refer to. If *be* were changed to *do*, *that* would refer to *practice(s) law,* and the sentence would be satisfactory.

that there, this here

That there and *this here* are pleasantly emphatic forms of *that* and *this*, but unfortunately not standard unless divided by a noun:

> *that* house *there*   *this* desk *here*

their, there, they're

Their is the possessive form. *They're* is the contraction for *they are*. *There* is used in all other senses.

then, than

Remember that *then* rimes with *when*, and that *than* has nothing to do with time.

there is or are

There is never considered the subject of a sentence; a verb following it therefore agrees with the following subject; "There *is* a man at the door"; "There *are* three men there." When *there* is followed by a compound subject of which the first member is singular, the verb may be either singular or plural: "There *is* (or *are*) a man and three boys on the raft."

they

The impersonal use of *they* ("*They* say he's rich," "*They* make good cars in England") is rather informal, and occurs more often in speech than in writing; but it is certainly standard.

this and that

For many centuries *that* has been used to indicate something comparatively remote in time or space, with *this* indicating something nearer at hand, and *it* noncommittal as to time or distance. These distinctions are still generally followed in regard to space, but a tendency has lately developed to use only *this* in regard to time.

He said we ought to try one more round. *This* (formerly *it*) seemed like a good idea at the time.

Last month I saw her with Dick. *This* (formerly *that*) surprised me very much until I discovered that Dick had a new Jaguar.

The tendency apparently comes from an effort to be dramatic by bringing everything into the foreground. It sounds to many of us rather frantic, and it certainly blurs some useful distinctions.

though

The simplified form *tho* has made more progress than *thru,* but not everybody accepts it.

through

The simplified spelling *thru* is heartily approved by some people, detested by others. Suit yourself, but if your instructor doesn't like it, you probably won't convert him.

till, until

These words are interchangeable. Use whichever you think sounds best in a given sentence, but notice that *until* has only one *l,* and *till* is NOT spelled *'til.*

Title of Paper

The title of a paper should be appropriate, short, and modest. Also, it should be considered a label attached to the paper, not a part of it. Usually it is best to write the paper before naming it. Then look for a few words that indicate the central idea. "An Accident at the Factory" is better than "A Serious Industrial Accident at the W. F. Hamline Furniture Factory." Let the reader find out for himself how good the paper is. If you put words like *amusing* or *exciting* in the title you may arouse his resistance.

If you do put down the title first, remember that your first sentence can't lean on it. If your title is "Why I Don't Like Strawberries," you can't begin "These berries . . ." You have to say "Strawberries" to explain, without the title, what you are talking about.

today, tomorrow, tonight

All these words are now usually spelled without a hyphen.

Topic Sentences

A topic sentence is one that expresses the main idea of a paragraph. It may or may not actually appear in the paper, but it should always appear in a good outline. In other words, any paragraph that cannot be summarized by a clear topic sentence has something wrong with it. See also pages 233-235.

toward, towards

Variant forms—take your choice.

Transition

Each paragraph should be a reasonably complete unit in itself, but the relation of ideas between succeeding paragraphs should be made clear to a reader. Often the connection (called *transition* or "going across") is made almost automatically by including in the first line of the new paragraph a word or phrase which ties it to the preceding one:

The success of *this* effort suggested the next step.
On the following day he tried a different approach.
Undiscouraged by *such* a reception, he continued his efforts.

Not every paragraph needs such a link with what has gone before, but it is well to remember that a connection that is perfectly clear in the mind of the writer may not be in the least clear to a reader unless it is specifically stated. Unless you are quite sure that the circumstances make the connection unmistakably clear, it is better to play safe and insert a connecting word or phrase—or even a whole sentence.

Transitive and Intransitive Verbs

Compare the two following sentences:

The man *saw* John.
The man *was* John.

In the first, *the man* and *John* stand for different people. The verb *saw* is said to be *transitive* (literal meaning, "going across") because it carries over the action from one to the other. And the complement, *John,* may be called the *direct object* because it receives the action of the verb.

In the second, *the man* and *John* stand for the same person. The verb is said to be *intransitive* because it does not carry over any action from one to the other, but simply links them. Since the complement refers to the subject it may be called the *subjective complement* (or a number of other things), but not a direct object. If we change this sentence to read "The man was there," *was* is no longer a linking verb, but is still intransitive.

This classification of verbs is quite important in some highly inflected languages, but in contemporary English:

1. Almost all verbs can be used both ways.

2. In many sentences it is impossible to prove which way a verb is used.

3. In such cases it makes little difference what it is called.

The nonstandard uses of such verbs as *lay, learn, raise,* and *set* can not be explained on the basis of this classification, since all four of these verbs are classified as both transitive and intransitive—though not in all uses.

transpire

This word *is* in the dictionaries. It should be allowed to remain there, undisturbed.

trite

See *clichés,* p. 266.

try and

"*Try and* get that finished tonight" is much more encouraging than merely "*try to* get it finished," since *try and* implies success while *try to* leaves the betting even. (It is only fair to add that many teachers disagree with this analysis, and condemn *try and.*)

twice

The only *t* or *t* sound in twice is at the beginning.

type

As a rough synonym for *kind* or *sort, type* is legitimate when it indicates a reasonably definite model: "this *type* of automatic ejector"; "a vehicle of the *jeep type.*" When the meaning is less specific, *kind* or *sort* is generally preferable: "that *kind* of thing"; "A person of that *sort.*" The use of *type* as an adjective, without a following *of,* invites ridicule:

> I don't care for that *type* book.
> He is a very *high-type* fellow.

un-

See *in-, un-.*

Underlining

Underlining in longhand or typescript is the equivalent of italics in print. The principal uses of *underlining* in college papers are:

1. To indicate the titles of books, periodicals, and newspapers (but not of articles, poems, etc. contained in such publications).

I have read reviews of Hemingway's Old Man and the Sea in The Saturday Review and The New York Times.

Kipling's story "Rikki-tikki-tavi" first appeared in The Jungle Book.

2. To indicate that words are being considered simply as words, and not for their meaning:

The expression the more the merrier is easier to understand than to explain.

I would use therefore rather than so in that sentence.

3. To give special emphasis:

It is never safe to leave a loaded gun in a car.

Underlining for emphasis should be used sparingly or it loses its effect. It is better to underline a few key words than a whole sentence. When you are in doubt about underlining, don't.

unique

This word originally meant "the only one of its kind." Such expressions as *very unique* and *most unique* are therefore weaker than the

simple *unique,* and are also often condemned as illogical by people who know the original meaning of the word. However, we might as well recognize that this word, like hundreds of others, has lost much of its original force, and is now often used to mean simply "unusual."

Unrelated Ideas

When a sentence contains two or more ideas, the relation between them should be made clear to the reader. Look at the following sentences:

He had played left tackle at Minnesota and he weighed 169 pounds.
Although he only weighed 169 pounds, he had played left tackle at Minnesota.
Although he had played left tackle at Minnesota, he was now down to 169 pounds.

There is a big difference between being good for his size and worn down from his past—and the writer shouldn't leave the reader guessing.

until

Only one *l.* Interchangeable with *till.*

used to

This expression is now used only in the past tense: "They *used to* live there." The *d* is not pronounced, but should be written.

very

The schoolroom theory that *very* should not be used to modify participles is a silly bit of pedantry. *Very pleased* is quite as good as *very much pleased.* However, *very* has been used so much that it is just as likely to weaken as to strengthen an expression. Radio announcers seem to realize this, and try to strengthen *very* by doubling it. Anybody else who uses *very very* should be condemned to listen to radio announcers until he begins to scream.

vice, vise

A bad habit is spelled *vice.* The tool may be spelled either way.

Voice

Latin verbs have two sets of forms called *voices,* active and passive. Thus *voco* means *I call,* while *vocor* means *I am called.* In English all the special forms of the passive voice have disappeared, and their places have been taken by combinations of the verb *to be* and past participles. We may therefore drop the term *voice* and speak simply of active and passive constructions.

When a verb tells what the subject does, we call it active:

A horse pulled the cart.

When it tells what was done to the subject, we call it passive:

The cart was pulled by a horse.

It is usually better to use active verbs, but passive ones are sometimes useful, especially when the subject is unknown, vague, or comparatively unimportant. See **Passive Constructions.**

Vowels and Consonants

The English alphabet is traditionally divided into vowels and consonants, as follows:

A, e, i, o, and *u* are vowels.
Y is a vowel except when it is pronounced as in *yes.*
W is a vowel when it follows another vowel in the same syllable, as in *draw.*
Y and *w* are consonants except in the uses mentioned above.
All the other letters are always consonants.
The table below indicates the long and short values of the vowels:

	LONG	SHORT
a	f*a*te	f*a*t
e	conc*e*de	b*e*t
i	b*i*te	b*i*t
o	n*o*te	n*o*t
u	c*u*be	c*u*b

This classification, which is based on the letters themselves rather than on the sounds they erratically represent, is worse than useless for a discussion of English phonetics. It is given here solely because it may be of some help in understanding spelling rules about the doubling of consonants and so forth. A full treatment of vowel and consonant sounds would require far more space than is available here.

vs.

This is an abbreviation of Latin *versus,* meaning "against." Used mainly to indicate the opponents in sporting events. The standard pronunciation is *ver'sus,* though *vee ess'* is now often heard.

wait for, on

To *wait on* a person implies service. To *wait for* him implies merely the hope that he will eventually join you.

wake, waken, awake, awaken

Waken and *awaken* are always regular, and *wake* and *awake* may be. The irregular past forms *woke* and *awoke* are also standard; in British use so is the past participle *woken.* All four verbs are freely interchangeable, and preferences differ.

want

The standard construction after *want* is the infinitive:

> I *want* you *to get* up early. (Not "I want for you to get up" or "I want that you should get up.")

You want to in the sense of "You ought to" is hardly standard.

want in, want out, ETC.

A neat and useful construction, unfortunately condemned in most schoolrooms and therefore not yet fully standard.

ways

We often hear *ways* instead of *way* in such expressions as "a long *ways* off." *Way* should be used in writing, unless you are trying to get a special flavor.

we

Aside from its definite personal use, *we* is often used impersonally. ("*We* often use *we* impersonally").

Some editors also use *we* instead of *I.* Whether this is modesty or the very immodest belief that an editor is a host in himself would be hard to determine.

Weak Verbs

See *Strong Verbs.*

weather, whether

It is too bad that these two words are so confusing, but you might as well learn them. Everybody talks about the *weather, whether* we like it or not; and the popular compromise (spelling both words *wheather*) results only in being wrong all the time.

well

See *good.*

(is) when, where

There is a general and natural tendency to use *when* and *where* clauses as definitions:

> A debate *is when* two sides argue.
> A junction *is where* two roads come together.

Since such definitions are usually clear, it is unfortunate that they are very generally condemned as illogical; but they are so condemned, and will probably be marked wrong.

where at

Where implies *at* which or *at* what place. An extra *at* is therefore unnecessary.

which

Amplifying clauses are regularly introduced by *which* rather than *that:*

The Carfrae Hotel, *which* has the best restaurant in town, is on Townsend Avenue.

Identifying clauses are more often introduced by *that,* but *which* is permissible if you like the sound better:

Here is a book *that* (or *which*) I think you may find useful.

while

Aside from being a convenient short way to indicate "during the time when," *while* may be used to indicate a mild opposition.

Jim was in favor of going by train, *while* Tom rather preferred the bus.

This usage is often condemned on theoretical grounds, but it has a long and respectable history.

who's, whose

Who's is a contraction of *who is,* and therefore needs the apostrophe. The possessive form *whose,* like all other pronoun possessive forms, is written without an apostrophe.

Whose with Inanimate Objects

Who and *whom* are used only of people, but *whose* is sometimes used to refer to things, simply because neither *that* nor *which* has a possessive form.

> That is the train *whose* whistle we heard.

Of course we might say "That is the train of which we heard the whistle"; but this would seem more like a balancing act than a natural sentence.

will *and* shall; would *and* should

A few grammarians still cling to the theory that the "simple future" and the "future of determination" are expressed as follows:

SIMPLE FUTURE		FUTURE OF DETERMINATION	
I shall	we shall	I will	we will
you will	you will	you shall	you shall
he will	they will	he shall	they shall

This is an oversimplification of British usage; and as regards current American usage it must be considered a pious wish rather than a description. Practice varies considerably, but the general tendency is about as follows:

1. In future statements the usual form is *will* (or *'ll*) with any subject, regardless of how determined the speaker is. "I *shall*" and "We *shall*" for the "simple future" are permissible but not necessary.

2. In questions, *will* is again the normal form with any subject, unless permission or consent is asked:

Will we have any left? (*Shall* is possible here, but even less common than in statements.)

If permission or consent is asked, *will* is abnormal with *any* subject, but *should* is established as an alternate for *shall*.

> Shall (*should*) we go?
> Shall (*should*) he turn on the light?

3. The separate "future of determination" has practically disappeared except in the drafting of constitutions ("The purpose of this organization *shall* be," etc.). Orders are written, "You *will* proceed," not "You *shall* proceed."

Shall still occurs in such sentences as "I am determined that he *shall* have a chance," but the more usual expression is now "I am determined for him to have a chance."

Would and *should* sometimes serve simply as the past tenses of *will* and *shall* after verbs of saying, thinking, etc.

> They *will* go.   He said they *would* go.
> *Shall* we go?   We asked if we *should* go.

In other uses, *should* is much more common than *shall* after *I* and *we*. Such sentences as the following are frequently used:

> I *will* be finished tomorrow—at least, I *should* think so.

The difference between the past and present forms often has nothing to do with time:

Will you pass the butter? (I expect you to)
Would you pass the butter? (It would be a favor)

I *shall* do it. (Definite statement)
I *should* do it. (Either a conditional statement, or a statement about duty rather than performance)

Should we go? (Asking for an opinion)
Shall we go? (Asking for a definite decision)

Of course not all speakers make such distinctions.

wire

As a substitute for *telegram* and *telegraph, wire* is now standard.

Wordiness

It is not necessary to reduce every sentence to the very smallest number of words that can possibly be used to express the ideas it contains; but it *is* important to use reasonable economy. If you are in the habit of saying things like "each and every one" for "each" or "in this modern day and age" for "now," you may reasonably expect your instructor to write "deadwood" instead of "goody-goody," and "D" instead of "B+."

would have

Would have is a standard phrase, but is sometimes misused in two ways:

1. In contrary-to-fact conditions:

> If Sheldon *had* (not *would have*) come, he could help us.

2. As a duplicate indication of past time in such sentences as:

> He would have liked to have seen that.

This sentence could be revised either to "He *would have* liked to see" or "He *would* like to *have* seen."

ye for the

The Old English letter for the *th* sound was thorn (þ). This disappeared from ordinary use, but many people continued to write þ for *the*. Unless they closed the top of the thorn very carefully, it looked more like *y* than anything else, and early printers often used *ye* to represent *the*. It was still pronounced *the* by the people who used it, but later generations, finding it in old books, misunderstood and mispronounced it. It is recommended only for those who like very dubious antiques.

ye for you

In older English, *ye* was the subject form and *you* was the object form. Now *you* is used for all purposes. In those dialects where *ye* still appears it is an all-purpose variant rather than a special subject form.

you

You is the normal indefinite pronoun in American usage:

> How do *you* get to the post office?
> *You* never know what the legislature will do.

All efforts to establish *one* as the normal form seem to have failed, though we sometimes use such substitutes as *a fellow, a man,* or even *a person.*

you all

In the South, *you all* is a polite plural, usually pronounced *you-all'* or even *yawl.* In the North it is pronounced *you'all* and used only in ignorance.

When a Yankee hears one Southerner say to another, visibly alone, "Won't *you all* come over this evening" he assumes that *you all* is used in the singular. What it actually means is "Won't you come over, and of course bring your family, and if there happen to be any odd cousins around of course they will be welcome too." It would be rude not to make the invitation completely general.

Perhaps it is natural that a mere Northerner cannot understand all this.

your, you're

Your is the possessive form. *You're* is the contraction for *you are.*

GENERAL INDEX

GENERAL INDEX

CORRECTION
CHART

Mechanics	**M 1** Abbreviations 307-308	**M 2** Capitalization 327	**M 3** Division of Words 346	**M 4** Margins, Spacing, etc. 124
P 2 Brackets 324	**P 3** Caret 327	**P 4** Colon 331-332	**P 5** Comma 332-335	**P 6** Dash 342-343
P 12 Question Mark 403-404	**P 13** Quotation Marks 404-405	**P 14** Semicolon 411-412	**Word Form and Choice**	**W 1** Adjective and Adverb Confused 310-311
W 7 Jargon 372-373	**W 8** Specific Word Needed 265-266	**W 9** Substandard Word Use Dictionary	**W 10** Unsuccessful Slang 34	**W 11** Wrong Word Use Dictionary
S 5 Fused Sentence 205-207	**S 6** Omission 387	**S 7** Overloaded Sentence 389	**S 8** Reference of Pronouns 407-409	**S 9** Run-on Sentence 205-207
S 15 Too Many Nouns 268	**S 16** Unrelated Ideas 425	**S 17** Weak Passive 393	**S 18** Wordiness 430-431	**Paragraph and Whole Composition**
C 6 Paragraph Length 180	**C 7** Shifting Viewpoint 413	**C 8** Title of Paper 421	**C 9** Topic Sentence 233-235	**C 10** Transition 422

M 5 Numbers 384-386	M 6 Spelling 157-161	M 7 Underlining 424	**Punctuation**	P 1 Apostrophe 319
P 7 Ellipsis 349-350	P 8 Exclamation Point 353-354	P 9 Hyphen 365-366	P 10 Parentheses 390	P 11 Period 394-395
W 2 Agreement: Pronoun-Antecedent 407-409	W 3 Agreement: Subject-Verb 312-314	W 4 Case 327-329	W 5 Cliché 266-268	W 6 Inflated Language 263-264
Sentence Structure	S 1 Dangling Modifier 341-342	S 2 Double Comparison 346	S 3 Double Negative 347	S 4 Faulty Parallelism 209
S 10 Sentence Fragment 203-205	S 11 Shifted Construction 208-209	S 12 Split Infinitive 415	S 13 Squinting Modifier 415	S 14 Subordination 264-265
C 1 Letter Form: Business 275	C 2 Letter Form: Social 272-274	C 3 Organization of Paper 117-121 174-180	C 4 Paragraph Development 231-238	C 5 Paragraph Division 180-182
Research Paper	R 1 Bibliographical Entry Form 301-302	R 2 Footnote Form 300	R 3 Footnote Needed 298	R 4 Mechanical Form 301-302